BLITZ

Blitz

The Story of 29th December 1940

M. J. GASKIN

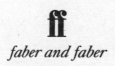

faber and faber

First published in 2005
by Faber and Faber Limited
3 Queen Square London WC1N 3AU

Typeset by Faber and Faber Limited
Printed in England by Mackays of Chatham plc,
Chatham, Kent

A CIP record for this book
is available from the British Library

ISBN 0-571-21794-X

2 4 6 8 10 9 7 5 3 1

To the Reader

ONCE, UPON A TIME . . .

It isn't the most original opening for a story perhaps. But in many ways it seems the only appropriate way to begin this one. 'Is it fiction?' I was asked more than once when I said I was writing a book about one air raid in the Blitz. The question made me boggle slightly – anyone who knew even a fraction of the tale I had to tell would have known why inventing something to make it more dramatic was such a far-fetched idea.

At the same time, as the hard evidence continued to pile up on my desk and bookshelves (and floor, and every available surface), the air of unreality seemed to grow with it. And I thought how much more 'realistic' a tale I could have made of it if it *were* fiction. How much more within the scope of recognisable 'human nature' I could have created my characters and their actions, and how much more logical and plausible a plot-line I could have crafted. And I remembered how playwright Peter Barnes had said that, whenever he wrote plays that were set in the past, it was always the bits the theatre critics found most implausible that were the things that had actually happened.

So, no. This is not a fiction – at least to the extent of my limited powers it is not. But there is nothing I can do to stop the story of that place, at that time, sounding as fantastical now as it appeared to the people living then and there.

How I empathised with those American foreign correspondents in 1940s London, trying to convey over distance, as I over time, just what this strange society was and what it did and how it did it. And how I blessed each one of them – and all those other correspondents, public and private, who wrote to friends and relations far away from the bombing, or to posterity – whenever they took special care to capture in detail some extraordinary commonplace of London life in 1940. For it is in these, as much as the grand narrative they counterpoint, that this story lies.

WHEN, DURING THE WRITING of this book, anyone asked how I came to pick on 29th December, of all Blitz days, to write about, I had to confess that, in truth, 29th December picked me. London is a city that constantly whispers stories into the ears of its inhabitants but, for a very long time, I was obstinately deaf to this one.

Perhaps I should have heard it as a child, taken to the Lord Mayor's Show as a birthday treat by my Dad, and afterwards to a fair where a spit-roasted beast attempted to bring a little medieval jollity to the concrete wastes of 1960s Paternoster Square. Perhaps I should have heard it later, working for the Royal Shakespeare Company amid the towering labyrinth of the Barbican complex: every lunchtime spent in the Green Room overlooking St Giles Cripplegate church – a bit of old, old London stranded in the midst of a very modern modernity – and never once thinking to ask myself the question: 'Why?'

In the end it was only much later, as I began wandering the silent Sunday City alone, trying to reacquaint myself with Shakespeare on a one-to-one basis, that the penny began to drop. Anyone seeking the sixteenth-century City of London knows that they will have to jump the fire-pit of 1666. But again and again I found another date – the same date – presenting itself. A plaque in this church. A footnote in that book. An odd patch of public garden among some of the world's most expensive real estate . . . The date 29th December 1940 had never meant anything to me. But, eventually, even I could no longer be that obtuse. OK London, I said. Tell me your story. And it did. And this is it.

London, June 2005

Contents

CODA

Introduction

IN THE SMALL HOURS of the morning of Monday 30th December 1940, press photographer Herbert Mason stood on the roof of the *Daily Mail* building in Fleet Street, watching as the City of London burned beneath him.

He had been waiting for hours to capture the definitive image that would encapsulate the drama of the long and astonishing night he had witnessed. Then the clouds of smoke before him parted 'like the curtain of a theatre' to reveal 'this wonderful vista, more like a dream – not frightening'. Against the flames, Wren's famous dome of St Paul's stood silhouetted and, almost miraculously, unscathed. Mason saw the light gleam on the golden cross above and clicked the shutter.

The image appeared on the front page of the *Daily Mail* the following day under the prescient headline 'War's Greatest Picture' and went on to become one of the icons of the Second World War. Today, two generations on, it is universally and instantly recognised as the quintessence of the London Blitz, the shining moment of Britain's finest hour.

But do we really know what we are looking at? Today, who has even heard of the night they called 'The Second Great Fire of London'?

WHAT HERBERT MASON photographed that night is now both world famous and unknown. But even at the time its meaning was not single or straightforward. In the hands of Herbert Mason, the camera did not lie. But the mythic simplicity of the image captured on the cover of the *Daily Mail*, heavy with the symbolism of hope and steadfast resistance, was by no means the whole picture.

Indeed, it was not even the whole photograph. More than half the area of the original print was cropped off for its first publication, taking away most of the thick black smoke billowing around the Cathedral and, more significantly perhaps, removing many of the hollow-eyed ruins dominating the foreground. Moreover, the brightness that seemed, in black and white newsprint, to halo the Cathedral and glint on the golden cross above was, in truth, no hopeful dawn but the lurid, multi-coloured glare of a still-raging firestorm.

Hours of relentless incendiary bombing by the Luftwaffe had set the

THE DAILY MAIL, Tuesday, December 31, 1940.

Daily Mail
FOR KING AND EMPIRE

NO. 13,941

TUESDAY, DECEMBER 31, 1940

ONE PENNY

LATE WAR NEWS SPECIAL

More Of A Pal Than Ever
SHERLEY'S
TONIC AND CONDITION POWDERS

Cycle Accessories
LIGHTWEIGHT FEATHERWEIGHT MOVEASY
Bluemel's

Hitler Planned Monday Swoop

London was to Blaze First

By NOEL MONKS, Daily Mail Air Correspondent

HITLER meant to start the second Great Fire of London as the prelude to an invasion.

This was the belief held in well-informed quarters in London yesterday.

The Nazis planned to set big fires burning all over London before midnight.

Relays of bombers laden with H.E. would then have carried out the most destructive raid of the war. The New Year invasion was to have followed.

The R.A.F. have given more attention to the invasion ports this past week than for two months or more. Clearly there are sound reasons for supposing that Hitler is still going ahead with invasion plans.

THE FACTS

Here are the real facts of Sunday night's fire-raising raid, as told to me yesterday:—

It was one of the biggest night attacks on Britain since beginning.

So R.A.F. night raiders were operating over the London area, though some were doing so between London and the coast.

Soon after 10 p.m. the German Air Command sent out instructions for all the bombers they engaged to return to their bases, as low water had taken a turn for the worse and fog was blanketing out their aerodromes.

It was the weather, then, and not any night fighters, that saved London from an even worse attack. The view that the aerodromes were flooded to be the fore-most of the war.

Up to 2,000 bombers were to have been used during the night.

One explanation given for the sudden release of London's inner A.A. barrage is that in the light of the fire by which most of London was lit up its position had been disclosed the positions of the guns.

Hold a few hours after dusk...

Here is a [...] how the raid started.

(1) The guns had stopped firing and

(2) the Flares lit up the aerodrome balloons, and the raiders could fly between them.

It is estimated that more than 10,000 incendiary bombs were dropped on the capital within three hours.

Had a bomb fallen [...] it really had been [...] part of Britain.

Because of that [...] the Channel [...] experiences [...] be cancelled.

Churchill Sees London's Ruins

MR WINSTON CHURCHILL, accompanied by his wife, visited the ruins of London's famous Guildhall yesterday and spent two hours walking through the City.

As they walked along people cheered. "One was cheered," Col. Moo-rey said. "Mr. Churchill smiled and lifted his hat.

They inspected a deep, underground shelter. So slowly of "Good luck" from the crowd. Mr. Churchill replied, "Good luck to you."

As they left this shelter a woman ran forward and asked: "When will you win the war?"

To the Churchill paused, turned to the woman, and said, "When we have beaten 'em."

Mr. Churchill looked grim and determined as he toured the damaged churches and other buildings.

The scene of his visit spread, and after a while a crowd of cheering Londoners were accompanying him on his tour.

Morrison on Radio To-night

MR. HERBERT MORRISON, Minister of Home Security, will broadcast after the B.B.C.'s 9 o'clock news bulletin this evening.

HAVOC COULD HAVE BEEN SAVED

By Daily Mail Reporter

MANY of Sunday night's fires in the City of London could have been avoided if fire-watching regulations had been properly observed.

That is the opinion of Commander A. N. G. Firebrace, the London Fire Brigade chief, who has just been transferred to the Home Office to help in organising local brigade duties throughout the country.

"It should be a point of honour," he declared, "for everyone to say 'I will not let this place burn down, both for my own sake and for the sake of my neighbours.'

"What is needed is not merely one roof-spotter—you want a rota to keep on the job, and even a party of half a dozen or so is better than no one at all in an emergency.

"Employees of the various firms should in every case form a rota and take turns—even on Sundays—to prevent the start of little fires by incendiary bombs."

Even on Sundays

The whole invisible details of the raid were reported to Mr. Morrison, who will broadcast this evening.

Berlin Radio Went 'All Quiet'

Berlin radio eliminated all reference to the destruction of churches and historic buildings in its broadcast account last night of the fire raid on London. Neither did it follow its usual practice of giving interviews with raiding pilots.

Bremen Radio's English announcer described it as a fierce mass attack, concentrated in the space of a few hours.

"A great number of fires were caused in a relatively small space," he said. "Although the area attacked presented itself on a smaller scale, the German Luftwaffe continued the bomb."

No reference was made to the appearance of the fires other than the eastern part of London."—B.C.F.

Four Raiders In Pacific

Daily Mail Radio Station

Four German raiders are now operating in the Pacific between Australia and China, states a Reuter message from Batavia.

Up to date, it was reported, 11 ships have disappeared in these areas. The ships have been of British, Dutch, and Norwegian origin.

100 to 1 Backing for Roosevelt

From Daily Mail Correspondent

WASHINGTON, Monday.

PRESIDENT ROOSEVELT is "tremendously pleased" at the reaction to his speech, in which he pledged more aid to Britain and declared that the Axis could not win the war.

Within 40 minutes of his end the President received 609 messages. They were 598 to 1 in favour.

This is how it was received by Senator Alban Barkley, leader of the Democratic Party in the Senate: A magnificent statement of our objectives.

End of Hitler?

Major-General Sam-he Moe, head of the Chinese Air Force, is in Washington conferring with Administration officials and Army and Navy leaders.

China Seeks U.S. Planes

From Daily Mail Correspondent

NEW YORK, Monday.—The United States Government has reported to be considering the extension of 600 warplanes to China for use against the Japanese.

500 Were Killed in Manchester

Mr. R. B. Adcock, Manchester's Town Clerk, revealed last night that in the severe raids on the city a week ago, about 500 people were killed.

WAR'S GREATEST PICTURE: St. Paul's Stands Unharmed in the Midst of the Burning City

LONDON LULLABY

HORLICKS

Herbert Mason's photograph of St Paul's Cathedral as printed in the *Daily Mail*, 31st December 1940

x

area of the ancient walled City of London ablaze from end to end. As this photograph was taken, there were still many painful hours to go before it would be possible even to start counting the cost.

As printed, the photograph might well be seen to echo Prime Minister Winston Churchill's bulldog-stubborn declaration of 'never surrender'. But those who saw the City's great Cathedral in hellish context tonight might more reasonably ask, 'How much more of this can London take?' Those who, at the very heart of the inferno, looked down from St Paul's on to the raging fires below – and would witness, when day finally dawned, the pitiful ruin and desolation that the cold December sunlight revealed – had even more cause to wonder.

WITHIN DAYS, Herbert Mason's picture was telling quite another story from the *Daily Mail*'s version to readers of the *Berliner Illustrierte Zeitung*, where it appeared, cropped even tighter, over tidings that 'Die City von London brennt!'. There was no missing those foreground ruins now, nor the import of the boiling cauldron engulfing the heart of 'britis-chen Hochfinanz' in London's biggest blaze, boasted the paper, since 'Jahre 1666'. German readers had followed their Führer's string of astonishing military triumphs over past months; now the conflict with England too, it seemed, was approaching its endgame.

AND TODAY? For us – at least for those of us under the age of seventy – Herbert Mason's photograph has become like an old illustration from a storybook, long since separated from its accompanying text. Torn out for its particular beauty, an illustration quickly loses meaning. We can imagine into it our own story, craft a tale better or worse than the original, but it is never quite the real thing. And then one day, discovering a few pages of typescript in a dusty junk shop, we recognise them with a jolt as belonging to that picture so familiar but, we now begin to realise, so barely understood from our past.

The accompanying text to Herbert Mason's mythic image is more extensive, and the tale it tells more complex and human, than we might imagine. Its pages are scattered widely across continents, and hardest to locate, sometimes, in the very Square Mile where one would most expect to find them. For the City of London is such a very modern city now, with such very modern concerns.

But then you happen down the wrong street one day while looking for something else; turn left instead of right; enter an alleyway that you have never noticed there before, even though you have passed the spot a hundred times; push at a door that stands a little ajar . . . and the City of London begins to give up its secrets. Some things, at least, about this ancient, storytelling labyrinth never change.

THERE ARE MOMENTS – a very few moments – when the whole rich pattern of human history seems to draw together to pass through a single point, as a finely spun shawl may be drawn through a golden wedding ring. And as the night of Sunday 29th December 1940 struggled on towards dawn, this scant square mile of English earth, walled round almost 2,000 years before to protect civilisation from the barbarous British, had become the world's only gateway from its weighty past to its unimaginable future.

Incredibly, all of Europe's long history had, over the past seven years, been captured and subdued to the will of a single individual, who had relentlessly imposed his obscene dreams on the Continent's independent peoples and nations. Equally incredibly, for six months past, the British Empire had stood, as it seemed, alone, holding the gate against Adolf Hitler's vision of the Nazi millennium to come. And now the very heart of that Empire, its heart of hearts, was in flames.

Was it a Turning Point? It was certainly a point on which very great forces were turning. The four most powerful men on earth – in Washington, Westminster, Berlin and Moscow – were playing their cards over the City of London tonight. The wind and weather were players, too. As if to complete a mythic contest, even the sun and moon took a hand.

Yet the outcome of this game – and the world's future – rested, just for this night, on the thousands of men and women doing battle beneath the choking black smoke that covered their city. True Londoners who, no matter where they had been born and what chance had brought them here, had taken on the protection of this ground as their own individual, and very personal, responsibility.

On that distant alien night in that distant alien city, built as much of stories as of stones, bespectacled bank clerks and pale drapers' assistants, lads on push-bikes, tea ladies in tin hats, elderly clerics and *mitteleuropean* refugees, librarians, secretaries, Cockneys and Colonials, fought alongside London's firemen, police and rescue workers, professional and volunteer, to write their own page in their city's long history.

And the epic tale of their successes – and even more, perhaps, their indomitable spirit in their defeats – should not be lost from London's long chronicles. For while the story of this night earns its small place in the sweeping histories of global war, it belongs equally to the voluminous, diligently recorded, carefully guarded annals of this small and ancient city. For the Square Mile might be just a dot on the map of the world in 1940. But then the world of 1940 was just a passing moment on the long time-line of the Square Mile.

It was a moment that might signal its total annihilation, of course. But old London had seen all that before, too.

Scale of | 0 | | 1 | | 2 | | 3 | | 4 Furlongs
Half a Mile | 0 | | 200 | | 400 | | 600 | | 800 Metres

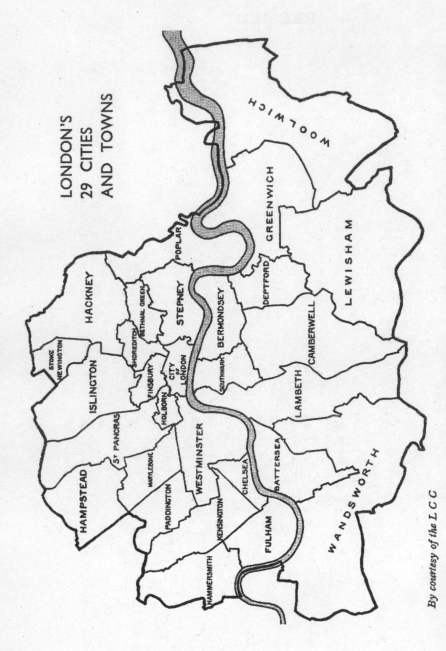

LONDON'S
29 CITIES
AND TOWNS

By courtesy of the L C C

From 1889 to 1965 the County of London covered the 117 square miles now known as inner London. Local government functions were divided between the London County Council (LCC), 27 Metropolitan Broroughs and the cities of London and Westminster.

PRELUDE

Chapter One

Home Service SUNDAY 29th DECEMBER
7.0 a.m. Time, Big Ben: NEWS
and summary of today's programmes
for the Forces

BBC *Radio Times* Christmas Edition, 1940

ACROSS BRITAIN, people were stumbling sleepily downstairs – or up from the basement, or in from the Anderson shelter – to put a match to the gas under the kettle, and to plug in the wireless and switch it on to warm up for the first news of the day: their first chance to hear how the rest of the nation had fared during the night. As they sipped their tea behind black-out curtains this Sunday morning, the familiar 'bongs' transmitted live from Westminster would herald equally familiar tones declaring: 'This is the BBC . . .'

THE 114TH DAY OF 'THE BLITZ' had begun. And all Londoners were starting the day in the reasonable expectation that at least some of them would be dead or badly injured in an air raid before the start of the 115th.

Perhaps not – there might be no raid at all. But since this business began back in the early autumn, there had not been many nights on which the capital had not been a major or minor target. If there was a heavy one again tonight, then your odds were perhaps one in 10,000 of dying; much the same of being seriously injured. Some people's chances were better than others, of course, depending on where they lived, the quality of their shelter and the job they did. But anyone could get caught out. It was the ultimate gamble – which, over the past four months, one in every five or six hundred Londoners had already lost. Thankfully, for Londoners at least, last night had been one of the quiet ones.

In Westminster, heart both of the British war machine and of the democracy it was defending, the deep-throated bell known the world over as 'Big Ben' tolled out across the capital in profound darkness. No glow drew the eye to the familiar clock faces. On the Thames beneath, only the faint reflected gleam of the Westminster Bridge fairway lights, marking a safe channel for emergency craft, showed that the dark waters were there at all. Office lights already burning in the wartime ministries along Whitehall were masked from the street by thick curtains or blackout boards. There was no moon and, unlike yesterday morning and so many mornings before it, no burning buildings to light up the London sky.

The brief December daylight – now lasting less than eight hours from dawn to dusk – was still far off, thanks to wartime daylight-saving. A peace-time Londoner glancing at his alarm clock now would have seen the little hand pointing to the six and burrowed contentedly back beneath the blankets, relishing his Sunday lie-in. But this was wartime; this was seven o'clock. And for many, seven o'clock on a Sunday morning was the start of just another working day – or the welcome end of one.

Gingerly, dimmed torch beams crept along unseen pavements, picking out the warning white painted on kerbstones, lamp posts, street corners and the trunks of looming trees along the Victoria Embankment.

One writer had become a connoisseur of the sound of footfalls on dark mornings, mostly shelterers returning to their homes – if they found homes to return to – after a night under ground:

> a light, but rather slow footstep means that it is probably a woman, carrying a child. You hear quite a lot of these. Too many – for these days in London. Then there will be the clatter of a family: the heavy tread of Dad; the swifter, tripping steps of his wife; the almost-prattle of the hurrying-to-keep-up anxiety of the kids. The stamp of the lonely man; probably if he is an old one, accompanied by the resentful tapping of a stick. All kinds of people, all ages, all states of fatigue, temper or stout-heartedness.

When the Night Blitz began, haste at daybreak could have ensured a couple of hours in your own bed before work. But as the weeks went by, the days shortened and hours of danger increased, workers scurrying home just had time to dump their shelter things, tidy themselves and set out again, still in darkness. Soon, they 'considered themselves lucky if they could find the time for a nice, quiet cup of tea'. The writer, American but a long-time Londoner, knew the importance of that.

'THIS IS THE BBC . . .'

Unseen by listeners, Broadcasting House dress code had relaxed from the perpetual evening dress of Lord Reith's regime into wartime's 'jerseys and sports coats, flannel bags and shirt sleeves'. And, three floors down for safety, the first newsreader of the day often rose to his work from a camp bed. But the traditional sangfroid with which the BBC News was delivered remained undiminished.

Though there had been that one night in October. Edward R. Murrow, writing in the tiny underground studio shared by the three big US radio networks, had heard the window separating him from the BBC engineers crack suddenly. And across Britain, listeners to the evening news had heard newsreader Bruce Belfrage pause momentarily at a muffled explosion. A distant voice called, 'It's all right,' and Belfrage gave a slight cough. 'I beg your pardon,' he said, before continuing.

A delayed-action bomb entering an upper window of Broadcasting House had exploded while being investigated, killing six and injuring many more. In the early hours, Ed Murrow had told early evening America of friends being carried on stretchers past his door to the first aid room, and of a pervading smell of iodine.

There had been more than stiff upper lip to Belfrage's reticence. Nor had the British censor who sat, finger poised on the cut-off switch, during Ed Murrow's broadcast had to enforce what Murrow's own common sense told him. Broadcasting House was target enough, without betraying more information to the German monitors listening in.

The same self-censoring caution lay behind the bland phrasing of news bulletins on so many mornings past. RAF 'jammers' were working flat out to confuse the Luftwaffe's radio direction finding; it made no sense to say whether their night-bombers were on target. 'Fires were started, casualties have been reported,' became standard raid-speak, in which even London might become 'a town in southern England'.

The anonymous city 'taking it' last night had been Plymouth. An intense raid, an hour long, eleven dead and about three times as many seriously injured. The death toll for a major raid was usually in the hundreds, with many more seriously injured. Though even the worst raids in this bombardment, the heaviest so far in human history, were killing only a fraction of the numbers envisaged in Britain's pre-war preparations.

Bigger news than last night's raid, on this last Sunday morning of this most momentous year, was further progress for Empire troops against the Italians in North Africa, and an RAF raid on the Channel ports from which any Nazi invasion of Britain must be launched.

THE NEXT NEWS would be at nine on the Home Service. Later the other, Forces, station would offer *News From India:* tidings from home for Britain's Indian community, including those troops evacuated from Dunkirk but not yet fighting with their compatriots in North Africa.

After the fall of France in June, a newspaper cartoon had shown British

5

defiance as a Tommy brandishing a fist from a small rock battered by stormy seas and declaring 'Very Well, Alone'. But that brilliant graphic simplicity hardly captured the complexity of all that Britishness represented in 1940. For though friends and enemies alike spoke of 'England' as the last bastion of democracy, what stood alone against Hitlerism now was not just the nation, or clutch of nations, occupying these islands, but a worldwide Empire and Commonwealth – as the cartoonist David Low, a New Zealander working for the Canadian Lord Beaverbrook, knew well enough.

This Empire and Commonwealth, made up of a bewildering array of colonies, protectorates, dependencies and independent dominions, meant that every fourth person alive was – in theory and largely in fact – a loyal subject of George VI, by the Grace of God, of Great Britain, Ireland and the British Dominions beyond the Seas, King, Defender of the Faith, Emperor of India. The issue was not as cut and dried as that for many of the King's subjects around the world, as you would see if you opened a newspaper this morning. But then again, for many – and for now – it really was. One young man growing up in the Caribbean later recalled his pride then in the world map on which so much was painted red:

> Big Australia, big India, rich Burma – little Jamaica! We felt proud to have the same colour, to be a family of nations. We felt proud that we had huge battleships like the *Hood*, which was the best in the world. We accepted all of the British traditions. We felt *safe*.
>
> The hierarchy went something like this. The Governor lived at King's House. From King's House the next step would be Buckingham Palace; and the next step above Buckingham Palace was the gates of Heaven itself!

From around the world, peoples of the Empire were responding to the peril of the Mother Country in their own way. The front page of this month's *News Letter* of the London-based League of Coloured Peoples offered its congratulations to Babatunde O. Alakija, the first African to be accepted for RAF pilot training; 300 vacancies in the Indian Air Force Reserve had attracted 18,000 would-be volunteers and the Secretary of State for India had announced that there were, overall, more volunteers from the sub-continent than could be accommodated in Empire forces at present.

The hard-pressed RAF also received gifts, ranging from 328 binoculars and telescopes, 'salvaged' by the Boy Scouts of the West Indies for its Observer Corps, to a squadron of Spitfires paid for by the people of Basutoland. Other presents to Britain included £300 to the children of London from the children of Mauritius: at a reception in battered

Buckingham Palace just before Christmas, thirty-five canteen vans to feed Britain's homeless, all gifts from the Empire, had been presented to Queen Elizabeth. In total, the Colonies and Dominions had so far donated around £17 million, mostly in individual gifts, to the fight against Nazism.

BBC pioneer Lord Reith liked to think that, in bringing great men and women to the humblest fireside, radio offered nothing less than 'a return of the city-state of old'. But in truth no city or state had ever been as intimate with its rulers as this vast Empire had become with the House of Windsor since Christmas Day 1932 when, in words written for him by his old friend Rudyard Kipling, George V had spoken: 'from my home and from my heart' to all those 'men and women so cut off by the snows, the desert, or the sea, that only voices out of the air can reach them'. The Christmas speech to the Empire had swiftly become, as new things so often became for the British, an instant, much-loved tradition. As much a part of the festivities as the tree or Charles Dickens or Brussels sprouts – and under the blazing sun on the far side of the world as much as in cold, grey Britain itself.

FOUR DAYS AGO, the new young king had spoken to the Empire. Though in south London, May Speed and her sister Ethel had nearly missed him altogether. They had been landed with so much Christmas washing up ('oceans of it!') that, by the time they joined their siblings at the wireless, *Christmas Under Fire*'s live broadcasts from around the Empire were drawing to a close, at a shelter party 'somewhere in Britain'. A Cockney woman who had lost all her windows in an air raid voiced the nation's loyal greetings to the King. Then came George VI.

His stammer made him a reluctant broadcaster, and many a loyal heart strained protectively whenever the voice halted. 'Time and again during these last few months,' said the King:

> I have seen for myself the battered towns and cities of England, and I have seen the British people facing their ordeal. I can say to them all that they may be justly proud of their race and nation. On every side I have seen a new and splendid spirit of good fellowship springing up in adversity, a real desire to share burdens and resources alike.
>
> Out of all this suffering there is growing a harmony which we must carry forward into the days to come when we have endured to the end and ours is the victory. Then, when Christmas Days are happy again and good will has come back to the world, we must hold fast to the spirit which binds us all together now. We shall need this spirit in each of our own lives as men and women and shall need it even more among the nations of the world. We must go on thinking less about

7

ourselves and more for one another; for so, and so only, can we hope to make the world a better place and life a worthier thing.

The King's message chimed perfectly with the sermon May Speed and her dear friend Etta Evans had just heard that Christmas morning. Which dwelt, May recorded in her diary, on the Christ-like qualities that disaster brought out in Man. 'Who would have believed that East Enders would have shown such courage, endurance & fortitude under bombings!'

Though public transport ran as usual on Christmas Day, she and Etta had decided to walk from the Speeds' Georgian villa in Brixton to the City of London. The ancient Temple church off Fleet Street was famous for its music: back in the Twenties, when Ernest Lough recorded O For The Wings of a Dove there, services had been ticket-only affairs. Today the choirboys were evacuated, and Ernest a grown-up auxiliary fireman, but the remaining choristers lifted the spirit. Listening to the carols ringing through the frosty air (the church had lost windows to bomb blast), May admired the bright fan vaulting above and wondered whether any of it would be standing next Christmas.

'No joybells and no decorations, but quiet and restful,' was her final verdict on the service. Church bells – the signal for invasion, or victory – were silenced this Christmas. But there had been plenty of decorations on the way home. The London Bridge underground platform was decked with holly, mistletoe, evergreens, silver bells and balloons: legacy of those who regularly sought shelter from the night-bombing in the Tube system.

IN BERLIN, George VI's Christmas Day message had left the Nazi Propaganda Minister cold when a transcript landed on his desk. 'Nonsense and slogans. Unimportant,' noted Josef Goebbels in his diary. He had too good an idea of the Führer's plans for those 'battered towns and cities of England' to attach any significance to the King's hopes for the future.

The only wonder to Goebbels was that the whole sorry business had not been over long ago. 'The only thing keeping them going is the famous English stubbornness,' he had noted in frustration some weeks back. 'Read an essay on the English: their best weapons are their phlegm and their stupidity. In their position, any other nation would have collapsed long since.'

Few entries in Josef Goebbels' diary would have raised a chuckle in British homes during the winter of 1940, but this would have been one of them. That foreigners found Englishness less a nationality than a form of mental weakness had brought a smile to English lips for centuries. Josef

Goebbels was saying nothing about the British that they had not paid good money to be told in the past: a long stream of best-sellers on the peculiar English by 'funny foreigners' proved there was a good living to be made in poking fun at the Island Race.

'Give plenty of space to our oddities,' his London publisher had urged Dutch academic G. J. Renier a decade back, when he sought to analyse how the rumbustious swashbucklers of English history had dwindled into the desiccated remnants he saw around him. 'You will be left with ample room for your pet theories . . . But never forget this: we are, and we want above all else to be, the odd islanders.' Renier's book, packed with sardonic observations on his hosts' strange habits, intellectual blind spots and sexual inadequacies, duly appeared in 1931 under the title *The English: Are They Human?* and was clasped to the bosom of the British book-buying public, reprinting steadily up to the war and beyond.

So Fleet Street, given the chance, would have cheerfully quoted Josef Goebbels' scorn of the English in 1940, as it did other German pronouncements that made it smile. Readers had already been treated to an SS newspaper's theory that London's resilience under bombing was due not to 'the British ability to "take it" or their proverbial toughness'.

> Rather England approaches death with sensual pleasure and smacks its lips. Psychopaths know of such cases where the pleasure of destruction is paralleled by the pleasure of self-destruction. There lies the solution of British toughness and endurance.

And last Friday's *News Chronicle* had printed highlights of Feldmarschall von Brauchitsch's Christmas message to his troops, under the headline: 'The War Is Already Won – Nazi Army Chief'. 'We are convinced that the war is already won and that the Führer will end it in the way needed by our nation for the security of its future,' the Feldmarschall had declared. All that remained was the Reich's 'last and most embittered enemy' which was, he said, 'protected by the sea only as long as it suits us'. No smile crossed Josef Goebbels' lips when he read these words: von Brauchitsch was a 'conceited dandy'. British newspapers might print the speech; Goebbels' Ministry of Propaganda would ensure it never appeared in a German one.

MAY SPEED, who had woken this Sunday morning to yet more bickering and tears among her many resident and visiting sisters, might well have had some sympathy with Goebbels' view on British 'stubbornness'. But she could have pointed to their self-appointed cook and domestic tyrant

9

Norah Speed, for one, as proof that not all the British were the phlegmatics of legend. 'You cannot speak to her reasonably,' May vented her frustration to her faithful diary this morning:

> If you do, she raves & falls into an hysterical weeping, in which there are no real tears. When she screamed coming to from gas the other day, she told me that as she returned to consciousness, she was thinking 'I won't, I won't.' That typifies her attitude. The war has affected her nerves very badly.

Norah, she wrote, 'wants to be a little Hitler. To rule us like children on old-fashioned lines.'

War had interrupted all their lives: May had given up work as a commercial artist and joined Ethel in the family's small textile business in the City (though she still retained ambitions as a writer); brother Fred had signed up as an air raid warden; and Norah had sacrificed her 'brain work' to run their household. Alas, though, for dreams of

> A happy co-operation for our mutual interest, as Ethel, Fred and I together could make it because none of us suffer from a swollen ego. None of us wants to boss the other and so we could live in happy accord. None of us wants the lion share of everything, the best helpings at meals, the best chair, the best place at the fire as Norah always does & always manages to get.

Those who had tried to contain the big Hitler through the 1930s might have recognised a profound truth in May's resigned sigh over their little one this morning: 'We have been fools I suppose, but have always let her have her way, for the sake of peace.'

How unlike poor, discontented Norah was the stoic little charlady Fred had deposited on them during Friday's raid for a 'wash and brush-up'. Tucking in to turkey stew (remnants of their Christmas dinner) in the Speeds' basement dining room at midnight, she had assured them over and over that: 'You have to be in trouble to know how kind people can be.' ('I could have howled,' May confided to her diary.)

There was indeed a strange, generous, almost egalitarian spirit abroad nowadays. The King had spoken on Christmas Day of 'good fellowship'; others talked, with approval or disapproval, of social revolution. A letter picked up by the Censor had spoken of 'a kind of *warmth* pervading England' and Churchill had marked the Censorship report with red ink at that point. There was undeniably something in the air. Though pinning it down was as hard as catching the Spirit of Christmas in a butterfly net. And this 1940 spirit had its own Scrooges too: big cheats and little cheats who clung to their cash boxes and cried 'Humbug!' whenever they heard carolling.

Perhaps the hopeful scenario that Charles Dickens had sketched out in the London of a hundred Christmases ago offered an insight into what his fellow-citizens were experiencing now, in these surreal days of human kindness amid inhuman savagery:

> a good time: a kind, forgiving, charitable, pleasant time: the only time I know of, in the long calendar of the year, when men and women seem by one consent to open their shut-up hearts freely, and to think of people below them as if they really were fellow-passengers to the grave, and not another race of creatures bound on other journeys.

For the unsentimental, very real, stark and practical wartime reality was that all Londoners knew themselves for fellow-passengers now. And who could say who was 'below' whom, when circumstances could place anyone's life in anyone else's hands in an instant?

What had most upset the old lady on Friday night was the family next door: 'nice people' evacuated from Jersey in the summer. The wife had arrived home from waitressing at the Devonshire Club to find not only her husband and her mother dead, but her baby too: found under the rubble 'with its little hot water bottle'.

'War is horrible,' said the old lady, 'but I suppose the German people suffer just as we do and are just as innocent.'

She was looking forward to the hospitality of the local rest centre. The teachers who ran it were 'ladies' she said, and the dinners wonderful: 'Angels' food', some of the others called it. This was her third time of being bombed out: her one regret was the loss of her piano. 'It had been a great comfort.' May's sister Ethel had given the old lady ten shillings, despite her protests, when Fred took her away. Later, after he had helped a fellow warden 'salve' the remains of his bombed flat (no casualties, luckily), he returned with news that a policeman and Home Guard had been posted to ward off the looters who had arrived within an hour of the bombing. You had to be in trouble to know how kind people can be – but to help people in trouble, you had to recognise that not every evil impulse in every human heart had been bombed into the milk of human kindness.

IT WAS A VERY DIFFERENT mood now, a very different world, from last Christmas. Long months of seeming inactivity had led then to the common complaint of 'Bore War'. The American press had even dubbed it a 'Phoney War'. But in spring 1940 it had suddenly blazed into the real thing with Hitler's slice through the neutrality of Scandinavia and the

Low Countries. Then came the devastatingly swift collapse, at the cost of many thousands of lives, of a French army billed as the strongest in Europe; the tragic, miraculous evacuation from Dunkirk; and Fascist Italy's last-minute entry into the war alongside its triumphant Axis partner. From Germany's invasion of Norway on 9th April, it had taken just two months to change the face of Europe and the future of the world.

It had seemed, initially, that it must be a future of purely German design. And yet, foreign correspondents noted with astonishment, France's capitulation had not provoked the expected despair in their allies across the Channel. The British seemed, if anything, rather more cheerful. G. J. Renier had claimed, as one of their inhuman oddities, 'the capacity possessed by the overwhelming majority of Englishmen to laugh or at least smile in circumstances where normal human beings curse or cry'. And after so many years of doubt, anxiety and the growing sense that Britain had not played the game by the Nazis' earlier victims, there seemed a kind of relief in knowing that they were, as one young man said, 'in the final now' – and on home ground.

American reporter Eric Sevareid had seen it in the faces of his British counterparts, heading for home as France crumpled. 'They seemed almost happy; they were British and their course was clear. They were sticking together now; all the British were together.' He had his own reservations about the odd islanders. But he decided to follow them to London rather than head straight for America. 'We knew, somehow, without inquiring, that England would continue to fight. I thought I had reasoned myself away from all youthful feelings of kinship with England, but now England seemed intimate, understandable, and terribly important.'

The day the Franco-German Armistice was announced, the *New York Times*'s London bureau chief Raymond Daniell found the Ministry of Information bar in Bloomsbury more cheerful than he had ever seen it: 'You could tell the correspondents from the officials at a glance. The former were long-faced and sad-looking. The latter were beaming.'

Unsure whether he was insane or 'the whole British government had gone daft', he canvassed his taxi driver. With his droopy moustache he was, thought Daniell, the spitting image of 'Old Bill', laconic British cartoon hero of the Great War trenches. What did he think of the news from France? 'Not too bad,' said the cabbie – a phrase US correspondents had learn to translate as 'OK'. But could Britain really beat Hitler alone? 'Well, we can't if we don't try, can we, Guv'nor?' he replied. When Daniell got to his office, the lift operator observed: 'Things are looking better, aren't they, sir . . . there's nobody left to desert us now.'

This mood was not confined to London. An Austrian Jew working in Devon recalled: 'We refugees thought we might as well go and cut our throats right away.' They decided the English were insane when the old foreman was applauded for saying, 'You don't understand us. Now we're rid of these bloody Frogs we're really going to go.' That evening the Local Defence Volunteers assembled. Looking at their shotguns and ancient pikes, the refugee told his compatriots: 'I don't know how they are going to win the war, but they are not going to lose it. People who do this cannot lose, they never know when they've lost.' It was a courage, he decided, 'born of ignorance of what they were up against'.

He had a point. Even after Dunkirk, no one had the true measure of the carnage the German military could inflict against a determined opposition. And unlike the French, unlike most of Europe – unlike most of the world in fact – the British had to look back hundreds of years to find war bloodying their own cornfields. On the other hand, most of the million-and-a-half LDV who mustered within days of the Government call were veterans of the Trenches. They knew something about war – enough to know that old soldiers with makeshift weapons could win no more than a little breathing space for regular troops racing to get into position. But, as their hero 'Old Bill' had said drily, last time around, to a disgruntled colleague sharing his shell-raked dugout: 'Well, if you knows of a better 'ole, go to it.' Britain was now in a more perilous 'ole than it had known in centuries. But if anyone knew of a better one . . .

Not that the Home Guard, as Churchill had quickly renamed the LDV, was all old men. Able-bodied chaps stuck in reserved occupations received guerrilla warfare training at the Earl of Jersey's home of Osterley Park, lent to the ad hoc Home Guard school launched by the publishers of *Picture Post*. This eccentric but deadly serious establishment offered such subjects as the manufacture of pipe bombs, camouflage (taught by a Surrealist painter) and how to inflict serious injury with a lady's hat pin. Instructors ranged from guerrillas just back after the Spanish Civil War to a man who had learned Scouting from Baden-Powell himself.

Eric Sevareid, who had scraped back into Britain on one of the last refugee ships from France, watched these 'bankers, brokers, and landlords – and once Sir Nevile Henderson, one of those who had tried diplomatic argument with evil' in training. He found plenty to dislike in Britain's social set-up but, he admitted, 'Whatever the faults of the British ruling class, they are not a very "soft" people; the tradition of physical courage, however poor a substitute for intellect, is with them still.'

> These gentlemen threw grenades, strung hidden wires, crawled on their bellies along the ditches, and gathered around their instructors, perspiring, eager for advice and praise. A stumpy, gnarled little Cockney Communist said very casually: 'Now I personally like to take my tank from a little bit to the rear – like this . . .' I wondered: Would the Hendersons do this if the tanks came? I was convinced they would.

This 'Cockney Communist' was presumably the same 'cripple of about 4ft 9in' whose handy hints were passed on in a family newsletter by an accountant from Hoare's Bank in Fleet Street.

> 'Forget the playing fields of Eton and the Marquess of Queensberry,' he bellowed, 'and remember that no way is too dirty to kill a German.' With the result that I now know all about how to use a knife and a cheesecutter. Always attack from the back, dear Uncle Basil. If you have to do it from the front, slit him up the stomach – but he'll squeal. He won't if knifed from behind.

Uncle Basil was Sir Basil Mayhew, vice-chairman of J. & J. Colman the mustard company, High Sheriff of the County of Norfolk and Parish Leader of his local Home Guard platoon. During the Dunkirk evacuations, the platoon's instruction to hold its post 'to the last man' had become to the last man and Aunt Beryl. As President of the Norwich division of the Red Cross, Lady Mayhew had insisted on setting up a First Aid Post and serving refreshments while the Home Guard filled sandbags and put up barricades. 'It seemed to be a bit dull to go to bed as usual, and also Dad had lumbago,' she excused herself to her family, recasting the whole adventure in the spirit of girlish lark. More seriously, she confessed that she found the

> 'present situation' quietly but deeply exhilarating, but probably it's a purely female (and British female at that) sort of feeling which no male could begin to understand. When other people have done your fighting for you, it's an incredible relief to feel you've come to a time when that blessed Ministry of Information poster has some meaning for you at last, and I think George [her son-in-law] is wrong about history – knitting mittens while others are making it is devastating, but actually making it is a different thing altogether. Alright, I know I'll feel very different when 'things go bump in the night', but here and now I wouldn't change places with anyone in history.

As THE BRITISH improvised their ground defences, a strange, epic battle had been fought in the skies above them. From the jousting of champions in the blue skies of high summer, it had shaded by autumn into the heavy bombardment of a medieval siege, bringing death in the dark on an as yet unparalleled scale. But though all the logic of warfare weighed against them, as 1940 came to a close, the British did not seem ready to concede the battle. If anything, they seemed to be just gearing up for the fight.

'Honestly Winnie, I am glad not to have been away from London so far,' one woman had written, after two solid months of Blitz, to a British officer's American wife, now back in the US and hungry for a true picture of how her friends were faring across the ocean.

> It is an experience which makes everything else look pale, and which justifies whatever feelings you ever dimly had about the English being something. The hopeless dimness of English foreign politics does seem part of the want of imagination which makes the heroism possible. I think all truly democratic people are bad at foreign politics because they are much more interested in making their own organization work . . . I hope in the end we will win a few battles and manage a bit of successful foreign intrigue, but we do seem to have lost the trick. Still we will win even at long distance of time and cost.

One thing that kept her going, another friend told Winnie, was the thought that there were hundreds of men whom she thought 'pretty small meat' who had stuck four years of this sort of thing in the last war. And, she wrote, 'if they can do it, I can, and so can anyone else. They were just ordinary people, and so am I.'

THERE IS A SENSE in which London was, had always been, a city written into being: story and history layered on top of one other till they were almost indistinguishable. At the beginning of this war, writer Storm Jameson had claimed that one of literature's tasks in this battle against the 'forces of regress' was 'to experience despair as a stage in courage . . . the thought of defeat as a reminder that no Dark Age has outlasted, or can outlast, the unquenchable energy of the mind'. And as a whole new literature of courage was being written in 1940, 'ordinary people' seemed to walk in to and out of the pages of storybooks till there was no telling where they belonged.

Nor was this just the much-derided Ministry of Information at work. Before the war, as London celebrated the coronation of George VI, a correspondent for the *New Yorker* had tried to explain to readers back home how British respect for historical precedent had overcome the little matter of bumping Edward VIII from the throne in favour of his younger brother

George. 'It's impossible for a foreigner . . . to understand the English from his foreign viewpoint,' she warned.

> He's got to try to understand them from the English viewpoint, which is nearly impossible, it being composed of local picturesque traditions observed as seriously as if they were universal scientific laws; a certain view of undeviating duty which, though it has been vaguely transplanted all over the Empire, flourishes best as a strictly island growth; and a combination of painstaking sentimentality and thumping realism, both drawn on in emergency as if they were the same thing.

'With their rational mind they empower democracy,' she assured her readers,

> but with their emotional imagination they still give credit, perhaps wisely, to that miracle-loving element in human beings which tends toward iconography, kings, prophets and special beings in strange, lovely garments. This element in other lands has recently found its less monarchic outlet in Nazi trappings, Fascist fanfares, a Communism which makes a shrine of Lenin's tomb, and, in America, a worship of cinema stars.

When, before this war, Eric Sevareid first wandered the streets of London, he had viewed them through the filter of 'Pepys and Dickens, Sherlock Holmes and a dozen others'. After a few days the veil fell and his candid American eye registered the cramped, class-ridden, dirty, draughty realities: 'Did the English, the remarkable English, masters of half the world, allow themselves to live like this?' But then war had come and he had escaped from France back to a London that was stranger, even, than fiction. At the end of October, on the eve of his departure home to his wife and new twin babies, he had agreed to Ed Murrow's request to make one last broadcast from London. 'I talked a little about France,' he wrote later,

> about Paris dying in her coma, about the cities which had broken in spirit, about London, which had not – London, which 'is not England' but which is Britain, which had become a city-state in the old Greek sense – and about a peaceable people who had gone to war in their aprons and bowlers, with their old fowling pieces, with their ketchup bottles filled with gasoline and standing ready on the pantry shelves. I quoted someone there who had written: 'When this is all over, in the days to come, men will speak of this war, and they will say: I was a soldier, or I was a sailor, or I was a pilot; and others will say with equal pride: I was a citizen of London.' I could not hold my voice quite steady and I felt ashamed of it; I felt that the broadcast was filled with bathos, mawkish and embarrassing to all who heard it. When I reached home a businessman told me he had listened while driving and had had to stop his car for a moment. A professor of English history told me he had heard it in his bedroom and had had to bathe his eyes

before he went down to dinner. In contribution it was a mite, but apparently it helped, and that was reward enough for any man among so many who did so much.

AFTER DUNKIRK, the world had wondered at the miracle of a third of a million men lifted from the beaches, over nine dramatic days by almost 700 ships, large and small. The new Prime Minister had warned that wars were not won by evacuations. But he had gone on to say that Britain would go on nonetheless, would 'never surrender', however long the fight, however high the price of victory, however savage the cost of defeat. And after Winston Churchill had spoken memorably for the British people on 4th June, the novelist J. B. Priestley, the following day, had spoken for the odd islanders.

Both men opened up the old English storybook but they were reading from different pages. The Prime Minister had invoked great heroes of fact and fantasy: even before the Battle of Britain began he was already comparing the young men of the RAF, with advantages, to Crusaders and Arthurian knights. But what Priestley had found most characteristic about this 'English epic . . . so typical of us, so absurd and yet so grand and gallant that you don't know whether to laugh or cry' were the seaside pleasure steamers among the flotilla of little ships assisting the mighty Royal Navy. Epitomising these 'shilling sicks' was the *Gracie Fields,* which had so often carried him home to the Isle of Wight but which now lay at the bottom of the English Channel.

What struck him about the whole thing, he told his BBC audience, was how typical it had been 'both in its beginning and its end, its folly and its grandeur':

> It was very English in what was sadly wrong with it . . . But having admitted this much, let's do ourselves the justice of admitting that this Dunkirk affair was also very English (and when I say 'English' I really mean British) in the way in which, when apparently all was lost, so much was gloriously retrieved.

He didn't need to labour the point. That all their country's great victories had been muddled through against the odds, that 'we British always lose every battle but the last', was an idea too deeply rooted in the national psyche to need explanation or justification. (Later, as things started to look up against the Italians in north Africa, a general won chuckles by opening a speech with 'Ladies and Gentlemen, unaccustomed as we are to military successes . . .' and loud laughter when he continued' . . . especially so early in a war'.)

PRIESTLEY ASKED, about the great evacuation: 'doesn't it seem to you to have an inevitable air about it – as if we had turned a page in the history of Britain and seen a chapter headed "Dunkirk" – and perhaps seen too a picture of the troops on the beach waiting to embark?' Now, half a year later, the odd islanders were all too aware that they were writing another, distinct, chapter for the history books.

The day would come (though who could say how far off?) when some-one, somewhere, would turn to the page of the story headed 'Blitz' and read this chapter right through to the ending not yet known; see pictures not yet taken that would encapsulate these strange and fateful days for later ages.

There was no way of knowing, for anyone writing their part of the 'Blitz' chapter in London on this Sunday morning of 29th December 1940, whether it would prove to have been the 'finest hour' Churchill had sum-moned them to, or a bloody, humiliating defeat that would draw the nation's long, dramatic history to a close and plunge the whole world into what Priestley called 'the black abyss at the end of a wrong road'.

The only thing the odd islanders could do now was to take things as they came.

One day at a time.

Chapter Two

29 December 1940 (Sunday). Yesterday: Into Berlin
early. Snow and frost. The Führer was here for a
day and has now gone off to the Obersalzberg . . .

Josef Goebbels' personal diary

HITLER WOULD PROBABLY STILL, Goebbels knew, be sleeping peacefully
at his spectacular mountain fastness. An early riser in Berlin, the Führer
had slept away whole mornings in his beloved Berghof.

Hitler had been visiting Berchtesgaden since he was a young man – he
had written part of *Mein Kampf* in the modest chalet that stood on the site
of his spaciously remodelled home. Visitors to his new Berghof invariably
noted the imposing Great Hall with its wall of window looking out on to
the magnificent, Wagnerian, Alpine view: a mirror for Hitler's sense of
destiny. 'The Führer lives here in the midst of the beauties of nature,' an
official booklet declared, 'a metaphor for human events.'

> Here he writes his major speeches which affect not only Germany, but give new
> direction to events in the entire world . . . As the mountains remain eternal
> despite the passing of millennia, so too the work the Führer has begun here will
> live for millennia in the history of his people.

It was in this Great Hall that, in 1937, Hitler had shared his thoughts on
Empire with British Foreign Secretary Lord Halifax. Though he railed
against it in public, Hitler saw something to admire in the British Empire
– *The Lives of a Bengal Lancer* was one of the Hollywood films that, while
banned across the Reich, was on constant standby in his private cinema.
But he obviously felt decadent British aristocrats needed guidance on
controlling lesser races.

'Shoot Gandhi,' he rapped out to the former Viceroy, whose, anguished
discussions with the Indian campaigner had made the first tentative steps
on the path towards independence. Lord Halifax could only gaze at Herr
Hitler in astonishment as he continued: 'And if that does not suffice to
reduce them to submission, shoot a dozen leading members of Congress;
and if that does not suffice, shoot 200 and so on until order is established.'
A vague gesture of demurral from the dumbfounded minister allowed the
embarrassing moment to pass but he confessed to the diplomat with him

that Hitler had 'bewildered' him: 'it was clear that he spoke a different language'.

An equally bewildered Neville Chamberlain had come here in September 1938, to discuss Hitler's claim to Czechoslovakia's German-speaking Sudentenland region (the final demand, Chamberlain hoped, in the Reich's pursuit of 'Greater Germany'). A few weeks later, Chamberlain had flown out of Munich clutching 'peace in our time'.

IN JOSEF GOEBBELS' lakeside retreat in the snowy woods west of Berlin, he was recording the happenings of the previous day, as he had every morning for the past twenty years. The diaries of Hitler's Propaganda chief would be a priceless gift to later ages – 'My legacy to my children,' he told his staff. A fascinating insight into how the Thousand-Year Reich was born: a process in which his own brilliance had been so integral a part.

'Behind Hitler sits a little man who laughs all the time,' a young Welshman had told readers of the *Western Mail and South Wales News* during the last-ever free elections of the German Republic.

> He has a narrow Iberian head and brown eyes which twinkle with wit and intelligence. He looks like the dark, small, narrow-headed, sharp Welsh type which is so often found in the Glamorgan valleys. This is Dr Goebbels, a Rhinelander, the brain of the National-Socialist Party and, after Hitler, its most emotional speaker. His is a name to remember, for he will play a big part in the future.

The time had been three o'clock on Thursday 23rd February 1933, and no journalist ever had a closer view of history in the making. Gareth Jones was flying with 'a mass of human dynamite' and his article read like prophecy in 1940: 'If this aeroplane should crash then the whole history of Europe would be changed,' he had written. 'For a few feet away sits Adolf Hitler, Chancellor of Germany and leader of the most volcanic nationalist awakening which the world has seen.'

By the time the Welshman returned to Germany at the end of May 1933, Hitler had already parleyed his 44 per cent vote into an absolute grip on the machinery of government. A process that, wrote Jones, 'makes the French Revolution appear almost like prolonged slow motion'. Hitler's Brown Shirts were now 'the masters of Germany. Every day in Berlin they march through streets bedecked with red, black, and white Nazi flags to the sound of those military marches which are rousing young Germany to a passionate militant love of their Fatherland.'

But, though they weren't aware of it, things had been about to change for the Brownshirts too. Three million *Sturm Abteilung* on the streets had been as essential to Hitler's rise as Goebbels' guile. But now he had law courts and new camps like Dachau to handle his enemies. And the SA was more of a hindrance than a help in his relations with the military establishment, whose dreams of revival he wished to harness to his own. In 1934's 'Night of the Long Knives', the *Schutzstaffel*, the ultra-loyal Blackshirts, obligingly eliminated several hundred of the more independently minded Brownshirt leaders.

The Blackshirt leader had gone on to make a favourable impression on at least one distinguished British journalist. Sir Philip Gibbs had played an honourable role in exposing the excesses of Allied propaganda in the Great War and did not want his countrymen drawn into another bloody conflict by anti-'Hun' hysteria. True, Berlin was not London: 'We do not like many things about the Nazi regime.' But everyone deserved a hearing. The 'good-looking' SS leader had spoken 'vivaciously and wittily' about the Reich's many problems and (often sadly rebuffed) affection for England. Gibbs also had, in fairness, to acknowledge the justice in his charges of British hypocrisy over colonies. 'Strangely attractive', Himmler did not, Gibbs reassured his nervous readers in 1938, 'look or speak like a man who would torture his prisoners.'

The more astute Gareth Jones was sadly unable, by then, to contribute his insights into the nature and capacities of the Nazi regime: he had been murdered in 1935 on an assignment in Japanese-occupied Manchuria. But even back in the summer of 1933, while much of the European Establishment was still giving Herr Hitler a cautious welcome as a bulwark against the Red Menace, the much-travelled Jones had found Germany's 'atmosphere of idealism combined with fear, of unbounded hope on one side and of whispered despair on the other' strangely familiar.

He had just been banned from the Soviet Union for revealing a massive famine in the Ukraine which the world's Moscow correspondents were still assuring their readers was not taking place. Now:

> When I added up in my mind the points of similarity between Berlin, Moscow and Rome I was astounded, for they clearly showed that the methods of the Nazis and of the Fascists are the same as those of the Bolsheviks, however much their aims may differ . . . You cannot argue with a Nazi, nor with a Bolshevik, any more than you could convince a fundamentalist believer of the validity of Darwin's theories.

Jones had been deeply dismayed by the quasi-religious fervour he saw around him. 'I have for my leader,' one leading Nazi had told him, '. . . a faith than which no faith, even in religion, could be deeper. Hitler can never be wrong, and his orders I shall carry out to the death.' As another inveighed, eyes sparkling, against the Jews, the Welshman felt himself 'transported back many centuries, to an age of witchcraft and black magic'. How could a society with which one had shared so many centuries of European Enlightenment become so profoundly incomprehensible?

Elements of Nazi ideology that had once seemed more farcical than dangerous had swiftly become concrete elements of the new administration. Obsessions and fetishes that had seemed ludicrous, fantastical, were enshrined in law. And, with his charming smiles to the foreign press and ruthless dispatch of domestic enemies, Josef Goebbels' role had evolved from architect of Hitler's rise to propaganda chief for his Third Reich. As Hitler's master manipulator of truth, Goebbels took considerable personal pride in what his Führer saw when he looked at his beloved maps at the end of 1940. For with just a few exceptions all of Europe – almost all the world – was now German, or occupied, or acquiescent.

NOT THAT LIFE was all roses, as Goebbels noted sardonically this morning. Saturdays were supposed to be relaxing but work had dragged him into the office yesterday just the same. The usual mixed bag: a question over who would sing the lead in *Die Meistersinger* on a propaganda tour of Holland; von Brauchitsch's ridiculous Christmas speech to suppress and, at the end of the day, a birthday party for the head of the SA: no one looking to survive in Hitler's court could afford to neglect any faction, even the long-eclipsed Brown Shirts. And he had boosted his own profile with a gift of a film projector, on which they had watched Propaganda's latest newsreel. Then it had been home to peaceful Krumme Lanke, his wife and angelic children, more paperwork, then bed at last.

Even Sunday would be no day of rest. He had a leader article to write for *Das Reich* today, rebutting Churchill's insolent speech to Italy, whose October invasion of Greece had met a spectacular popular resistance that threatened to drive it from Albania too. The valorous Greeks were Britain's great heroes now, and the collapse of Italian Fascism Churchill's current best hope. In his broadcast before Christmas he had urged ordinary Italians to consider the desperate position to which Mussolini had brought them: 'we have always been such friends'. Goebbels sometimes admitted to his diary that Churchill's speeches were not without talent.

But if Churchill saw Italy as the soft underbelly of the Axis, he was well aware that Germany itself was not yet in the field. Goebbels too, though contemptuous of his Italian counterparts, knew Hitler would not easily let his Fascist mentor fail, even if Mussolini's blunders were an unwelcome distraction from Reich priorities.

THE FÜHRER'S first visit, on Christmas Eve, to the airfields bombing England had not been quite the triumphal progress envisaged six months ago when Goering promised to sweep the RAF from the skies. 'Again and again the German High Command believed that the last of the doggedly fighting Spitfires must have been shot down,' recorded one Luftwaffe pilot.

> Yet again and again as the days became weeks and the weeks became months, our bombers were still being engaged in combat by more fighters taking to the air, undaunted by the large numbers of the RAF who crashed to their deaths every day.

The 'Battle of Britain' that the British (and Canadians, New Zealanders, Poles, Czechs and the others who flew with them) had fought between 10th July and 31st October 1940 had been hailed by their friends as a victory to rank with Trafalgar or the defeat of the Armada. But from the German perspective there had been no such battle and – in the Goebbels-controlled press, certainly – no defeat. The Battle *for* Britain continued: the Luftwaffe simply chose to fly by night now, not by day, with London rather than airfields the main target.

THUS THE BATTLE that was not a battle had shaded into the *Blitzkrieg* that was not a *Blitzkrieg*. For London's 'Blitz' was not really the 'lightning war' that had been seen rolling out across Europe in newsreels at all. Germany's tactic – air raids to disable and demoralise before ground troops rolled in – had been developed in Spain, had won it Warsaw and Rotterdam and had driven its enemies before it across France in a tangle of fleeing refugees and regrouping troops until Paris had been surrendered without a fight. But, when it came to Britain, as one of Lady Mayhew's sons had written to her cheerfully, did not Shakespeare talk of 'This precious jewel, set in a silver sea, Which serves it in the office of a tank trap?' While Hitler's planes could reach England, his tanks, as yet, could not. Luftwaffe strategists had concentrated on bombing Britain's aerial defences to destruction – and had been succeeding. So what had possessed Hitler to try to bomb London into submission in the autumn of 1940?

In one sense he could not resist it, as a chance of forcing a speedy peace; in another, he could hardly avoid it. London was the largest capital city in the western world: one inter-war guidebook proudly boasting that, if you included 'Police London, Postal London, Telephone London, Water

London, Electricity London, Transport London', the original 'Square Mile' had grown into a metropolis close on 700 square miles in extent and peopled by a quarter of the population of England.

Hitler had decreed that London should be bombed only on his express command. But which London? The 'greater' London area had naturally taken its share of attacks as part of the Luftwaffe's focus on air defences and factories. At Croydon, where Britain's premier civil airport had been taken over by the RAF, six servicemen and more than sixty civilians had been killed when Croydon Airport was bombed on 15th August. The first bombs on the London County Council's 117 square miles of inner London had fallen two days after that. And a week later, on a Sunday night when homes were destroyed in a number of London suburbs, a bomb fell on the 'Square Mile' itself for the first time since 1918. It landed just a few hundred yards north of St Paul's Cathedral, destroyed commercial property on the corner of Wood Street and Fore Street and blasted the porch of one of only eight City churches spared by the Great Fire of 1666, shattering its stained glass and littering its floor with broken cherubs.

High explosive dropped from several miles up in the dark is not a precision weapon. So the bomb blast that turned the course of the war can only be ascribed to a highly portentous serendipity.

St Giles Cripplegate was rich in London history: Shakespeare's bastard nephew was christened here, Cromwell was married here and it was the last resting place of John Milton. Inside the church, memorials to Elizabethan sea-dog Martin Frobisher, martyrologist John Foxe and map-maker John Speed (honoured ancestor of the Speeds of Brixton) had escaped the bombing relatively unscathed. But outside, Milton's statue had been bounced from its vantage point. He made a telling image for photographers next morning as he lay, stonework and dignity intact, gazing blindly up at the vacated plinth and his words from *Paradise Lost* that sought to 'justify the ways of God to men'.

There was no question that London had been bombed now, as Churchill had always expected it would be, sooner or later. He ordered swift retaliatory raids on Berlin: Goering had promised the German people that no British bomb would ever fall on them; the Nazis must be shown that they could not act wholly without unpleasant consequences for themselves.

In physical terms, the British raids achieved very little. The RAF, who had to cross many more miles of hostile territory than the Luftwaffe, in the dark, were mostly way off target. But though their bombs did not make much impact on Berlin, they certainly made an impact on Adolf Hitler. On 4th September, an incandescent Führer promised his ecstatic Berlin audience revenge on 'Europe's last island':

> if the British Air Force drops two, three or four thousand kilos of bombs, then we will drop in one night 150,000, 180,000, 230,000, 300,000 or 400,000 kilos, or more, in one night. If they declare that they will increase their attack on our cities, then we will raze their cities to the ground. We will stop the handiwork of those night-pirates, so help us God! The hour will come when one or the other of us will crumble, and that one will not be National Socialist Germany.

Having publicly threatened British cities, in private he offered the British Government one last chance to sign up to his vision of the future. On 7th September, the Foreign Secretary received an offer, through an intermediary in neutral Sweden. The world would be divided into two economic spheres: the 'continental' organized by Germany; the 'maritime and colonial' by Britain and the USA. Britain would keep her colonies, though Germany might be compensated elsewhere – colonies of other European states were up for discussion.

> Political independence of European countries now occupied by Germany to be restored, including 'a Polish state' but excluding Czechoslovakia. Economic division of Europe must, however, be brought to an end.

If this offer was rejected, the war would intensify: 'special mention was made here of the loss to Great Britain of Egypt, the Middle East and ultimately India'.

As Hitler dangled this carrot of 'peace', his bombers demonstrated – from Docklands to Buckingham Palace – the weight of his stick. It was a combination he had always found effective in the past.

After four days and nights of heavy Blitz, Lord Halifax cabled back the Cabinet's reply: 'His Majesty's Government did not enter into this war for self defence aims, but for facts and general purposes affecting the freedom and independence of many states in Europe,' he wrote, and the indiscriminate bombing of London and the 'many horrible crimes' committed on Germany's neighbours had only stiffened Britain's resolve. 'His Majesty's Government do not wish to prolong the war for a day longer than is necessary,' wrote Halifax. 'It therefore lies with the German Government to make proposals by which the wrongs that Germany has inflicted upon other nations may be redressed' – though there must be 'effective guarantees by deeds not words' of his sincerity.

Halifax asked the British Ambassador in America to share this exchange, in confidence, with Franklin D. Roosevelt:

I feel that the President should know at this moment when Hitler is battering London with indiscriminate attacks from the air he is also following his familiar technique of trying to seduce us with superficial fair promises of an illusory peace at the expense of everyone but ourselves. I am sure that the President understands that we are not unmindful of our responsibilities and that we shall meet all attacks and all blandishments with firm resolve to rid the world of this scourge.

Hitler had no option but to remain locked on to the track that he had chosen. And thus, by deciding to savage London, Hitler had postponed Britain's inevitable defeat yet again. For the RAF might well have been destroyed if the Luftwaffe had been allowed to stick to its plan of targeting airfields: Fighter Command had lost so many squadron commanders and experienced fliers that, on 10th August, it had agreed to cut the original six-month Operational Training period to just two weeks.

'It was burning all down the river,' RAF Air Vice-Marshal Keith Park wrote of the view from the air over that first September weekend. 'It was a horrid sight. But I looked down and said, "Thank God for that," because I knew that the Nazis had switched their attack from the fighter stations thinking that they were knocked out. They weren't, but they were pretty groggy.'

REPORTS FROM HIS AIR CREWS and stories in the neutral press kept Hitler well informed on the physical damage he was inflicting on London. And Luftwaffe film of cities burning beneath them told their own tale. But though Goebbels' Propaganda team broadcast hopefully on 3rd October that 'London is facing riots, the authorities prove to be helpless, and everywhere there is wildest confusion', in truth no clear picture was emerging about just when the British would break.

'Obdurate and cocky . . . ,' recorded Goebbels in his diary. Then:

wild devastation . . . London's psychological situation is deteriorating daily . . . Churchill's monster is not yet on the point of collapse . . . people's morale is holding up . . . the English are tough. They are still holding out, after a fashion . . . waves of pessimism emanating from London . . . We receive reports that morale in London has reached rock bottom. Some even claim that riots have taken place. I do not place much credence in these . . . The British press in general has recovered its arrogance and cockiness, doubtless on orders from above . . .

Though on this last point, Goebbels should have known it needed no Propaganda Ministry to impose cockiness on Fleet Street.

'Apart from a relatively small minority,' Dutchman G. J. Renier had declared in 1931, 'the English are convinced that they are, that they own, and that they produce, all that is best in the world.' And should they ever forget it, Fleet Street was there to remind them. Over a matter of months, Renier had gleaned from British newspapers that their readers enjoyed the best landscape, the best women, the best radio voices, the best zoo, the best airline, the best underground stations and posters, the best pictures, the best legal system, the best police force, the best secret service, perhaps the best civil service ('I deeply regret this "perhaps",' tutted Renier), the best Post Office, the best homes, the best servants, the best gourmets, the best home farms and gardens, the best Press (naturally), the best domestic architecture, the best fashions, the best patriots, the best education system and (most brazen of all in Renier's view) the best climate in the world.

Britain even, he was startled to learn from the *Manchester Guardian*, had the best cooks in the world. 'We did not find an honest British bun anywhere in Europe,' declared an ex-president of the National Association of Master Bakers, Confectioners and Caterers, after a fact-finding mission to the Continent, during which Viennese bakers expressed themselves greatly impressed by the Eccles cake. G. J. Renier, too, had been impressed:

> Well might Mr Lloyd Dumas, an Australian journalist, declare to the *Daily News* (June 24, 1929): 'You English are so modest.' Well might the London Correspondent of the *Manchester Guardian* (January 16, 1930) write, 'We are the most self-deprecating people on earth.'

Wartime only extended the areas in which the British newspapers, struggling manfully against their innate British modesty, could tell their equally modest readers that they were the best in the world. For whether they demonstrated amazing stoicism now or champion-grade grumbling, the most conscientious obedience to official regulations or the most refreshing anarchy in subverting them, every option, being equally capable of being described as 'typically British', was equally – by definition – 'the best in the world'.

Josef Goebbels might have spent a long time puzzling over a story that appeared in this Sunday morning's British press, for instance. A shipload of citrus fruit from South Africa had made a news story in many papers: the *Sunday Times* had found a decorous Saturday queue forming at 8 a.m. at Woolwich market, disposing of several crates of oranges and 'plenty of

27

lemons' within two hours. What, though, of the oddly jaunty tone in the *Sunday Express* front page account of 'The Man With The Oranges'?

> Shoppers in Croydon's open-air market got a surprise yesterday when a man arrived pushing a barrow loaded with oranges.
>
> So did the man with the barrow.
>
> Within a split second there was a great squeeze of women round the barrow.
>
> Hats were knocked off, coats were torn, blows were exchanged.
>
> Hands reached out to grab the oranges, the owner of which fought vainly to defend his property.
>
> At last with his hands scratched and bleeding, he forced his way through the crowd and went for a policeman.
>
> When he returned, the women had gone.
>
> So had the oranges.

When Hitler awoke to begin his day in Berchtesgaden, master of more of Europe than any man since Charlemagne, Britain would remain a troubling thorn in the Reich's western flank, keeping him from progressing to the full glory of his destiny. The Führer had once harboured serious hopes that the powerful and (for the most part) ethnically acceptable Imperial race might be his ally and friend. But he had fed, perhaps, too well on Gary Cooper's tall, straight, beautiful embodiment of Hollywood's version of Empire in *The Lives of a Bengal Lancer*. If he had screened a Will Hay comedy at the Berghof occasionally, or a musical comedy featuring Gracie Fields or George Formby, he might perhaps have had a better idea of why he had spent his Christmas Eve visiting the airfields of France rather than driving through London at the side of some acquiescent British leader.

'THE FÜHRER HAS NOTHING but contempt for England,' Goebbels had recorded in mid-October. Then, six weeks later: 'For England the Führer feels only pity. The Empire is destroying itself. There is scarcely any chance of salvation for England now.' Hitler seemed not to relish the idea of actual invasion, though: 'He is shy of water,' Goebbels recorded after their conversation of four days before Christmas. 'He will only do it as a last resort.'

Earlier in December, as Goebbels and Hitler had watched a Ministry newsreel together, the Führer had seemed very pleased.

> The shots of London burning make a particularly profound impression on him . . . Nevertheless he does not expect the immediate collapse of England and probably rightly. The ruling class has now lost so much that it is bring up its last reserves. By which he means not so much the City of London as the Jews, who if we win will be hurled out of Europe, and Churchill, Eden, etc., who see their

personal existences as dependent on the outcome of the war. Perhaps they will end up on the scaffold. We can expect little resistance to them from the masses at the moment. The English proletariat lives under such wretched conditions that a few extra privations will not cause it much discomfort.

In the meantime, Hitler was planning a propaganda coup to astonish the world. He had decided not to bomb over Christmas, Goebbels recorded: 'Churchill, in his madness, will do so, and then the English will be treated to revenge raids that will make their eyes pop.'

In the event, the RAF had also refrained from bombing over Christmas. Still, the spectacular reprisals the Führer had planned would not go to waste. Goebbels noted the RAF bombing of the invasion ports on Boxing Day with satisfaction: 'We give it a big splash in the press. The English stayed away because of the weather, then, and not because of Christmas. We can exploit this kind of opportunity very well.' It was, he wrote, 'excellent grounds for retaliation'.

Chapter Three

29th December 1940

Dear Salmon,

Fire situation in London – 24 hours to 0500 hours
The last twenty-four hours have been perfectly quiet from our
point of view – no incidents of any kind have been reported.

From Lambeth HQ, London Fire Brigade

Daily report of Air Raid Fires to E. C. H. Salmon, Esq, MC, JP,
Clerk to the London County Council

EACH MORNING, a small piece of headed notepaper about four inches by
six was despatched along the Albert Embankment from Fire Brigade HQ
to County Hall, giving a brief account of how the LCC region had fared
since yesterday.

London is a clerkly city. Throughout its long history, on wax tablets
and papyrus, on vellum and then on paper – acres and acres of paper –
neat rows of names and dates and figures had kept its daily life brisk and
businesslike over the best part of two millennia. How many jugs of wine
sold today; how many dead of plague this week; how many mortgages
defaulted this quarter-day; how many ships safe to harbour this year and
how many lost. And as the great sprawling city was being destroyed piece
by piece in 1940, the same careful drawing-up of accounts continued all
across the capital.

Paper was scarce, like everything else nowadays. But in occurrence
books, reports, and the forms sent in to HQs from fire service watchrooms, ARP posts, rescue and salvage depots, first aid posts, hospitals and
mortuaries, the quiet heroism of efficient accounting captured the essence
of each night's battle, extracting order out of chaos so that London might
better survive tomorrow. Once each night's crisis eased, neat records were
collated to quantify the night's horrors, passing vital information back up
the line so the capital's scarce resources could be better allocated for the
days and nights to come.

No one would argue that London had been best prepared for what it
was going through now. But the idea that it was simply, as ever, a case of
'muddling through' undersold some fearsomely unmuddled thinking in

official circles, in both national and local government, and from the highest rank to the lowest.

Major Frank 'Gentleman' Jackson DSO, Great War veteran and Officer Commanding the London Fire Brigade and Auxiliary Fire Service, believed in keeping reports succinct. In terms that were technically specific – a 'small' fire required one pump, 'medium' two to ten, 'serious' eleven to thirty (more than that was 'major') – he distilled the story of each night's Blitz into precisely what the Council needed to know straight away.

Yesterday morning, for example, Major Jackson had pondered his report on Friday's raid:

Dear Salmon,
   A very heavy night. 532 fires in all — 5 serious, 34 medium and 493 small. 20 pump fire at 48 'X' station Choumont Road School . . .

A twenty-pump fire – especially at a fire station – would have been a memorable event in peacetime, with the head of London's fire service in personal attendance. But this was not peacetime and there was no need to become hysterical: Commander Jackson had picked up his fountain pen and deleted the word 'very' before adding his signature.

Friday night's raid had ended the capital's longest-ever break from raids since the Blitz began: London's unprecedented two-week pre-Christmas lull had been followed by Christmas Eve and Christmas Day (no bombing by either side: a truce said some, bad weather said others). On Friday the bombers had returned to the capital in force. But then last night all had gone quiet again for the London Fire Brigade.

The last big London raid before Christmas, on the night of Sunday 8th December, had produced a record 1,316 fires. Though, as Major Jackson pointed out to County Hall at the time, over a thousand of them were 'small' – nothing like the first great raids of September. No, what struck him most forcibly about the raid three weeks ago – and his report had highlighted it – was the way a relatively small number of HE (high explosive) bombs had been accompanied by an unprecedented number of IBs (incendiary or firebombs).

Such new developments were always noted: as the reports already neatly clipped into County Hall files showed, this Blitz was proving not so much a ravening beast as a fast-mutating virus. And both sides of the fight were learning what it was, or might become, as its form changed day by day, night by night.

In a sense, it had begun a quarter of a century ago, with the very first

German bombs dropped on London. And the chain of events linking those bombs to these, though invisible to the passing years, took on a dreadful inevitability when viewed with hindsight.

ONLY A FEW hundred Londoners had died over three years in raids in the Great War. The 12,000-plus in just three months of this one showed the progress made in the technology of death. But the very first Zeppelin raid in 1915 had destroyed the bedrock of centuries of British defence policy forever, by showing that a strong Navy would no longer be enough to maintain Britain's independence.

In all, the Great War had killed more than eight million people, brought down four empires and impoverished most of Europe. No one had doubted that killing machines would be even more effective in future wars, and most of the world had believed that nothing like it should ever be allowed to happen again. Stanley Baldwin's jeremiad of 1932 had already, even before Hitler took control in Germany, laid the foundation stone for a policy of appeasing rather than confronting ambitions that were backed by force. 'I think it is well, also,' the once-and-future Prime Minister had told the House of Commons, 'for the man in the street to realise that there is no power on earth that can protect him from being bombed. Whatever people may tell him, the bomber will always get through.'

What he offered the man in the street, though, was more debilitating than simple despair. 'The only defence is in offence,' Baldwin had continued, 'which means that you have to kill more women and children more quickly than the enemy if you want to save yourselves.' With defence not only desperately difficult but inherently barbarous, how could any decent, civilised nation contemplate it? And how could any decent, civilised politician argue for spending money to develop it?

In 1932 Japan, having invaded Manchuria, bombed Shanghai. The League of Nations condemned both invasion and bombing; Japan withdrew from the League and received no further sanction. In 1935, Fascist Italy bombed and gassed its way into Abyssinia. 'Apart from the Kingdom of the Lord,' declared Emperor Haile Selassie, 'there is not on this earth any nation that is superior to any other. Should it happen that a strong Government finds it may with impunity destroy a weak people, then the hour strikes for that weak people to appeal to the League of Nations to give its judgement in all freedom. God and history will remember our judgement.' The League had sat on its hands. From 1936 to 1939, Italian and German fliers bombed towns and cities in support of Franco's coup against the Spanish Republic. 'If you tolerate this,' declared a pro-Republican poster showing a dead child, 'your children will be next.' But the democracies had tolerated it. When Hitler finally made his move, the free world's will to resist was so feeble that Austria and then Czechoslovakia had been swallowed up without a bomb needing to be dropped.

And then finally, in 1939, the Great Air War that all this caution had been designed to avert had happened anyway – and the Luftwaffe had won it. The British had lost the War, but they had refused to believe they had lost it. So, after more than two decades, German bombers had returned to London to convince them.

HITLER HAD BEGUN with the spectacular in docklands that Londoners came to call 'Black Saturday'. On 7th September 1940, 'Gerry' Knight, LFB Station Officer at Pageant's Wharf rang in: 'Send all the bloody pumps you've got. The whole bloody world's on fire!' Firewoman Betty Barrett, who took the call, was startled: 'He had never used that sort of language to me.' But she had no option but to repeat it, word for word, up the line to New Cross Fire Control, whence it proceeded to Lambeth HQ to become legend throughout the service.

Station Officer Knight himself was dead by then. The Surrey Docks fire he died fighting, amid stacks of blazing timber, was thirty or forty times the size of any London fire between the wars. But it was only one of nine over that weekend that called for a hundred appliances or more. Warehouses blazed out of control and destruction lit up the sky as a stream of more than 250 bombers circled incessantly, from Black Saturday into Sunday, around the fatally recognisable loop in the Thames known as the Isle of Dogs. London had 2,000 fire appliances (a number considered sufficient, in peacetime, for the entire country) and half of them had been at work in docklands that weekend.

AUXILIARY FIREMAN FRANK HURD, who was preparing for duty in Euston again this morning, was an old hand now. But, as with many AFS men, when the bells had 'gone down' on Black Saturday as he waited for the supper call to the mess room, it had been his first real fire.

Each LFB station now had six wartime sub-stations, U, V, W, X, Y and Z, manned by auxiliaries under LFB officers. The splendidly named Aylmer Firebrace, who had headed both the London Fire Brigade and the Auxiliary Fire Service until war broke out, admitted that there had been 'a good deal of pull devil, pull baker' as the professionals trained the auxiliary men for the task ahead. Not to mention the women, who would staff watchrooms, and drive officers, food, messages and, most dangerous of all, petrol cans to the appliances working at fires.

To the LFB, AFS men were largely 'Taxi Brigade': three-, four- or five-man crews pulling a small trailer pump behind a London taxi, van or car. The LFB, in AFS parlance, were 'The Red Stuff' (even after most heavy appliances were painted wartime grey). Frank, though, was an AFS 'Red Rider', and had clung to his 'heavy' that Saturday afternoon as it raced across London to East Ham. His station Sub Officer was given charge of the fire at Beckton Gasworks, which supplied most of the East End, and ten crews had fought for control all night as gasometers blazed, bombs fell, ack-ack barked and 'a huge mushroom of flame shot into the air from the docks followed by a dull, rolling roar' when an oil container went up.

'It surprised me how quickly we got used to sensing whether a bomb was coming our way or not,' Frank wrote.

> At first we all lay flat every time we heard anything, but after an hour or so we only dived for it if one came particularly close. Even so, I had a funny feeling inside each time I heard it coming. (It took quite a time to overcome that. It wasn't exactly fear, but I don't know now just what it was.)

He had finally got back to Euston, exhausted, at eleven o'clock on that Sunday morning, sixteen weeks ago. And though AFS shifts were officially forty-eight hours on and twenty-four off, he had been back at work again that night – a fair indication of the punishing pattern ahead. 'Since that time,' Frank had written in early December, 'London has been subjected to raids almost every night till now . . . and in that time I have seen a variety of sights, but it will be a long time before the memory of that first night raid is forgotten!'

BILL REGAN HAD GONE without sleep for about seventy-six hours that first Blitz weekend. He had been enjoying the sun in his garden in Poplar with his wife Vi after a quiet shift with the rescue service when three blocks of bombers droned out of a clear blue sky. 'My husband yelled at me to take cover,' recalled Vi, 'then he was gone – to join his colleagues at the Heavy Rescue Depot in neighbouring Millwall.' She hadn't seen him again till Monday.

Vi had spent the next hours in their Anderson shelter, alone, listening to bombs and the sound of neighbours trying to soothe their screaming children – the Regans' own little girls were, thankfully, evacuated. Then an ARP warden called her out: time bombs near some oil storage tanks might explode at any time. Carrying her neighbour's child wrapped in a blanket, Vi followed the warden through streets alive with flying sparks. 'Great canopies of billowing smoke blotted out the sun, and barrage balloons were falling down in flames . . . We were literally surrounded by terrible fires and the air was hot even to breathe.' Taken to crowded Glengall Road School, Vi watched in horrified fascination as the eerie glow of fire fell through a corridor of gaping windows on to the wall opposite and she listened to the 'fierce crackle of flames and the constant crashing of falling masonry, so near us, dear Lord – so near'.

THE ONLY SHELTER Australian auxiliary ambulance driver Bert Snow had managed to find during this raid was a bomb crater, where he and his part-ner waited while a Heavy Rescue crew of ex-construction workers used their combination of structural knowledge and heft to extricate a casualty from a collapsed building. Bert was full of admiration for the ex-major who directed the rescue as bombers roared overhead.

> His calm efficiency was an inspiration to everyone. When Mick and I arrived we were greeted by the Major as pleasantly as guests arriving for a party. 'Welcome, lads,' he said, 'we'll soon have him out now. We have been able to shake hands with him.'

Bert had been less impressed that 'certain Civil Defence personnel, com-plete with uniforms and steel helmets' emerged from the public shelters at the sound of the All Clear and 'tried to boost their rather flat egos by attempting to take control':

> some residents of London's East End were not renowned for their command of Oxford English but were able to express themselves, and those who had spent the night in the open were not in any mood to be pushed around by those who had dodged the dangers. Very clearly the late arrivals were told where to go and what to do and while much of the advice was physically impractical, they got the message.

Newspapers had printed inspiring tales of thumbs-uppery and cheery Cockney banter from bombed-out East Enders after the raids. And, though they may have over-egged the pudding – and given few column inches to the 'bad apples' Bert Snow saw – the truth was certainly unlike the mass panic predicted in many fictions, and some official reports, through the 1930s.

One of Winnie Bowman's friends, summoned from Chelsea to the East End that weekend by the Women's Voluntary Service, had driven over with her friend Jeannie to find, as she wrote to America, very little in the way of smiles and jokes but there was also very little in the way of the defeatist kind, in fact when I say there was very little, I should say there was none. There were very few complaints also in spite of the fact that many of the people whom I took in the car from place to place were without any possessions at all except what they had in small paper bags.

'Most of us were scared stiff the first week,' she confessed later. 'We didn't show it much but we damned well were. Then I suppose the "soldiers of the front line" business came over us and we found there was no point in being scared and also it was a bad thing to be, so we stopped being.'

Some of her passengers had been through hell. Trapped in a rest centre encircled by flames, they had been led by wardens through burning streets to a second centre, which had then received two direct hits.

Their behaviour was so wonderful that it hardly seemed possible they had been through what they had and were still going through it too. There was only one thing that brought it home to one and that was the sudden hardening of every muscle of their faces when the siren went in the middle of the day.

She and Jeannie had, at that moment, been enjoying a welcome respite in the back kitchen of 'a funny little East End emporium'.

The owner had stayed all night with fires nearly all round serving food to the AFS men who were fighting the fires. You can imagine how tired and worn they were and yet with a piece of gas about as high as a millimetre they still insisted on making us a cup of tea.

Taking refuge in a shelter alongside those who had already suffered so much, they found

practically no talk of horrors at all, the air raid wardens, in bedroom slippers mostly, went and fetched beer from the pub, which was miraculously still intact, tea and water. The women who had been up all night in this horror were amazingly clean, it was a thing that astonished Jeannie and me that they all appeared to have found something clean to put on and have given themselves a hearty wash . . . All the week I did this work, and the more I saw of those people the more I wondered. I've always loved them and got on with them, but I've never known just how grand they were before.

OVER THE FOLLOWING three months to 8th December, in only three twenty-four hour periods had no bombs fallen anywhere in the London area. And Major Jackson's succinct reports from Fire Brigade HQ had told the tale to County Hall.

Later today, the Chairman of the LCC's Civil Defence and General Purposes Committee would approve the submission of thirty-three names to the Home Office for medals for acts of gallantry by firefighters during September's raids. Two days ago a note had arrived saying that Winston Churchill himself wanted the first batch of awards to London fire staff issued as early as possible in the New Year, and that these 'should relate to some of our best cases'. The problem they had was of keeping the numbers within bounds since there was 'already in the fire service a high standard in assessing gallantry for a start'.

As a flick through the files would show, it was a rare central London station that still had all its six sub-stations intact. Things had been 'fairly quiet' on 2nd November after a 'lively' start, reported Major Jackson:

> 24 'Z' sub-station (Ricardo Street LCC School) was hit by a high explosive bomb . . . One woman auxiliary was killed and one LFB sub-officer, nine auxiliary firemen and two women auxiliaries were injured and removed to hospital. It is not thought that their injuries are serious . . . The auxiliary fireman who was reported missing when 58 'V' station was hit the previous night was extricated early yesterday and found to be dead.

A few days later, two of the injured from Ricardo Street 'succumbed to their injuries' and within the week the death toll had risen to five.

'Dispersal' was the watchword of wartime planning: if air raids could not be prevented, their effectiveness could be minimised. So, dispersal of industrial capacity, dispersal of people into many small air raid shelters rather than gathered together in large ones, and dispersal of emergency services too. The LCC already had buildings with open yards scattered conveniently across its territory: Edwardian temples of education whose 'three vast storeys and a pinnacled roof' rose up, according to one 1940 Londoner, 'like feudal castles dominating the two-storied houses from which they draw their hundreds of small serfs'. With their small serfs evacuated to the country, many schools became either rest centres for the bombed-out or AFS sub-stations. Some, like Saunders Ness in Poplar, were both.

Even well sandbagged from blast, though, Edwardian buildings were not designed to withstand high explosive. The 7th November report recorded another tragedy for the Service:

> I regret to say that No. 86 'W' Station Cavendish Road School received a direct hit from a HE bomb, 13 of the staff being killed and 19 injured. At the time the bomb dropped the men were at supper in the mess room and this accounts for the high casualty list. One of the women drivers was killed . . .

A week later it was Invicta Road School, with twenty-two extricated, eight dead and four more 'believed under debris'. But it was another comment from that report – 'On the instructions of the Regional Fire Officer, fifty men left this morning to help with the fires at Coventry' – that had proved most significant. The Coventry raid signalled a major mutation in the Blitz virus: frustrated by the capital's refusal to crumble, the Luftwaffe had begun to combine raids on London with sudden, massive attacks on provincial cities. The Reich coined a new word *Coventrieren*: to destroy a city as it had just destroyed Coventry. The reports were 'horrendous', Goebbels confided to his diary. 'An entire city literally wiped out. The English are no longer pretending; all they can do is wail. But they asked for it.'

Through November and December, London's firefighters responded to calls from other forces as more cities were 'Coventrated'. On 23rd November, fifty men, eleven officers and fifteen pumps were ordered to Birmingham with a water unit, two lorries carrying hose from Home Office stores, two canteen vans with food supplies for 200, and four dispatch riders – of whom only three returned alive. More help went to cities like Bristol and Southampton and Liverpool as they were blitzed in their turn.

On Christmas Eve, more than 400 London firefighters and almost 300 from outer London brigades went to Manchester after its vicious raid of the previous night – in which, as in the 8th December raid on London, firebombs rather than HE dominated. Commander Jackson's deputy Mr Kerr, called in off leave in Kettering, had spent Christmas Day in Manchester securing, with considerable difficulty, a 'sausage and mash Xmas dinner' for the London men.

HEAVY RESCUE MAN Bill Regan had been inspired by Samuel Pepys (borrowed from his local library) to start a diary of his own dramatic times – whenever he could find the time and paper to jot things down on.

Sometimes a blank sheet made the best listener: people had quickly become immune to one another's dramas. There was compassion for victims of tragedy. But bizarre near-misses and comical survivals were tolerated on a strict 'I'll listen to yours if you'll listen to mine' basis. 'It must be terribly dull in heaven or hell these days,' one of Winnie Bowman's friends had written to America, 'with everyone telling each other their bomb stories.'

The men of the Heavy Rescue had more bomb stories than most. Bricklayers like Bill Regan, carpenters or the like, they had once, wrote one woman, been regarded as 'scum' but were now seen as public saviours. Working for borough councils under clerks of works and district surveyors, they were a common sight at any 'incident' (the dry official understatement for any event requiring the emergency services) where the different services were distinguishable by the colours of, and letters on, their 'tin hats'.

Extracting the living and the dead generally involved tunnelling rather than digging through the debris – often in the blackout, amid broken gas and water mains and with bombs still dropping – so, yes, they had a story or two to tell. Though Bill made space for funny stuff too.

Every emergency worker, it seemed, had their bird-in-a-birdcage story: Bill's was of a parrot rescued in its squashed-up cage who, undaunted by its adventures, had delighted the whole depot by giving 'a most wonderful recital of obscene language . . . It finished off with two words, repeated very rapidly: "F— Hitler, F— Hitler, F— Hitler" – my sentiments exactly.' Though 'scandalised', the canteen ladies 'still fell about laughing' – as did Vi, who was volunteering there at the time.

Bill's gave plenty of space in his journal to the wonder that was Vi. He had come home in that first week to find a rope blocking off the street. There was an unexploded bomb opposite their house, where he found Vi, sweeping fallen plaster into the road.

> She showed me [the] hole where the UXB had gone, and wasn't concerned about it. Warden Herbie Martin had tried to persuade her, and her Mum and Dad, to take shelter in Saunders Ness school but they declined. Vi said she wasn't afraid of dying, provided she didn't have a lingering death. Surprisingly, this took away the worry I had at the back of my mind while on duty.

Frank Hurd had been putting a few of his firefighting adventures down on paper, too, over the quiet watches of the past few weeks. And in October, a bomb had penetrated the road by Euston Station, blocking the Underground tunnel below and breaking and igniting a gas main, which had then begun to burn off the insulation from the electric cables under the road. Firemen were not allowed to extinguish burning mains, as the gas build-up could explode; on the other hand, if the insulation burnt through and water from the firemen's hoses fell on bare wires . . .

Afterwards, Frank and his crew had been captured for posterity by an *Evening News* photographer in a picture embodying every Ministry of Information cliché in the book. Firemen, mugs in hand, with a large teapot, laughing on the doorstep of a diminutive, toothless old lady whose home they'd saved. London Could Take It, all right. London would Go To It. London would Carry On.

THAT WAS THE THING about the British propaganda. It was propaganda. But a lot of it was also true. Life imitating art or art imitating life, it was your choice: follow one line of reasoning and you soon fell into the other. American editor/proprietor Ralph Ingersoll made a brief fact-finding tour specifically to discover the truth behind what was coming out from London-based correspondents. After a guided tour round the East End by 'a little man we discovered by his Anderson shelter', he joked that he must have been a Ministry of Information plant: 'We should have had the dialogue on a sound track to use with the film *London Can Take It*.'

And this 'business as usual' meant, he wrote:

> just what it says. By day. Not by night, but by day. The night is something else again. But by day it's business as usual. It really is. How can I make it clear? There is a sense of frustration about trying to convey something so commonplace.

It was not 'bombs, or bomb damage nor even 8,000 people sleeping in rows in a subway' that was really typical of London in the Blitz, he explained, but men and women just going about their daily lives, seemingly oblivious of the destruction around them.

Make all the exceptions that you liked but, yes, most Londoners had learned to 'just get on with it'. Yes, a cup of tea really was viewed as the universal panacea for all ills. And yes, they were all perhaps just a little bit crazy. On one occasion, Ed Murrow was riding in a taxi when a couple of HEs came down. The driver

> hauled his ancient cab to the curb, where it was rocked by the blast of the bombs. He slid back the window and said, 'He'll do that once too often, once,' closed the window, and drove on. I have never understood exactly what he meant by that.

EVEN THE DEPICTION of air raids as one long community sing-song had a tenuous link to reality. In the East End, pacifist stretcher-bearer Nev Coates experienced one of his first alerts in the basement of the People's Palace in the Mile End Road. He had gone to hear *La Traviata*, and Luella Paikin and company had sung on through the raid like the troupers they were. Patrons were then invited to wait till the alert ended in the basement. Where Nev's morale had remained remarkably unboosted by the audience's insistence on an archetypal Cockney sing-song until the All Clear sounded in the small hours of the morning.

Most people agreed that the worst way to experience a raid was alone. And anything that drowned out the noise or gave you something else to think about was a damn good idea. So some people sang loudly, some prayed quietly, some found themselves muttering the same meaningless phrase over and over and over. Some concentrated on writing their diaries; one woman, more 'jittery' since she was bombed out of her central London flat, wrote letters to a friend – it was almost like saying her prayers, she told her.

She now spent raids, alone, in the relative safety of the central corridor of the mansion block where she rented a room and confessed that, for 'lily-livered cowards' like her, the real strain was of '*listening*' all the time – for the vicious tone of an aircraft coming low, then for the first bomb to fall, then for the last bomb of the 'stick', then for that vicious tone again.

Once a neighbour wandered by, looking for a book his wife had left behind in the bathroom. She explained why she slept in the corridor:

> He says tut, tut they've been bombed out twice, once in their flat in Maida Vale & once in Mount Royal. What is my name. He is in the police & gives me his name, but I have already forgotten. Bye bye I'll see you later he says & departs along the corridor. This dashing in & out of people's lives is all part of the war. People are suddenly friendly: they would like to have a last chatty conversation before a bomb wipes them out: they would like to leave a nice impression.

One of the biggest strains, she scribbled mid-raid, was the need

> to have your faculties alert as to which corner you'll flatten yourself in if it's a direct hit & to be sure to have one's handbag near one – identity card. My body shall *NOT* go in one of those ghastly cardboard boxes in which civilians unclaimed are dumped in.

She might have been comforted to know that, if the worst happened, the most strenuous efforts would be made to ensure she never would end up in an anonymous cardboard coffin. The duty of care to the dead was taken very seriously, with every body part logged and directives on such matters as the special funeral requirements of different religions.

'One thing that impressed me,' wrote a landscape painter who had joined the ambulance service and been put on mortuary vans,

> was the extraordinary lengths the authorities went to, to establish the number, sex and, if possible the identity of those killed. Everything was in such a state of chaos that at first one did not appreciate the amount of thought which had gone into preparations for this civilian war. I know my own impression at first was that they had been completely caught napping, but obviously there were some far-seeing types around, as my own experiences bore witness.

Legions served the dead. The Heavy Rescue men and, once even they had departed, the mortuary van crews sent out with shovels and sieves; the mortuary attendant who murmured 'poor soul' or 'poor fellow' as remains were brought in and who worked, observed the painter, 'to make them as human as he could, before relatives came to identify them'; the stalwart WVS ladies who conducted families through this harrowing ordeal and offered tea and sympathy afterwards; and, of course, all those clerks docketing and registering and filing the details that might make all the difference to someone, someday. The horrors of war and human compassion had perhaps never been brought together in such stark contrast, marking out this civilian killing ground from the battlefields of old.

LONDON'S PRE-CHRISTMAS 'LULL' ('that word will go down with all our other war words in the story of the struggle between the devil and Democracy,' the 'lily-livered' Londoner told her friend) had been a chance for all the emergency services to catch up on their backlog. Bill Regan's crew had been called back to look for bodies left behind at an incident when all hope of life was abandoned. This was 'hand-work' and Bill and his old workmate George Jillings had drifted off together as usual: 'We fitted well together.' Bill had helped build one block and knew its layout. As he worked his way down the long corridor,

> George called me to help him with a doormat he had found but could not pull clear. It was black, and of a thick curly texture, so I fished around for a while, loosening the packed rubble, then George came back with [a] length of iron rod to prise it out. I told him it was a bloke, and I knew who he was, Warden Herbie Martin.

It was the ARP man who had tried to persuade Vi and her parents to take shelter here at Saunders Ness School during the first week of the Blitz.

Bill and George went to tell the others and found them gathered around more bodies in the AFS block. Two teenage firewomen had been asleep in the 35 'U' dormitory, in knickers and shifts, when the bomb fell – and seemed to be sleeping still.

The rubble had packed so tightly around them that the unmarked bodies were perfectly preserved, their limbs not even rigid. 'I looked around at the other men,' Bill wrote,

> and most of them looked shocked, and a bit sick; we had usually found bodies mutilated, and were usually lifted out by hands and feet and quickly got away. Major Brown sees one man being sick, so he fishes out a bottle of rum to be handed round.
>
> By now I was feeling a bit angry at the prospect of these two girls being lugged by their arms and legs . . . I could not let them be handled like the usual corpses.

I know I would have belted the first one who handled them with disrespect, but nobody makes a move to shift them, and are just standing there, gawping.

I looked up at George, and I just said, 'Stretcher – blanket.' Then I put my right arm under her shoulders with her head resting against me, and the left arm under her knees, and so carried her up. I laid her on the stretcher, 'You'll be comfortable now my dear.' I did exactly the same with the other one. I stood up and waited for some smart Alec to make a snide remark, but nobody did. I cooled down a bit after I had smoked a cigarette. I wonder why I had been so angry?

He told the Major about Herbie and returned to the depot, feeling depressed. If there was any comfort to be drawn, it was the bleak Blitz comfort that three families could now at least plan funerals, and their worst Christmas would not be burdened with the extra agony of not knowing where their loved ones lay.

Bill himself had worked on Christmas Day. With only one room now habitable at home there had been no question of bringing Joan and 'Little Vi' back from their Oxfordshire billet to Poplar. But Bill had got Friday 27th December off in lieu – which meant a precious long weekend to visit the girls.

They had gone bearing gifts: including *three* helpings of the chocolate handed out to the Heavy Rescue men as a 'token of appreciation for the courage and dedication of our brave, unflinching rescue workers'. As he handed over his contribution, Bert Forbes had told Bill that he was worried about his weight, while Billy Bracken said he was taking care of his teeth – 'This was true, I had seen him take them out after every meal and give them a good scrub.' But though he took his colleagues' reasons for sacrificing their treats 'with a block of salt', Bill also took the chocolate.

I did not try to thank them, I just said they were bigger liars than Tom Pepper. Bert said he knew he would be expert at something and thanked me for pointing it out to him. Billy just said, 'Come away Bert, he'll be licking our boots next.' I think they like me, but there we are, people have peculiar fancies.

IT HAD NOT taken long for staff at the LFB's Lambeth HQ to total up the zeros coming in from its sixty-plus fire stations this morning for the report to County Hall. Most unusually, though, it was not the Officer Commanding who had composed today's brief update for the LCC.

Like Bill Regan, Major Jackson had worked over the Christmas, allowing his Deputy, Mr Kerr, to get away to Kettering (even though the Manchester raid had put paid to his quiet Christmas). Now Kerr was left in charge at Lambeth while Jackson permitted himself a rare few days

43

away from the capital too (though he was never off duty in this war, and would only be about fifty miles away and, as ever, on call in case of real emergency).

Did Mr Kerr, at the start of his first full day in command, flick back through Major Jackson's reports to find a suitable wording to use today? If so, he would have found no particular reassurance in the clean sheet he had to report this morning. In the ever-changing physiology of the Blitz, it was not always possible to discern significant patterns until later. But it was perhaps unsettling to read the London Fire Brigade report written exactly three weeks ago at the start of the day that had ended with a 'record number of fires'. For the report on the morning of Sunday 8th December had carried exactly the same cheerful news as on this one: 'A perfectly quiet night – nothing to report.'

Chapter Four

It seems odd that only one machine should have been despatched from Takoradi during the week ending December 27, when no fewer than 44 are piled up there waiting. Is there a breakdown in the handling work at Takoradi? Could we have a report on conditions there? Quite soon they will have the second instalment from the *Furious* upon them. WSC

Memorandum from Winston Churchill to Air Chief Marshal Sir Charles Portal, Chief of Air Staff, 29th December 1940

THIS BEING A SUNDAY was no reason to expect the flow of detailed directives and pointed memoranda from the PM to dry up: in this case, about a bottleneck in Ghana endangering the supply of bombers to Cairo. Churchill's stream of questions, suggestions and demands could tax and infuriate the professionals under his command. Sometimes his interventions were inspired; sometimes an unnecessary diversion from the task in hand. Often both, as he reapportioned the Empire's woefully inadequate resources to ensure that there would be a tomorrow in which to regret and repair the mistakes made today.

For all the certainty in his bulldog speeches, he knew his nation was clinging to a sheer mountain-face – and while the 'broad sunlit uplands' of Churchillian rhetoric might well await above, when he looked down into the abyss the prospect was frightful. So he looked down rarely, concentrating instead on the search for the next foothold. If the ascent was successful, there would be years of peace in which to speculate on how it *could* have been done.

'SHORT WORDS ARE BEST, and the old words, when short, are best of all' was Churchill's rule of thumb, both in writing and in speaking. They made his short, sharp memos crystal clear. And in his speeches they enabled him to reach a whole city, country and empire as one – as well as that other, vital but uncertain, audience across the Atlantic.

One Londoner detected a primeval note: 'Churchill's voice is that of an aggressive old man of the tribe defending his cave home from wolves,' wrote an LCC lecturer who was this morning weekending with friends in

Epping Forest: 'The voice of a man who knows he has to win or there will be no tribe.'

The Prime Minister might have acknowledged the truth in this. Long ago, as a Victorian soldier fighting in Kipling's 'savage wars of peace', he had paid tribute to the suicidal courage of the Dervish enemy:

> 'Mad fanaticism' is the depreciating comment of their conquerors. I hold this to be a cruel injustice . . . Why should we regard as madness in the savage what would be sublime in civilized men? For I hope that if evil days should come upon our own country, and the last army which a collapsing Empire could interpose between London and the invader were dissolving in rout and ruin, that there would be some – even in these modern days – who would not care to accustom themselves to a new order of things and tamely survive the disaster.

He had not then expected to lead this last stand. But now a lifetime in the hurly-burly of the public presses had honed the robust tongue in which to rally his London tribe, his British tribe, his tribe of 'English-speaking peoples'.

He already had a couple of last-ditch war-cries up his sleeve: 'The time has come, kill the Hun' and 'You can always take one with you'. For now, though, he was playing at the top of his game in Old Testament prophet style. In this 'War of the Unknown Warriors', he had said in the summer, 'let all strive without failing in faith or in duty, and the dark curse of Hitler will be lifted from our age.' He conjured up a task desperately difficult – but not impossible. Like a latter-day Napoleon of Notting Hill he declared: 'The vast mass of London itself, fought street by street, could easily devour an entire hostile army; and we would rather see London laid in ruins and ashes than that it should be tamely and abjectly enslaved.'

CHURCHILL WAS, considered twenty-nine-year-old Yvonne Green in Chelsea, a good 'puller-up of socks'. A thirteenth-generation Canadian, Yvonne was now at the Heart of Empire. 'London is the best place to be in,' she had assured her anguished mother back home. 'There is nowt one can do about it now. Anyway my blood is up and I'm dying to have a poke at the Germans.'

> If one has the mischance to land in the garden, he's going to have a hot time before I'm through with him. I'm glad to be Johnny-on-the-spot with a chance of taking a crack at them complete with saucepans of boiling water aimed with great precision from the kitchen window.

Yvonne's husband had been, like many servicemen, horrified to find his wife facing bombs while he was safely tucked up in camp in the country and he had moved her out of London nearer to him. But 'Maman Chérie,' she had written in October. 'Here I am back in London again, to your horror & my satisfaction.'

She would, she wrote, 'rather face Goering's worst than die from pernicious boredom' and had now joined the Auxiliary Fire Service. But, she assured her mother, 'when I'm not on duty I sleep downstairs very snugly in the basement. Don't alarm yourself when you don't hear from me because I have given instructions that if anything should happen to me you should be informed *immediately* – so no news is good news – remember that.'

IF PEOPLE FELT Churchill's defiant words echoed and amplified something that they already, deep down, knew, they were probably right. The Prime Minister was resonantly Shakespearean, not only in his combination of high-flown imagery with broad humour in unexpected places, but also in his shameless plundering of the common stock of English literature. He advocated that beginners keep a box of poetry scraps at their side when composing speeches. And the screeds of half-remembered poetry rattling round the brain of any Londoner with the barest LCC board school education reverberated whenever the Prime Minister spoke.

A decade before, he might have seemed hopelessly out of tune with the modern world. But the modern world had been smashed to bits and his language now seemed appropriate to the scale of what was at stake. 'Everybody is reading Churchill's speech,' wrote one London woman. 'What a superb phrase-maker he is: "Death and sorrow the companions of our journey, hardship our garment . . ." That is worthy of Milton or Burke or the Authorised Version itself.'

In his speeches – or at least their final sections, which is where he generally drew up his big guns – Churchill cast his hearers in their own Shakespearean epic: conjuring up their past, recording their present and moulding their future all at once. And just as anyone with a penny in the London of 1600 could stand at the Globe and imagine himself Hamlet, so anyone in the London of 1940 with access to a newspaper or a wireless found themselves a mighty warrior: fighting – and perhaps dying – for freedom.

An American observer of the odd islanders – who might have been accused of succumbing to Ministry of Information propaganda, had he not been writing almost a century before the MoI was even thought of – claimed that: 'The difference of rank does not divide the national heart . . .

47

Every man carries the English system in his brain, knows what is confided to him, and does therein the best he can.' The strength of this most successful nation in the world lay, wrote Ralph Waldo Emerson in the 1850s, in: 'A great ability, not amassed on a few giants, but poured into the general mind, so that each of them could at a pinch stand in the shoes of the other.' Britain's position as 'top nation' might have slipped a little since then. But if duty had called upon eighteen-year-old City clerk Colin Perry to stand in Winston Churchill's shoes in 1940, he would certainly have done his best to fill them.

Colin had watched a sad stream of East Enders, old and very young, trailing westward through the heart of the City on a September Monday morning after the first weekend of the Blitz. It told 'the callousness, the futility of war', he bashed out on the office typewriter back in Lombard Street. Yet, hard as he fought against finding 'glamour' in the scene:

> As I stood, just a few minutes ago on the Bank crossing, surveying the broken windows of the Mansion House, the bomb crater, listened to the newspaper men crying their news, the noise of exhausts of thousands of cars and lorries and buses, the smatterings of conversation from the passers-by, the smiles and laughter of City clerks and girl typists, it was superb to see the courage and greatness of it all . . . We are not English for nothing, and as one looks back upon all the perseverance of the past, feels the tingling of the blood, one sees now why we are the greatest nation on this earth, and one is lost in the greatness of it all.

Printer's son Colin might have left school at fifteen, but he was unafraid of the ringing phrase. He was a great reader: his lunch hours at the ABC tea rooms in Cheapside were usually divided between silent contemplation of The Girl who dined there, and silent debate with the likes of H. G. Wells, J. B. Priestley, pacifist Professor Joad and Winston Churchill himself. ('The ABC Girl made to speak today but I was reading Vera Brittain,' he had noted sternly one lunch time.)

American Eric Sevareid, on his first visit to London, had gazed in amazement at the ranks of these timid City clerks in tea rooms, heirs to all the generations of timid City clerks of English literature, shovelling down food, noses in a book or a newspaper, never acknowledging one another by word or look. 'Do the English know they are shy?' G. J. Renier had asked in 1931, and Sevareid's reaction had been somewhat similar. In 1940, he decided that this was what held them together in a crisis: 'One could panic in his heart, but two together could not show it, nor a hundred in a group. They neutralize one another and therein lies the thing that makes the British slightly different.' He had been forced to change many of his ideas about the British, he wrote, 'but never to change the first impression that they are afraid of one another. They are afraid of nothing on earth except one another.'

On the Tuesday lunch time of that first Blitz week, Colin Perry had arrived at the ABC to find it closed, amid a mass of smoking ruins. But thoughts of never again crossing paths with The Girl were driven from his mind by the arrival of Winston Churchill himself, come to inspect the damage. The crowds cheered, and stuck their thumbs up for the cameras, and Colin was transported. It fulfilled the prophecy, he wrote, 'that we would rather see London in ashes, but free and ours, than standing under the will of Hitler' (a neat digest of the Prime Minister's own words of six weeks before).

The following day, a Hamburg newspaper assured its readers,

Another two weeks of attacks will make normal life and work in London impossible. In other words, the complete evacuation of London's 8,000,000 workers is the immediate danger the country has to face. When this happens, Germany will have attained its main objective, the clogging of all highways of other cities with homeless refugees, who must be transported, fed, housed.

But Churchill, simultaneously, had pooh-poohed attempts to 'terrorize and cow the people of this mighty Imperial city and make them a burden and an anxiety to the Government'. Hitler little knew, he said 'the spirit of the British nation or the tough fibre of the Londoners, whose forebears played a leading part in the establishment of parliamentary institutions and who have been bred to value freedom far above their lives'.

That might sound too high-flown for some, but not for Colin Perry. He had found himself pictured on the front page of that Wednesday's *Daily Telegraph*, walking alongside the Prime Minister, and felt that he would like to put a caption to the photograph: 'Present – Future'.

This chilly December morning, though, Colin was steaming through warm oceans East of Suez. The American oil company he worked for had decided to move out of the City and he had ached to Do Something: to, 'lead this very world unto a better way of life, and point out all our futile ways and make a name for the very brave'. Unable without a School Certificate to follow his first instinct to be a fighter pilot, he had penetrated the mysterious East End and signed up for the Merchant Navy. Which, a friend had reassured him, was even more dangerous since pilots were only a target when actually flying.

NOT EVERY LONDONER affected the grand heroic style. At the end of that first week, another young City worker had written to her sister in the country. 'How quickly one gets to total warfare'.

> Monday was a pretty awful day – I only had to walk from Moorgate, which is really no hardship, and quite good for the figure. The streets were full of glass and there was a terrible bomb at the entrance to London Bridge, but today I walked through exactly the same way and now they have cleared the streets and bunged the glass back it really doesn't look so bad.

There was still no water or gas in the City, she wrote and, when she got home, she sheltered from the bombs that whistled and screamed around the house on the nursery day bed. ('It is smelly but soft, and I can smell mice all night. What Hitler makes you put up with.')

'I feel like a refugee already rushing round with blankets and pillows, and bags galore,' she wrote,

> or I think it is rather like some dreadful journey in a fourth class carriage across Central Europe, with no washing and no lavvys, and you have to drink cold water, when you are dying for a cup of tea. Anyway these awful journeys always end, and when you get there, the place looks marvellous. Well, here's hoping. I should be furious if we gave in.
> Keep your tin hat on. Lots of love.
> Effie

The Prime Minister didn't always affect the grand heroic style either. A female air raid warden who was no natural Churchill-worshipper admitted that he had found the measure of her own community with a 'somewhat risky' speech after the Blitz had been raging for a month. The casualty rate was, he said, grievous but only a fraction of pre-war expectations. Moreover, with so many bombs falling on already-ruined buildings, the law of diminishing returns meant it would take Hitler ten more years to flatten even half of London. (After which, he said drily, 'progress would be much slower'.)

Far from being appalled, the warden found that her neighbours, in the firing line most nights, were 'cheered and amused' by the joke: 'Fancy the 'ole man thinking up that one!'

The impish sense of the ridiculous that made some of his more respectable fellow-MPs consider the Duke's grandson 'not quite a gentleman' endeared him to many in the country at large. Arguably the most quintessentially British act of domestic policy in the whole interwar period had been the banning of political uniforms in 1936 – deflating the pretensions of all Britain's would-be dictators and taking half the fun out of fascism for its more timid or naive supporters. Churchill himself adored a uniform but, these days, he took equal delight in being seen in his practical Blitz cover-all 'siren suit', which the baby-faced Prime Minister cheerfully referred to as his 'rompers'.

A DECADE AGO, as 'strong man' politics looked set to eclipse the very idea of democracy, G. J. Renier had pointed to Winston Churchill as Britain's own would-be dictator. And just last month, after his return to Washington, the US Ambassador to London, Joseph Kennedy, had caused consternation on both sides of the Atlantic by declaring that 'democracy is all done in Britain' (as it might be in America too, he continued, if it got into this war).

Certainly Britain's Prime Minister this morning enjoyed, in theory, something of a dictator's powers. Journalist Ed Murrow had been witness in the summer to the 'British revolution' – not on the streets, he explained to his American listeners, but in a quiet announcement to the House by the leader of the Labour Party followed by a vote that 'swept away the freedom acquired in the last thousand years'. Henceforth every person in Britain – all their property, their cars, their houses, all the land and all the factories – were at the disposal of the war effort.

It certainly showed determination to fight on. But Murrow harboured a deep fear, which he never lost, that democracies can all too easily come to mirror the tyrannies they are fighting. In the intervening six months, therefore, he had watched, with a certain wonder, this very British brand of totalitarianism in action.

MPs of all parties had continued to harangue Churchill and his ministers about their use of the absolute powers they had been given. And, even more astonishingly, Churchill and his ministers had continued to bow to MPs' correction. Murrow later concluded that, whatever action was most decisive in this war, for Britain it had been the decision to win or lose under the rules of parliamentary procedure.

But then Parliament was far more deeply rooted here than democracy. And that sense of ancient English right which Ed Murrow's own nation had inherited, more deeply rooted still. Churchill had been a Tory in his time, then a Liberal, then a Tory again, and he now led a coalition of many parties. But he was always, as he so often said, a 'House of Commons man' to his bones. And his awe for the parliamentary process in general and the House of Commons in particular did not disappear just because he now led the Government. While he sought, as ever, to dominate and control the

Chamber with his mastery of words, he also relied on the Chamber to stop him turning into the monster he could so very easily have become. And his fury when MPs challenged his decisions would have been as nothing to his despair if they had not.

'Parliament' – literally a 'Speaking' – was the sacred space of Churchill's tribe, where the bitterest disputes were fought out with words rather than the knives, fists, coshes, guns or clubs found elsewhere. It was no mere bagatelle that the opposing front benches of the Commons were set, as all new arrivals were gleefully informed, at two swords' lengths apart. Nor that, for hundreds of years, the Commons Chamber had shut its doors against the King and his officers.

Archaic rules and quaint rituals were constant reminders that MPs' powers were theirs only for a day. What persevered was the basic parliamentary principle – so seemingly simple, natural and obvious when it worked, but so rarely found across all the wide sweep of world history – that the argument should go not to the arm that was strongest but to the cause that was just. And that the just cause would somehow emerge, by the grace of some mysterious amalgam of God and 'the people', if you talked about it long enough.

'His Majesty's Loyal Opposition' had long been as essential to good governance here as 'His Majesty's Government' since, in the words of one Victorian theorist of liberty,

> Complete liberty of contradicting and disproving our opinion, is the very condition which justifies us in assuming its truth for purposes of action; and on no other terms can a being with human faculties have any rational assurance of being right.

CHURCHILL KNEW, none better, that the sanctity of the institutions protecting English liberty had been hard won over many centuries. Mere democracy, by contrast, was a relatively fragile structure: new democracies, fully equipped with new parliaments of various designs, had proliferated across Europe after the Great War. But unless every faction that knew – absolutely *knew* – their beliefs were right consented to lodge their trust in the achingly slow and ludicrously haphazard parliamentary process, then democracy meant nothing at all. Because the day would always arrive – and usually sooner rather than later – when one faction would find it imperative to stop all this ridiculous folderol and consign their opposition to the dustbin of history. And if they could muster the guns and the *oubliettes* and the execution chambers to do it, then any nation could be sent straight back to the political Stone Age overnight.

Lord Acton's dictum that 'Power tends to corrupt; absolute power corrupts absolutely' had long been a commonplace of British politics. So Churchill (who also knew, absolutely *knew*, his beliefs were right) took genuine pride in having to face his critics in the House every week; pride in having his bitterest opponents scrutinise every aspect of his own guns, *oubliettes* and execution chambers; and pride in the fact that, if Parliament didn't like what he was doing with them, it could turn him out of office overnight (even as he used all his political cunning and rhetorical tricks to ensure it never would).

AND IF Parliament had failed in its duty, English liberty still had one last line of defence. Walking down King Charles Street once en route for Number 10, his policeman bodyguard recalled, Churchill rounded furiously on a whistling newspaper boy.

'Stop that whistling!'

'Why should I?' said the boy.

'Because I don't like it. It's a horrible noise!'

'The boy strolled past us,' his bodyguard recalled, 'gave a side glance at Mr Churchill and said, "You can shut your ears can't you?"'

It was hardly a clever riposte. It wasn't witty; it wasn't even anatomically feasible. But the Prime Minister was chuckling as he entered the Foreign Office Yard. And Sergeant Thompson heard him repeating to himself: 'You can shut your ears, can't you?'

Churchill could be vain, and a bully, but he could also appreciate being taken down a peg or two. For what separated the nation Churchill led from those he was fighting against was not the extraordinary courage of the boy who kept on whistling – but the centuries of struggle and sacrifice that had gone into ensuring that it took no extraordinary courage for a newspaper boy to keep on whistling when the King's first minister told him to be quiet.

IT WAS NOT JUST the official documents arriving daily in the Prime Ministerial red boxes – or those mysterious buff-coloured boxes that were strictly for his eyes only – that commanded Churchill's attention each morning. He insisted on scanning the newspapers too. Though it often infuriated him, the Prime Minister still valued Britain's free press (with all the caveats that phrase required these days), not least its lively letters columns, as additional eyes and ears on the state of the nation. He was sent detailed reports on the state of public opinion from the Ministry of Information but, for him as much as anyone, newspapers cut through red tape to highlight hidden problems – as in the uproar over the appalling state of official and unofficial shelters when the Blitz began – and warned him of sceptical rumblings and vague misgivings that might not reach him through official channels.

American newsman Quentin Reynolds had no truck with those who disparaged Britain's wartime press. They were still, he guessed, 'the only comparatively free newspapers in the world.

'Of course we have never had freedom of the press in America so we don't know much about it,' he went on provocatively. 'Always our newspapers have been dominated by advertisers. No publisher will deny that. Here the editor of a paper means something. He actually writes almost as he pleases.'

He cited Fleet Street's campaign against 'Cooper's Snoopers': an early Government attempt to monitor public opinion. Minister Duff Cooper had paid for large newspaper advertisements in rebuttal of the campaign: 'The papers in which his advertisements appeared attacked him the hardest.' In the end it was the Minister, not the journalists, who backed down. (The fact that official monitoring of opinion had gone on regardless, though by different and less overt means, was neither here nor there.)

Many newspapers today trailed an upcoming *Daily Herald* series on 'The Twelve Riddles of 1941':

Will Hitler invade Britain?
Will America enter the war?
What next in the air?
Can we smash the U-boat campaign?
Can we take the offensive in 1941?
What will happen in the Balkans?
What are Stalin's plans?
Will our blockade win?
What will happen to Europe's neutrals?
What will happen in the Far East?
How will the world pay for the war?
Where do we go when we win?

Even a seven-day-a-week Prime Minister was hardly sufficient to knit these puzzles together into a strategy for survival through the approaching year. Fortunately, Churchill had found more days in the week than that.

Typically he would work late into the night – 3 a.m. was not unusual. Then start again early next morning and, with space for an expansive luncheon and nap, work until dinner, after which dictation into the small hours began once more. A young civil servant once found a secretary typing at the foot of the PM's bed while he expatiated, in red dressing gown and cigar in hand, throwing out occasional endearments to black cat Nelson resting on his feet. Mrs Hill could have responded that this was nothing: before the war she had been required to mount a ladder to take notes while Mr Churchill was bricklaying (though female staff were never called upon, as some male ones were, to attend him in his bath).

For the Prime Minister's prodigious work rate and eccentric hours represented not just the 'war effort' but business as usual at the old-established firm of Winston Churchill & Co. Ltd. Throughout the Thirties he had poured out a staggering flow of words: speeches, journalism and histories, galvanised by his political mission to expose Hitler's machinations and his need to repair his own fortunes in what had seemed destined to be his years of political decline.

When he was, against all odds, recalled to very pinnacle of political life, one of his first jobs as Prime Minister had been to prepare MPs for a prospect more terrible, even, than he had envisaged. In secret session, he warned the Commons that he had been informed that the nation might have no defences against night bombers on 250 nights a year.

This was 'one of those things you can only tell by finding out,' he had dictated, when he prepared his characteristic 'psalm-style' notes for that speech:

Folly underrate gravity attack impending.

But if 100 to 150 bombers employed
entitled to remark:
  Not very cleverly employed.

Hardly paid expenses.

Learn to get used to it.
  Eels get used to skinning.

Steady continuous bombing,
  probably rising to great intensity occasionally,
  must be regular condition of our life.

Britain's response, he said, would be more effective. It was 'A test of our nerve against theirs' and no one could tell the result.

This supreme battle depends upon
  the courage of the ordinary man and woman.

Whatever happens, keep a stiff upper lip.

'God was very good to the English,' Quentin Reynolds wrote one night as bombs dropped a block away from his West End apartment. 'He made each one of them half a fool.'

An Englishman is fool enough to believe that one Englishman can lick a dozen Germans. The RAF kids aren't boastful, but each one is foolish enough to believe that he and his Spitfire can lick a dozen Messerschmitts. Women and old men in the villages have built street barricades and they are foolish enough to think that they can defend their villages in case of invasion. The fact that each Englishman is half a fool gives him a tremendous psychological advantage over any German who is no fool at all, but instead is a reasoning methodical being who knows the rules and abides by them.

The Englishman is also foolish in this respect: he thinks that his personal liberty is the most important thing in the world.

And in Winston Churchill, perhaps, the English had found the one man fool enough to lead them.

There were those, inside Parliament and out, who maintained a deep scepticism about the Prime Minister. And even some of his greatest supporters had, as it were, only half a mind to believe him. But the foolish half a mind that responded to his words helped the sensible, logical half that visualised the Nazi on their own front doorstep to hope for the best. Not of the Nazi, but of themselves: 'Winston's speeches send all sorts of thrills racing up & down my veins & I feel fit to tackle the largest Hun!' wrote Nell Carver, who was at work in the City this Sunday morning, after she heard his first speech as Prime Minister. Adding: 'Probably if only a small one threatened my hearth & home I should creep into a corner – but that is as it may be!'

'We have before us many, many months of struggle and suffering,' Churchill had said that day:

> You ask, what is our policy? I will say: It is to wage war by land, sea, and air, with all our might and with all the strength that God can give us: and to wage war against a monstrous tyranny, never surpassed in the dark, lamentable catalogue of human crime. That is our policy. You ask, what is our aim? I can answer in one word: Victory – victory at all costs, victory in spite of all terrors; victory, however long and hard the road may be; for without victory there is no survival.

IN THE *SUNDAY EXPRESS* this morning columnist Nathaniel Gubbins, one of Churchill's favourite reads, was poking fun at Fleet Street's clumsier attempts to serve the national interest: 'The newspapers have been playing some funny tricks with us lately,' he wrote.

> Conscious of their important role in helping to maintain the national morale, there are times when it seems they can't make up their minds whether the masses need pepping up or having some of the pep knocked out of them.

When there is bad news on the front page the leader writer orders us to cheer up and keep smiling. When the news is good he warns us not to be too cocksure about victories . . . we can't say what harm it does the imperturbable British masses, we can only record that it demoralises an excitable temperamental thing like us.

The paper's film critic, meanwhile, laid into the 'morale-boosting' short films produced for the MoI by the 'bearded boys of the Documentary School'. Though he gave full marks to the one he had just seen. Its last scenes shot four mornings ago, *Christmas Under Fire* was already on its way to a thousand British cinemas and to 16,000 in the USA. Shelterers at Kensington and Leicester Square Underground had given up their sleep as cameras rolled back and forth along the tracks on Christmas Eve, filming until the current was switched back on at half past four. They rose to the challenge 'splendidly', said the director: 'I couldn't have had a finer cast.'

'The most poignant moment in the picture,' wrote the *Sunday Express*,

which shows you the Christmas trees, the puddings, the bombed shops and theatres, the toys of war for 1940's children, the shepherds in uniform, and the spotters on roofs – most poignant of all is where Quentin says, 'No bells ring in England to celebrate the birth of the Saviour. No church bells are allowed to be rung in England.'

This, and the scene of choristers in the chapel, with the dramatic 'cut' to peaceful families sleeping 'Underground', are the most moving thing in this great little film.

'Quentin' was, of course, Quentin Reynolds, and his use as narrator was not merely a sop to the USA. A pro-British message in an American accent – any American accent, even that of as besotted an Anglophile as Quentin Reynolds – was reassurance that, though the United States was not in the war yet (and with luck might not even need to be), Americans understood what Britain was fighting for and were, or soon would be, backing them to the hilt.

THE PRIME MINISTER could not afford to be so sanguine. Not for nothing was the hard-pressed British Government paying out precious dollars to have so many prints of *Christmas Under Fire* made across the Atlantic. At the end of 1940, London was waiting on, and courting, favourable decisions from Washington as anxiously as the governments of Abyssinia, China, Spain, Czechoslovakia, Poland and Finland had ever waited on, and courted, London's. And Churchill's hopes and fears were caught up in the same tangle of high principle, practical politics and sheer bloody survival instinct that theirs had been. For he knew his nation must soon follow all the others into the abyss if the American people could not be brought to see that this was already a world war, even if not all the world was fighting. That the continued existence of Nazism posed a threat to all democracy everywhere. And that Britain's long-term survival was vital for their own defence.

As the British Prime Minister worked on this morning, in the White House, six hours behind, the American President slept. Sometimes Franklin Roosevelt's dreams were troubled by thoughts of fire – a particular terror since he was struck down by polio. His wife Eleanor had fled from the room in tears on the day he proudly demonstrated how, if trapped by flames, he would escape by slowly dragging himself by his elbows across the floor, pulling his useless legs behind him. Whatever else they might say about Franklin D. Roosevelt, no one could deny his physical courage.

It would take something more than physical courage, though, to escape the fires haunting White House dreams these days. US Military Attaché General Raymond Lee, before he left for his posting in London in June, had asked a State Department adviser about the 'hemispheric defense' idea being floated in Washington, establishing a 'no-fighting' zone round the North and South American continents. Didn't the proposers realise, he asked, that it was impossible in practice, and that the United States didn't have sufficient forces to defend so many Latin American nations? The adviser agreed, but said that it sounded good and encouraged some of the weaker ones to stand up for themselves. General Lee said that it was like having a pyromaniac loose in town – yes, you sent for the firefighters, but you also called in the police to catch him and throw him in jail.

Independently, the Secretary of the Interior had reached for the same fiery imagery. 'It seems to me that we Americans are like the householder who refuses to lend or sell his fire extinguishers to help put out the fire in a house that is right next door,' he had written to FDR in August about Britain's plight, 'although that house is all ablaze and the wind is blowing from that direction.'

Before Christmas, the President too had spoken of fire. Not of pyromaniacs, or the dangerous way the wind was blowing, but with his accustomed relaxed, unthreatening, common-or-garden folksiness. 'I don't think there is any particular news,' he had opened his press conference on 17th December, 'except possibly one thing that I think is worth my talking about . . .'

'Suppose my neighbor's home catches fire,' he said,

and I have a length of garden hose four or five hundred feet away. If he can take my garden hose and connect it up with his hydrant, I may help him put out his fire. Now what do I do? I don't say to him before that operation, 'Neighbor, my hose cost me fifteen dollars; you have to pay me fifteen dollars for it.'

Well, he said, he had been working on a new notion. 'A very overwhelming number of Americans,' he told the assembled press, were now clear that Great Britain's successful defence of itself was the United States' 'best immediate defense'. 'It is possible – I will put it that way,' he said, 'for the United States to take over British orders, and, because they are essentially the same kind of munitions that we use ourselves, turn them into American orders.' Such portion of the arms that seemed right and proper at the time could be leased or sold to Britain, where they could be more useful to America's defence than sitting in warehouses.

'Now what I am trying to do is eliminate the dollar sign,' he said. 'That is something brand new in the thoughts of practically everybody in this room, I think – get rid of the silly, foolish old dollar sign.'

What precisely did that mean? This evening President Roosevelt was to make one of his famous Sunday night 'Fireside Chats' to America. Friday's *Daily Express* had carried news of an appeal made to him by 171 famous Americans, asking that his broadcast make clear both that it was the settled policy of the US to ensure the defeat of the Axis and that everything was being done to defeat the 'plausible but fatal' arguments of those who would appease Hitler. So was tonight's speech to be, at last, an unequivocal US commitment to British survival? This Sunday morning, Winston Churchill was among the world's millions who were still in the dark on that question.

'FOR YEARS Mr Roosevelt has been regarded in democratic Europe as a great moral force,' a young London social worker wrote in her diary, 'the only statesman in the world who has made a stand for ordinary decencies and the underdog.' She had been, she added, 'like every other visitor to America before the war . . . shocked to hear the remarks some Americans made about their President.' And remarks made about Mr Roosevelt by his enemies could indeed be vitriolic. Communist. Fascist. Imperialist. Liar. Warmonger. Traitor.

But, as Britain's most powerful friend in the world at present, it was criticisms made of him by his friends that best explained Winston Churchill's current anxieties.

'You are a wonderful person but you are one of the most difficult men to work with that I have ever known,' FDR's Secretary of the Interior once told him. 'You won't talk frankly even with people who are loyal to you and of whose loyalty you are fully convinced. You keep your cards close up against your belly.' The President even admitted as much to his Treasury Secretary: his philosophy was, he said, 'Never let your left hand know what your right is doing.'

'Which hand am I, Mr President?' asked the Secretary, to which Roosevelt replied, 'My right hand – but I keep my left hand under the table.' It was, noted the 'right hand' in his diary afterwards, 'the most frank expression of the real FDR . . . but thank God I understand him.'

Churchill's relationship with FDR was still young and tentative and he did not yet understand him. But he was already aware that Britain's last best hope did not always keep both hands above the table. And from the distance of London this morning, looking from his right hand to his left and back again, it was difficult to guess which one the politically ambidextrous President used most naturally.

ECONOMICALLY, Churchill had gone for broke when he became Prime Minister. The previous administration had budgeted for a three-year war. After Dunkirk, when so much equipment was destroyed or left behind in France, Churchill had scrapped the budget and told the Armed Forces to order what they needed to survive. Partly because he held on to the hope that American support would come, but mostly because . . . what other choice was there? Having put the British people into the hazard – and the Empire – did it make sense to try to preserve the balance of payments?

US Military Attaché General Lee, with some idea of what the British were spending – in blood as well as money – was rooting for them to succeed. They would be bankrupt at the end of it, he wrote in his diary, but would deserve practically limitless gratitude from rest of the world. Churchill, with a more accurate picture this morning of Britain's dwindling resources than General Lee, knew bankruptcy was a much more immediate prospect than victory. And it was not gratitude he needed now.

Still on its six-week journey across the Atlantic, a letter written before Christmas to Winnie Bowman expressed her friend's frustration at an American she'd heard on the wireless:

The bloke said that America wanted and needed to be told what we wanted in the way of arms etc. I blew into a fury and said did they want more to make them realise how badly we needed stuff . . . did they want bits of people to be

60

taken over there to be displayed in the streets before they realised how much a country at war needed help in armaments?

'Of course,' she admitted, 'I was wrong and the man was right. We should state what we need and how much, but I thought afterwards how many women in the world must have made just those remarks when Helsinki was being blown to pieces. Mustn't the Finnish women have felt the same?'

'We are certainly suffering for our past sins,' she admitted.

None of us ordinary people wanted help sent to China [against the Japanese], we wanted none of our young men to have gone and died for them, many of us were glad that we saved ourselves by sacrificing Czechoslovakia and now we are learning a very hard lesson for being complacent because the race that needs our help is on the other side of the world from us.

Now Britain looked to the other side of the world for help itself. And Winston Churchill's only qualm about saying exactly what was needed from America was that the figures might frighten its President away.

THE BRITISH, wrote the head of the European Division of the US State Department in 1939, 'regard us as a Dominion gone wrong, but if they frankly regarded us as a foreign country, albeit a friendly one, relations would be better.' A foreign country, moreover, that had forbidden itself to take sides in any war, even economically by selling arms or extending credit, unless it was itself attacked. Because that, it was widely believed in America, was how they had been dragged into the last war by tricksy Britain and France, who had then stiffed them on the bill.

Congress had passed laws through the 1930s to prevent the sale of war *matériel* to either side in any war. A couple of months into this war the laws had been amended so that anyone could buy arms – provided they could pay for them, cash on the nail, in dollars or gold, and collect them in their own ships. This obviously favoured Britain, which had the merchant fleet for 'cash-and-carry' that Germany lacked. Many Americans (including their President) had assumed that the fabled wealth of the British Empire could sustain such a situation for a long time to come. Many Americans (including their President) had also not been wholly sorry to see Britain having to pay up.

Even so, many big US manufacturers seemed reluctant to produce the arms Britain was paying for, even on new plant it had been required to pay for too. Cassandra (the acerbic William Connor, Churchill's particular bugbear from the *Daily Mirror*) was revealing in his column for tomorrow the number of aircraft that had arrived from America during the first year of the war. A year, he wrote, 'in which it was gaily alleged on repeated occasions that five hundred aeroplanes a month were reaching this country from the United States.'

> September (1939), thirty-four; October, nil; November, four; December, fifty-three; January (1940) forty-one; February, nineteen; March, two; April, twenty-three; May, nineteen; June, ninety-seven; July 173; August 278.
> Total for the first year of the war, 743.

'America,' he concluded, 'just isn't anywhere near this fight yet.'

THROUGHOUT THE AUTUMN, blitzed Britons had taken considerable comfort from a US Presidential election in which both candidates espoused the slogan of 'All Aid to Britain, Short of War'. President Roosevelt had coined the phrase and in early September General Lee in London had asked the visiting Chiefs of US Army and Air Force War Plans what exactly it meant.

He was told that nobody knew: that it depended on what the President thought from one day to the next. Lee pondered on whether people in Washington ever considered that they had no God-given right to declare war. One day they might wake up to find Germany and Japan had declared war on them – that was their style. Or was that, Lee wrote in his diary, what the President was after?

British hopes for FDR's re-election in November had been unanimous. Although, if anything, the Republicans' surprise choice candidate had been more forthright in his declarations on the campaign trail. 'If Britain fails,' Wendell Willkie declared in one newsreel, 'we are utterly, and savagely, alone.'

> Almost no nation on earth, except Britain, owes us anything but disillusionment and ill-will . . . We must send and we must keep sending aid to Britain: our first line of defence and our only remaining friend.

Well, Roosevelt had won his unprecedented third term. But British hopes that this would mark a big new aid initiative had been dashed. In the judgement of the *New York Times*'s Raymond Daniell: 'What they really were afraid of came to pass to some extent anyway. That was a hiatus in industrial production, a slackening of the American defense effort, and a cooling of the sentiment for helping Britain.'

Chapter Five

First Sunday after Christmas
        10.30 am

        Mattins Ps 8 Te Deum and Benedictus *West* in C
        Litany
        Hymn before Sermon, no 180 (A & M)
        Sermon [preacher The Rev J O Hannay M A]
        Hymn after Sermon no 189 (A & M)
        Introit. JESU, the very thought of Thee no 178 (A & M, Pt 1)
        Holy Communion.
        Byrd (three-part)
        Hymn no 318 (A & M)

Notice of services at St Paul's Cathedral for Sunday, 29th December 1940

THE GREAT WEST DOORS of St Paul's Cathedral were opened only for great state occasions: royal jubilees; thanksgiving for famous victories; funerals of great warriors such as Nelson and Wellington. So the congregation mounting the great stone steps for *Hymns Ancient & Modern* this morning were drawn by a twinkling Christmas tree to the smaller, more everyday, entrance to one side. Inside, another tree was piled round with gifts for evacuated children and the men of the minesweepers. A collection box appealed to Blitz Londoners to remember the less fortunate at this season of goodwill.

The trees were gifts from the King: a relatively recent innovation championed by the Dean of St Paul's against those members of the Chapter and congregation who considered them pagan. They had quickly become a popular tradition, which the Dean and Chapter had decided 'should not be abolished by Hitler'. Maintaining traditions – even short-lived ones – took on extra meaning in the face of a threat that could end everything. Though there could be no services after dark (they could not black out the huge windows), services otherwise would continue as normal, 'whatever the noises from outside'. But, as the war progressed, it became clear that business as usual was developing into one of the most memorable chapters in the long history of their remarkable establishment.

LONDON HAD BEEN still in its post-Roman doldrums, and Westminster no more than a marshy island popular with duck hunters, when the newly baptised King of Kent paid for a Christian cathedral to be built on top of Ludgate Hill in the neighbouring East Saxons' city of London. (A later legend, that it replaced a Roman Temple of Diana, was only finally squashed when, a thousand years later, circumstances gave Sir Christopher Wren ample opportunity to investigate the site thoroughly.)

Thus when the Very Rev. W. R. Matthews, Dean of St Paul's, sat down with the Cathedral Chapter in April 1939 to discuss the threatened war, they had all been aware, he wrote, that 'our own great Cathedral was not by any means the first to have been built upon this spot'.

Taking the long view can bring perspective, but the Cathedral's history hardly inspired confidence. Built AD 604. Burnt 675. Rebuilt then burnt and ransacked by Vikings 962. Rebuilt again, then destroyed in the 1083 fire that razed most of the City.

The greatest St Paul's of all, begun in 1087 and more than two centuries in the building, had lost its famous spire to a bolt of lightning three years into Queen Elizabeth's reign. Then, of course, the whole edifice had been consumed in the Great Fire of 1666 – enter Sir Christopher Wren. His Cathedral, completed in 1709, was less than twenty years off its quarter-millennium. But who would give odds on reaching that?

The building immediately before their own was so well documented as to be almost as familiar to the Dean and Chapter as Wren's. And the dramatic story of its destruction was of more than academic interest now.

They knew, for instance, from blackened fragments in the crypt, that fire turned white marble monuments black. The best statuary was therefore shifted downstairs and packed round with sandbags. Most precious of all was the lone survivor of the Great Fire, though even that bore its scars. Black scorch marks showed where, centuries earlier, flames had licked the base of the effigy of sexy poet turned sombre churchman John Donne, who was Dean of St Paul's in the 1620s. He had posed for the sculptor in his shroud: having taken to the church late after a lifetime of disappointment, he was not a cheery soul.

Nearing death, he had grimly reminded his congregation: 'Never send to know for whom the bell tolls; it tolls for thee.' No bells tolled at St Paul's in 1940. But Dean Matthews, who had spent many a wartime night lying by his doom-hungry predecessor, required no special reminders about the fragility of this life: 'There have been moments when this juxtaposition seemed only too appropriate and when I felt that only Donne could have done justice to my feelings.'

SINCE LONDON'S marshy subsoil was judged too soft to support modern skyscrapers, new building had been limited to 100 feet: in practice, seventy feet or even thirty-five was more common. So St Paul's, with its golden cross soaring 365 feet above Ludgate Hill, had sailed into the twentieth century with its effortless pre-eminence on the skyline, and the psyche, of Londoners intact. Only the many church spires and Wren's Monument to the Great Fire shared its airy domain.

A sudden, much-publicised alarm about its structural safety in the 1920s had prompted journalist H. V. Morton to make his first visit to its famous Whispering Gallery: 'When Americans had talked to me about it I had lied and pretended that I knew it. So I determined to wipe out my shame.'

> 'I thought,' I said to the verger, 'that I'd better go up there before it comes down here.'
>
> 'That won't be for a long time, sir,' he said, with a reassuring smile, a sentiment I passed on at step two hundred and forty-one to a charming old lady, who asked if I thought it was 'quite wise' to go right to the top.
>
> What a climb it is! If ever I go foolishly walking or climbing in Switzerland again, I will get into training on this spiral staircase. Once up and once down every day, and no mountaineer's muscles would be firmer, no walker's wind less treacherous. It is a fine, free and uncrowded gymnasium.

Most Londoners had, like Morton, taken St Paul's for granted. But, at the end of 1940, a small band of loyalists exercised regularly in this 'fine, free and uncrowded gymnasium'.

The Dean and Chapter had decided, in their April 1939 meeting, to re-form the St Paul's Watch that had protected the Cathedral from Zeppelins; the Surveyor to the Fabric of the Cathedral volunteered to lead it. Cathedral staff would do the job by day and most volunteered to take a turn at night too, but more members would be needed. So, as in the last war, the Watch recruited architects above call-up age, who could offer both a feeling for the building's beautiful but complex geography and the prospect of availability 'for the duration'.

The Surveyor asked the Royal Institute of British Architects for 'men from forty to sixty who can walk up stairs and not fear heights or fire' and who could volunteer one or two nights each week. Over sixty RIBA members (including poet John Betjeman), responded; some of the older ones still had their Watch badges from twenty years earlier.

Brisk and businesslike questions left volunteers in no doubt of the risks:

1 can you bring a helmet
2 have you an overall, if not wear old clothes
3 have you a respirator, what kind is it
4 night and hours of duty
5 date of commencement
6 next of kin

St Paul's Watch was, claimed architect-turned-bomb-damage-inspector A. S. G. Butler, 'the best club in London with English, Scots, Irish, Welsh, Americans, Dutch and Czechs'. Some personalities emerged from the darkness in his letters to his mother: sculptor Edgar Frith, 'looking rather saintly after doing every night ARP in Kennington slums'; art connoisseur Colin Anderson, 'Head of the Orient Line – ex-Eton and ex-Greek god and all that'; and much-loved Cathedral Librarian Gerald Henderson, universally known as 'Dracula'.

'St Paul's is quite fun,' Andrew Butler wrote to his mother after his first stint.

Got there at a ¼ to nine, full of food. Our HQ is the crypt. Given smart, dark blue very rough boiler suits to wear. Did several hours of gentle drill with hoses, chiefly joining them together and rushing round with them in the dark. No squirting practice yet. All doors inside are open and we tear about everywhere. There are two OPs [observation posts] like in the war on the roof where we will later do watch-out and telephone down position of raiders if any and when incendiaries are coming down. Others of us then rush with squirts and stirrup pumps and buckets of sand and long-handled scoops. We are learning to take over from the much younger Cathedral staff who will be called up.

The Dean gives us hot tea at about 3 a.m. in a carpenter's shop under the garden and then we can repose if we want, on mattresses and pillows in a museum place. It seems awfully safe because you can always nip into a cranny with 8 ft walls around you.

I have in my 'gang' C. Farey who is the greatest living architectural draughtsman, a rich, very jolly architect called Phipps *and* Edgar Frith, sculptor, also a quantity surveyor. Some do two nights a week and Frith and I did 'effects' from the top of the cross. Marvellous look of London dead and black and a moon, climbing iron ladders in the dark with small lamp in mouth. We smoke nearly everywhere except actually in the church!

At seven next morning, he had ridden home to Chelsea on the number 11 bus looking 'frightful in oldest jersey and cap', slept for an hour, breakfasted, then slept again for ten hours solid.

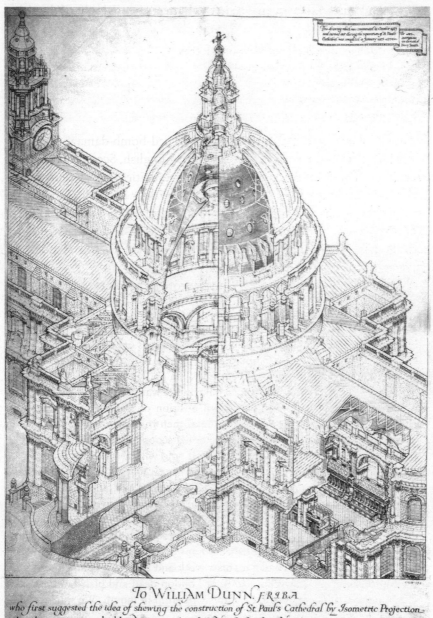

To WILLIAM DUNN, F.R.I.B.A
who first suggested the idea of shewing the construction of St Paul's Cathedral by Isometric Projection
this drawing is inscribed by MERVYN EDMUND MACARTNEY, F.S.A. Surveyor to the Fabric ~
Measured and drawn by R.B.BROOK-GREAVES *in collaboration with* W. GODFREY ALLEN
Valuable assistance has been rendered by Matthew Dawson F.R.I.B.A. *&* E.J.Bolwell

'A ship with six decks': the night and day responsibility of the St Paul's Watch

ANDREW BUTLER later lectured newer Watch members on the task facing them. The Cathedral should be thought of, he said, as a ship with six decks. At the bottom, the long crypt set half underground with the cross-shaped Cathedral floor above. Above that the Triforium, at which level it was still possible to move round the cross shape through corridors and hidden passages such as the picturesquely named Shinbone Alley.

Over the Triforium, neatly hidden from the passing public by false walls, Wren had created an array of flat and pocket roofs: 'good receptacles for incendiary bombs'. Then came the eight main roofs over the nave, choir and transepts, linked on the fourth 'deck' by the circular Whispering Gallery. More steps took you to the fifth level, where the Stone Gallery ran outside the base of the dome. Stairs inside the dome linked to a sixth and final 'deck': the Golden Gallery around the base of the massive stone lantern. Atop this lantern, the golden ball was large enough to hold ten people; finally came the cross.

Watch members had also to master the four towers beneath the drum, two more flanking the great West Doors, plus some thirty stone staircases and metal spirals linking decks, towers and multifarious roofs in eccentric ways. Some, wrote Butler, 'make a point of by-passing where you want to go and either land you in a little room where the Lord Mayor washes his hands or fling you out of the building into the churchyard, in the dark.' Some areas were accessible only by ladders. There were no lifts. And you had to know all the staircases, and the mile or so of dark corridors, well enough to navigate by the light of a small hand-lamp since explosion or fire might block any one of them without warning.

Wren had presented the Watch with yet another problem in creating a larger dome than the Cathedral structure could really carry. His method was 'ingenious', conceded Dean Matthews, but 'a source of embarrassment to those responsible for its defence'. Put bluntly, Sir Christopher's famous dome was a cheat. The lead shell dominating the London skyline arched high over the smaller, sturdier dome seen inside. This shell was supported by a network of stout wooden beams braced against an eighteen-inch-thick brick cone built over the inner dome. Get an HE or IB in amongst that lot and there was no telling what might happen.

'Volunteers for the Dome patrol were selected from amongst those with heads for heights and with a leaning towards acrobatics,' wrote the Dean:

They were expected, if necessary, to walk along the slender beams of the Dome to reach their bombs or to thrust the nozzles of their stirrup pumps into the heart of an incipient fire. The Dome was not a healthy place in the height of a blitz and the patrol was changed at half-hourly intervals. Men have told me of the awesome feeling they experienced when carrying out their patrols in the darkness of the Dome while the battle raged around them and of how the din seemed to be magnified by the Dome like the beating of a drum.

The Cathedral had two near-misses during the first, fateful City raid of 24th August, and the Watch had been busy ever since. 'Terrific at St Paul's last night,' Andrew Butler wrote to his mother after one watch.

> Searchlights whirling, two fires blazing and bangs but not very near. Hardly any sleep. We patrol round inside the dome, popping out of eight little doors and on to the roof with a telephone to the crypt. The Dean has really joined in. Comes every night and does it with us. Rather sweet. Somebody was so tired on Wednesday night that they just sat down and said 'is it Monday or tomorrow?' Days and nights get so muddled.

IT WAS NOT JUST St Paul's. All over the City this morning, volunteer and paid firewatchers were going on duty. Not as many, sadly, as there should have been. And not every company had prepared its staff for the challenge of war as thoroughly as Hitchcock, Williams & Co. of St Paul's Churchyard. But then the celebrated textile wholesaler – supplier to the Empire of Sports Hats and Tams, Straws and Felts, Ribbons, Umbrellas, Maids' Costumes, Corsets, Coatees, Mackintoshes and the like – did have an exemplary record of civic responsibility.

Old Mr Hitchcock had been one of the Victorian City's anti-Scrooges: a founder member of the Early Closing Association that won shop assistants their afternoon off. And employee George Williams – a saved sinner – had used his free time to start a Bible class. Over the years, George had risen to partnership and his Bible class had grown into the Young Men's Christian Association. Even now, YMCA members from around the world dropped in to Hitchcock, Williams to pay tribute to their late founder, whose grandsons ran the firm in 1940.

Four hundred Hitchcock, Williams employees had, like the three young Mr Williamses themselves, gone off to fight in the Great War; one in five had never returned. Now many of the survivors buckled down again, shovelling a hundred tons of sand into sandbags, donating blood at St Bartholomew's Hospital, plane-spotting by day and firewatching by night. One older employee penned a wistful picture of the new life blossoming amid the serious business of war.

> As I wander through the shelters,
> And glance that way – or this,

69

I see some charming tableaux
Of nice young man and miss!
As knee to knee they sit, and smile,
They seem to say, 'This is worth while.'
How welcome if 'twas said to me:
'You're not so old at fifty-three'!!

Hitchcock, Williams had signed up for Home Office and Fire Brigade lectures, and trained their staff for the emergency ahead. For months, battery torches were secreted in unlikely places to represent burning incendiaries and staff wrapped each other enthusiastically – sometimes over-enthusiastically – in bandages. Rescue practice, wrote Mr H. A. Walden, historian of the firm's war, uncovered several 'unsuspected "he" men': especially when 'victims' were lady members of staff. 'Encores were frequent; in fact two engagements were subsequently announced.'

No 'he' man himself, Mr Walden had, under the influence of two large sherries from Mr Hugh Williams, 'recklessly agreed to enter the forbidding realm of letters' and edit the firm's wartime journal. *The Log* carried news of strange reunions of Hitchcock, Williams men in the heart of Africa or mid-ocean lifeboats, and regaled far-flung employees with the old firm's lively adventures at home, through hidden staff talents for writing, cartooning and that endless versifying endemic among Blitz Londoners.

Something of the breaking down of class distinctions noted everywhere in wartime London crept even into the well-ordered beehive of Hitchcock, Williams. Live-in junior staff and domestics were joined by firewatchers of all grades, from warehousemen to the three young Mr Williamses themselves, while the General Manager 'lived in' now, too, taking the opportunity of quiet Sundays to compile what Mr Walden called a 'sustained and interesting series of articles on historic City Churches and buildings'.

The management organised dances and film shows, concerts and whist drives; rehearsals for a Noël Coward comedy were well advanced. Only a few 'in the know' had escaped on the night when the ladies of the Millinery Department staged a secret mass sew-up of pyjama sleeves, legs, pockets and buttonholes to enliven the hours of darkness. Rival dormitories, bearing names like 'Hotel Splendor' and 'The Squeezin' Hotel', pitched against each other at the ping-pong table. And a darts league was organised with fire squads of nearby textile firms such as Messrs Cook, Son & Co. (St Paul's) and Bradbury Greatorex of Aldermanbury. *The Log* commemorated one famous victory, over Messrs Rylands and Sons Ltd of Wood Street, with a lengthy epic:

> . . . And so our men were victors,
> We'd won by 4 to 3,
> Like heroes they refrained to boast –
> Dartistic Modesty! . . .

It was too cold for deck quoits this morning, but daylight patrols often also relaxed with a game on the roofs overlooking the Cathedral:

> . . . Let Hun Armadas come in soit!
> Like Drake our Firemen take no froit,
> They calmly play and quite enjoit,
> This playing with the nimble quoit . . .

Hitchcock, Williams and St Paul's had shared many adventures since the Blitz began, the most celebrated in the very first week. On the Thursday morning, as the two o'clock watch of Hitchcock, Williams' Fire Party assembled under the direction of General Manager Mr Lester, they had heard the shriek of a bomb followed by a heavy thud. The sound of guns masked the sound for Andrew Butler inside the Cathedral, and he was unaware of the peril until a 'rather perturbed official' came to inform the Watch that a huge HE had just missed the South West Tower and now lay, fifteen feet down, still armed with 1,000 kilograms of explosive.

A bomb disposal squad, led by Canadian Lieutenant Robert Davies of the Royal Engineers, turned up and police cleared the area – though some Watch members remained on duty at the far end of the Cathedral. Hitchcock, Williams, too, clung to the idea of business as usual: its Fire Party helped man the police barriers and were allowed to let through fellow-staff arriving for work, so long as they went straight to the basement shelters until the bomb was made safe.

They were in for a long wait. The long-delay fuse on the huge bomb (nicknamed a 'Hermann' by Luftwaffe pilots after fat Reichsmarschall Goering) had an anti-withdrawal device for which there was, as yet, no remedy. Instructions were to blow up such bombs *in situ* but the disposal squad was not going to give up St Paul's without a fight.

As they tried to dig 'Hermann' out, they found it had entered the ground at such an angle that every movement took it closer to the Cathedral's foundations. Three of the squad were overcome by fumes from a broken gas main. Then the gas caught fire. A heroic gasman blocked off the main and digging began again.

All through Thursday the work went on and all through Friday. Hundreds of Hitchcock, Williams staff came and went without once being able to get up to their workrooms or showrooms. St Paul's Watch maintained their vigil up on the Cathedral roofs during sporadic raids.

On Friday night, Mr Lester had to conduct his 'rather weary' Hitchcock, Williams crew to a public shelter further off after an NCO from the bomb squad warned that the whole thing would either 'come up' or 'blow up' within two hours. But it didn't. On Saturday, Mr Frisby of Ribbons, acting as go-between with the digging party, brought back

> frequent reports of hope and despair, ranging from 'up in the afternoon,' or 'a couple of hours,' then 'before dark'. He explained the special difficulties being encountered by a bomb settling down in the soft sub-soil. As fast as the squad dug, the bomb penetrated further by its own great weight.

It was twenty-seven-and-a-half-feet down by the time steel hawsers were got around the bomb, now slippery with London clay. The hawsers were attached to two lorries waiting to drag the eight-foot-long bomb out into the open. The lorries pulled. The hawsers snapped. The whole operation was repeated. The lorries pulled. The hawsers snapped again. As darkness fell, work was abandoned.

It was Sunday morning when the bomb finally came up. A lorry, with Lieutenant Davies at the wheel and a car with a red flag in front tore through empty City streets. At a 'bomb graveyard' in Hackney Marshes 'Hermann' was safely detonated, making a crater only a little smaller than the dome of St Paul's itself.

'The bravery and fortitude of the bomb-disposal squad is not forgotten,' wrote Mr Walden afterwards:

> These men went about their grim task with complete sang-froid. They showed signs of some excitement, however, when, their work completed, Mr Frisby entertained and thanked them at the local hostelry! Here was no delayed action in dealing with the affairs in hand. Lt Davies RE as leader of this gallant band, was awarded a well-earned George Cross.

So too was Sapper George Wylie, a Scots-born East Ender, and there was recognition as well for the gasman who cut off the main. This was among the first actions recognised by the award created by the King on 23rd September, acknowledging civilian gallantry on a par with the military Victoria Cross. The King was said to have been incensed when his generals said Davies could not get a VC as he was not working 'in the face of the enemy'. No one could tell him he shouldn't get a George Cross.

The Cathedral had experienced another narrow escape in October, when an HE hit the eastern end. If it had penetrated the roof or church floor before blowing up the results would have been devastating. But it had exploded on the keystone of the vaulting, piercing a hole in the roof ('unfortunately missing the reredos', wrote architectural purist Andrew Butler) and reducing the High Altar below to rubble. This actually made rather a fine composition for press photographers: autumn sunshine pouring down on the rubble with the power of revelation. American journalist Ernie Pyle found Londoners 'both philosophical and proud'. 'They go and look at it without sadness and they say, "We would rather have it that way in a free London than have it whole like Notre Dame in an imprisoned Paris."'

ON BLACK SATURDAY, members of St Paul's Watch had stood on the colonnade witnessing hell coming to docklands. 'We were a silent company as we gazed upon this apocalyptic scene,' wrote the Dean, 'each no doubt pondering many things. At last someone spoke, "It is like the end of the world," and someone else replied, "It is the end of *a* world."'

In the past, the destruction of St Paul's Cathedral itself had been used as a symbol of the impermanence of earthly certainties in general and British power in particular. The poet Shelley had imagined, with a certain relish, its 'shapeless and nameless' ruin standing, Ozymandias-like, 'in the midst of an unpeopled marsh'. In the same 'vast solitude', Macaulay had seen some future New Zealander 'take his stand on a broken arch of London Bridge to sketch the ruins of St Paul's' while for Horace Walpole it was 'some curious traveller from Lima' documenting the scene. And scientific soothsayer H. G. Wells (now in his seventies and writing in today's *Sunday Express* on 'The World of My Heart's Desire') had, in 1898, conjured up the Cathedral, 'dark against the sunrise, and injured . . . by a huge gaping cavity on its western side'. St Paul's still dominated London's skyline – but this was the silent, ruined London left behind after an attack from Mars.

Wells confessed that, when his novel *The War of the Worlds* prophesied attacks from another planet, he had shared his generation's 'easy complacency' that war between humans was on the wane. 'The world before 1900 seemed to be drifting steadily towards a tacit but practical unification.' Though not through the kind of world parliament attempted in the League of Nations. In those days of poor communications and 'limited facilities for peoples to get at one another and do each other mischiefs', he wrote:

> 'Business' was much more of a world commonwealth than the political organisations. There were many people, especially in America, who imagined that 'Business' might ultimately unify the world and governments sink into subordination to its network.

73

In old age, and in a reality whose dealing-death capacity was fast catching up with his wildest imaginings, Wells had turned with new urgency to 'the things we must do and the price we must pay for world peace if we really intend to achieve it'. Published in January, his book *The New World Order* had been the subject of lively debate in London throughout 1940. The *Daily Herald* had run a month-long series on whether, to quote the book's subtitle, 'it is attainable, how it can be attained, and what sort of world a world at peace will have to be'.

Wells himself proposed a new Declaration of the Rights of Man (man meaning, he explained, 'every individual, male or female, of the species . . . without distinction of race, of colour or of professed belief or opinions'). But futurology was a game anyone could play now and everybody did. Had not the King himself, this Christmas, emphasised the 'real desire to share burdens and resources alike', which would be needed 'in each of our own lives as men and women and . . . the nations of the world'?

Picture Post promised a thoroughgoing 'Plan for Britain' in next week's issue: a Britain now forced 'into an acknowledgement of our dependence on each other'. When it came to devising a better world, it declared: 'This is not a time for putting off thinking "till we see how things are". This is a time for doing the thinking, so that we can make things how we want them to be.'

Things were already changing. Unemployment was disappearing; wages rising; rationing and price controls meant most people had enough food, even if it was dull. Meanwhile high taxes – progressive income tax ranging from 7/6 up to 18/6 in the pound (37½ to 92½ per cent) and a 100 per cent tax on war profits – meant that the upper, upper-middles, lower-upper-middles, upper-lower-middles (and all the other subtle social gradations of class by which the privileged of Britain excluded each other) were starting to feel the pinch.

Some complained and others took evasive action – but by no means all. A volunteer social worker received her income tax assessment: 'I nearly fainted!' she wrote in her journal. 'It's a good thing it's deducted at the source or it would hardly be collected at all.'

> Last year I thought the amount was crippling, this year it is just three times as much without any increase in the income. This automatic slicing off of two-thirds of one's income, plus taxes on every conceivable object, from checks to sugar, is a sobering process, but everyone takes it with a mere shrug of the shoulders. The days when we fulminated about taxes are past. The war costs what it costs, and that is that.

One woman, who sorted clothes at a WVS depot by day and volunteered as a first-aider in the Underground one night a week, seemed sanguine about her reduced prospects. 'I don't think the war will shatter life as we have known it completely,' she wrote cheerfully to Winnie Bowman.

> After all, none of us had standards that were luxurious. We would all have been happier for regular jobs with small secure incomes attached. I think our standards will be much what the standards of the Dutch or Swedish people were. A large moderately salaried middle class, a well-to-do working class, and no wealthy people to speak of and no money competition. Of course we won't have the kind of life you can get in America but I don't think it will matter. The one thing that worries me is that we are hardly likely to have the standards of taste which existed in Sweden etc. So our Co-ops will likely provide much more ugly things for all of us.

Even the Prime Minister, though steadfastly refusing to be drawn into a declaration of war aims, gave some thought to what he expected to be a 'short lull' after the war was over, in which there might be an opportunity to establish a few basic ground rules of national and international justice. Privately, he expressed the view that 'the more closely we followed the Sermon on the Mount, the more likely we were to succeed in our endeavours'. However, 'all this talk about war aims,' he said, 'was absurd at the present time'.

VERA BRITTAIN would have disagreed. A peace campaigner who had poured all her hopes into the League of Nations, she had lost her brother and her first love in the last war, and was sure international friendship would have to be the way forward after this one. Driven by 'an irresistible impulse of gratitude towards Providence and Lieutenant Davies' bomb-removing squad', she had come to St Paul's last month and had left with a free booklet of prayers.

Expecting the 'customary ecclesiastical propaganda about the holiness of this war, the righteousness of our cause, and the necessity of our victory if the impeccable standards of the British Empire were to prevail throughout the world', she was pleased to find it did not exclude even the enemy from what it called 'the common need of mankind, bewildered, frightened, embittered, led astray by delusions which end in despair'.

'Only cowardice, hypocrisy or a bad conscience makes men afraid to know the truth about themselves,' declared the booklet, listing, 'our national sins and weaknesses which war has laid bare':

We had sought peace, but did not know or would not face the price which must be made for having it. We tried to *keep* peace rather than to *make* it.

We had prided ourselves on our empire, but had begun to lose our strength and honour because we had put power and wealth before responsibility and duty.

We had set ourselves to achieve recovery, prosperity and security, but they were to be for ourselves, our nation, or even for some classes and sections within our nation, rather than for mankind.

We had perverted the true order of human life, by making wealth and profit, rather than the satisfaction of human need, the aim of our industry and commerce.

We had been blind to the continuance of needless suffering and waste in human life.

We had forgotten God, and believed that we could build a better world by our own skill and effort.

Vera Brittain was encouraged to believe that not all the truth lay with the recent Sunday paper that argued the British were irrevocably hardened by the Blitz: 'A nation cannot watch its holiest monuments being battered, with system and premeditation, and then meet the enemy afterwards in a forgiving, tolerant spirit.'

'Can it not?' responded Vera. 'If not, then it has already lost the peace; and if it loses yet another peace, the war of 1965 will annihilate our children and our London too.'

Chapter Six

Sun 29th Decr 8/2 in Phones – very slack. It's so nice &
peaceful on Sundays after the rush & bustle of week days.
Room 18 is now crammed full of Telex, Circuit Tables &
Meter Wires & what not, but we have some order now.

Nell Carver's diary for 1940

LOOKING ABOUT HER this morning, Post Office supervisor Nell Carver
was finally starting to warm to the basement office where they had been
moved after their old office, up above, was bombed on the first Wednesday
of the Blitz.

'Since the Londoner had never thought of London as anything but the
world's center,' Eric Sevareid observed wryly, 'it did not surprise him that
the world's attention was now fixed upon London, when upon occasion he
observed that this was so.' The Central Telegraph Office, by St Paul's tube
station, had long been London's centre and the world's centre rolled into
one for Nell Carver.

Though she had spent Christmas Day at home with her mother and
elderly aunt, she had worked Christmas Eve and late shift Boxing Day. 'A
really jolly time,' she recorded in her diary. 'Edith was also late & after we
were all off I produced my bottle of sherry & Biscuits & Edith had a box of
chocs so altogether we celebrated well and truly! A very pleasant end to a
good Xmas.' She had not got home until about midnight but fortunately
there had been no sirens.

Thanks to an early shift next day, Nell was home in time for Friday
night's raid, which she saw out, as usual, with Mum and Auntie Mary in
the kitchen (taking to the cupboard under the stairs if things sounded near,
as recommended if you had no better shelter). But her Saturday shift had
ended at eight last night and, with an eight o'clock start this morning, she
had been more than happy to overnight in one of the CTO's basement dormitories. In the privacy of her diary, Nell admitted to being 'apprehensive'
during raids at home: she hated the 'trapped & helpless' feeling as you
waited for another lot to come down.

At the beginning of the war, Mum had rejected the Government offer of
a corrugated-iron Anderson shelter for the garden – £7, or free if you

77

earned less than £250 a year: 'She says it would be better to be bombed in the warm than to get pneumonia!' And in due course they had been.

One week after the bombing of her office, Nell, Mum and Auntie Mary had been toasting Nell's birthday in port:

> Just finishing a glass apiece & about to go up when the whole house seemed to be torn apart by something we didn't hear fall. It was not so much a crash but like a shattering wind & thick dust rose up all round the room. We leapt from our seats & crouched together near the fireplace & waited, holding our breaths, for the roof to fall in. Nothing further happened in the Kitchen but everywhere we could hear crashing glass both inside and out . . . wardens and rescue parties had sprung from nowhere & were running along, banging on each door and shouting 'Is everyone all right in there?'

They said that you never heard the one that killed you and, if the land-mine had made a direct hit, that would have been that. They might have died of blast too: wardens often found people dead without a mark on them. But blast was a powerful and eccentric destroyer and had left the three Carver ladies unharmed on this occasion, even while it damaged their home beyond repair.

They had decamped briefly to friends in Leatherhead. Nell would have liked to stay on but Mum and Auntie Mary insisted on returning to the old neighbourhood. The determination with which the more ancient residents of bombed boroughs stuck to their patch – what one ambulance man called the 'I was born in Stepney, I've lived all my life in Stepney, and I'll die in Stepney' attitude – was something of a headache for those who looked after them.

An air raid warden urging her Finsbury folk to safer havens, found that

> The blind, the crippled, and the very old would say, 'Yes Miss; thank you Miss; I'll go Miss,' but they never went. They were a liability to us, particularly at the start of each raid; but since they would not be evacuated, the wardens were very considerate of them. Even the toughest, who had spent their whole lives among race-course gangs, generally had their 'specials' whom they carried or helped down to their shelter immediately the sirens went.

Last night, the wardens of West Norwood would have had the where-abouts of Mum and Auntie Mary noted down among what the Finsbury warden called 'the multitudinous things a warden needed to know':

> from the names of the residents in each house, and which shelter they used, hydrants, cul-de-sacs, danger points in the area, to the whereabouts of the old and infirm who would need help in getting to shelter, telephone numbers, and addresses of rest centres etc.

Recently, wardens had been advised to compile lists of the rooms where people spent raids. Hard-won experience taught that this would give Heavy Rescue a vital head start when deciding where to tunnel.

Meanwhile, in the City, Nell had her own charges to help watch over: the influx of displaced City mousers to the CTO basement over the past months. They were 'bombed-out "Orphans of the Blitz" & as such are made much of by the whole staff,' she wrote: 'They must tell each other, I think, that there is "Bed and Breakfast" here.'

ON HIS BRIEF fact-finding mission from New York, *PM* editor Ralph Ingersoll had found the most striking aspects of Blitz life were 'the normalcy of life by day and the dramatic suddenness with which that life stops at sundown'. Though he had adjusted to it, he just 'couldn't get over' it at first: in London, 'The two worlds, the world of peace and the world of war, exist side by side, separated by only a few minutes of twilight.'

The winter solstice was only just passed and days were short now. Sunrise had been at 9.08; sunset would be at 4.37 this afternoon, with the blackout imposed fifty minutes after that. Like a creature from mythology, London had been returned from the world of war to the world of peace for this brief space, after which it would be consigned again to the netherworld for another gamble with fate. And Londoners had learned to make the most of the interval.

THERE WAS A PROFOUND stillness stretching out for mile upon mile across London this morning. George Orwell had pictured the capital, just before the war, 'like an enormous plain that you could have ridden over':

> Whichever way you cross London it's twenty miles of houses almost without a break . . . Miles and miles of streets, fried-fish shops, tin chapels, picture houses, little printing-shops up back alleys, factories, blocks of flats, whelk stalls, dairies, power stations – on and on and on. Enormous! And the peacefulness of it! Like a great wilderness with no wild beasts.

It was, he wrote in 1939, one giant target for bombs.

And today, being an English Sunday, it was closed.

There were odd pockets of activity this morning, like the raucous Sunday market in 'Petticoat Lane' on the City of London's north-eastern edge. And all across the capital, behind factory walls, shift workers were singing along to *Music While You Work*. But in general the quiet calm of this world of peace might call to mind those popular terms from a year ago, of 'Bore War' or 'Phoney War'.

Yet this war was no phoney. And if things seemed boring – as ineffably boring as only an English Sunday, focus of a century's determined efforts by the Lord's Day Observance Society, could be – wasn't that a blessing?

People had learned to be grateful for their boring English Sundays: a triumphant prize won by the 'Few' who had driven the Luftwaffe from the daylight skies. Grateful for the chance to go to church in peace, to dig the allotment, to read the papers, to practise the banjo, listen to the wireless, write letters, stroll between the slit trenches and gun emplacements in London's green spaces, see friends and relations. Grateful, like Nell Carver, for a 'nice & peaceful' shift at work. It was hard to resent the slow drag of hours that might prove to be your last.

'This is a City, now, uncanny, as if the devil incarnate is descending on her borders,' City clerk Colin Perry had written in his diary in the first week of Blitz. 'It is queer, unreal, eerie . . . What is coming? What is threatening this ancient and magnificent City? You read novels, of the unknown, like H. G. Wells and his Martian invasions, and you feel we must be one too.'

Colin was not alone in detecting an interplanetary scale to the conflict. 'We are involved in a conflict in which more than the victory of only one country or the other is at stake,' Adolf Hitler had told workers at a Berlin arms factory just before Christmas. 'It is rather a war of two opposing worlds . . . I grant that one of the two must succumb. Yes, one or the other.' He had only ever wanted peace, he said, but this was a war he would wage, 'as long as I have breath in my body'. Because: 'This struggle is not a struggle for the present but primarily a struggle for the future.'

FACING LONDON's destruction by Martians, H. G. Wells's narrator had contemplated the multiplicity of 'hopes and efforts, the innumerable hosts of lives that had gone to build this human reef'. And, despite the depredations of bombing, during the working week a coral reef – legacy of generations of individual lives, growing ever larger over ages, vibrant natural habitat for millions of diverse living creatures – remained an appropriate image for this great metropolis, which was, wrote Wells: 'Delicate in her incidental and multitudinous littleness, and stupendous in her pregnant totality.'

But wander the almost empty streets of Nell Carver's City of London this morning and it was less a prolific reef than a bare lump of dead coral – a mere agglomeration of tiny skeletons – that came to mind. For ironically London's sooty heart, one mile square and 2,000 years deep, where the whole dynamic story of city, nation, empire and modern world had begun, was the one place in the crowded capital this morning where the dead outnumbered the living. On this peaceful Sunday, as the modern world that it had done so much to create stood poised to destroy it, the City belonged once again to citizens past.

Mouldering in honoured tombs or consumed – tomb, church and all – by the Great Fire; crumbled to dust in plague pits on the City's edge; stacked in tiny churchless churchyards or neatly tidied to the suburbs by Victorian railway builders, their corporeal remains had suffered many translations. But in church safes all across the City they lay – bridal couples, corpses and new-born, cheek-by-jowl – bound together for eternity in ancient church registers compiled by centuries of diligent clerks and clerics.

It was the railways, overground and underground, that had emptied these old City parishes, whisking workers from shop, factory and office to their respective suburbs at the end of each working day. By 1860, Dickens was already calling this 'The City of the Absent' and relishing, as he wandered its alleyways and churchyards, the 'Sunday sensation in it of being the Last Man'.

There were, he observed, City streets where you could tell the weekday trade just by sniffing the air:

> Rot and mildew and dead citizens formed the uppermost scent, while, infused into it in a dreamy way not at all displeasing, was the staple character of the neighbourhood. In the churches about Mark-lane, for example, there was a dry whiff of wheat; and I accidentally struck an airy sample of barley out of an aged hassock in one of them. From Rood-lane to Tower-street, and thereabouts, there was often a subtle flavour of wine: sometimes, of tea. One church near Mincing-lane smelt like a druggist's drawer. Behind the Monument the service had a flavour of damaged oranges, which, a little further down towards the river, tempered into herrings, and gradually toned into a cosmopolitan blast of fish.

This last of course denoted boisterous Billingsgate down by London Bridge, which had already been selling its wares to Londoners for centuries when Dickens came – and which had lost none of its distinctive Sunday morning aroma in 1940. US Military Attaché General Raymond E. Lee, on a recent quiet weekend reconnoitre of bomb damage in the City, had noted that even the Germans couldn't drive that away.

When Dickens walked the echoing City, its live-in population had already dropped from the quarter of a million-plus of Shakespeare's day to a little over 100,000; eighty years on, and the Square Mile was home to a mere few thousand, mostly office caretakers and their families. Their numbers were boosted now by wartime necessity. But every firefighter, policeman, Home Guard, firewatcher, ARP man or essential office worker like Nell Carver in the City this morning had a hundred ghosts to keep them company.

AND IF YOU THOUGHT that they didn't realise that, you would be wrong. One should never underestimate the romantic and fantastical hearts of buttoned-up City folk, whose workaday world occasionally burst out to observe, with processions and red roses and horseshoe nails, traditions so old that no one knew why they did them but did them anyway. This was a City of old gods and mammon, and only a very insensitive soul could have been unaware of the very peculiar atmosphere pervading this very peculiar square mile on this silent, sooty Sunday morning.

Nell Carver had found her guide to it in her beloved Sam Pepys, model diarist and admirably efficient civil servant. The General Manager of Hitchcock, Williams & Co. discovered it whenever he pushed on the door of one of the City's many churches and found it open. To the east, you could sense it in the ex-soldiers in Tudor garb, tin hats and gas masks fretting over the well-being of the ravens that kept the Tower of London standing. And it was strong, too, at the City's administrative heart.

Hemmed in on all sides by the factories and warehouses that had made the City rich, the Guildhall was centre of City government and hub of its wartime ARP. And Mr R. H. Lott (City formality could make a 'Mr' even of an office boy) had this morning reported alongside his older colleagues in the Corporation Fire Guard, for twenty-four hours' duty protecting the Guildhall complex.

Mr Lott worked in the Remembrancer's Office, an ancient establishment whose original role had been to record the Corporation's business correspondence: respectful complaints to Elizabeth's Privy Council about the unruly playhouses; permissions for church collections to ransom Englishmen out of slavery on the Barbary coast; orders, in the run-up to the English Civil War, to suppress the 'mutinous and disorderly conduct of sundry persons of the Artillery Yard who had assumed to themselves the right of choosing their own captains &c'. The office paperwork was a lot less colourful these days. But then he was not here today for the paperwork. If there was a raid today, seventeen-year-old Mr Lott was going to be one of the first up on the roofs, watching out for fires. And two fourteen-foot wooden giants, standing on a massive wooden balcony beneath the massive wooden roof of the Guildhall's medieval Great Hall, would be as precious as anything under his protection.

You might have to go to a secret country location now to see the Corporation's treasured letters of greeting from Queen Victoria and Henry V; the confirmation of its privileges from William the Conqueror to the City Fathers who had kept the port of London in order in Saxon times. But, too large to be evacuated, the massive eighteenth-century figures of 'Gog' and 'Magog' bore witness that London's history went further back than all that – further back, even, than the Romans. For these giants had been vanquished by Brutus, grandson of one of Homer's Trojans, and he had gone on to found a New Troy here on the banks of the Thames, way back before the days of such other famous London kings as Lear and Lud and Cymbeline.

All of which was complete nonsense of course. You might as well believe Sir Thomas Malory's tale of the City Christmas long ago, when the Once and Future King had proved his claim to England by drawing a sword from a stone in the Cathedral churchyard. Or try to explain how, each Christmas, a City merchant who helped Henry V pay for Agincourt was transformed into a leggy young woman in tights and high heels. But then no one ever said London's history had to be sensible – or even true – to have meaning.

When ancient civilisations fell, something of them survived in their stories, cast up after many adventures and narrow escapes on the furthest shores of new empires. So if London – the upstart trading post that had sprouted beside a bridge on the far edge of someone else's empire – were to fall now, might it too live on in such nursery tales?

For history showed that all great empires followed one another into the dark. More than forty years ago, Kipling had warned that the day was inexorably approaching when 'the Captains and the Kings depart', the 'far-called . . . navies melt away' and:

> Lo, all our pomp of yesterday
> Is one with Nineveh and Tyre!

It had seemed such a far-distant prospect in the 1890s – almost as remote as Wells's Martian invasion. But in the dying days of 1940, with Kipling himself only five years gone, the barbarians were already at the gate, and the heart of Empire lay open and virtually unprotected as a War of the Worlds raged in earnest.

There wasn't a square foot of the Square Mile that hadn't featured in half a hundred tales at one time or another. So in far-flung libraries and school-rooms, ages hence, might silent Eastcheap weep again for bad, boozy Falstaff, carried to Arthur's bosom by the turning of the Thames tide? From

Cheapside's lone tree, in a disregarded churchyard on the corner with Wood Street, might the song of a thrush once more catch the heart of Wordsworth's Poor Susan? Or would ghostly Cornhill witness City clerk Bob Cratchit, on his way home to Camden Town, sliding on the ice like a schoolboy in honour of another Christmas Eve?

Perhaps President Roosevelt had found the streets of London rising more vividly to mind in Washington this Christmas Eve. As he read *A Christmas Carol* to friends and family as usual in the White House, acting out all the parts – Bob, Mr Scrooge and the Ghosts of Christmas Past, Present and Yet to Come – did thoughts of London's future strike a special chord in his audience? When the City peals rang out to celebrate Scrooge's Christmas conversion, did the thought intrude of just what church bells might mean if Londoners heard them now? For the solid, physical City of London seemed – was – infinitely more fragile now than the skein of stories that had been spun out from it over the centuries.

You could find Dickens' world almost intact, for now at least, at paper-makers Grosvenor Chater in Cannon Street. The smooth, cream-wove pages of Grosvenor Chater ledgers had consumed the working lives of generations of clerks since the eighteenth century. And their own sales ledgers were so huge and heavy that warehousemen had to be summoned to haul them up and down a winding metal staircase from the fireproof safe in the basement.

Counting House clerks still worked in formal dress here from Monday to Friday at tall, sloping wooden desks, seated on high stools which 'needed some agility to mount and . . . soon imparted a mirror-like surface to the seat of the trousers', according to one with cause to know.

Though now, on Saturday mornings, sports jackets and flannels were permitted, 'preparatory to the afternoon's football or cricket', and all work ceased, as at most City firms these days, at half past twelve. Many businesses had downed pens even earlier this week. Boxing Day had ceased to be a Bank Holiday for the duration but many City firms had chosen to close down with whatever modest celebrations had been held to mark Christmas Eve. A few fire guards were on duty today at Cannon Street and a few more at Grosvenor Chater's stationery factory in Old Street. But for many locked and shuttered City firms, the long, un-Scroogelike Christmas holiday would last right through until tomorrow morning.

OUTSIDE THE CONFINES of its ghostly weekends, the City still retained much of the old, lively, intimate character of its past – the busy and businesslike London of medieval guilds, of Georgian tradesmen and apprentices living over the shop, and of Victorian merchant adventurers who sealed bargains on a handshake with men they'd known all their lives. On weekdays, narrow City streets echoed with the horns of vans and bells of box-tricycles fighting for space with horse-drawn carriers' carts (permitted again in greater numbers since petrol rationing). Warehousemen in brown dustcoats pushed great cane 'wheelers' through the streets, disgorging neatly tied brown paper parcels for the 'Country' at the great, steaming railway termini, while at the GPO's King Edward Building, goods were still optimistically dispatched to the furthest reaches of the Empire.

GPO responsibilities now ranged from the delivery of Christmas cards to the telephone links that held Britain's air defences together; from delivery of the dreaded death telegram to very special specialisms for the top-secret code breakers of Bletchley Park. And while its inner workings behind the bright red pillar boxes and bright red telephone kiosks might remain a mystery to most Londoners, the sheer physical presence of the GPO was inescapable in the City.

The massive King Edward Building opposite St Paul's Station (which was actually called Post Office Station until three years ago) dealt with all London's internal and foreign post, despatching mails to and from the rest of the country by private underground railway to Clerkenwell's Mount Pleasant sorting office. Connected to 'KEB' by a bridge, Nell Carver's battered five-storey Central Telegraph Office employed 3,000 staff in a clearing house for all Britain's national and international wire services. A hundred yards east, 15,000 telephone exchange lines went through the Wood Street building containing three London exchanges and parts of two more. The huge new Faraday Building in Queen Victoria Street on the far side of St Paul's housed the headquarters of the whole national phone system.

Over the centuries, as its postal monopoly extended to accommodate new technologies, so too had GPO premises in the City. For where better – in peacetime at least – to maintain the hub of a global information network than where Charles II had established the General Post Office in the first place: right at the heart of the City of London?

For it was not mere civic hubris on the part of the Corporation that identified its own square mile as the heart of the British Empire. Westminster might govern the country. But merchants, not governments, had financed the English trading expeditions that had shaped the world.

There was barely a place on the planet that had not been affected, for good or ill, by the contents of City ledgers over the centuries. And there was barely a place on the planet that would not be a matter of intimate concern to someone in the City when the ledgers were brought out of the safe and opened up again tomorrow morning.

FOR A GRAPHIC PICTURE of what it had cost to make the slogan 'business as usual' a reality in the City of London so far, one might turn to the company diary of the publisher of, among other publications, *Cabinet Maker*, *Fruit Grower* and *The Nursery World*. Benn Brothers shared Bouverie House in Fleet Street with Ernest Benn book publishers (another branch of the same famous philanthropic and political family) and, latterly, with the Fire Brigade Union, which had been bombed out of its own premises. The week before Christmas had been their quietest since the Blitz began: 'work proceeding as normally as possible in war-time conditions; nothing to report'. But the first, terrible fortnight of the Blitz had been recorded in the diary by the Chairman:

> The staff has rallied in the most wonderful style. Only two members of it failed to report for duty through fear of the consequences of air raids to themselves or their families. One is not strong and has been given leave of absence; the other has resigned and left London. One of our cleaners, Mrs West, who had been with us for 20 years or more was, unhappily, killed with her husband while they were in a public shelter near their home in Southwark.
>
> Miss Walker had the front of her house in Mecklenburgh Square ripped out. Homer had a delayed-action bomb in his garden, and others, including Flatt and Harrington, have had to leave their homes temporarily for the same reason. Reed, of the post room, spent one night helping to dig out bodies of neighbours higher up the Poplar street in which he lives. Hillier and one or two others who live in the same part of London have been spending the night in the Bouverie House air raid shelter and, incidentally, relieving the housekeeper (Castle) of some of his nightly burden.

Nevertheless, it was not till October (when staff were forced to work elsewhere while 'the redoubtable Captain Davies, of the St Paul's bomb fame' defused two time bombs in Fleet Street) that the Chairman noted gravely: 'The monthly cheques to our suppliers could not be got out on the 20th of the month for the first time in my memory.'

The mains had been cut off for some time afterwards but, fortunately, Bouverie House was all-electric (except for the staunchly gas-lit *Gas World* offices: '*Gas World* staff gnash their teeth while working at the will of the hated rival,' recorded the Chairman with quiet amusement). Water had not been a problem either, since Bouverie House had its own well. There was no telling what you might find in the City at pub cellar, church crypt and office basement level. Even if Fleet Street buildings were new, the land had been in occupation for over a thousand years – perhaps nearer two – and the further down you dug, the further back you went.

Bouverie House staff now shared their basement, during raids, with members of the public. This was common practice: caught in a raid, one woman had taken refuge in the basement of nearby *Punch* and found an assortment of regulars settling down quietly for the night on the warm, dry sleeping platforms the proprietors had constructed from back issues.

All companies with more than thirty staff were legally obliged to provide adequate shelter facilities; those with extra capacity put up signs. 'A shelter is anything that protects you,' American Ernie Pyle explained to readers back home. 'It may be an underground restaurant, a store basement, a bank vault.'

> Every block is dotted with shelter signs. The official ones are black metal plates clamped to lamp posts, like street signs. They have a big white letter 'S', and underneath in small letters is the word 'Shelter' and a white arrow pointing to the building in front of which the sign is affixed. Each sign has a little V-shaped roof over it to keep the dim night-light from shining upward.
> Every block has a dozen signs of white paper, pasted on building walls, saying, 'Shelter Here During Business Hours' or 'Shelter for Fifty Persons after 5PM' . . . I know buildings in London that go six stories underground. When the banshee wails in London's West End you wouldn't have to run fifty yards in any direction to find a shelter.

Passers-by in the City were equally well served. True, during a false alarm in the first days of the war, Hitchcock, Williams' Mr Lillycrop, manning the Paternoster Row door to a staff shelter, 'had to forcibly persuade one panicky stranger that he must find a "public" shelter'. But the capacious basements of a deserted City had little problem accommodating chance visitors in the Night Blitz. Some people even made a regular trip in from home each afternoon, bundling their bedding on and off buses and trains, to use a shelter that they found congenial. Surface shelters nearer at hand, meanwhile, often stood empty. Locals didn't trust them, and with reason. Ambiguous Government specifications had led to many being constructed with inferior cement. LCC lecturer Leslie Paul knew of one in Poplar where blast had sucked the walls outwards; the heavy, flat, blast-proof concrete roof fell and crushed everyone inside.

If *Punch*'s basement was quiet, a livelier time was on offer at Lloyd's of

London in Leadenhall. It had recently been the venue for the 'Man in the Shelter' spot on the BBC's *In Town Tonight* and regulars put on their own Christmas pantomime. It was run by the Friends Ambulance Unit, and to stretcher-bearer Nev Coates, who had sung carols there with the FAU choir on Christmas Eve, it was a 'model shelter'. With all lights but the Christmas tree and their own hurricane lamps extinguished, they had performed their whole repertoire for a silent audience then: 'The lights went up, hubbub once more and tea and buns for the chaps.'

It was the last of five performances that night, over a wide spectrum of shelters – including Stepney's notorious Tilbury. This was not a model shelter: in fact American journalists were regularly brought here by their British colleagues to show them how bad things could get. Together with the luxurious Dorchester Hotel, with its curtained-off section labelled 'Reserved for Lord Halifax', it was something you had to see for yourself.

'The Tilbury' was the largest shelter in London: a network of railway tunnels in which shelterers had broken through from the official area, designated safe for 3,000, into private warehouses. Up to 14,000 East Enders of all nationalities sheltered there nightly. Like 'Mickey's Shelter' nearby, where nearly 10,000 crowded into a space meant for only 5,000, things had been almost unbelievably sordid and unsanitary at the start. But, just as Mickey Davis, a three-foot-three-inch local optician, had rallied volunteers to knock the latter into shape, so the Tilbury was, by Christmas, a world away from its darkest days. It still didn't suit everyone – but it suited those it suited. You certainly didn't lack for company at the Tilbury.

In Fleet Street, the Benns' more decorous shelter attracted about a hundred regulars, though numbers had dwindled over the holidays. The dozen or so staff who had slept here on and off throughout the Blitz had got three clear nights away. Later today, well ahead of the few minutes of twilight that separated the world of peace from the world of war, just a sprinkling of staff would again join the regulars.

WANDER OUT through the maze of City streets this morning, among locked and silent pubs and shops and churches, Georgian workshops and Dickensian warehouses, great modern financial institutions and small factories, and you might hear singing. A hymn perhaps? It was Sunday after all. Or was it perhaps a less heaven-directed ditty?

> Our John's a fireman bold
> He puts out fires.
> He went out to a fire last night,

'Cos he puts out fires.
It set fire to some dynamite:
Where poor John's gone we don't know quite,
But where he's gone he'll be all right
'Cos he puts out fires.

You might have happened across one of the many AFS sub-stations or annexes tucked into every conceivable niche across the Square Mile.

These were the idle 'ten bob a day darts players' that the public had disdained only six months ago. Even now, you could hear some hair-raising stories about some of the AFS from the fastidious, mostly ex-Navy men of the old Brigade – just as you could hear tales of spit-and-polish bull among some old-school officers from the men and women of the AFS. But, as Aylmer Firebrace always said, the only way to really learn about fires was by fighting them, and over the past few months the LFB and AFS together had become the world's experts.

The City of London was very much on the minds of the men at London Fire Brigade HQ in Lambeth this Sunday morning. As it was every day as they waited to see what the Luftwaffe had planned. And as it had been every day since the Brigade first came into being.

The City was no stranger to fire: just as there were seven Troys, each built on the ruins of the last, so there had been many Londons before this one. But of all the City's Great Fires, it was the first one, which had almost ended London in its infancy, and the last, which began in Pudding Lane and swept away four-fifths of the City, that were etched on the conscious-ness of every Londoner.

After Boudicca's fire, the Romans had rebuilt their young Londinium grander than ever. But after the Legions left, their elegant villas and tem-ples had been recolonised, their pillars cracking and crumbling as oppor-tunistic native vegetation put down roots. The rational grid of Latin streets had been lost for ever and it was from a green wilderness that the Saxons and their successors had carved the eccentric spider's-web of roads, lanes, passages and alleyways that put the fear of God into London's fire chiefs in 1940.

And for every London fire officer of the past two-and-a-half centuries, the date 1666 had been not something out of the history books but a brand on the soul. If you sought Sir Christopher Wren's monument, it said in St Paul's, you should 'look about you'. But for the monument to Londoners' stubborn refusal to bow to authority, just wander the maze of ancient streets that still hemmed in his masterpiece in 1940.

Their wooden houses might have gone forever in 1666, but Londoners did not sacrifice their ancient rights to anybody's Grand Design without a fight. With a pack of hungry lawyers at their elbows, property owners had ensured that their old labyrinth was rebuilt in brick and stone to much the same plan as before. The wide avenues and grand squares of Wren's imagination never left the drawing board and the Square Mile remained the key LFB 'danger zone' into the twentieth century.

The Barbican clothing district was one obvious worry; the bonded warehouses full of wine and spirits down by the Tower another. Then there were the great publishers' warehouses along Paternoster Row; the imposing head offices of financial institutions that declared their prestige with cavernous entrance halls, sweeping oak staircases and mahogany panelling; the four- or five-storey buildings crammed with multitudinous tiny companies making the most of the City's unique trading advantages. And, above all of these concerns, and connecting them all, those narrow, winding, ancient City streets and alleyways, which made the passage of fire engines so difficult but the passage of fire so very, very easy.

ONE OF FRANK HURD'S essays described a fire in the City. He called it *In Lighter Vain* – though you perhaps had to be a Blitz-seasoned AFS man of twenty-four to fully appreciate the joke. He had been despatched from Euston to the Square Mile just past midnight: 'If you know the average width of a City street,' he wrote, 'you might be able to imagine what it was like trying to pilot a tender with trailer pump to a given point when about thirty pumps are doing the same thing, but to several different places.'

'His' fire was in a cul-de-sac about 300 feet long, lined with clothing warehouses. Fire had reduced one of them to a shell, with its roof, contents and collapsed floors making a lively bonfire inside.

Flames were also issuing from a broken gas main through wide fissures in the road. 'Pretty rotten really,' wrote Frank, as the only gasman they saw that night turned up with a very small tool bag and left again, saying it was too big a job and, anyway, he didn't know where to turn the gas off.

'We were working with our backs against one side of the street, aiming our jets into the warehouse, with the street alight in front of us.' They dared not let their jets hit the shaky wall:.

> An eighty-foot-high wall collapsing into a twenty-foot road, with a line of flame one side and only a very narrow path on the other side past debris and pumps. Not a pleasant prospect! And of course, if we didn't bring the wall down, 'Jerry' might.

That night the fires 'seemed gifted with an almost human sense of humour or obstinacy'.

> Out of sympathy with the fire on which we were working, the top floor of the building against which we had our backs kept bursting into flame. There was not enough room to get any more branches to work, and not enough water to supply them in any case, so this necessitated us going across the road (over the burning cracks) with a charged hose, facing about and directing the jet into this new fire. When that subsided we had to work our way back to our original position.

'This sounds easy,' he remarked with breathtaking insouciance,

> but it has to be tried to realise what it means. (I wonder why water has such an uncanny knack of finding its way *up* a tunic sleeve – most uncomfortable!)
> . . . We had been at work now for about four hours (it wasn't too comfortable) when some bright spark decided to get a branch working from a roof behind and to our left. Unfortunately, he couldn't see just where his jet was going, with the result that most of the water came on us! Consequently, the atmosphere was charged at frequent intervals with rather impolite requests to the chap to put his water elsewhere (I will not tell you just where we told him to put it).
> It wasn't until 4.30 in the morning that a nice man told us to relieve each other at the branches and go to a canteen van about a quarter of a mile away for refreshment. That quarter of a mile was just one climb and slither over debris, but we made it. Who wouldn't with that goal in view.

'Perhaps I have made light of a serious situation,' concluded Frank – who was down for AFS duty again tonight – 'but thank God we can laugh at this sort of thing.'

Chapter Seven

SUNDAY for the Forces
1.15 THE WORLD WE'RE FIGHTING FOR
4 – What does God expect of it?
The Rt Rev Monsignor R. A. Knox

Home Service SUNDAY
1.15 JEWISH CHANUKAH
SERVICE
Order of Service
I will praise thee (Psalm cxviii, 21-24)
Address by the Chief Rabbi
Benedictions on Kindling of Chanukah
Lights
'These Lights'
Rock of Ages, let our song praise thy saving power
   (Mo-oz-tzur – Chanukah hymn)
Priestly Benediction
Music by the Cantor and Choir
   of the Great Synagogue Choir

BBC Radio Times Christmas Edition, 1940

IF ANY NAZIS had been criminal enough to listen in to the BBC on Christmas Day, even those who had already removed all Nativity references from their Winter Solstice Festival and sought to replace Christian holidays with a cycle of great dates in the life of the Führer might have envied the effrontery of Britain's so-called democracy. An unelected Head of State who was also Head of the Established Church? Broadcasting to the world via his nation's only official broadcaster? Which was itself incorporated by Royal Charter?

How they would have scorned, though, the poor use made of that concentration of power this lunch time. For in an almost exclusively totalitarian Continent, an officially Protestant nation's sole broadcaster was offering listeners a choice: between the urbane, whodunnit-writing, limerick-loving Catholic priest Ronnie Knox, and the celebration of the Jewish Festival of Lights by the Chief Rabbi of the British Empire.

'THE CHANUCAH LIGHTS of 5701 will long be remembered by those many Jews – and non-Jews too – who saw them kindled in London air raid shelters this year.'

The *Jewish Chronicle*'s offices in Moor Lane in the City, closed today, had already begun to compile reports from the holiday season. About 300 people – 'including a number of non-Jews who followed the service very attentively' – had attended the service conducted under Dickins & Jones department store in the West End.

> The service started with the lighting of the candles and chanting of prayers, followed by two psalms and the recital of the Kaddish by shelterers in mourning. Then came a sermon by the Rev. E. Nemeth, in which he said that Hitler was attempting to do the same as those against whom the Maccabeans fought over 21 centuries ago. 'We are called upon to make many sacrifices in our time,' he said, 'and the Festival Chanucah comes to hearten us.' Then came the singing of the Maoz Tsur and, finally, the National Anthem.

Nearby, in a Broadwick Street shelter, a children's Chanucah service had been followed by a tea party and games.

Rabbi and air raid warden Rev. H. Mayerowitsch of the Great Synagogue had conducted up to five services a night in the City and East End during the eight-day festival.

> The celebrations were greatly enjoyed by all who were present, including the non-Jewish shelterers, who openly expressed the pleasure it gave them to join their Jewish friends in their religious celebration. As Chanucah coincided with Christmas, Mr Mayerowitsch took the opportunity of addressing the Christian shelterers, and conveyed to them, on behalf of the Jewish shelterers, the compliments of the season.

There had been some early obstacles to harmony in a multi-faith shelter on Senior Warden E. I. Ekpenyon's patch, as he later explained in a broadcast on the BBC's African service.

> In this shelter I am talking about the shelterers were peoples of many nations, with a variety of beliefs. They were young and old people, and children. The bombing of London forced this mixed crowd to be in one another's company, though their ways and manners and views of life in some cases were as opposite as the north and south poles.

The wardens had their work cut out keeping the peace:

> Some of the shelterers told others to go back to their own countries, and some tried to practise segregation. A spirit of friendliness and comradeship was lacking. If this spirit had continued it would, as certainly as the night follows the day,

have led to riots. So I told the people that the British Empire, which is also known as the British Commonwealth of Nations, is made up of peoples of many races. I said that though I am an air raid warden in London, I am still an African. I also said that I am one of many peoples of other countries that make up the Empire.

Then I spoke of the three classes in the shelter – namely, His Majesty's subjects, protected persons and guests. These last were refugees from other countries. I said that this third group of people who were in my shelter, and who were not interned, were entitled to the protection of the Union Jack. I said that this being the case I would like to see a spirit of friendliness, co-operation, and comradeship prevail at this very trying time in the history of the Empire. I further warned my audience that if what I had said was not going to be practised, I would advise those who did not agree to seek shelter somewhere else. For to remain in the shelter and to behave in an unfriendly way would force me to report them, because they were trying to create disunity in the Empire.

A few grumblers had left but most responded well. And, by dint of good administration by the Post Warden and provision of concerts, dances, film shows and darts matches, 'gradually friendliness and merriment spread in the shelter': culminating in their happy Christmas Day children's party which had left 'laughter and happiness on all faces'.

IT HAD NOT always been thus. For all its reputation for tolerance, London had its dark stories: the English road to heaven had once been flanked by flaming and disembowelled heretics with the best of them. Yet British society had somehow, over time, lost the trick of the iron orthodoxy of thought that had half the world in its grip. British theorising about The Good Society rarely rose above 'common sense' tempered by 'common decency'. But over the centuries, they had somehow cleared a breathing space around other people's right to be wrong, and it had made London a favoured refuge for those fleeing the hell that is Heaven designed by one's enemies. 'If there were only one religion in England,' Voltaire had written after his time there, 'there would be danger of tyranny; if there were two, they would cut each other's throats; but there are thirty, and they live happily together in peace.'

The breadth of London ecumenism was too much for some refugees. In 1902 one newcomer had been given a sightseeing tour, shown how to get a reader's ticket for the British Library then taken to a church service – of English Marxists. Who, after a speech on social revolution, had risen to sing 'Lord Almighty, let there be no more kings or rich men'.

'I could scarcely believe my eyes or ears,' recorded Leon Trotsky, his sense of intellectual decorum deeply affronted. His guide, an old London hand, sympathised: 'There are many revolutionary and socialistic elements among the English proletariat,' V. I. Lenin assured him, 'but they are mixed up with conservatism, religion and prejudices, and can't somehow break through to the surface and unite.' Through the dramatic political battles of the intervening decades, zealots of all persuasions had despaired of this nation's apparent inability to grasp the importance of orthodoxy in *anything*. Largely uncaptured by the twentieth century's more glamorous ideologies, it remained mildly derisive of zeal itself.

National borders cannot keep ideas out but different societies prove more fertile soil for some concepts than others. Where but in the 1930s and those parts of the map shaded pink could one read, in a school textbook,

> Look at the children in Fig. 64. They are not any different to yourselves; they are fellow human beings. The Almighty did not create a lower order of beings who like to live in slums. They arrive there by a perfectly obvious process. A farm is laid down to grass; an industry dwindles; a new labour-saving machine is installed. Economically it may mean a few pounds in somebody's pocket, but more often than not it means a few more inhabitants in a slum area; and it may happen to any of us.

– and then learn that the solution was 'a very simple one – we have only to play the game of life as fairly as a game of cricket'?

Call it tolerance and fair play; call it hypocrisy and indifference. It was certainly not to the taste of a German journalist who had lived in London for some years before the war. He scorned the vaunted freedom of the British press and free speech of Speaker's Corner. Far from England being free, he told German readers in 1939, 'one needs an annual licence to hunt, to drive and to own a car, for his dog and his radio, to be a market crier or to get married'. One's glass of beer might be snatched from one's hand at 'last orders' – which could be half an hour earlier than on the other side of the street. Worse: 'Anyone who leaves his car parked for 15 minutes on a 60 foot wide avenue at an English seacoast resort will return to find a policeman giving him a ticket.' And yet still, he marvelled, the English believed they lived in a country with no police shenanigans.

Faith in their bobbies was part of the 'small unprinted catechism' of freedom that was not, he revealed with disgust, chanted only by politicians: 'It is rooted in the mind of each Englishman'. He gave an example:

> There was a night watchman in my neighbourhood with a mangy hound. He let the dog run as it wanted, despite an infectious disease, and did not stop it from chasing other dogs. Since I wanted to keep my own dog healthy, I politely asked him one evening to keep better watch on his dog.

95

The answer was rather vehement. But what was most remarkable was that one of the three young Englishmen in the area shouted to me: 'It's a free country.'

The German had decided to retreat with dignity intact, resigned to the fact that these misguided oafs would take it as a victory.

A Frenchman who broadcast home regularly via the BBC in 1940 also noted his hosts' myriad eccentric restrictions on one's freedom in the matter of speed limits and licensing laws. Nevertheless, he wrote, England maintained a disconcerting freedom of thought, unhampered by the weight of the surrounding community, not found in other societies. It had a 'charm, to which one may or may not respond' and created, he wrote, 'a species of freedom that charters and codes cannot establish'.

Though impervious to many aspects of English 'charm', one American had been startled to find herself, before the war, agreeing with her husband Henry's contention that there was much more intellectual freedom in a small English town than in its counterpart at home. 'In America small-town neighbours hurry to find out what one thinks and often indicate rather oppressively that it damn well better be what they think,' she wrote, 'whereas in Yeobridge nobody tries to find out what we think because it has not occurred to anybody that a well-bred person thinks at all.'

AMERICANS HAD ALWAYS been a special breed of 'funny foreigner' and Margaret Halsey's *With Malice Towards Some* had been a best-seller on both sides of the Atlantic in 1938. Her lecturer husband, on an exchange year at a West Country college, was a convinced Anglophile. Newcomer Margaret was less convinced: she loved many things about England but hated others. The real revelation, though, had been just how foreign it was. She had felt she was living 'not in another country, but on another planet', and Henry had agreed: 'It keeps you wondering whether you have died or just not been born.'

During their year in England, the couple had escaped, briefly, to the real world. It was only about 200 miles from London to Paris, the distance from their native New York to Baltimore. But twenty-two of those miles were over water, and that had made all the difference. 'At the end of one day in Paris,' wrote Margaret, 'where I do not even know the language, I feel more at ease than I ever have in England.'

It is not only being warmed with wine and good food and central heating and not having to breathe coal gas and the smell of cabbage. It is that Parisian women go in at the waist – a thing which, living in England, you are apt to forget that women can do. And the people in the cafés look as if they were talking

96

of things they were interested in and knew about . . . Our long winter's nap in Devonshire has its points, but it is exciting to be back in the world of men again, where people have blood and brains and stomachs, not to mention various other convenient devices.

Those words had been published only a few dozen months ago. But the apparently solid and immutable fact of the France-that-had-been was dissolved like a dream. And the passionate putting-the-world-to-rights debates in Parisian cafés had been silenced, perhaps for ever.

Josef Goebbels, visiting in October, had been captivated by the 'ancient magic of this wonderful city, which is pulsating with life once more. Big military presence.' Goering had taken him to dine at Maxim's, which had become a favourite with Luftwaffe crews relaxing after their *Bomben gegen England*. (An exchange rate fixed in Berlin made a pilot's pay go a long way in Paris.) Goebbels didn't begrudge them the luxury: 'They have earned it. The army grumbles about it, but they should keep their mouths shut.'

Back in grubby old London, meanwhile, things were still pretty much as Margaret Halsey had left them. She would certainly have recognised the smell of coal gas and cabbage – as evocative as the taste of *madeleines* – that pervaded the capital as London sat down to Sunday lunch today. And recognised something, too, of the dozy, dreamlike placidity of this strange society where passions ranged all the way from 'not too bad' to 'mustn't grumble'.

SIDNEY CHAVE couldn't grumble, even though his family was sitting down to bully beef from a tin rather than a traditional roast. Shopping in Streatham yesterday, lab technician Sidney and wife Lee had discovered only one-and-fivepence-worth of meat left in their ration books to last them and toddler Jillian for the rest of the week. Fortunately tinned food, like fruit and vegetables, wasn't rationed: it was a matter of getting what you could find and taking what you could get.

Still, their Christmas Day dinner had been grand. 'We sat down to roast veal,' he recorded in his diary,

(which Mummy was lucky to get), roast potatoes, a few new, boiled potatoes – a gift from Jock Tweed – cabbage from the garden, and our runner beans stored from the summer. Then we followed on with Christmas pudding and mince-pies. We drank a toast in sherry to absent friends and relatives in the forces.

Britain had long ago ceased to be able to feed all its population. But U-boats were in the midst of what their captains dubbed their 'Happy Time'

97

in the Atlantic, so it had to do its best to limit the need for imports. The old motto of 'Waste Not, Want Not' had been joined by 'Dig for Victory'. Gardens, allotments, window boxes, parks, city squares – even the drained moat of the Tower of London – were turned over to vegetables. Margaret Halsey had bemoaned their cuisine's dependence on the Brussels sprout but the British were now becoming aware that there was even such a thing as a wholly vegetarian meal. Aided by 'Gert and Daisy' on the wireless and an army of cookery writers in the press, Food Minister Lord Woolton was teaching British housewives about nutrition and encouraging experiment with what was available: primarily 'Potato Pete' and 'Dr Carrot'.

Some vegetables needed no 'selling'. A fourteen-pound bag of onions, discovered in the lost parcels section at Mount Pleasant sorting office, had made a news story in today's *Sunday Times*. The loss of the Channel Islands – and the disappearance of the French 'Onion Johnnies' who sold their wares from bicycles – had made onions even more precious than tomatoes.

Though all food was news now. Today's *Sunday Express* revealed that a Government price ceiling aimed at curbing profiteers had led to many turkeys being taken off the market in the week before Christmas. With 20,000 in cold store in London alone, 'turkey will be in season throughout 1941, and may suddenly appear on the menu any day from now until next October'.

Rations were to be cut in the New Year. 'Meat supplies and other important food-stuffs are going to be reduced in amount,' noted Sidney Chave. 'Tinned food must be kept as an iron-ration. We are asked to eat less cheese. But this will not hurt us.' Ration book juggling was fairer than the privations of the poor in the last war: he had heard the lady introducing the King's Christmas speech speak of queuing for potatoes then.

In Sutton, Viola Bawtree, who had been through that war herself, was not inclined to grumble either, since she had been really lucky over Christmas too. She and her siblings shared a large house and, as with the Speeds in Brixton, things could get fraught. With turkeys so expensive, Sheila had ordered the largest chicken she could get for £1 – and had been terribly upset when Sainsbury's had sent round two small ones instead. But though they were nine for dinner, it was, Viola recorded in her journal, 'the nicest Xmas dinner I can ever remember! . . . Everyone had plenty on both holidays & the cold chicken lasted for *three* more dinners . . . & then nice soup.'

Talking things over after church today, she and Eric had agreed that

'Christmas might have been much worse & had been rather wonderful.'

> Then he added that everything all through had been wonderful, that Germany
> had the power to smash us & yet we'd come through & then I added my bit,
> that in all our own experiences too, things had been wonderful, right from the
> beginning. It's amazing & heartening to think back & realise what we've been
> brought through.

Viola had particularly welcomed the Christmas truce – though newspapers claimed it was the weather that kept the Luftwaffe away. This was a
bad way of looking at things she felt: she was sure the German High
Command refrained from bombing in the hope that Britain would refrain
too and give their people a peaceful Christmas: 'I hope we did refrain.'

The only cloud over her bright Christmas had been the Christmas Eve
newsletter from All Hallows Barking church, by the Tower of London.
The church had sustained some damage in the 8th December raid, it said,
and Viola hoped that the Toc H lamp, symbol of the international volunteer network founded by its vicar Tubby Clayton, was still burning.

PERHAPS IT WAS just as well that LCC lecturer Leslie Paul had eaten early
today (chicken and left-over Christmas pudding with his friends in
Epping) and was on his way across London by the time the BBC got into
its religious stride. For he was, to borrow a vogue phrase of these Blitz
days, browned off with God on the wireless. The BBC's religious music
was extremely good, he thought, but 'Oh by God and Lucifer', its ser-
monising! Most days:

> Just before eight we have a sermon, 'Thought for the day', then a fullblown ser-
> vice for schools just after nine, then the morning service at 10.15, then by Christ
> a little evening sermon called 'Think on these things' which usually tells us that
> God is like the wireless, or goodness like a struggling little flower, or good deeds
> like stones flung in a pond, or evil like a traffic jam, obstructing the good flow
> and so forth.

On a recent *Think on These Things*, 'The Think they Thunked on us
was, yes, Mallory's climb of Everest.' And, he wrote gloomily in his journal, 'I expect it will be Captain Scott tonight.' He would have protested
publicly about the BBC, but for the fact that he was 'trying to get work out
of them (you see how venal I am: no doubt if they give me enough work
I'll turn high Anglican myself out of sheer gratitude)'.

Leslie Paul's own spirituality owed not a little to the Red Indian beliefs
he had encountered first through the Boy Scouts. Perhaps it was not surprising that he had detected an 'old man of the tribe' note in Churchill's

speeches. Having broken with Baden-Powell's Scouts on a point of principle, Leslie Paul had founded, at nineteen, the socialist, pacifist Woodcraft
Folk, committed to camping in the open air, common ownership of the
means of production and striving to 'understand and revere the Great
Spirit which urges all things to perfect themselves'.

It was a Woodcraft Folk party that had dragged him away early from
his rural idyll ('Cold sweet air. Dove gray sky. The dim pastels of the end
of December') this weekend. Though war had never been far away. His
beloved Epping Forest was only on the fringes of the Tube network, and
the Plain was riven with tank-trap ditches and pitted with bomb craters.
One from a thousand-pounder looked, he thought, like an extinct volcano.

Still, he was enjoying his last days of freedom. He had been passed fit for
the Army on Christmas Eve and found that he minded less than he
expected. It was ironic, he wrote, 'that I, who all my life have fought for
peace, who founded a youth peace movement, must find myself a soldier,
and a soldier of Tory England.' But: 'Under her scabbed crust of Toryism
England is a good place,' he added, a little self-consciously. 'The flesh is
young and healthy.'

> I do not fight for privilege: for the hardfaced business men who have brought us
> to the edge of ruin . . . I am not fighting for the old school tie . . . for the dead
> hand of the older universities on culture and the professions . . . for the
> Anderson attitude to liberties and civil rights, for the Simon attitude to control
> of capitalism and hostility to checks on exploitation. For none of these things. I
> hate them only one degree less than Hitlerism.
>
> For the right, however, to run our own country. For the right of the elemen-
> tary schoolboy to enter politics and the professions. For a New Deal and a New
> Order here. Yes I will fight for those things. Maybe we won't get them if we are
> victorious. But we shall certainly never get them if we don't fight, I feel. Or if I'm
> wrong I'd better be a conscientious objector.

IT WAS A CHOICE many young men faced. One of Sir Basil and Lady
Mayhew's sons had gone through considerable struggles with his conscience, serving first as a London fireman, then as a stretcher-bearer in the
Royal Army Medical Corps (winning a Military Medal at Dunkirk); finally, since the fall of France, as a full combatant. A brother in the Army confessed to feeling 'vaguely disappointed' by this last move:

> Perhaps it's because genuine convictions are so admirable in themselves, espe-
> cially when unconventional and unpopular . . . They also bear witness that as a
> nation we really do believe in Freedom of Conscience and in man's not being
> made for the State.

'It is a great social accomplishment,' wrote one registered conscientious objector, 'that this country has written into its laws the right of a man to follow his conscience against the will of the majority.' Described at his tribunal as a Christian anarchist, he couldn't help thinking of his visit to Germany in the summer of 1939.

He had felt the violence of the threats against Poland at a rally in a Hamburg city centre bedecked in red, white and black banners; in Berlin he learned a little of the fear stalking that city from a Jewish family; and on his last night, as he watched searchlights practising through the blackout, he had talked with a man who said he, too, would refuse to fight. His German counterpart's fate must, he knew, have been death.

DESPITE THEIR 'slight air of concern for a misguided youth', a tribunal of five 'old gents' had registered Nev Coates, though conditionally, as a conscientious objector too: convinced of his sincerity by his membership of the Friends Ambulance Unit.

It was certainly no soft option. Its initial six-week course, set up by Quaker veterans on the estate of Dame Elizabeth Cadbury, was even more demanding than the Home Guard's at Osterley Park. Weekly route marches built up to a final seventy-mile bike ride to Stratford-upon-Avon followed by a twenty-four mile, eight-hour march back. (Nev had managed to fit in *The Merry Wives of Windsor,* a packet of chips and water from the Memorial Fountain before his overnight march home.) 'We were unconsciously anxious to prove something to ourselves and this march was part of the process,' he decided, ending his diary entry with: 'Devotional at 9.00 was a chance to be thankful for the joy and experience of life.' Like many FAU, Nev was not a Quaker but all were welcome at Devotionals: in Stepney, where he would be on duty again tonight, he found it 'a good thing to sit together in silent worship with anti-aircraft guns and possible bombs creating havoc outside'.

LIBERAL DEMOCRATIC theory notwithstanding, pacifists could still find themselves in prison if they ran into an unsympathetic tribunal, refused a suggested non-combatant occupation or were suspected of pro-Axis sympathies. One London member of the Peace Pledge Union came home one evening to find two detectives waiting in the lounge with his father. They questioned him about his beliefs, and asked what he would do if he met a German parachutist.

'I would offer him a cup of tea,' I said. At this point Dad butted in. He said,

'Are you entitled to ask these questions? My sons are loyal subjects but they object to war.'

The detective explained that he just wanted to make sure that I would not assist the enemy in the event of an invasion of this country.

I said I certainly would not assist anyone to destroy life. Upon being asked whether I would divulge the whereabouts of the Hendon Aerodrome, I said I would not.

'That is what we want to know,' the detective said.

And that had been pretty much that.

Arnold Spencer Leese's Special Branch interview had been, predictably, more dramatic. And – in his own account anyway – predictably heroic. Before the war, the hapless Leese, self-proclaimed 'Anti-Jewish Camel Doctor', had found his Imperial Fascist League quite cast into the shade by the rise of Oswald Mosley's British Union of Fascists. And not only by Mosley's wealth and connections: 'On one occasion,' he claimed, his meeting had been attacked

> by a large body of Mosleyites which greatly outnumbered our men . . . I was attacked by 26 men, thrown to the ground, half-stripped of my clothes, struck on the face with a leaden 'kosh' and much bruised by kicks . . . Newspapers, describing this battle said it was the biggest fight that had ever been seen at a London meeting; our enemies deliberately smashed as many chairs as they could, knowing that we, who had no large fund behind us, would have to pay the owners of the hall for them.

One might have been more inclined to sympathise were it not for what the IFL might have done with greater numbers if they could have recruited them. But with such bizarre articles of faith as 'the League of Nations was entirely sponsored by the Jews to ensure future wars', it had been reduced to ruses such as public debates with League supporters (who then paid to hire a hall) in order to air its views.

With invasion imminent, about a thousand BUF were imprisoned under the Government's special wartime powers in the summer of 1940, though many were later released into the services. Leese, meanwhile, evaded the police for months before they tracked him down at home.

'I seized a thick stick, which I always had close to me throughout the time I had been "on the run", and crept out on to the landing,' he recalled. A plain-clothes detective was inspecting the linen cupboard.

> I crept up behind him and could have brained him, but I simply said: 'What the hell are you doing in my house?' He turned round quickly with his hand in his pocket and just then a uniformed man came along the passage behind me, so I

backed into a corner and then there followed a sort of parley. I told them the facts and pointed out the dirty work they were doing for pay.

They replied that they were ignorant men who had been ordered to make this arrest and if anything happened to them, others would follow to do it. Reasonable enough, that, for morons!

Eventually they rushed me and a long struggle ensued; I did what I could, but there were two of them, each as strong as I was, and twenty years younger. My wife tried to help me and was, afterwards, fined £20 for it! At last they got me to the head of the stairs and then uniformed men came rushing up the staircase, the first one waving a revolver. This made the force against me overwhelming, which I took to be the only excuse for calling off resistance.

In his cell at Guildford Police Station, Leese recalled with pride, 'I smashed everything breakable and tore the noisome blankets into strips and stuffed them down the WC.'

Refusing to pay for the damage, he was given a month's imprisonment and then, when his time was up, was transferred to Brixton – handcuffed to a conscientious objector – as a detainee under '18B' wartime security regulations. There, Leese complained to the Governor of 'certain penal conditions I found myself under, contrary to law'.

His reply was: 'My good man, don't you know that there are a lot of people outside who would like to have you all shot and that you may consider yourself lucky to be alive?' That gives an idea of what the Mug-in-the-Street had been told about us detainees!

Later, in a camp run by the military, Leese went on hunger strike. Threatened with proceedings for conduct prejudicial to good discipline by a Captain Petrie – 'a Jew whose real name was Steinthal,' claimed Leese – 'I laughed in his face, which he buried in his hands.'

What Leese was holding out for was a question to be asked in the House of Commons: 'As soon as I knew the question could not be stopped, I ended my hunger-strike (50 days, less 10 days in the middle on minimal food).' The question was duly asked, and an Under-Secretary to the Home Office

said it would not be proper for him to state the reason for my detention except that it came under Regulation 18B. So I achieved little of public importance by my strike; but I prevented my export to Isle of Man, and my wife was able to see me every week almost throughout my detention.

Whatever strain it put on the nerves and patience of its loyal officers, the British Establishment rarely found the need to resort to the 'kosh' to deal with the likes of Arnold Spencer Leese. 'I want to be fair to all,' Home

Secretary and Minister of Home Security Herbert Morrison said in an interview in today's *Sunday Express*, 'including Fascists – they're human beings.' He defended the use of 18B in the emergency that had faced the Government after Dunkirk but agreed that it was quite exceptional. 'In peace time the British would never stand for it – at least, I hope they wouldn't!'

Chapter Eight

Home Service SUNDAY
2.30 SCOTTISH ORCHESTRA
(The Choral and Orchestral Union of Glasgow)
Leader, David McCallum
Conductor, Warwick Braithwaite
Overture: The Barber of Seville *Rossini*
Ballet music: Rosamunde   *Schubert*
Symphony, No. 7, in A   *Beethoven*

BBC Radio Times Christmas Edition, 1940

'As I WRITE, Beethoven's 7th is now being broadcast,' wrote Isabelle Granger to her friend Harrison Brown in Canada this afternoon. 'It is my favourite. Tonight is the Christmas Oratorio and we have records of two Brandenburgs – could life be better?'

Andrew Butler of St Paul's Watch called these dawdling Sunday afternoons 'that awful time in London when it looks as if everybody must be in a stupor or dead in their dining rooms'. But for Londoners who had learned to live in the moment, sometimes the moment could be sublime.

Isabelle's letter was certainly better-tempered than her last one. She apologised for her pre-Christmas grumpiness this afternoon, giving the excuse that 'living with a very short man in the house is a perfectly impossible position for tall women'.

She and flatmate Elisabeth Gruber ('Lilibet') had been happy to offer Freidl the hospitality of their small basement flat in Chalk Farm after he was released from internment and he planned to make a home in London soon for his wife and baby, now evacuated to the country. But in the meantime his funny little ways – not least an obsession for turning the gas off at the mains during air raids – had proved wearing: 'I can't think why those under 5' 4" should be so masterful & lustful for power in two rooms.'

Freidl has been interned as an 'enemy alien': all citizens of enemy countries had been taken into custody after Dunkirk. Even though, as the Home Secretary agreed in today's *Sunday Express*, 'two-thirds, maybe even four-fifths of the aliens were quite probably friendly to this country'. The process of review moved relatively quickly considering the reputation of British bureaucracy – 64,000 of the 74,000 interned had already been redesignated 'friendly aliens' and released. But it was too slow for some – and too late for others. There had been suicides and, in July, the luxury liner *Arandora Star*, carrying detainees and prisoners of war to Canada, had been torpedoed by a U-boat with the loss of more than 800 lives.

One of the terrible ironies of Churchill's draconian 'collar the lot' directive had been that it disproportionately punished the refugees from Fascism who were cooped up with Fascists. Journalist Ritchie Calder pointed out that the internment of 20,000 'enemy' Jews also left behind a disproportionate number of wives, 'helpless and lonely', in poorer London districts. Their noted presence down the Tube in raids helped promote the idea that Jews were more highly strung that the stoical British, feeding into the low-level but pernicious anti-Semitism that swirled around London. Calder regretted that the many Jewish firefighters, ambulance drivers, stretcher-bearers, wardens and doctors he had seen risking, and losing, their lives above ground were far less visible to travellers.

Sometimes the topic turned to anti-Semitism at Bert Snow's ambulance station in Stepney. Station 101 was made up, he wrote, of 'English of nominal Christian heritage, Jews of English and foreign ancestry, an Irishman and myself, an Australian'. His first experience of Passover bread was at the station, while some of his Jewish mates were cheerfully tucking into bacon and eggs: 'Neither the Jews nor the Christians of 101 were seriously involved with their religions.' Politics was another matter: 'Two of the men were Communists, some were Communist supporters, while others were strongly anti-Communist. This mixture, stimulated by war and war propaganda, frequently produced some very interesting ideological discussions' – not least over Bert's pacifism.

The East End had witnessed big clashes with Mosley's Blackshirts before the war and, though Mosley was interned, no magic wand had eradicated the undercurrents he'd fed on. One of Bert's mates, arriving at Aldgate East station, heard: 'Get out your passports boys, we are now about to enter Palestine.' Bert himself had seen a Jew accidentally step in front of a woman leaving a bus at Aldgate,

> whereupon the husband pulled her back and said in a loud voice, 'Stand back for the Chosen Race, dear.' Some of the waiting Jews responded with angry mutterings and resentful looks, while others laughed at the self-appointed humorist.

That was the dilemma: laugh it off or be thought over-sensitive? Some of the 101 crew had seen a comedian who made a joke, supposedly about the Local Defence Volunteers. His patter went: 'I am now LDV' – 'What do you mean you are LDV?' – 'I live down Vitechapel.' 'Some of the Jewish ambulance drivers,' recalled Bert, 'referred to him as a bright bastard.'

THOUGH DELIGHTED to have Freidl at liberty, he was a prime example, Isabelle Granger told Harrison Brown, of her contention that 'the raids seem to be more upsetting to men, on the whole, than to women'.

> Don't think I am indulging in a bout of feminism please, but whether it is generations of 'protecting' weeping women while they work, or some quite other reason, they seem to take it more heavily. They speculate on the origin of every sound and impute the most sinister origins to a slammed door or a cock's crowing – everything is a bomb (a long way off, of course – you can't fool us with a bomb within our earshot) or a flare or a land mine or shrapnel.

One visitor would close his eyes and call for silence every time he heard an engine, trying to locate its position. (Though it was often no more than a lorry and, in any case, wrote Isabelle, what on earth was he going to do if he did locate it? 'It is best to give most noises the benefit of the doubt I find if you want to have a happy evening.') Another chap threw himself to the floor: 'I do this in the street if a plane dives,' admitted Isabelle, 'but not at home: it leads nowhere.'

For the most part now, though, she found London life 'not epic like the Greek resistance, but very satisfying and full of delight'. Her sadness was for the French: 'At times I am irrationally angry that so much praise is lavished on us – the people of England – and that, for perfectly obvious reasons, it can't be shared by France.'

A language teacher before the war, Isabelle was an untypical Englishwoman, having not only travelled widely in Europe but having made many friends there too. They could get a little fractious in exile: over one weekend, Freidl told her he could never get on with Czechs; a charming Czech lawyer told her all Germans were animals; a Hungarian insisted that Austrians were 'idiots and dreamers' while a Scottish friend said the Czechs here were 'not Czech Czechs, but Jews and so not a truly representative body that could be relied on as Czechs'. And then, she wrote, 'they all unite to be glad they are not as corrupt as the French!' She and Elisabeth wondered how nations would deal with 'this kind of blather' after the war.

One bright note in Isabelle's grumpy pre-Christmas letter had been her appreciation of the Prime Minister's common sense on such matters:

I was glad to see Churchill's reply to G. Strauss, who asked that we should aim at 'the complete humiliation and defeat of the German people', was 'I consider we shall be content that they shall be defeated.'

Among the 'isolated strangers here who thread in and out of our lives', she wrote, Mr Fulte from Nuremberg was a favourite: 'like a fairy tale character incorporating all the traits of the Germans who are as nice as they can be . . . one of his brothers was murdered in the '38 pogroms.'

THERE HAD NEVER been a time in London's history when it had not been a cosmopolitan city: it was a port, after all, that had been founded by foreign invaders. But there could never have been a time in London's history when it was quite as diverse as now. London had long offered a home for the world's exiles and adventurers; now the world was gathering, it seemed, for a last defence of this city.

Colonials of many races, citizens of independent Dominions, refugees fleeing the Nazi Juggernaut, and the foreign soldiers, sailors and airmen planning their fight-back under their governments-in-exile all shared the streets with those who had simply come as they had always come – from across Britain and the world – to be Londoners.

For while newcomers found that it took years to become British, and a generation or two to become English, you were a Londoner the minute you found someone who had had a little less experience of the city than you had. Now more than ever, wrote Scotsman Ritchie Calder, the true Londoner 'includes in his metropolitan-cosmopolitan synthesis almost every nationality and every colour'. He pointed to the Chinese drinking a toast to 'Us Londoners', the refugee who declared 'our Spitfire boys are *wunderbar*' and an American journalist who, dug out of a bombed shelter, asked, 'Can I call myself a "Londoner" now?'

And, of course, he could – if his burial hadn't qualified him, then the joke on his resurrection certainly had. Not that it had been much of a joke. But, as Winifred Bowman's friend explained in one of her letters to America, 'We just have to laugh, Winnie, and find jokes in everything.'

Maybe our jokes seem feeble to you but we're ready to find anything to laugh at these days, and a damned good thing. When the war is over I am only going to laugh at the very funniest, subtlest and wittiest of jokes . . . maybe!

'You would not mind London at all now,' Isabelle Granger had assured Harrison Brown. 'It seems shorn of most of its worst aspects and glares stubbornly and gaily at us all encouragingly . . . The people who are here now are here for a purpose, and they are purposeful and determined and very good tempered people.' She tried to give a picture of how the face of the capital he had left had changed:

> Everywhere are red, apple-faced New Zealanders, Australians (they are all so fruit-like, I can not think why), and Polish airmen, and French soldiers in Kepis, and flowing cloaks and Czechs and Norwegians in their greenish-grey uniforms – all sorts of languages and uniforms: the red bobs of the French sailors' caps come jogging cheerfully along the Strand.

Her omission of Canadians from the list might have been simple tact, since Harrison had travelled in the opposite direction as war approached. But they were here all right: the Station Master at Leicester Square counted as one of his favourite memories of the whole war the night he had to summon a Canadian Military Policeman to evict a drunken Canadian serviceman who would not leave the platform.

It was a heavyweight bout that he witnessed: Canadians provided wartime London with an object lesson in what happened if you took an Englishman and fed him well from birth. 'Such a wonderful fight,' recalled the Station Master, the like of which he had never seen again, 'not even amongst the professional men in the boxing ring . . . It went through my mind that they were probably lumberjacks in their own Country.' His only regret, he said, had been that two countrymen 'that had left their own Country to help us in our hour of need', should be fighting one another.

A WHOLE NEW BATCH of Canadians had only just arrived. Canada's newly appointed Historical Officer, Major C. P. Stacey, was among 1,400 troops who left Nova Scotia aboard the 27,000-ton RMMV *Capetown Castle* just before Christmas. And his account of his crossing showed something of the Battle of the Atlantic that had been waged, day in day out, ever since this war started. For there had been no Phoney War at sea: 112 lives were lost when the liner *Athenia* was torpedoed on the very first day of the war; by December 1940 Allied shipping losses totalled 4,500,000 tons, with a corresponding large death toll.

A mail boat designed for the South Africa run, the *Capetown Castle* was not as well heated as might be wished for the North Atlantic in December. But she was comfortable, modern and fast. Or would have been, were it not for the two other troopships and the Dutch cargo ship she sailed with. By travelling in packs, unarmed and lightly armed ships secured a naval escort; the price they had to pay was that of travelling at the speed of the slowest vessel.

Two destroyers had escorted them on their first day, then an older battleship for a further four, leaving them about halfway across the Atlantic. Six destroyers – two Canadian, two British, one French and one Polish – were steaming out to bring them in but somehow the rendezvous was missed and the destroyers hunted in vain for three more days while the convoy negotiated the perilous Western Approaches alone and at just thirteen knots.

There were regular boat drills and, from reveille on 20th December, all ranks slept fully dressed and carried lifebelts; that afternoon the *Capetown Castle*'s Lewis guns practised firing and from the 22nd they were manned throughout daylight hours. Rifle parties were allotted positions. The next afternoon the ships began to zigzag – a standard evasion technique which tended to scatter the convoy for long periods. At dusk, the *Capetown Castle* was given Admiralty permission to leave the convoy and proceed at best speed. And on Christmas Eve, flying kites to deter low-flying air attack, the ship received a cheery wave from the pilot of a passing Royal Canadian Air Force flying-boat and Major Stacey saw his first British naval vessels on this side of the Atlantic.

Christmas Eve was 'fairly thoroughly celebrated by all ranks' that night and on Christmas morning the *Capetown Castle* started up the Clyde. As it passed the great shipyards, where 'an almost incredible amount of naval construction' was in progress, the troops swapped good wishes with people on the banks and on other vessels: 'Perhaps the warmest single greeting we received was from the coloured crew of a Liverpool freighter.' By nine-thirty on Christmas night, Major Stacey was on a train bound for London. Though he never learned the fate of the slow Dutch merchant ship.

Despite their importance to daily life, and the risks they ran, the men and boys of the merchant marine were often the 'forgotten service', rarely accorded the recognition given to those in uniform. The King had tried to remedy this in his broadcast at the outset of the war: 'You have a long and glorious history,' he said, 'and I am proud to bear the title Master of the Merchant Navy and Fishing Fleets.' And just before Christmas, the *Daily Mirror* had pictured him inspecting Caribbean seamen who were, it wrote, like sailors from around the Empire and Allied nations, bringing 'food and munitions to us in spite of U-boats, mines and bombing planes'. (Not to mention carrying back the British exports that helped pay for them.)

The League of Coloured Peoples' *News Letter* (which 'recognised Maxted from Barbados and Prince from Jamaica' among those pictured) said these seamen played a very important part in warfare: 'We hope they will not again be forgotten as they were after the last war, when the League of Coloured Peoples had to take action in order to get their nationality which had been wrongfully abridged, restored to them.'

'IT IS QUITE TRUE that the English are hypocritical about their Empire,' wrote George Orwell, adding: 'In the working class this hypocrisy takes the form of not knowing that the Empire exists.' There might be a widespread feeling that the Empire was a Good Thing – reflected in the nobility with which her children were rallying to the Mother Country. But the grand Imperial history celebrated by a Victorian poet like Rudyard Kipling or a Victorian soldier like Winston Churchill had always been something of a minor or a passing enthusiasm with the British public.

The really popular past – the one 'Dig for Victory' tapped in to – was an older, pastoral dream that permeated left and right wing alike. Many Englishmen saw their own, beautiful little island mirrored in the little patch of earth they laboured over. Not Eden exactly, but perhaps a post-Fall Merrie England, which had discovered the compensatory arts of brewing and baking, growing food, domesticating wild animals and playing country sports.

See these simple men on their allotments or ancestral acres, with their pie and their pint and their dog by their side, while indoors their wives salted and bottled and canned their harvest against shortages, and one might imagine that time had stood still in England for thousands of years.

Until, that is, one considered where such simple pleasures as the tobacco in their pipes, and the sugar in their tea, the tea itself, the cotton shirts on their backs and the rubber for their gumboots came from; how the processes which made them available had over the past 500 years changed the whole world utterly; and what it cost to supply them now through wartime seas.

Mention a banana this afternoon and people would sigh and say that was just one of those things they were learning to live without. Few outside London's small colonial communities, some specialists in the City, the Cabinet and Colonial Office – and perhaps the King and Queen, who had seen more of the Empire than most – had any inkling of the devastated economies whose route to market was now patrolled by U-boats. 'What do they know of England,' Kipling had asked, 'who only England know?'

One night at Blackwall police station, a call from the man on the door had brought Sergeant Grey to the top of the station steps, where he found seventeen dark faces looking up at him: 'A soft pleasant voice said, "Are we on the right road for Tilbury?"' The men, all from the Caribbean and new to London, had left the Tube at the end of the line and had started walking east from Aldgate in the hopes of finding their vessel. 'I have never seen men so weary, except some of my own mates,' recalled Sergeant Grey – who told them they were still many miles short of their goal.

> Well, it was the Canteen downstairs, tea and a bun (or what was going), a wash, the lavatory, then the two cells on the benches & wood floor . . . The Skipper or he in charge, came to me in the office and what a pleasant chap he was. I explained to him, where he was, the Raid and that he was walking into it.

The captain regaled Sergeant Grey 'with his adventures from a West Coast port and his journey to London – 3 days of keeping his crew together'. The Skipper had known nothing about the Blitz but was able to enlighten the Sergeant in his turn: 'He told me of his education in Jamaica – and proudly stated that Education (Public) had been known in that country for 300 years (I didn't dispute it).' When they left at dawn, the captain insisted on paying for what they had eaten and pressed a 'Roosevelt Election Piece, the size of a shilling' on Sergeant Grey as a memento of their meeting. 'I have often thought of that Skipper and his Crew,' Sergeant Grey wrote years later. 'They were such a good crowd – it coloured and helped my race relations so much.'

Londoners still had much to learn about the reality behind those patches of pink on their school maps – and the tiny dots so small that their names had to be underlined in red to be seen at all. The tide of stories that flowed out through London docks to the ends of the earth had not returned in equal measure.

Nevertheless, in his review of *We Fight For the Future: The British Commonwealth and the World of Tomorrow*, Professor Basil Mathews argued in this month's LCP *News Letter* that, if Britain went under, the colonial peoples would lose 'that freedom which we have never fully reached, but towards which we are well on the way'. His central thesis was one recognised by New World Order theorists from Leslie Paul to Adolf Hitler: 'The root difference between victory and defeat depends on whether we think of the war as an end or as a beginning.'

ANOTHER CONTRIBUTOR to this month's *News Letter* had been 'nosing about' in shelters and 'hospitable dance halls' since his own shelter was destroyed. His experiences 'amply corroborated', he said, 'the opinion of various newspapers that "Londoners can take it"'. And he was pleased to record that 'the contribution of the coloured population in proportion to its numbers is pretty considerable'.

> In London especially one is amazed at the numbers of coloured men who have accommodated themselves to the novel circumstances of the war, and are to be found working with characteristic lightheartedness and punctiliousness as Wardens, AFS men, members of Stretcher Parties, First Aid units and Mobile Canteens.

He mentioned Air Raid Warden Headley, a mining engineer from British Guiana, Trinidadian fireman G. A. Roberts, and Jamaican boxer 'Buzz' Barton, now working in First Aid. He expressed some surprise, though, to find League member, interior design student, film extra and sometime artist's model Granville 'Chick' Alexander working hard at a number of incidents: both in a first aid party and helping out in a mobile canteen. 'When I asked whether he wouldn't prefer the peace and quiet of Jamaica he replied, "Not likely! and miss all the fun?"'

LCP founder Harold Moody himself, as readers of the *News Letter* well knew, ran an exemplary first aid team by night, in addition to his regular duties as a Peckham GP. And it was perhaps to be expected that the capital's medical services had a high degree of internationalism. Nev Coates had noted in passing that the doctor who had summoned him and his FAU colleague Hugh to their first, horrific 'incident' was an Indian. And this morning's papers carried the first news of a 'soft-voiced' Egyptian doctor who, with his Scottish colleague, had prised an unexploded bomb from the floor of the children's ward of an Ealing hospital and carried it 200 yards in a tin bath lined with blankets for safe disposal.

THIS AFTERNOON, Luftwaffe crews were already thinking forward to tonight, and to the challenges they would face in getting to target '*Loge*'. But still Londoners – of all nationalities – were just getting on with being Londoners. In Chelsea, Yvonne Green ('Papoose' to her mother; 'Canada' to her colleagues in the Auxiliary Fire Service) was off duty. 'I am a bit later than usual in writing you my weekly letter,' she excused herself to 'Maman Chérie',

> but with Leonard home it didn't give me much time. However from what you tell me it seems to make no difference to you receiving them at regular intervals, so one must just hope than one catches a mail sailing soon & that having caught it, it won't go down to the bottom of the Atlantic.

Their Christmas had been 'very nice but quiet', she wrote. She sent thanks for her Christmas gift of silk stockings ('worth it's weight in gold'); Leonard had bought her a camel coat with a hood: 'just the thing'. The only disappointment during his lovely leave was *The Great Dictator*: 'We couldn't have picked a worse day for it – Boxing Day – with queues of people stretching for miles in all directions around the three theatres at which it was showing.' In the end they decided not to bother.

At least in London you were allowed to see it. Yesterday's *Daily Express* had carried a small wire story that, in Argentina, the Mayor of Buenos Aires had banned the film at the request of the Italian Embassy. It did have a lot of fun at the expense of the buffoonish dictator 'Napaloni', though Chaplin's main target in the film was 'Adenoid Hynkel, Dictator of Tomania'.

The main talking point of the film was Chaplin's big closing speech as a humble Jewish barber mistaken for the dictator. 'Soldiers,' announced the pseudo-Hynkel,

> do not give yourselves to brutes, men who despise you, enslave you, tell you what to do, what to think, and what to feel, who drill you, diet you, treat you like cattle . . . use you as cannon fodder . . .
>
> You the people have the power to make this life free and beautiful . . . Then, in the name of democracy, let us use that power. Let us all unite. Let us fight for a new world, a decent world that will give men the chance to work, that will give youth a future and old-age security.

Some critics had called the speech inappropriate for a comedy, but Leslie Paul (who had seen it on Friday afternoon) thought that any other ending would have been inappropriate.

> For the dictators are not just vaudeville. Men are dying for the ambitions of men very like Hynkel and Napaloni, or dying in opposing them. People around me, familiar friendly people – the greengrocer, the laundry boy, the clerk in the Catford bank, the little boy who used to ask me for fag-cards on the way to Scouts – dying for all this Freudian tomfoolery.

ISABELLE GRANGER had watched in despair as the evil of Nazism spread across Europe without, seemingly, anyone lifting a finger. Her flatmate Elisabeth had got out of Germany early, but spring 1938 had been spent helping Austrian friends get visas after their country's absorption into 'Greater Germany'. The 'wise and lucky ones swarmed over at once' but by the middle of that year they were either 'trickling out or shooting themselves'.

Isabelle and Lilibet had spent Christmas Eve 1940 at the Krotts'

Heilige Abend party. 'I moved Evi (now 11) and Ilse (now 7) from Vienna two years ago – just before Christmas 1938,' she wrote to Harrison Brown.

> Irma and Heini and the baby (Heidi) followed in March 1939 and last year the children were with friends in the country as their parents could not afford to keep them. Now Heini's dental practice is beginning to flourish it is the first time they have all been together since pre-Hitler Vienna in 1937.

It had been a lovely evening: 'We were lucky to get immigrants like the Krotts here',

> and they mean to stay here which is consoling, as we want some of the Good Europeans left here for after the war. They are lovely children, and magnificent parents with unbounded courage and intelligence – it is our great good fortune that they are here.

She felt this was Britain's chance to atone for past sins: 'Death and a grave in the Abbey seems too easy a way out for Chamberlain,' she had written bitterly after his funeral in November, 'but how much luckier for those of us who will live till after it is all over. I always wanted to die before war broke out, now we are bombed every night I do so want to see the end, and to go back to Germany is an obsession.'

By chance Beethoven's 7th, still playing on the wireless now, had been playing while she wrote that letter too, 'the slow movement, perhaps one of the most heart-rending of all musical conceptions': 'How can the Germans, who are the creators of the music I am listening to, do these things?'

THE INTERNATIONAL MIX at the Krotts' *Heilige Abend* party had been completed by a Japanese diplomat. Mr Inone had been particularly delighted by the company of little Heidi, thought Isabelle: she served as a kind of substitute for his own baby, evacuated back to Tokyo with his wife by his embassy. He had been 'puzzled at this gathering of official "enemies" whose loving kindness knew no bounds', wrote Isabelle: 'He is always apprehensive – quite rightly too in view of official Japan's lack of cordiality! – of English reactions to him, but we like him as a person and that this should penetrate his official mind is a splendid thing I think.'

The Japanese currently stood neutral in the European conflict in 1940 – as did Germany and Italy in Japan's war with China. But in September Japan had concluded a formal Three-Power Pact with Germany and Italy, recognising Japan's right to establish a new order in Asia and the right of Germany and Italy to do the same in Europe.

'A very happy New Year to you, my dear,' Isabelle signed off her long letter to Harrison this afternoon.

I look forward to 1941 with unbounded confidence, and happiness. Not that I think it will be easy, but so long as there is a struggle against all the bad things of 1930–39 I am happy to join in it.

Very much love to you,
Isabelle

SOMETIMES IN THIS WAR it was instructive to spin the globe and see how different the world could look from a different vantage point. While Britain was looking hopefully westward to America, America might well look nervously at the growing friendship between Germany to its east and Japan to its west.

The Three-Power Pact united Germany, Italy and Japan in defending one another from any new country entering their current conflicts – a clear message to the United States to steer clear. On the Friday before Christmas, Hitler had confided to Goebbels that he now believed that 'Fear of Japan' would prevent America risking war with Germany. But then the RAF had come over and, though their conversation continued in the shelter, Goebbels' diary recorded no more of the conversation.

Elsewhere, though, September's Three-Power Pact had also caused another nation to eye Germany to its west, and Japan to its east, even more warily than before.

Fears in Moscow about the German-Japanese pact had been assuaged, to a certain extent, by a friendly assurances of German Foreign Minister Ribbentrop that it was exclusively directed at 'the warmongering agitation in America', which at that stage of 'the final defeat of England' was seeking 'a last outlet in the extension and prolongation of the war'. These pro-war elements, he wrote, must be brought to their senses by being faced with a triple enemy. An invitation to Berlin for Herr Molotov, he added, would follow.

Looking the world situation now, the lesser known half of that famous Victorian quote about the corrupting influence of absolute power seemed remarkably prescient. History, Lord Acton had written, taught that 'Where you have a concentration of power in a few hands, all too frequently men with the mentality of gangsters get control.' And as anyone knew who had familiarised themselves with gangster politics, from *Richard III* to *Little Caesar*, a mobster's closest friends needed to be no less wary of him than his enemies.

Trust, in anyone or anything, had long since been purged from Josef Stalin's soul, but he prided himself on his shrewdness in international politics. He felt he had played a very cool hand in what he called the 'poker game' of autumn 1939. When the Western Powers had responded with nose-holding reluctance to his suggestion of an anti-Fascist alliance, he had concluded a non-aggression pact with Germany instead. He had his ideological differences with Adolf Hitler. But, up to his elbows in blood from the torture and murder of enemies and friends alike, he had no ethical qualms about carving up Europe with him. The Nazi-Soviet Pact had been, Stalin boasted, 'all a game to see who can fool whom': 'I know what Hitler's up to. He thinks he's outsmarted me but actually it's I who's tricked him.' Signing it had ensured, he said, that war 'would pass us by a little longer'.

His pact with Hitler had astonished everyone, including Hitler's supporters and his own. In London, an Anarchist hospital porter found unused X-rays being shied at him when he broke the news to a Communist Party radiographer with whom he'd often crossed swords in the past. Later, he discovered her in tears.

For loyal members of the British Communist Party this was still, at the end of 1940, an imperialist war in which, even after four months of Blitz, it was the British Establishment and not Nazi Germany that was the British People's real enemy. At least, that was the official Party line coming from Moscow.

Stalin's calculations, like so many other people's, had relied on the mighty Western Powers keeping Hitler busy on his western flank for years – and the fall of France in June 1940 had come as a terrible blow to him. 'Couldn't they put up any resistance at all?' he complained bitterly. 'Now Hitler's going to beat our brains in!' But then von Ribbentrop's friendly invitation for his Prime Minister to visit Berlin had arrived, and his self-confidence had returned.

During their November meetings, Molotov had been as unimpressed by Hitler in person as he was by his ideology. And while the Führer tried to direct his attention to the great opportunities opening up for the Soviet Union in Iran and India now that the British were all but defeated, Molotov had continued to press home (encouraged by cables from Stalin) the trickier issues outstanding between them: Finland, the Balkans, and the Straits from the Black Sea to the Mediterranean. The talks achieved little, but they convinced Molotov that he had found the measure of the man he was dealing with.

On the night before his departure, Molotov had joined Goering, Ribbentrop and Rudolf Hess for a farewell banquet – which was interrupted by an air raid. 'Our British friends are complaining they have not been invited to the party,' joked Ribbentrop. But Molotov permitted himself a jibe of his own: if Britain was finished, as Ribbentrop had been claiming: 'Then why are we in this shelter and whose bombs are those falling?'

Two weeks later, he had responded to the draft of the 'Four-Power Pact' they had been discussing with a string of provisos and caveats to show that the Soviet Union was not going to be pushed around.

And now today, a coded message had arrived in Moscow from Berlin. Stalin believed a spy 'should be like the devil; no one should trust him not even himself'. So the message that had been received, addressed to the Head of the Intelligence Department of the Red Army, on Sunday 29th December 1940 would not be enough to convince the Soviet leader that, this time, he had misplayed his poker hand quite disastrously.

It was unlikely, at first sight, to convince anyone. For, once decoded, the astonishing message revealed: '"Alta" reports that Hitler has ordered preparations for war with the USSR. War will be declared in March 1941.'

Chapter Nine

Home Service SUNDAY

3.45 THE SAVIOURS – 2
A play sequence specially written for
broadcasting by Clemence Dane
'The Hope of Britain'
Merlin . . . . LEON QUARTERMAINE
Arthur . . . . MARIUS GORING
(of the Queen's Royal Regiment,
by permission of the officer commanding)

BBC *Radio Times* Christmas Edition, 1940

WHILE THE REST of the Square Mile maintained an air of holy calm as the chilly afternoon drew on towards dusk, in one unholy quarter Sunday was not divided from the week, in war or peace. Here, business as usual meant the ever-changing, never-changing business of news: last night 'Sundays' like the *Dispatch* and *Pictorial*, *News of the World* and *Observer* had pounded off the presses; this evening, the first editions of the *Daily Telegraph & Morning Post*, *Express*, *Mail*, *Mirror* and half a dozen other national dailies would have the machine rooms roaring once again.

'Fleet Street' was more than just a location – a bare quarter mile or so of the ancient track that linked the City of London with royal Westminster but predated them both. Over the centuries it had come to mean the whole news-disseminating business. Modern news agencies like Reuters-PA and Associated Press now crowded round the same churchyard at its eastern end where William Caxton's apprentice Wynkyn de Worde had moved in AD 1500, bringing the Street of Ink's very first printing press with him. Odd newspaper offices might be scattered as far afield as Covent Garden and Cheapside – and Broadcasting House, off Oxford Street, had established a rival locus for news – but in the winter of 1940 'the Printers' Church' of St Bride's remained at the heart of the modern news business.

Rebuilt after the Great Fire (for the seventh time in its history), St Bride's boasted a peal of twelve great bells that had once been the pride of this parish. 'PROSPERITY TO ENGLAND' was engraved on one;

'PEACE & GOOD NEIGHBOVRHOOD GOD SAVE THE CHVRCH & QVEEN 1710' on another. And crowds had gathered to hear lusty local youths ring changes with names like 'Oxford Treble Bob Maximus' and 'Stedman Cinques' by the hour.

But this City parish had emptied like all the others, and its distinctive English music had found no favour with the incoming press barons. A special effort had been made for George V's Silver Jubilee in 1935, and another for his son's Coronation in 1937. The last time the bells had rung was for the Lord Mayor's Show in November 1938. When – if – they rang again, the news agencies that hemmed in St Bride's on all sides would pump out across the world the news of invasion – or victory.

And night copy boy Frank Backhouse, cycling in for a punctual four o'clock start now, would be one of those who would carry that message to the Central Telegraph Office on the far side of St Paul's. Frank worked at the Canadian Press news agency offices in the Associated Press building on the corner of Tudor Street and Dorset Rise. He slept in the AP basement, too, at the end of his shift: 'He could ride his bicycle home at midnight as he used to do,' wrote D. E. Burritt, CP's senior staff writer, but 'he considers any kind of travel "a bit scruffy" at that time of night'.

To Frank's adolescent embarrassment, Mr Burritt picked him as a sample of Cockney resilience for readers back home – though, coming from East Dulwich, Frank was not, strictly speaking, a Cockney at all. Still, nor was anyone much, these days. The old rubric about Bow Bells, often mistakenly ascribed to the East End's Bow Church, really referred to St Mary-le-Bow, opposite Colin Perry's ABC tea rooms in Cheapside. So there were very few true-born Cockneys about nowadays – though if you defined them more loosely by their general 'h'-lessness, Cockneys were spread, like Hitler's bombs, right across the capital.

D. E. Burritt was keen to get across to Canadians the reality behind the slightly phoney-looking cheeriness they might have seen on newsreels. Young Frank, he wrote, 'isn't the kind to go around talking "thumbs up".'

> He's even a tougher type – he gets to work on time and goes out into the dark nights on his errands and he re-appears in his little tin hat even faster than he used to. These little narrow streets of old London are no place to loaf during air raids.

His office had been bombed once and his home twice; his mother was evacuated to the country for her health; his father left for the factory before Frank reached home each morning. Yet this 'happy-go-lucky' lad whose baggy clothes lacked all semblance of a crease long before he ever started sleeping in them . . . still whistles incessantly, goes to the movies, plays football when possible, and has no concrete complaint against conditions . . . 'I'm better off than a lot of people,' says Frank in an accent that sometimes needs interpretation for Canadians 'Anyhow we've got to go through with it.'

A dip into Frank's sixpenny Boots diary for 1940 gave a snapshot of what 'going through with it' meant. A fairly typical October entry read:

I got up 7 o/c. Caught 63 home. Indoors 8.20. Had breakfast. Warning 9 o/c. Saw planes high up in sky in a clear, bright sky. All clear blowing up as 9 fighters coming back 9.35. At 9.50 warning. Plenty planes heard. Saw some. All clear 10.55. Stopped in. Listened to wireless. Heard planes, went post box. Planes still knocking around. At 12.10 – whiz-bang. 3 bombs fell. Shook kitchen windows. Saw 15 planes overhead about 12.20 making South. No water in main. Someone said bombs fell over Nunhead way. All clear 12.35. Dinner 1 o/c. During eating bombs fell. Warning given after. I shot to Bike 2.10. In CP 4 o/c. I ate 7.30. Warning 7.40. All clear 9.15. Warning 10.15 till 6.30 am. I slept.

Sometimes, if things got particularly lively, the day's entry spread over on to the pink blotting paper interleaving the diary's pages.

Frank had worked through Friday night's raid – 'Two bombs fell on Ward Lock's building while I in Leito's café,' he noted briefly – but had been off last night. He could have spent Saturday afternoon at the football and might even have got a game: conscription was playing havoc with professional fixtures. Up north, for example, Blackburn had played Manchester United yesterday and, reported today's *Sunday Express*, 'Three short, Blackburn asked for recruits from the crowd . . . Got 'em, including a goalkeeper. Tried hard but crashed 9–0.'

However, Frank Backhouse had neither forgotten nor forgiven, wrote D. E. Burritt, the afternoon that his 'bob' had not been refunded when an air raid stopped play. Frank and Doreen had been to see Randolph Scott in a cowboy flick yesterday instead and, fortunately, there had been no wartime interruptions. (Stanley Champion, also on his way in to the City this afternoon, had not been so lucky yesterday. Having spent the morning at work in his factory in Old Street, boarding up windows and doors blasted by a landmine in Friday's raid, he had gone to the pictures in Romford with his friend Arthur – and the cinema had been rocked by a left-over time bomb.)

No one bashing out copy on Fleet Street this afternoon could be wholly unaware of their historic legacy. If words mattered to you, stories mattered to you, then the maze of lanes and alleyways cobwebbed around this village high street – crammed with presses and pubs, picture agencies, block-makers, 'caffs', more pubs, stationers, myriad associated printing trades, three churches and yet more pubs – was steeped in the romance of your trade. It was a world of adrenalin, gossip, history, humour, friendly journalistic rivalry – and the other kind.

Fleet Street ran from the Fleet River (now disappeared into a Victorian sewer) at the bottom of Ludgate Hill to Temple Bar (also disappeared, thanks to Victorian road-widening, into rural exile in Hertfordshire). The Bar had been a kind of ceremonial roadblock established when the City Corporation extended its jurisdiction beyond the walls in the Middle Ages: beyond it, the highway to Westminster resumed its Saxon name 'Strand'.

In Fleet Street, the exploits and excesses of recent newsmen, kept alive in village gossip, bobbed on top of a bottomless well of ink and alcohol. At Hoare's Bank by Temple Bar, the shades of clients Jane Austen and Lord Byron glided past a prone Ben Jonson, who had hosted a boozy literary club here when it was still the Mitre Tavern. Dr Samuel Johnson had drunk at the Cheshire Cheese across the road, in the network of alleyways leading to the house where he produced his *Dictionary*. And Samuel Pepys haunted the street literally from end to end, having been baptised in St Bride's and thwarted in groping a 'pretty modest maid' during a sermon at St Dunstan's-in-the-West (she mounted a spirited defence of her honour with a hat-pin).

If you were a fireman attached to No. 62 Station Whitefriars in Carmelite Street, or any of its five sub-stations or half-dozen annexes tucked into this labyrinth of courts and alleyways, you had a different handle on the romance of Fleet Street. Hoare's Bank? That had a useful well left over from the days when all bankers lived over the shop, though now with a modern pump. St Bride's and St Dunstan's shared the challenges of wood-lined spaces roofed in lead common to all the City churches. And Dr Johnson's five-storey house in Gough Square, rescued from dereliction before the Great War by press baron Cecil Harmsworth, now operated as a rest and arts centre for the AFS.

And while firemen might not know that the black-and-white-fronted Ye Old Cocke Tavern once boasted Dickens, Thackeray and Tennyson as regulars, all were aware that the cluster of tall, thin, half-timbered buildings at the western end of Fleet Street marked where the Great Fire was eventually halted in 1666 – an added responsibility if fire ever swept along Fleet Street again.

Fleet Street was not just about the writers and editors in the offices above ground but was fundamentally about the huge, noisy printing factories below. Long before writing became a paying trade, this street had been run by printers – some said it still was. To be 'In The Print' was to belong to a jealously guarded working-class aristocracy, as hard to break into as the upper-class one. For while any fool could pick up a pen and write, it took brains and a seven-year apprenticeship to learn the crafts of the printing trade. And for the fire service, the romance of the locale was overshadowed by the huge drums of paper, pots of hot lead, printing inks, photographic chemicals and fearsomely flammable celluloid film stuffed into every nook and cranny.

AMERICAN JOURNALISTS had their own relationship with this street. As wordsmiths they could hardly help having a personal relationship with London – with the fogs and the stones and the streets, if not always with the people. Eric Sevareid, despite no British ancestry at all, described his first arrival as 'a little like coming home after a long absence and finding everything changed and no recognition in the eyes of the family'.

Ernie Pyle had arrived here just three weeks ago – and for a newspaperman, his timing had been lousy. It was the day after the big 8th December raid and thus, until Friday night's show, he had not really experienced a blitz at all. Not that he had run short of copy. Ernie was not a war correspondent, nor even a newsman as such any more. For the past six years, he had been granted a roving commission by the Scripps Howard newspaper chain to wander the highways and by-ways of America, writing about what he saw. Ernie Pyle's style was friendly and his business, people. From the dirt-poor farmers of Indiana he had grown up with, to the lepers of Hawaii, easy-going Ernie seemed able to depict humanity with genuine warmth and a gleam of dry humour.

The news pouring out of Britain had given him an almost overpowering urge to be there. Not to 'see what it was like' or in pursuit of a 'story', but because of a feeling deep inside that even he could not put into words: he simply wanted to go. There was, he felt at the end of 1940, 'a spiritual holocaust – a trial of souls' taking place across the Atlantic and 'the immersion into fear and horror of London bombings' could not but have an enriching effect on his own spirit.

The reality had turned out to be less melodramatic. He had arrived by flying boat from Lisbon around lunch time, at a little town that – but for the sticky paper criss-crossing the shop windows – was straight out of a Dickens novel. It was 'so peaceful, neat and secure', he wrote, that by the time he had been ashore three minutes he was 'in love with England'. He and George Lait of the International News Service were offered a cup of tea and had been put through a very British version of the third degree, which Ernie said made you feel you were just sitting there chatting. Their baggage was searched and their letters read, but the Customs man had courteously asked Ernie to remove each letter from its envelope for him: 'He evidently thought it would be prying for him to do so!'

It was all a bit of a revelation to Ernie, whose only contact with the English hitherto had been with ex-pats who gathered in clubs and hotels for their afternoon gin and tonics and considered themselves 'superior to anything else on land or sea'. The English at home, he told his readers in his first dispatch from The Front, were 'lovely, courteous people'. 'I don't mean to us visitors so much as to each other. It is true they are especially nice to Americans right now, but I noticed that they were just as thoughtful among themselves.' This was, he heard later, quite normal, though people tended to be rather kinder now than previously.

Their official grilling over, Ernie and George had boarded a train and chuffed in First Class luxury through fields that looked, through the small clear panel in the centre of the black-painted window, more like parks than farms. They had read the London papers, drunk more tea and eaten ham sandwiches. Here and there they spotted a well-camouflaged gun emplacement or a forest of barrage balloons in the distance – which Ernie had expected to form a protective ring but which actually sprang up across a town 'like candles on an eighty-year-old's birthday cake'.

They peered out with interest at their first bombed buildings – which looked surprisingly like they did on the newsreels – at ploughed-up cricket fields and at rows of suburban gardens with vegetables planted in the earth on top of Anderson shelters. Then a conductor came in to pull down their window shades and they had spent the rest of the journey in the faint blue light adopted on all trains in the blackout.

When they arrived at Victoria Station, it was so dimly lit Ernie could barely see the elderly porter who greeted him with: 'Well he hasn't come yet, sir, he's more than a bit late tonight' (the 'he' being Jerry of course). And the nervous journalists had trailed the porter as closely as baby ducks as he kept up a constant commentary through the gloom: 'I had a gentleman a bit ago and he said, "Could I speak with you for a second?" I said, "Yes, indeed you may. Time's up." The gentleman didn't get it at first . . . You might as well have a bit of a laugh . . .'

A taxi had dropped George at his office near Fleet Street then gone hunting for Ernie's destination. After driving up and down and shouting for advice from the few people on the streets, the cabbie gave up and tried to make him get out and walk. But Ernie, though genial, was no pushover: after some grumbling and some more bellowing to passers-by, he was delivered right to the door of the United Press.

'The men were surprised to see a stranger walk in from America unannounced at that time of night,' wrote Ernie. But phone calls were made and an office boy despatched to hail another cab to take him on to a hotel. After a drive of a few blocks, the taxi had swung down what seemed to be a blind alley and Ernie had a momentary fear that this might be a stick-up. But then the door was opened and a torch was shone on the floor of the taxi by the doorman of the Savoy hotel.

The Savoy was, it transpired, Main Street USA for newsmen, and within twenty minutes Ernie had been in the hotel's underground dining room with the one person in all of London's millions whom he had known before he arrived – Ben Robertson of New York's *PM* newspaper. As Ernie tucked in to soup and chicken, two Chicagoans – Larry Rue of the *Tribune* and Bob Casey of the *Daily News* – dropped by to make his acquaintance and Frank Owen, editor of Lord Beaverbrook's London *Evening Standard*, came to chat about how the war was going.

The Savoy was a favoured watering hole for those who wanted to keep their fingers on the pulse, and for reasons that had hardly changed across 700 years. Mighty baron Simon de Montfort had built his mansion here on the Strand, in a commanding position on the north bank of the Thames, slap-bang between Westminster and the City of London. If you wanted ready access to both King and cash, there was no finer spot in England to park your dining table. The fact that, in 1940, that dining table was in a bomb-proof shelter, which also offered dormitories and its own hospital ward, was a welcome bonus. For US newsmen, it was like living midway between Washington and Wall Street – if Washington and Wall Street were a ten-minute cab ride apart.

The meeting of writers and politicians was nothing new here either: Froissart and Chaucer had been frequent guests when the Savoy Palace was home to John of Gaunt, then the most powerful man in England. But he had also been the most hated, and when revolting peasants flooded into London in 1381, they broke into his palace, threw his treasure into the Thames and built a huge bonfire of all his goods. Unfortunately, these included some gunpowder barrels, and the whole thing had been razed in an orgy of explosion and flame.

On the evening of Sunday 15th September 1940, a rather more self-conscious Peasants' Revolt had taken place as the Communist Stepney Tenants' Defence League marshalled about a hundred East Enders in Embankment Gardens by the back door of the Savoy hotel. The sirens went and the crowd, led by a heavily pregnant woman, demanded shelter in the basement. As they trooped into the elegant Art Deco hallways, they were met by a larger than usual foreign press contingent – forewarned that something was on for tonight.

The hotel manager, faced with the proletarian masses demanding equal rights with the bloated capitalist elite that was his clientele, consulted the police. Officers were not empowered to throw the demonstrators out, he was told – though if the staff themselves ejected them, the police could handle them in the street. On reflection, the manager decided it was more seemly to accommodate the newcomers in the dormitory section of his shelter for the duration of the raid.

Some wandered out into the restaurant section, where diners were being entertained by Winston Churchill's son-in-law, the Austrian-American musical comedian Vic Oliver, and a few hecklers demanded to know why he wasn't performing in an East End shelter. Then, after about fifteen minutes, an unexpected All Clear sounded and the demonstrators were persuaded to leave. They hung around in the Gardens for a while, waiting for the next Alert, but when it came they were firmly escorted to a deep public shelter nearby.

It was hardly the Storming of the Winter Palace, and the exercise was not repeated, but it made a great story for the foreign press. And by the time it had passed through the filter of Goebbels' Propaganda Ministry, German readers read that howling mobs of poor Londoners had been gunned down by police as they attempted to storm the West End playgrounds of English plutocrats.

BY THE TIME Ernie Pyle arrived, the nearest thing to the common people you found dining at the Savoy were their elected representatives – eating, presumably, on their behalf. Two young Members of Parliament were among Ernie's dinner companions on his first evening in England: 'You're a welcome sight,' his new friends told him cheerily. 'We've all told our bomb stories to each other so many times no one listens any more. Now we've got a new audience.'

At midnight, as Ernie lay in a bed for the first time in forty hours, it had all seemed too good to be true. 'This can't last,' he thought. 'This isn't the way the people live.' But, he told his readers, 'it's mighty good for your soul on your first night in London'.

Over the next three weeks, Ernie had tramped the streets of London, capturing the mood in the minutiae of blitzed London for the people back home. In the interests of research, he went into a snack bar and asked the waitress just what the Bovril stuff was that he saw advertised everywhere like Coca-Cola back home. 'Why sir, it's beef juice and it's wonderful for you on cold days like this,' she replied. 'It's expensive, but it's body-buildin' sir, it's very body-buildin'.'

'So I had a cup,' Ernie told his readers. 'It cost five cents, and you just ought to see my body being built.'

Each night he returned to the luxury of the Savoy, where the water was always hot, the radiators warm, and where he was served (to his secret shame) with two eggs, ham, toast, jam and coffee for breakfast every morning. It was a 'flossy' hotel, he wrote to his wife: expensive at 23 shillings or $6 a night, and 'as Quentin Reynolds says, "They shilling you to death here." But this is the center of things and about twenty American newspapermen are here.'

His room was as elegant as it was comfortable – the heavy blackout curtains were lined with brown satin – but his observant eye had been caught by an odd, walnut-sized object lodged under the radiator. It proved to be stone and looked like a toe from a statue. There was a sculpted frieze on the roofline of the Savoy . . .

When the maid came in, Ernie asked: 'Have the windows ever been blown out of this room?' 'Why yes, just a few days before you came,' she replied. 'But they put them back in you know.'

'Taking a gander' out of his window, he wrote, he found that a corner of the room next door wasn't there at all. This may well have been David Anderson's room. He had been away working the night shift at the *New York Times*'s London bureau downstairs that night and thought his colleagues were ragging him until he went up to see for himself – and came back down looking very pale indeed.

Anderson's next-door neighbour had not arrived home till just before dawn, after an evening spent 'with some of Fleet Street's merry andrews in Emile's friendly and convivial establishment', according to his *NYT* chief Raymond Daniell. It seems he didn't notice his door hanging awry and had simply swept away a coverlet laden with thick broken glass and plaster, crawled under the blankets and slept. He had woken to find a waiter and a guy in striped pants marvelling at his lucky escape.

RAYMOND DANIELL, who lived at the Savoy too, understood if readers at home sometimes found accounts of Blitz London implausible: when working alongside his English office staff – Miss Carter, Jack Lea, Willy Fieldhouse, Harry Bagnall, Bill Long – he could never quite shake the feeling that he was playing a part in a Noël Coward comedy.

But he denied that London-based journalists who sent back reports of plucky Brits had gone native, were too dumb to see through British propaganda or were – worst of treasons – colluding in an attempt to lure their homeland into an unnecessary war. 'It is impossible to be neutral in thought when a city one has grown to love is being smashed to bits wantonly, when one's friends are being killed and injured every day, when one's own home has been wrecked.' But, he wrote, 'journalistic integrity is quite another matter'.

America's London press corps had not been bought or sold: 'They are not pro-British; they are pro-American; and if at any time their country's interests happened to clash with those of Great Britain they would be the first to point that out, for that is what they are there to do.'

After all his team's hard work getting stories and checking information, he was dismayed to discover that people at home seemed to believe that London's wartime correspondents

> wrote their stories and tossed them into a hopper where a group of men bent upon suppressing the truth and getting the United States into the war rewrote the stories and sent them on in any form that happened to suit their purposes at the moment.

While there were restrictions on what you could write about militarily sensitive matters, he had found: 'little or no censorship at the source and absolutely no pressure exerted on correspondents to color or slant their stories to favor either the present government, nor for that matter the British cause'.

He recalled one occasion when he had got mad. A lowly bureaucrat in the censor's office asked for permission to 'kill' one of his stories. You had the right to argue your case – right to the top if necessary – and there was no way Raymond Daniell would spike this particular story, written up from a press agency report.

A riot had broken out in Aberdeen when an attempt to burn Hitler in effigy had been attacked by pro-Nazis. This was something the American public had a right to know, he argued. Until the censor politely pointed out that the riot had taken place not in Aberdeen Scotland, but in Aberdeen, Washington State, in the United States of America.

ERIC SEVAREID, back in America today, was one US newsman who had resisted the idea that his country's security depended on Britain's survival. It was not that he was unaware of the creeping horror of Nazism, which he had witnessed first hand on his pre-war travels. Third-generation Norwegian-American, he had grown up, like his wife, among the German communities of Minnesota, and much in Munich over the last Christmas before the war had spoken to him of his childhood: the wide streets, the large, clean, cosy kitchens, the turkey and mashed potato, the Christmas cookies and the lighted tree in the parlour window. But 'because Germany was part of our intimate lives', he wrote

> we knew well how it should have been, and therefore we could see very clearly how, in this December of 1938, it was utterly warped and changed. The place had been poisoned: the place was sick, heavy with a fog of unhappiness that was composed of suspicion and hostility, private shame and self-reproach – and public, belligerent, and arrogant justification.

Every charming Bavarian building bore its delicate traditional paintings of Bible scenes and the messages of brotherly love, 'and on the door of every house beneath the holly and the wreath was the stark and ugly placard, black print upon blood-red paper, which carried the same words everywhere: "Juden Unerwünscht".'

Even at Oberammergau, when they visited the house of the late Anton Lang who had played Christ in the famous Passion Play three times, they found a small red and black sign tacked to the counter by the cash register. 'You see, we have nothing to say about it,' explained the sweet-looking girl at the counter. 'They just come and put it up and we have nothing to say about it.' Surely, Eric suggested, it wasn't necessary here of all places? Were there even any Jews here: they hadn't seen any. 'There was one,' she answered. 'He was a Catholic, too. They took him away.'

The following Christmas, 1939, the Sevareids had been in a France at war and fearful; and for Christmas 1940 they were back home in the United States – but a United States that Eric now felt was itself in great danger.

It had not been until after Eric left Blitzed London, though, and was waiting in neutral Lisbon among spies and refugees of all nations, that he had finally decided his 'more acute colleagues' had been right all along: 'There was no possible living with Fascism, even for a strong America . . . Europe was small, and with Europe gone the world was very small.'

America would have to spend all its resources preparing for an attack that might come without warning or, if it took the appeasing course, 'every Fascist-minded man and group inside my country would rise in power and prestige':

> it would mean the end of education in freedom as I had known it; would mean that the Silver Shirts and all men of darkness like them would move out of the dim parlors and into the city halls . . . The Nazis meant it when their legions sang that tomorrow the world was theirs. They could do it; and they could do it either by arms or by the defeat of men's minds. They had allies everywhere, in Minneapolis as well as Tokio or Buenos Aires.

Before this war began, received wisdom in certain influential circles on both sides of the Atlantic, as among the German elite before them, had been that Hitler was one of those useful poisons of pharmacology: nasty but not so dangerous in himself as he was efficacious against the scourge of Communism. In 1937, the US ambassador to Berlin had shared his fears about these influential circles with the *New York Times*:

> a clique of US industrialists is hell-bent to bring a fascist state to supplant our democratic government and is working with the fascist regime in Germany and Italy. I have had plenty of opportunity in my post in Berlin to witness how close some of our American ruling families are to the Nazi regime . . . A prominent executive . . . told me point blank that he would be ready to take definite action to bring fascism into America if President Roosevelt continued his progressive policies.

However, it was probably true to say that among American, as among British, appeasers, active supporters of the Dictators were far less common than the perilously wise 'realists' who might prove equally fatal for Britain's immediate prospects.

A month into the war, a young British aristocrat whose husband had just rejoined his regiment received a bright, newsy letter from an old dancing partner, writing from Wall Street. 'If you are counting on us Americans to come over and liquidate the stupidities of your post-war British Governments I suspicion you will be disappointed,' he had written cheerily.

> The feeling here is intense against involvement although sentiment is pro-Ally. Americans, you know revere sagacity – and there are some of us who think Hitler has the finest brain in Europe, if not in the world today – and that with such a leader Germany is sufficiently powerful to do a lot of unpleasant things if you insist. It would seem foolish to me to go on, killing hundreds of thousands and squandering pounds sterling to the ultimate end of fostering communism in all Europe.
>
> I honestly don't think you have a chance of defeating Germany and, if you do, the communists will take over.

Of course this does not make pleasant reading, but I must say, after the Baldwins and MacDonalds etc, you English should enjoy a little realism.

Life here is about as usual, all the night clubs are opening up in new decor, Martinique, Hawaii and other exotic islands . . .

And as Hitler went from success to success in Europe, the Nazis became, for some, really not so nasty after all, nor the ills they cured restricted to Communism alone. In the summer of 1940, *Harper's* journalist E. B. White returned from his Maine farm to mix again with smart New Yorkers, and found that it was not just clothes that had changed with the fashion: 'people had remodeled their ideas too – taken in their convictions a little at the waist, shortened the sleeves of their resolve, and fitted themselves out in a new intellectual ensemble copied from a smart design out of the very latest page of history.'

One man he spoke to reasoned that

perhaps the Nazi ideal was a sounder ideal than our constitutional system 'because have you ever noticed what fine alert young faces the young German soldiers have in the newsreel?' He added, 'Our American youngsters spend all their time at the movies – they're a mess.' That was his summation of the case, his interpretation of the New Europe.

'Such a remark leaves me pale and shaken,' confessed White, who was informed by another sophisticate that America's democratic notion of popular government was 'decadent and not worth bothering about – "because England is really rotten and the industrial towns are a disgrace"'. And by another that

anyone who took *any* kind of government seriously was a gullible fool. You could be sure, he said, that there is nothing but corruption 'because of the way Clemenceau acted at Versailles'. He said it didn't make any difference really about this war. It was just another war.

Yet another announced that he 'wasn't going to be swept away by all this nonsense, but would prefer to remain in the role of innocent bystander' which he said was 'the duty of any intelligent person'.

For E. B. White, a liberal for whom the promise of America still meant something fundamentally about freedom and democracy, the experience was shattering. 'I feel sick when I find anyone adjusting his mind to the new tyranny which is succeeding abroad.' At forty years old, he said, he resented 'the patronizing air' of people who found in his 'plain belief in freedom' a sign of immaturity: 'If it is boyish to believe that a human being should live free, then I'll gladly arrest my development and let the rest of the world grow up.'

Hitler had poured scorn on the 'knights of the goose quill' who wrote against Nazi ideals; E. B. White accepted the title with pride.

I am inordinately proud these days of the quill, for it has shown itself, historically, to be the hypodermic which inoculates men and keeps the germ of freedom always in circulation, so that there are individuals in every time in every land who are the carriers, the Typhoid Mary's, capable of infecting others by mere contact and example.

It was no coincidence, he said, that tyrants burned books and destroyed their authors. 'A writer goes about his task with the extra satisfaction which comes from knowing that he will be the first to have his head lopped off.'

In my own case this is a double satisfaction, for if freedom were denied me by force of earthly circumstance, I am the same as dead and would infinitely prefer to go into fascism without my head than with it, having no use for it any more and not wishing to be saddled with so heavy an encumbrance.

IT WAS STARTING to get dark now in London, but it was still morning in America. And in the Oval Study, the President was hard at work with his White House speechwriters, still shaping tonight's 'Fireside Chat'. Despite the folksy title, Franklin D. Roosevelt's 'Fireside Chats' were Presidential messages of weighty significance. Like Churchill he believed in using simple language. But where Prime Minister Churchill addressed his tribe as ancient warrior to ancient warrior, President Roosevelt talked to America like a friendly liberal lawyer chewing the fat in the parlour with his small-town neighbours.

He had taken office first amid his country's worst domestic crisis since the Civil War. And with the economy on the verge of meltdown, he had given Americans back their hope with his first inauguration speech of 4th March 1933: 'The only thing we have to fear is fear itself – nameless, unreasoning, unjustified terror which paralyzes needed efforts to convert retreat into advance.'

On the following day, the German electorate had placed the levers of power of their own nation within the grasp of Adolf Hitler. And over the intervening years, fear had become a much more complex political factor in the President's thinking. For too little might now perhaps pose as much of a threat to his great nation as too much.

'So many Americans,' H. G. Wells had written in *New World Order* at the start of 1940, still look on at world affairs like spectators at a ball game who are capable of vociferous participation but still have no real sense of participation; they do not realise that the ground is moving under their seats also, and that the social revolution is breaking surface to engulf them in their turn.

He was certainly not exaggerating America's sense of isolation. When Raymond Daniell first sailed out of New York on the USS *Washington* on 1st September 1939, he had thought it 'a ferry between two worlds, a link between the known and the unknown'.

It was a little like embarking on Charon's barge for a voyage across the Styx, for in Europe the forces of destruction and death that many feared might cause the collapse of European civilization had at last been unleashed after a succession of abortive efforts to hold them in check.

And in a long, friendly letter, Queen Elizabeth had sent to Mrs Roosevelt (whom she and the King had met on a royal visit to the United States, at the President's invitation, in the last summer of peace) she had written that she had been much moved by the generosity and kind messages she had received from across the Atlantic. However

In one of the nice letters I have received from America, a lady wrote of 'the sorrows of your world'. It seemed such a curious distinction. Her world and our world are apparently different! I did not feel that at all when I was with you last year.

EVEN SEPARATE worlds might not stay separate for ever. The events of the night before Halloween 1938 had been widely treated as a joke afterwards. And they had indeed had their ludicrous side. But was it really such a joke that President Roosevelt's voice coming over the airwaves on a Sunday night two years ago had helped to convince many Americans that the United States had been invaded by Martians?

About ten minutes into NBC's hit variety show that night more than a million listeners had begun to fiddle with their radio dials, just in time to catch a 'reporter' on CBS (who based his horrified tones on a famous recording of the *Hindenburg* crash) telling of a spaceship landing in a small New Jersey town.

Having missed the explanation that they were listening to a play based on *The War of the Worlds*, they heard fictitious music programmes interrupted by newsflashes echoing Ed Murrow's innovative live reports during the Munich Crisis of only a month earlier. And the very familiar tones of the 'Secretary of Interior' (actually referred to as the President in a draft script till CBS objected) had made a statement. 'One man insisted he had heard "the President's voice" over the radio advising all citizens to leave the cities,' reported the *New York Times* the next day.

There was considerable panic, though some took the news more stoically. The next day's *NYT* reported that evening services in Harlem brownstones had become 'end of the world prayer meetings' as 'less faithful parishioners rushed in . . . seeking spiritual consolation'.

Afterwards, amid a mixture of chagrin, public laughter and private anger, some people detected a deeper significance: 'A sane people,' wrote Eleanor Roosevelt:

> living in an atmosphere of fearlessness, does not suddenly become hysterical at the threat of invasion, even from more credible sources, let alone by the Martians from another planet, but we have allowed ourselves to be fed on propaganda which has created a fear complex.

'Mr Hitler made a good deal of sport of it, you know, actually spoke of it in the great Munich speech,' Orson Welles had told H. G. Wells two months ago, when the two men were brought together on 28th October 1940 for a radio interview in San Antonio, Texas, to celebrate the show's second anniversary. 'And it's supposed to show the kind of corrupt condition and decadent state of affairs in democracies, that *The War of the Worlds* went over as well as it did.'

Mr Wells had been angry with Mr Welles for not consulting him before the radio dramatisation, but had been mollified since. He made light of the 'most delightful' young Orson's 'bit of Halloween fun', even giving a 'plug' to the twenty-five-year-old's forthcoming film *Citizen Kane*. But there had been something rather uncomfortable about the conversation between the old man and the young, the Old World and the New.

'You aren't quite serious in America, yet,' said Mr Wells. 'You haven't got the war right under your chins, and the consequence is you can still play with ideas of terror and conflict.'

'Do you think that's good or bad?' asked Mr Welles brightly. There was a short pause.

'It's the natural thing to do until you're right up against it.'

'So it ceases to be a game?'

'And then it ceases to be a game.'

THERE HAD BEEN something a little uncomfortable too, about a conversation that took place just two days earlier between US Military Attaché General Lee and Sir Edward Villiers of Britain's Ministry of Information.

They had been on a weekend visit to Fleet Street, to see what bombs had done to that large, peculiar enclave of buildings and gardens known as The Temple, between road and river at the western end of the street. This had once been, General Lee recorded in his diary, the garrison of the Knights Templar. (And it was they who had built its early-twelfth-century round church with the wonderful acoustics, which still echoed to the famous Temple choir for May Speed at the end of 1940.)

The Knights had only survived for a couple of centuries though. The barristers, pupils and clerks of Middle and Inner Temple had already been well ensconced here when Wynkyn de Worde arrived at St Bride's at the other end of the street in 1500 – and they had been here ever since.

The lawyers had gradually and eventually inherited title to the whole property. Though whether they had also inherited the independence from City control that this ground had enjoyed under the Crusader Knights was a question that had been fought out, sometimes with depositions and sometimes with fists, down the centuries. The final judgement was hazy: suffice it to say that the Middle and Inner Temple could close their gates against the Lord Mayor himself if they chose. And that this intricate maze of lawyers' chambers, gardens, libraries and oak-lined halls was still guarded in 1940 by The Temple's own, independent fire service with its own engine. It cooperated with the LCC Fire Brigade as necessary though and, in Tanfield Court, the AFS men and women of 62X enjoyed watch-room, mess and sleeping facilities – but its pumps were housed at Unilever House up by St Bride's.

The Temple had received quite a battering by October 1940, and Sir Edward Villiers had been nonplussed when General Lee began to laugh as they inspected the damage. Lee explained that it quite tickled him to think some fresh air had been let into these dusty old lawyers' offices after all these years. Noting Ted's unwillingness to share the joke, he decided that his friend had probably written him off as an uncivilised American.

Perhaps it was because he was a military man. An American lawyer might have felt differently about this spot. For, just after Christmas 1214, in the days of the Knights Templar, a group of disgruntled barons had come to the Temple to thrash out the wording of a great charter of rights with the King's Marshal – who had then to persuade the King to sign it. Which King John did, upriver at Runnymede, the following summer. When John died, William the Marshal's first act as Regent had been to reissue this 'Magna Carta' in the name of John's nine-year-old son Henry III; and when William himself died, a few years later, he was buried, complete with knightly effigy, here in the round Temple church.

The most perfect remaining copy of this ancient document was now in Washington – a treasure taken to New York for the 1939 World's Fair and too precious to entrust to the seas when the Fair closed in 1940.

No one could argue, 725 years later, that the liberties King John promised to English freemen then – 'to be had and held by them and their heirs, of us and our heirs for ever' – had always been faithfully delivered. No one could ignore, 725 years later, how many English had been not freemen then, but serfs: owned as surely as the land they worked on. But so long as ink remained on vellum, two in particular of Magna Carta's sixty or so articles survived, like E. B. White's Typhoid Marys, to carry the *bacillus* of liberty forward into the increasingly totalitarian world of 1940 and link the aspirations of many peoples:

> No FREEMAN shall be arrested, imprisoned, dispossessed, outlawed, exiled or harmed in any other way, nor will we act against him, or send others to do so, except by the judgement of his peers and according to the law of the land.
> To NO ONE will we sell, to no one will we refuse or delay, right or justice.

Britain was a notoriously pragmatic, untheoretical society. 'Our realm of England,' a Scottish King of England had acknowledged in a 1608 charter confirming the lawyers in their Temple properties, 'is sensible that great part of its welfare is justly owing to the ancient and proper Laws of that Realm, tried through a long series of ages, adapted to that populous nation and approved by constant experience.' Over the intervening centuries, laws had been put on and taken off the Statute Book by successive parliaments until, like the Temple church itself, only a professional eye could tell what was medieval and what Victorian restoration. But in 1940 the principle of the Rule of Law to which even monarchs (and their ministers) could be made to bow was still, in a very real sense, the same that had seemed 'ancient' to a Stuart king.

And as arguments raged over the summary imprisonments of 18B in the leaders and letters columns of Fleet Street newspapers, and among the people's representatives just along the road in Westminster, the ideas thrashed out in the Temple by the barons and William the Marshal in 1214 – even before Simon de Monfort had forced King John's son Henry to accept the notion of a 'parliament' – had been picked up and handled as practically as a tradesman might take a familiar, well-used spanner or wrench to a misfiring engine.

And the fact that so many 'enemy aliens' were free again this Sunday showed that the rusty old engine of English liberty could still be made to work – eventually.

IT REALLY WAS getting dark now.

At the far end of Fleet Street, from among the international press agencies, Wren's wedding-cake spire rose gracefully above St Bride's. Up in the tower, with pull-ropes removed, the great bells waited silently for history to call upon them again, for good or ill, still carrying the evocative hopes and good wishes of an earlier London to their neighbours of a future of 'prosperity to England' and 'peace and good neighbourhood'.

In this very different age, the forty or so parishioners joining its seventy-two-year-old vicar Arthur Taylor for evensong tonight were not summoned by church bells, but by a mechanical musical carillon. And Verger Leonard Morgan had picked an appropriate tune from its choices to play on this last Sunday of 1940 – at least, it was only a few days premature. The title of the tune he had chosen was: 'The year has gone beyond recall with all its hopes and fears.'

FUGUE

Chapter Ten

SECRET
Copy of letter at folio 33A on FC/S 19883
From: Air Ministry,
London, SW1

S.7815/DCAS 29th December, 1940

Command and Control of Special Experimental Units
Sir,
I am directed to inform you that consideration has been given
to the command and control of special units employed on
experimental work of an operational character. The units
under consideration are:
    The Special Duties Flight, Christchurch,
    The Fighter Interception Unit, Ford,
    No. 93 Squadron, Middle Wallop,
    New Air Mining Units to be formed in the immediate future,
    'Pegasus' . . .

*Letter from A. T. Harris, Air Vice Marshal, Deputy Chief of the Air Staff
to Air Officer Commanding-in-Chief, Headquarters, Fighter Command,
RAF Bentley Priory*

AT AD ASTRAL HOUSE in Kingsway, off the Strand, Arthur Harris would be working late into the evening tonight as usual. There at the Air Ministry, as at Fighter Command out at Stanmore, the heady, hectic atmosphere of the Battle of Britain had long since been supplanted by the gloomy, frustrating – but equally hectic – atmosphere of the Night Blitz. The skies over Britain were perilous for any German flyer who ventured over in daylight now. But once darkness fell – as Churchill had warned the House of Commons in secret session back in June – those skies pretty much belonged to the Luftwaffe.

Like an endless game of 'Scissors, Paper, Stone', over progressively shorter intervals technology developed in strict secrecy by one side burst upon the enemy with great suddenness – to be met by hurried counter-measures from the other. The Prime Minister was fascinated by what he called 'the Wizard War' being waged between scientific brains. But Air

Vice Marshal Harris, whose letter clarified the chain of command for the various RAF units aiming to provide Britain with some sort of night defence, knew they were all still very much in the experimental stages.

Which one might turn out to be a war winner and which a dud could only be judged in the heat of battle. And there was no time to waste: Britain might be 'taking it' magnificently, but everyone at the Ministry was painfully aware of just how impotent the RAF was after dark. The British Isles sat cupped in a European coastline under total Nazi control. And the many Luftwaffe airfields ranged along it had a single purpose: '*Bomben gegen England*'.

Not that German crews could view Britain as, to use the RAF slang, 'a piece of cake'. As the summer days had taught them to respect the fighter planes of the RAF, so during these winter nights the British Army's anti-aircraft batteries kept them on their toes. Although the guns had not brought down many planes, the mere fact of ack-ack banging away helped, like the RAF's forest of barrage balloons, to keep the Luftwaffe flying high. This not only helped to remove dive-bombing and machine-gunning civilians from its repertoire, but made precise targeting difficult. The survival of key installations like the bridges across the Thames, despite so many attempts to destroy them, could be laid to the credit of London's ack-ack batteries.

And in the fast and furious Wizard War, improved detection apparatus was making the British guns more accurate, as Junker 88 pilot Peter Stahl had discovered for himself last month. Recording his experience of a raid on London, Stahl wrote: 'the sky is alive with hundreds of exploding AA shells. Not only that: tonight they seem to have got not only our correct altitude but also our speed and lateral position!'

> The shells burst ahead and behind us and any attempt at evasion seems point-less. Things are so bad that I catch myself several times wanting to give up, drop the bombs blind into the night and get out of here, but I persevere.

When he did release his bombs there had been a blinding flash, then everything seemed to return to normal. Like most British successes against the night bombers, this one had not come until after the mission was over. It was only as he was flying back over the North Sea that Stahl realised shrapnel from a bursting shell had fallen into his throttle controls: he had a runaway engine.

He switched it off and flew on his single good engine until, crossing the coast, 'friendly fire' from their own ack-ack nearly did for them at last.

Despite radioing in, and sending out identification flares, the

deadly game of searchlights and light AA guns follows us all along the coast. In the end, my crew give up firing the identification flares and start shooting back with their machine-guns in earnest. We are so incensed that we are actually hoping we have hit some of those silly AA dopes!

Approaching the airfield, he put down his undercarriage for a one-engine landing but, coming in too low, he felt a blow on the port wing, and the plane scraped along the ground in the pitch dark and stopped. The crew called out to one another through the blackness. It could have been worse. Hans the bomb-aimer had smashed his arm against the instrument panel; Hein the radio man had flesh wounds to the face where the whole radio apparatus had slammed into it; Theo the air-gunner couldn't stand up; Peter himself had injured his right hand. They were freed, with difficulty, by soldiers who smashed in the jammed cabin roof and a doctor was quickly on the spot.

But when the soldiers told him that there were no serious injuries, he had abandoned his patients to crawl in to the cabin to unscrew their valuable aircraft clock.

This is too much for our Hans, particularly as Theo, stretched out on the ground, begins to complain about pains in his groin. When the handsome doctor appears again, Hans calmly walks up to him, removes the clock from his grasp, and then hits him in the face with his good hand with such force that the medicine man slithers down the wing and falls flat on the grass below. That is the last we ever see of this particular doctor; he was transferred elsewhere double quick. And so ended another flight to London.

Goebbels had noted problems of morale amongst flyers back in October: 'It seems to them as if they are fighting a kind of aerial Verdun,' he recorded in his diary. The Battle of Verdun had been Germany's longest, bloodiest defeat of the Great War. Hitler had been determined never to get his troops in this war trapped in the grinding hell of the trench warfare that he had known in the last one. But no leader gets to fight exactly the war he plans. And here he was after all, after more than a year of war, with his Luftwaffe trapped in the grinding hell of a trench warfare of the air that it was never designed for. The switch to night flying had reduced the scale of losses to manageable levels but it hardly reduced the stresses on crews.

AS THE YEAR ENDED Britain, as at so many times in its history, was finding its best ally in its weather. Though even that had not been as decisive as had been hoped. The weather was bad tonight – the RAF meteorologists reported:

Weather Low Countries and Northern FRANCE:- Cloud mainly 8/10ths to 10/10ths at 2,500ft in the West at first, at 1,500 ft in the East and locally 800 ft in occasional rain. Low cloud increasing rapidly at 1,000 ft in North-west FRANCE early in the period and locally 300 to 600 ft covering hills in a period of moderate rain. These conditions spreading Eastward over the whole of Northern FRANCE during the period with visibility generally poor. In the East winds WNW moderate in the West, wind freshening from South-west becoming fresh or strong with gusts of gale force locally on the Coast.

The question was, would it be bad enough? As Peter Stahl's diary recorded, German crews were often ordered out on *Fledermaus* operations in terrible flying weather or – in some ways even more stressful – were stood down at the last minute. On one night earlier this month, the fog had been so thick that Stahl's driver got lost on the way to the aircraft and his crew were already strapped in and ready to go when the operation was aborted; on another, he had been running his engines in driving snow when the cancellation came.

The inescapable fact was that the airfields of northern France, Holland and Belgium were a long way from Berlin, where the decisions were taken. And if the decision in Berlin was a 'Yes', it took a lot of courage all the way up the chain of command to send back a 'No'.

Whatever decisions had been passed down from Berlin today, Peter Stahl would not fly tonight: on three weeks' blessed home leave, he was, he wrote, 'glad not to have to wear a uniform for a short while'. On a raid earlier this month, he and Hans had been thoroughly alarmed by an ominous fiery red spot in the sky, growing larger and larger on the horizon as they approached the target. They had suddenly realised it was the rising moon ahead of them and burst out laughing with relief , but 'considering our overheated nerves', wrote Stahl, such silly mistakes were not to be wondered at.

Night after night we witness all kinds of similar apparitions in the skies over England that we cannot explain: searchlights that wink or flash in an unusual way, signalling something to the night-fighters or other air defence devices; intermittent lights on the ground; and illuminating flares that are hung in the air above, below or behind us. All these things are sinister to us because we have no idea what they mean and we cannot do anything about them.

Arthur Harris in the Air Ministry would have been delighted to hear all this. But he would have known just how little material difference it had made, so far, to the Luftwaffe's ability to strike at British cities, virtually at will.

THE ANGUISH of the RAF at present was that Britain's air defences were the best in the world but not yet good enough. The interest of the privileged outsiders who were allowed in to study them was that Britain's air defences were not yet good enough – but were the best in the world.

When US Military Attaché Raymond Lee had visited Fighter Command, which co-ordinated Britain's response to air attack in the summer, he had been stunned by what he saw. He had been beguiled by the old-world style and *politesse* of the British military but confessed to his diary that he hadn't expected to find them running one of the world's most modern and complex organisations. He had not suspected that the British could have developed and run this swift and complex technical set-up, which reached out over their coast to meet the Luftwaffe before it arrived.

Descending deep into the two large underground rooms, where there was no sound but the murmur of messages to and fro, he witnessed in astonishment the telephone switchboards, the message boards studded with electric lights and the huge table maps where the enemy were tracked moment by moment, twenty-four hours a day.

Felicity Ashbee, who worked in the first (and most secret) of the two map rooms that held the whole defence operation together, had soon got used to seeing top brass gather on the balcony to see how the war was going.

THE FIRST INTAKE of Women's Auxiliary Air Force personnel drafted in for 'special duties' at Bentley Priory included many who had attended boarding schools 'of the "gentleman's daughters" kind', recalled Felicity (as she also had 'for two hated and inglorious years!'), but many creative types too. Felicity's best friend Pyddy had been a film continuity girl while, in her first billet, Felicity shared a chaste double bed with a six-foot lesbian ballet photographer. (Who looked, Felicity thought, like nothing so much as the Sandeman Port advertisement, for she continued to wear her own long black cloak and sombrero until the WAAF could find a uniform big enough to fit her.) During their uneventful Phoney War shifts, the WAAF positions had been 'encumbered with books, knitting, letter-writing materials, even chess-sets' – anything to keep bright girls from going crazy with boredom.

Felicity sometimes amused herself by making sketches of the officers – even 'Stuffy' Dowding himself, 'with his little-boy hair-cut and his glumly brooding expression'. The Air Chief Marshal had reason enough to brood, for he had spent the pre-war years in planning and preparation for a task that might well prove impossible. The force Dowding commanded was, General Lee discovered in the summer of 1940, the most important barrier between Britain and invasion.

Even this remarkable linchpin of British defences had begun in an archetypally British amalgam of genius and skin-of-the-teeth improvisation. Dowding had first visited the dilapidated stately home that was to be his HQ in 1936. Lofty reception rooms, fifty feet by thirty by twenty feet high, had once hosted parties for the likes of the Prince Regent, Wellington, and Lord and Lady (Emma) Hamilton. Dowding had immediately set about making the best of what he had been offered.

He had always realised that telecommunications would be key to his whole operation. Britain was not alone in having radar – in fact the early German radar was technically superior to the British in some ways. It was the efficient networking of the information radar provided that would give Britain the edge through the summer of 1940. Central to his vision of air defence was a Central Operations Room which would gather and distribute all available intelligence and, he wrote briskly, 'the Ball Room seems to be most suitable for the purpose',

> ... although this of course may not be desirable as a permanent location owing to the fact the Priory is extremely conspicuous from the air and the rooms would be very difficult to render gas proof. I do, however, wish to make a start immediately so that the delay in the production of my permanent Operations Room may be reduced to a minimum and only by immediate experiment can be determined the requirements necessary for the purpose.

Balconies of scaffolding and timber were speedily erected within the Adam-style interior and draped with cables and angled lamps in classic Heath Robinson style. From these balconies senior officers had a bird's-eye view of the great maps on tables below, and of how the situation in the air was developing.

In the early, quiet months, Felicity had captured the improbable scene in the small magazine started by the Bentley Priory WAAFs:

> ... Into the misty sky the guns nose out
> From sand-bagged rings; sinister snouts of steel.
> The stone bowl where the fountain used to spout
> Is clogged with leaves. The stucco facings peel.
> But the cracked bell in the Italian tower
> Discordant, fairy-like still tells the hour.

Boots on the lawn, boots on the wide stone stair,
Boots on the cellar flags, boots up above,
Blue cloth with wings, and gas-masks everywhere,
Where Nelson may have wandered with his love.
Did the bell warn them that their joy would pass?
And stranger-feet would trample on the grass?

The one saving grace of pre-war economies in Defence had been that, with so little money to spend, the Air Ministry had concentrated its efforts on radar and on developing and producing decent little fighter planes rather than bigger and more expensive bombers. Even so, new technology takes time. The first production-line Spitfires were not delivered till the summer of 1938 and only the first five stations of the coastal radar chain, around the Thames Estuary, were operational by the time Chamberlain had faced Hitler at Munich.

As planes continued to be produced and gaps in the radar chain closed up, digging went on relentlessly in the gardens of Bentley Priory through the bitter winter of 1939 to reproduce a more refined version of the above-ground map rooms in a huge air-conditioned and gas-proof underground bunker. The system was finished only just in time for the start of the Battle of Britain: in the final switch-over, the GPO telephone link-up of all the out-stations with the new HQ was, miraculously, 'completed in the short space of two and a half minutes', according to the official records.

The main difference for the girls in their new workplace, recalled Felicity Ashbee, was that

> instead of entering by Regency portals and marble staircases, we now squelched over duckboards covering seas of mud as we went truly underground to our new, and much more 'purpose-built' accommodation. True, the woodwork was in places rough and unfinished and calculated to ladder even the tough grey lisle stockings which now encased our legs . . . but the new premises were at least functional.

It was this bunker, known to staff as 'the Hole', that had so impressed General Lee and was the brain co-ordinating the RAF response in the Battle of Britain.

RADAR STATIONS were dotted along the coast, housed in small huts or even vans, each with a dedicated phone line into the Filter Room where WAAFs were gathered around a huge map that showed the eastern coast-line of Britain from the north of Scotland down to the South Coast and round to Cornwall.

As soon as the first green blip appeared on a radar screen on the coast indicating raiders over the sea, the station called it through to a Filter Room WAAF, who marked the grid reference on the table map with a brightly coloured 'tiddly-wink'. Ingeniously, this showed both the position of the raiders and the time they had appeared, since its colour matched the relevant five-minute division on the large clocks on the wall.

Once the sighting had been confirmed by a second station, or visually through binoculars by the Observer Corps, the male Filter Officer interpreted the path of the incursion and put down a matching arrow on the trail of the tiddly-winks. 'Some despised planner had even got around to making sure there were good angles of vision,' noted Felicity,

> especially for the three Tellers, who, once the raids started, needed every help to cover the mass of multi-coloured tracks between the dodging heads of plotters bending over to put down their counters, and of Filter Officers 'filtering' the true tracks from them.

As a Teller herself, she continuously 'told through' the grid reference of the point of the leading arrow to the Operations (Ops) Room. There, more WAAFs (including Felicity's friend Pyddy) stood with long magnetic wands, ready to move the markers that showed the progress of encroaching aircraft on a table map that now covered the whole of Britain, divided into sectors and also showing the RAF fighter stations available to respond.

From the balcony of the Ops Room, senior officers rang through the information they could see on this table map to Sector HQs, which had their own Ops Rooms which in turn gave orders to 'scramble'. At a distant fighter station, someone would play merry hell with a fire bell, and young fighter pilots would put down their tea, throw down their newspapers or wake from their blessed armchair dozes and prepare to do battle in the skies within two minutes.

On the speed and accuracy of transmission of information from the radar stations to the fighters stations, many lives depended. A single 'action' involved many thousands of messages and the concentration needed in the Filter and Ops Rooms was exhausting. The twenty-four hour day was split into six watches, with three groups of WAAFs taking two four-hour watches each with an eight-hour break between. At the end of each week, the rotation changed so they went all round the clock over a three-week period. Their only break was the occasional, glorious twenty-four- or forty-eight-hour pass.

OVER THE SUMMER and early autumn, the RAF had held the fort – just. How close run it had been was witnessed by Churchill himself, who watched the decisive air battle of 15th September, later known as Battle of Britain Day, from the balcony of a very similar Ops Room at Group HQ No. 11 in Uxbridge, commanded by Air Vice Marshal Keith Park.

Goering had planned two separate hammer blows on London, either side of noon, that Sunday – a total of 500 to 600 planes – and he expected little or no resistance from the battered RAF. The Luftwaffe was attempting to repeat the first devastating Blitz of the previous weekend and the Prime Minister found himself witnessing the drama from the 'dress circle'.

Ranks of lights showed the readiness of each squadron at the Sector's six fighter stations. The At Available light showed it could be in the air in twenty minutes; At Readiness in five; Standing By in two. A further light showed a squadron had taken off and another that the enemy had been sighted. A red light indicated that the squadron was in action against the Luftwaffe and, when the top row lit up, that the squadron – or what was left of it – was heading home.

As message after message came in to Uxbridge that day, of twenty-plus, forty-plus, sixty-plus, eighty-plus raiders, more and more lights had moved up the board to red. Park had phoned Bentley Priory to request that squadrons from No. 12 Group be put at his disposal in case more bombers came while his men were rearming and refuelling. The Prime Minister asked what further reserves could be called into play and, Park recorded, he 'looked grave' when told there were none. 'Well I might,' Churchill wrote later. 'The odds were great; the margins small; the stakes infinite.'

But on this occasion, as he saw for himself, while the lights showed the RAF fighters coming in to land, the discs representing the Luftwaffe forces were being pushed ever eastward across the map. The Germans were going home.

It was thought, and reported, that 183 German planes had been shot down by the RAF that day: almost one in three. In fact it was more like one in ten. But Goering had expected a walkover. He could not countenance repeating losses of that magnitude on a daily basis and the Luftwaffe had increasingly taken to bombing under cover of night.

NOT THAT THIS would stop some Londoners going out on the town tonight – it was still the holiday season. On his visit a couple of months ago, *PM*'s Ralph Ingersoll, staying at the Dorchester, had been struck by the unreality of the scene as couples danced beneath the bombs:

> It's a ghost of a room in which people danced and drank in 1917 and 1918. It's peopled with French officers and Polish officers, Englishmen in gay Guards' uniforms, young Americans from the Eagle Squadron, which is the walking ghost of the Lafayette Squadron from Paris. The girls the officers have with them are very beautiful – very – and are beautifully and immaculately dressed, with their hair exceedingly well waved . . . A Negress and a distinguished-looking Englishman. A handsome young lady smoking a cigar. Monocles are in female as well as male eyes . . . The colour of the faces is high and the note of the conversation slightly hysterical. Many are drinking champagne . . . Someone said, 'Wouldn't it be wonderful if a bomb came in now? It would be like watching the *Titanic* sink all over again.' . . . Then somebody said, 'But why shouldn't they come here and dance? What else should they do? Most of these girls drive ambulances or run canteens or help some place.
>
> Why shouldn't they get dressed up and come here and dance? Even if it isn't their war any more.'

For this was Grand Finale, Ralph Ingersoll believed, for what he called 'the "international set" – the people who are always in Biarritz and Cannes at the right time of year in the right hotels'.

He was not alone in believing that this war was about to end not only many of these gay lives, but this whole way of life. The Polish Ambassador, Count Edward Raczynski, recording his impression of life in London after the fall of France, wrote: 'For some time now, the privileged classes have ceased to believe that their material prosperity was an effect of Divine will.'

> Nevertheless, as long as they were able to believe that the social order was unchangeable, they could enjoy their advantages without self-reproach, Today, when classical economic doctrines have been exploded, we have not even that excuse for clinging to a system that is inconsistent with Christianity and with the sense of justice which lies deep down in all of us.

And: 'as at other turning-points in history, it suffices to put the question in order to answer it. So far, the change has taken place in Britain rapidly but more or less painlessly.' The working-class standard of living, he judged, had suffered little as rationing ensured that there were no actual shortages; high taxes meant it was the wealthy who would have to change their lifestyle.

Certainly everyone knew that things were soon going to get tougher – for everyone. And people wanted them to be tougher, reported Ernie Pyle:

> With Germany bearing down harder in her U-boat strangulation campaign,

there is more talk in the newspapers and among groups about stricter regulation of food. The striking thing about this talk – and I think it is an example of British character – is that the people want the Food Ministry to cut down on food faster than it is doing.

You can hardly conceive of the determination of the people of England to win this war. They are ready to take further rationing cuts. They are ready to eat in groups at communal kitchens. Even the rich would quit their swanky dining rooms without much grumbling.

'If England loses this war,' Ernie told his readers back in America, 'it won't be because people aren't willing – and even ahead of the government in their eagerness – to assume a life of all-out sacrifice.'

THERE WERE FEW evening shows as such at cinemas any more but, this late in the year, even those who went to the pictures in the afternoon could emerge into the blackout: making the transition from the world of peace to the world of war by way of the world of the imagination. The irony was not lost on film-goers, who often emerged into a world more dramatic than the one they had been watching on the screen.

Today, audiences had been queuing longest to laugh at Chaplin's pseudo-Hitler in *The Great Dictator*, or take refuge from their own war in America's battles of eighty years ago in *Gone With the Wind*. Two of Hoare's Bank's firewatchers who would be on duty tonight had chosen to escape reality altogether with Alexander Korda's Technicolor fantasy *The Thief of Bagdad*, which had opened on Christmas Eve. May Speed, who had seen it on Boxing Day, thought it

the most beautiful colour film I have seen. Vivid oriental colourings as a background for brown bodies. Fairy tale imagery, geniis, magicians, magic carpet, a beautiful Princess – or she should have been but I didn't think she was – all very absorbing. It is an Alexander Korda production with Sabu as the thief, June Duprez as the Princess and Conrad Veidt as the villain of the piece, the evil magician.

The American journalist William L. White and his French colleague Marguerite had chosen *The Great Dictator*. Bill White was often known as 'W. L.' back home in Kansas, to distinguish him from his father. William Allen White, the 'Sage of Emporia', was owner of the *Emporia Gazette*, and the voice of the Midwest and of small-town America through his syndicated columns. Father and son were not of one mind on this war. Bill was one of the Americans convinced by what he had seen that Britain was fighting for democracy and that it was America's fight too. His father was one of the most powerful voices of 'internationalism': the belief that this was not America's war, but helping Britain was the best way of keeping America out of it. William Allen White loyally accepted an article W. L. had sent for tomorrow's *Gazette*. But he had added his own comment: 'W. L. White . . . says that the British feel that America should get into the war – a position which his father does not agree with.'

ALTHOUGH BILL WHITE's call to arms had not borne fruit thus far, Britain already had cause to be grateful to William Allen White. Democratic President Roosevelt had unofficially relied on the patriotic Republican's rallying of internationalist public opinion: first behind the idea of relaxing the Neutrality Laws in November 1939 to allow America to sell arms to the Western Powers, and then behind sending fifty mothballed Great War destroyers to the British to help protect their convoys in September 1940. That Roosevelt had managed to secure, in return, the right to establish a string of military bases on British territories from Newfoundland down to the Caribbean – a shrewd deal which, he told Congress, represented 'the most important action in the reinforcement of our national defense that has been taken since the Louisiana Purchase' – had been all to the good.

The 'White Committee' – the Committee to Defend America by Aiding the Allies which William Allen White had chaired – had operated by appearing to be always one step ahead of the President. And the President had operated by letting it seem so. William Allen White had been one of the 171 prominent citizens asking the President for a firm stand in his 'Fireside Chat' which was due later tonight. But with this he had finally reached the outer limit of his political landscape.

Other members of the Committee were pushing for more support of Britain, even for America to provide its own convoys, but William Allen White believed this would drag the United States into a war that could last thirty years. Three days ago, New York mayor Fiorello La Guardia had sent him an open letter charging: 'When the going was good for the Allies, you and others were strong in saying what you would do. Now that the going is bad, you are doing a typical Laval.' Laval was a French collaborationist with the Nazis – things were starting to get bitter in America.

IN LONDON, meanwhile, life was sweet – at least it was if you were Win Marshall, who was in love and writing – amid the 'serene air of domestic bliss' pervading an Earl's Court flat – to her fiancé.

The sun had set and the curtains were drawn ready for the blackout, which was due in about ten minutes. 'Vera is tired, after cooking a marvellous roast dinner for Nina and me, so I have tucked her up in her eiderdown in the lounge in front of the fire, given her a hot-water bottle for her feet and with the wireless giving the news in German, am indulging in the usual four pages of nonsense.' Win and her soldier boyfriend Teddy exchanged daily love letters (an impressive tribute to the efficiency of the wartime GPO): partly in English and partly in French, as Teddy was in Intelligence and needed to practise his languages.

Win had originally come to London from Australia to study piano with the famous Solomon and her anxious parents had been doing everything they could to get her to come home. They had withdrawn their financial support in a last-ditch effort to force her return, but she wrote that leaving London now would feel like desertion. She worked every second night with the WVS and was now looking for a full-time job too.

On Boxing Day, she had firmly turned down Teddy's offer of financial help: 'I shall ask Solly for my bill, pay him, and tell him that I shall have to leave off lessons for a while until my future is more assured. He'll understand and I'm sure he'll let me go on again as soon as I can afford it.' She was far from downcast by her lot: 'My dear I absolutely loved your letter this morning,' she had written. 'It was a grand tonic and I see you're made of the right stuff too. Between the two of us we've got pretty high ideals, and we're young too, and we love each other. Oh no! The world's not such a bad place after all.'

This Sunday had been heavenly, she wrote to Teddy:

We've done absolutely nothing today, and haven't even been outside, except to fill the coal-scuttle. After lunch the girls made me play to them and I picked a few pieces at random from the pile I brought from Australia with me. I was delighted to find that I could play them so much more easily than before . . . Joan rang this afternoon – her bloke had wired her 'serious trouble, can't come', so she was feeling depressed and wanted to talk to me. I couldn't leave Nina, but I shall see her tonight. This chap is in charge of Defence in Yorkshire, so hope the trouble wasn't too serious.

You can't imagine how loath I am to go out these lovely days in 28D Bolton Gardens. I practise and dream by the fire, and am quite happy for 24 hours out of the 24. Vera comes home from duty and I fuss around after her and she's always interested in everything that I do.

I feel that this flat has traditions which I must carry on – traditions of hospitality, friendship, good humour and consideration.

With all my love.

Win

IT WAS CLEAR tonight that the weather over the Channel was going to be bad. But it was not bad enough. The command came through that the planned raid on the target – Codename: *Loge* – was to go ahead. In airfields across northern France, and in the Low Countries, more than a hundred bombers began taxiing on to the runways.

But the real key to the operation lay with just ten black-painted Heinkel 111 of Kurd Aschenbrenner's Kampfgruppe 100, waiting to take off from a small airfield at Vannes on the south Brittany coast. Each one bearing the Viking ship emblem of their unit on the side of its nose, and each one equipped with the sophisticated and expensive X-Gerät (X-apparatus) that made them crucial to this operation.

IN THE SUMMER, shortly after he was made Prime Minister, Churchill had received the unexpected and deeply disturbing news that the Luftwaffe was developing a way of navigating not only at night but in total, moonless darkness – which negated the RAF's daytime supremacy even before it had been established.

British bombers had been forced to adopt night-flying almost from the outset: the long journey across Occupied Europe to German targets in daylight would have been suicidal. Almost unbelievably in the light of subsequent developments, the RAF had largely rejected radio navigation in favour of dead reckoning and navigation by the stars. But either way it required visual confirmation of the target to be certain. If Bomber Command had been able to get a truer picture of just how far adrift its bombs were falling in these early months, Churchill would have been much more despondent about its prospects of crippling the German war machine.

The Luftwaffe also used dead reckoning – navigating using fixed points, including direction-finding radio beacons, combined with the aircraft's track and groundspeed, to determine actual position. But their Knickebein ('Crooked Leg') radio navigation system promised an extra precision. By flying high, a plane could follow a VHF beam for something like 250 miles – enough to take in most of Britain. Knickebein worked by intersecting two VHF beams. Using an aural signal, a pilot flew along one beam until the second was detected, telling him when he was over the target. Like a torch-beam, the radio beam spread as it travelled so, after 180 miles, each beam was a mile wide. But with the help of even a sliver of moon you could get visual confirmation. And, in the case of London, the distinctive loops and bends of the friendly Thames glinted like a curved blade into the heart of the city.

Knickebein was certainly ingenious but – and this had been the RAF's basic objection to radio navigation in the first place – it could be sabotaged by the other side. The RAF's radio countermeasures organisation, No. 80 Wing, was on to the Knickebein operation with impressive speed, with the help of top-secret intelligence provided by Station X at Bletchley Park. The beams, nicknamed 'headaches', were countered with 'aspirins' – transmitters that interfered with the signal. Transmitting beacons were also 'Meaconed': their signals copied and re-transmitted from a British location so as to confuse a pilot and send him flying out to sea rather than over land as he expected. It was a significant home victory for Britain in the Wizard War.

But if, in this 'Scissors, Paper, Stone' game, Knickebein was a stone that could be quickly wrapped up by the paper of British electronic countermeasures, within weeks the British paper had been cut through by the scissors of the more sophisticated 'X-Verfahren' (X-system). And finding a stone to blunt these blades was not going to be a quick or an easy process.

X-Verfahren was a technological generation on from Knickebein, hard to detect and even harder to counter, and its exceptional accuracy had been demonstrated in trials as early as 1936. It, too, used intersecting signals. But each transmitter sent out not one beam but a fan of beams, coarse and fine, which were then picked up by two separate receivers on the aircraft. In all, an aircraft's X-Gerät included two special receivers, two aerial systems with masts, two decoders, two audio units and a clock (X-Uhr) which could be set to co-ordinate 'fall time' of bombs with the aircraft's height, automatically producing the precise moment for release.

This specialised equipment was not wasted on all and sundry. At the start of 1940 Kampfgruppe 100, the sole X-Verfahren bomber wing, consisted of just twenty-six Heinkels He 111 H, of which twelve were fully operational. The wing was then making practice flights, without bombs, over London and the Thames Estuary. On 13th February, Gruppe commander Oberstleutnant Joachim Stollbrock had disappeared off the North Kent coast after an encounter with three Supermarine Spitfires of No. 54 Squadron. If he had crashed on land, and his plane been examined, Britain's cities might have been spared a great deal of agony during the ensuing months.

As they might if the KG100 pilots captured during the Norway campaign had revealed their secrets. But they knew enough to say nothing of their special training, even among themselves. Yet vague comments made carelessly by less knowledgeable air crews began to stir suspicions. Intelligence coming in from Station X was keenly scanned for any reference to the mysterious 'X-system'.

The RAF detected unusual signals emanating from the Cherbourg area for the first time in early September 1940. But, unaware that a few aircraft were equipped with these special receivers, it was thought that they must be for the use of German shipping.

After a varied war service, Kampfgruppe 100 was moved in early August 1940 to Meucon, a small, private aerodrome surrounded by woodland near Vannes in Brittany. The wing's initial role was to target British aircraft factories, docks and other specific targets in provincial cities. But when Hitler had turned his ire on London, Kampfgruppe 100 was there too: eight aircraft arrived in the early stages of the first Night Blitz of 7th September, dropping over fifty HE and oil bombs on docklands before departing.

Its operational records give a clear picture of the wing's life over the next few weeks: September 8/9: *Loge*, 10/11: *Loge*, 11/12: *Loge*, 12/13: *Loge* . . . It was not until October that its London forays were once again interspersed with provincial targets, and on 14/15 November thirteen of its planes had contributed forty-eight high-explosive bombs and over 10,000 incendiaries to the razing of Coventry.

The Coventry raid had been the start of KG100's new career as a pathfinder. As British countermeasures made progress against Knickebein beams, X-Gerät was used to guide other planes in by dropping thousands of incendiaries precisely on target. The fires set by KG100 operated as a beacon to the planes that followed with their heavy bombs.

The Heinkels of Kampfgruppe 100 had eight bomb chutes. Each chute could carry either a single 250-kilogram bomb or four 50-kilogram ones. But now they each regularly held four BSK incendiary bomb canisters, each of which in turn held thirty-six one-kilogram incendiary bombs. Eight chutes, four canisters, thirty-six bombs: a total payload of 1,152 small, lethal firebombs in each aeroplane, and all delivered with precision by a system that British countermeasures could not deceive.

KG100's special place in the destructive raids on provincial cities could not long escape British surveillance, and on 5th December a Fighter Command Operational Instruction had gone out with the information that these leading raiders often approached the coast at dusk and stuck rigidly to a very narrow beam for the last thirty kilometres of their approach:

It is intended to take all practicable steps to intercept and destroy these special aircraft by:

(i) Searching for them out at sea in the afterglow of sunset.

(ii) Intercepting them either at sea or overland by normal methods of control.

(iii) Despatching fighters to locate them in their very limited cone of approach to the target.

Interception at night was, of course, a desperately difficult task. A fighter plane, which was perhaps only as long as a London bus, might have to patrol a sector of night sky that stretched several miles in all three dimensions. But the RAF was now to be aided by Airborne Interception (AI). This was an on-board radar installation – of only three miles' range so far but a development that might yet prove to be the stone to blunt the scissors of X-Verfahren. Just six nights ago, a Bristol Beaufighter from Middle Wallop, equipped with AI, had located a Heinkel III of KG100 in the afterglow and had shot it down over the Channel. It had meant that a thousand fewer firebombs fell on Manchester that night. But it was still very early days both for AI and for the fearsome new Beaufighter.

Chapter Eleven

Home Service SUNDAY
1474 kc/s 203.5m 1013 kc/s296.2m 767
kc/s449.1m 6.145 Mc/s48.82m
5.15 CHILDREN'S HOUR
5.15 'Chanukah'
The light that did not fail, by Maurice Pearlman
A programme arranged by the Joint Emergency
Committee for the Religious Education of Jewish
Children evacuated from London
A story for all ages – 'The Shepherdess'
by Elizabeth Kyle
5.45 Children's Hour Epilogue

BBC *Radio Times* Christmas Edition, 1940

'GOODNIGHT CHILDREN, Everywhere!' Uncle Mac's familiar farewell
ended the programme that had sought today, as on practically every day
since its launch in 1922, to draw listeners together, as families and as a
nation, in a regular, cosy, tea-time ritual. Even though, in many homes
tonight, it had been more of a useful distraction for parents making last-
minute preparations for yet another stint in the Anderson or the basement
or the cupboard under the stairs. And although, in many others, it had
been a painful reminder of family members far away.

Some children had listened tonight in the relative safety of the British
countryside, separated from their parents; others would spend tonight in
the bosom of their families in dangerous London. It would have taken the
wisdom of Solomon to decide which was worse. Hardest fate of all,
though, was that of the 10,000 children of the *Kindertransport*, young
Jews brought out of Europe just before war broke out: listening to the
2,000-year-old tale of their people's miraculous salvation knowing that
their parents, aunts, uncles and cousins were still trapped in the dark,
nightmare world on the far side of the English Channel.

THERE COULD BE FEW more potent symbols of the two worlds now at
war than a document placed on the files of the Education Officer of the

LCC in 1939. It listed 'Schools known to have more than 20 Jewish children' and there were entries against well over a dozen different postal districts in the LCC area. Mostly the schools came in ones or twos, but the number rose to eight in the Orthodox community around Stamford Hill and Stoke Newington, and peaked at sixteen in the E1 area covering Whitechapel, Mile End and Stepney.

The document's sinister appearance reflected not what it was, but what it might have been in the files of practically any other Education Officer in Europe. And – who knows? – for what it might yet become in the hands of some Nazi *Gauleiter* if London ever succumbed to the blandishments or the bombs of the Reich. For the present, though, it remained just what it was meant to be: a list compiled by the LCC, at the prompting of the same committee that had arranged tonight's *Children's Hour*, to ensure Kosher meals were available to Jewish evacuees.

AT THE BEGINNING of October, Josef Goebbels' usually upbeat diary had recorded: 'Serious problems of evacuation of children from Berlin.' When Goering's boast that Berlin would not be bombed proved empty, evacuation had been hastily entrusted to the Nazi Party's People's Welfare (NSV), who had 'proceeded very clumsily in this area', wrote Goebbels testily, and had

> created enormous discontent. And I had expressly ordered that the process should be carried out without compulsion. I summon the ten Berlin Kreisleiters [district leaders] and read them the riot act. They are to warn the local Party branches immediately and bring order back into the situation. Unfortunately we cannot clear matters up through the press. But I hope things will work out even so.

The Führer wanted the situation resolved quickly so Goebbels made a speech and recorded: 'Complete peace has been restored.' But the rumours – that children were being taken away for poison gas experiments – had resurfaced. Goebbels had the rumour-mongers arrested but Hitler was 'quite furious' a week later to find the stories still abroad. Goebbels blamed 'reactionaries, former communists and clericals. The whole pack of them must be eliminated.'

It was hardly surprising if German mothers reacted badly when the NSV knocked on their doors demanding their children. Over the previous year, hundreds of babies and toddlers had been removed, often forcibly, for 'special care', never to return. Midwives and doctors were now required by law to register any child of three or under with symptoms of mental retardation or physical deformity. And the transfer of these children to a 'Children's Speciality Department' signalled death by injection or gradual starvation as part of the Nazi programme to purify the Aryan race.

Adult 'defectives' were also part of the programme of racial hygiene: as things stood at the end of 1940, the Nazi regime had so far killed many more Germans than had RAF bombers. The euthanasia was not discussed openly, but clearly enough information had filtered out to thoroughly frighten the mothers of Berlin.

ON THIS SIDE of the Channel, the British evacuation had not been without its own problems. With a million ad hoc fostering arrangements created over three days at the outbreak of war, how could it be otherwise? But for all its shortcomings, that operation had been Britain's first – and for a long time its only – major campaign victory of the war.

The British Government had decided that babies and toddlers were to be evacuated with their mothers. But even the tiniest schoolchildren headed off to points unknown with schoolmates and teachers, to be met and accommodated by far-flung billeting officers.

The headmistresses of the LCC's Stoke Newington Church Street Junior and Infant schools had called a joint emergency meeting for parents at the start of September 1939, on the eve of departure. One of the teachers recalled the solemn mood in the packed school hall, 'the mothers sitting, the fathers standing behind, mostly in silence', as the headmistresses ran through the drill for tomorrow.

> You will want to see them off so please stand around the playground walls and wave them off cheerfully as they march out. Shed your tears after they have left and please remember the teachers, they also have had to leave their homes and families and they have the great responsibility of looking after your children – a responsibility they all take very seriously.

Amazingly, the next morning the stiff upper lip had held almost intact. 'The children were cheerful,' the teacher, Miss Hellar, recorded, 'the adults also outwardly.'

> And as we marched out of the playground into waiting buses the parents all waved and so did the children. It was a most moving sight – the courage of the children and their parents. The only tears I saw shed that day were those of the young bus conductor who put his head in his little ticket box and wept all the way to Finsbury Park where we disembarked.

At Finsbury Park, the school party had become the responsibility of the hard-pressed railway companies – who were balancing this mass exodus with the equally urgent needs of the troops and equipment of the British Expeditionary Force being despatched to France. The Stoke Newington children were allotted a train to Barnet (where rows of very welcome portable lavatories stood waiting) then another took them on to Stevenage. Here Miss Hellar's group split off from the rest of the school and travelled by bus to a village where they were greeted by the vicar and given a large welcome tea in the village hall by some local ladies. Another bus then took them on to their final destination, where a group of 'Aunties' were gathered on the village green to claim their new family members.

Such complex operations were taking place all across the country that day and the next, assisted, marshalled and eased at various points by the doughty ladies of the WVS.

Some children had been sent even further afield – though overseas evacuation had been available to relatively few parents, and taken up by even fewer. Only 3,000 child refugees had been placed under a tentative Government scheme. Then it was stopped altogether, in the aftermath of the sinking of the *City of Benares,* in which seventy-seven children were lost. Roughly 10,000 children had already been placed abroad privately with relations or foster carers but Winston Churchill, who had always opposed the idea of evacuating children abroad, had stepped in to prevent it for one of his own young relatives: the symbolism of a Churchill fleeing danger was too powerful a propaganda tool for the enemy. Lord Rothschild's children, too, had been kept in Britain by their father, hostages to 'their blasted last name'. 'If I sent those three miserable little things over,' he is said to have remarked, 'the world would say that seven million Jews are cowards.'

TONIGHT's *Children's Hour* had been designed to bring alive the ancient story of the Festival of Lights to Jewish children far from home. But it was also entirely appropriate to the programme's ethos that it should try to help form a bridge of understanding between Jewish evacuees and their host communities.

'Through example in song and story rather than by formal exhortations,' the BBC's first director of education had laid down, *Children's Hour* should foster 'Sound notions on such subjects as fair play, pride of country, personal cleanliness, good manners, thrift, "safety first", sympathy with animals and birds, tidiness in public places, respect for the aged, self-restraint, etc.'

Try to dissect what precisely was meant by 'sound notions', or to un-tangle the easy confidence behind that casual 'etc.', and you came face to face with the British conundrum. For if you were any kind of a chap at all, no further explanation was necessary; if not, then none was possible.

However, lest the *Children's Hour* ideal of the British child smack too much of the lisping, curly-headed improbable paragon of virtue, 1922 had also seen the birth, like the programme's evil twin, of Richmal Crompton's well-meaning but incorrigible William Brown. And you would find plenty of 'Just Williams' at large in London tonight.

In shelters across the city, an army of valiant, kindly women with a robust sense of humour, sent by the LCC and Save the Children Fund, would attempt to keep shelter children peacefully occupied during the hours before bedtime. Though warden Barbara Nixon recalled with amusement that one lady had arrived saying how much she 'loved little children' but had given up after half an hour on the grounds that these weren't children but *'animals'*.

One tactic that Barbara herself found effective, if politically dubious, was to get children to form their own shelter committee, ensuring that 'at least two of the inevitable tough gang were on it'. One nine-year-old – regarded, 'even by the locality, as certain of a scholarship to Borstal' – had proved an exemplary librarian for his shelter's stock of fifteen books. However, during an altercation with a wiry seven-year-old over a box of Meccano, the box had come down 'bosh' on the smaller boy's head, accompanied by the deathless line, heard in political organisations of all complexions down the ages: 'You're not committee – you're only ordinary – you can't have it.'

It was not unusual, wrote London Regional Fire Officer Aylmer Fire-brace, for children to escape the ministrations of parents and shelter mar-shals altogether, and come out during raids to 'assist' the firemen. He heard of a pair of 'treasures' aged about ten who, told in no uncertain terms by a fire officer during one heavy raid to get back to their shelter, had simply retired to a safe distance from which one shouted in righteous indignation: 'T'aint your bloody war, mister!'

In Stepney, the FAU had read children in Nev Coates' shelter *A Christmas Carol*, in installments, climaxing on Christmas Eve. After which Nev, dressed as Santa, distributed presents from the Shaftesbury Society. He'd been Santa again at their party yesterday. There had been Christmas and/or Chanukah parties in most shelters over the past week, and thousands of London shelter children had received extra gifts of sweets, chocolate or money from actor Conrad Veidt, villainous Jafar from *The Thief of Bagdad*. Veidt, already a star in Germany when Hitler came to power, had defiantly registered himself as Jewish (which he wasn't, though his wife was) under the Nazi race laws and had also defied the Führer's personal request to turn down, 'for the sake of the Reich', the title role in a British production of *Jew Süss*. Arrested by the SS, only the vigorous efforts of the London film studios, backed by the British Foreign Office, had got him safely to England, where he had stayed, becoming a British citizen in 1938.

WHETHER TO EVACUATE their children away from London dangers or keep them close had been an emotional labyrinth that parents had to nego-tiate for themselves at the outbreak of war – and then again and again as the threat ebbed and flowed.

West Ham fireman Cyril Demarne and his wife were one of many cou-ples who had brought their children home this Christmas holiday – and would not be sending them back in the New Year. On her latest visit to Wiltshire, Alice had consulted the billeting officer in pretty Bradford-on-Avon on a subject of much debate between her and her husband.

If they were both killed in London and their home destroyed, what would happen to the children? 'I don't rightly know,' the billeting officer had replied. 'I suppose they would be sent to an orphanage.'

'We had seen the effect of bombing over the past three months and did not need to be told that London was no place for small children,' wrote Cyril. 'On the other hand, the threat of invasion seemed to be receding. The kids missed us and how we missed them!' They decided that the youngsters should come straight home with their mother – for good.

They were so young that it took a while for Alice and Cyril to discover what deep fears their little hearts had harboured in their exile: 'There were many older children who fed them lurid tales of London's ordeal.'

With little home to speak of, Bill and Vi Regan had no choice but to leave their girls in the safety of the country. But they had just enjoyed a wonderful weekend in Lidstone with them. An RAF officer driving back to his base had offered to give them a lift as far as west London. It would be a squeeze to get three into the tiny MG, and Bill and Vi would have to travel across London by Tube, but it meant a few more hours with Joan and Little Vi. And, as Bill said, 'Who could resist the chance of a fast ride in the best little sports car to date?' As *Children's Hour* came on the wireless, they had already been speeding past Oxford.

SOME PEOPLE THOUGHT that letting the working class choose where their children lived was simply ducking the issue. Writer F. Tennyson Jesse had impeccable liberal credentials. She had been outraged, for instance, by Lord Halifax's insistence on talking about Christianity's fight against Nazism: 'It is an insult to Mohammedans, Hindus, Jews who are fighting for the same cause.' And she had scored some notable successes against unjust 18B internments with her letters to the *Manchester Guardian* (she had been rung up for details by a civil servant and the individuals had been freed forthwith). But when it came to removing Cockney children from their parents, she believed compulsion was the only answer.

> When one sees the difference that has been made in those of them who have been kept in the country since the scheme was first started, one can have no doubt about the rightness of the plan . . . far better for a whole generation of parents to be penalized by the loss of their children than for the children to be penalized by losing this marvellous opportunity.

She was keen – though not hopeful – that boarding schools would be set up after the war to remove poor children permanently from their parents' pernicious influence.

In truth, though, one of the great discoveries being made in this war and this Blitz was the devastating impact on children of separation from loved ones, as opposed to extremes of danger or relative deprivation at home. Social reformers had focused for so long on what the home life of the working-class children of London lacked, that what it actually provided had been largely overlooked.

Even though they made up the vast majority of its population, the 'h'-less of London had remained something of a heart of darkness to the aspirate classes: just another alien tribe of Empire. Dutch academic G. J. Renier wrote in 1931 that he had discovered Englishmen who were nevertheless human among the 'h'-less – but he had been referring to the rural burr he'd met with in country pubs. He could not speak for the urban equivalent, which was to be seen in its most natural form, he assured his readers airily 'in the police courts'.

Few but social workers and campaigning journalists had penetrated the intimate lives of this alien tribe that was becoming the discovery of this war. American writer Jack London, at the turn of the century, had told London friends that he wanted to explore the dockland slums and they had just laughed. 'But we know nothing of the East End,' they had said. 'It is over there, somewhere.' And they had waved their hands 'vaguely in the direction where the sun on rare occasions may be seen to rise'. Persevering into 'The Abyss' and bartering his gentlemen's clothes for workman's gear:

> Presto! in the twinkling of an eye, so to say, I had become one of them . . . The man in corduroy and dirty neckerchief no longer addressed me as 'sir' or 'governor'. It was 'mate' now – and a fine and hearty word, with a tingle to it, and a warmth and gladness.

George Orwell, going 'Down and Out' in the 1930s, had experienced a remarkably similar initiation: 'My new clothes had put me instantly into a new world. Everyone's demeanour seemed to have changed abruptly. I helped a hawker pick up a barrow that he had upset. "Thanks mate," he said with a grin. No one had called me mate before in my life.' Now, in 1940, large numbers of middle-class Londoners were finding a new world when they put on overalls.

Andrew Butler of St Paul's Watch, in his new day job of Chelsea bomb damage inspector, had discovered the joys of not having to mind where you sat on a bus and being greeted by the conductor as an equal. And a journalist, when training to be an auxiliary fireman under an instructor as 'gentle and patient as a Nanny', was helped along during a tea break by a 'brick labourer' who, he wrote, 'sat beside me, patted me on the knee and succeeded with infinite patience in teaching me a running bowline.' After a dressing-down from a tougher instructor, he had also been initiated into what he liked to call 'the secret proletarian society of the wink':

> In the changing rooms, the canteen, in the yard waiting to parade, in the street, men were always winking at each other. Sometimes a long slow wink accompanied by facial contortions, sometimes a quick blink. At first it seemed a little pointless, even silly – like cockney gestures – thumbs up, etc. – performed out of context by a bad imitator. Then one realized that it meant quite a lot. It was the underdog sign by which those under authority commiserated with each other.

Perhaps 'commiserated' was too strong: the wink, he decided, conveyed a three-part message, 'Never mind. It's all part of the racket. What the hell!'

> By the end of the three weeks I was exchanging some thirty or so pregnant winks a day. I found myself winking at all kinds of people out of training-school hours; disappointed at getting no response I winked harder, then realised I might be taken for a lunatic or worse and glared down at my feet.

ONE NINE-YEAR-OLD Londoner (nine years and thirty-four days old precisely tonight) who was experiencing the warmth of working-class family life amid the terrors of war was Ronald Weir. He had lived through the whole of the Blitz so far right in the heart of London: a stone's-throw from St Paul's at the north end of Blackfriars Bridge, with his mum Rose, dad Gus and older brother Stan. Ron Weir's dad was caretaker of Bridge House, and the family home had been moved up to converted offices at the top of the building when their basement flat was turned into an air raid shelter for the business tenants.

To Ron, if not to his anxious parents, this was a great improvement, since the elevated position gave him a bird's-eye view of the Home Guard's weekend manoeuvres in the road below as they prepared to defend the City street by street. And he could make a splendid battlefield for his own armies of toy soldiers on the hinged lid of the bath in the living room.

During daylight raids, the Weir family had joined the office tenants in the basement shelter. Ron had whiled away one of them by writing a letter full of his Blitz news to his grandmother, which he neatly folded, addressed and adorned with a drawn-on stamp. 'dear nan. this letter is from CORPORAL RONALD WEIR,' he informed her proudly.

> Mum has made me two stripes and Ive got three medals and a home guard band on my right arm and one of the boys out of an office has given me an air gun. I was glad with that book grandpa made for me. during the day I play draughts with Curly Bert Piper & dad. mum does knitting all day long. most tenants bring there typewriters down and make a machine gunning noise. we've got the wireless down the shelter and the tenants like hearing the wireless go until they cut it of and we've got the electric fire down here too. there are several bangs going on while I'm writeing this letter they may be bombs they may be guns we don't know what it is anyway we hope we will be safe in our shelter.
>   well cherio nan we hope to see you soon
>   x x x x x x x x x x x x x x x
>   P.S.
>   Iv'e asked grandpa to give this to you he gets there quicker than the postman tat-a nan
>   We all give you many good wishes to you and Jolly good luck
>   From CORPERAL Home guard – Ron
>   x x x x x x x x x x x

Later, during night raids, the Weir family had the shelter pretty much to themselves. At first they had stayed in their beds on the top floor until the sirens went, when Ron would get from his bed, dress hurriedly and be rushed down, still half asleep, in the lift to the basement amid the noise and flash of guns and bombs. Once safely in the basement, he later recalled, they would then spend some hours sitting half asleep round the electric fire, flinching as the bombs fell, and hoping they would miss them.

This had made everyone so jumpy and bad-tempered that Mrs Weir had moved the family's sleeping quarters downstairs permanently, making beds on the bench seating: it wasn't very comfortable but it was worth it. And the Bridge House basement had just witnessed a cosy family Christmas, with Ron's dad even lighting a proper Yuletide fire in the fire-place of one of the empty basement offices.

AT 5.20 P.M., five minutes into tonight's *Children's Hour*, the first British radar station had reported the first enemy aircraft far out over the sea, tracking in from the direction of the Channel Islands and the Cherbourg Peninsula.

Soon, in the Filter Room at Bentley Priory, growing clusters of coloured tiddlywinks were followed by coloured arrows; the courses of the incursions were told through to the Ops Room, and as the forces built up from other compass points – 'ten-plus raiders', 'twenty-plus raiders' – the officers on the balcony above picked up their phones. The information was fed through to Balloon Control and to the anti-aircraft batteries, and in the Isle of Wight, Solent, Portsmouth, Slough and Thames & Medway the guns began blasting away into the night sky to give the planes a noisy reception as they came over.

But there would not be, as in the bright days of August, calls from sector HQs to fighter stations ready to fling planes and men into the air at two minutes' notice. Earlier today, the Spitfires of 66 and 611 Squadrons, Hurricanes of 145 and 257 Squadrons and Whirlwinds of 263 Squadron had been ordered up against incursions over the south and East Anglian coastlines. The RAF had damaged two enemy planes at the cost of two of their own, with two fatalities. But after dark, Fighter Command's resources were extremely limited, the odds were stacked against them, and the calls made few.

On the table of the Ops Room, the WAAFs used their magnetic wands to push the markers further and further in, and it became clear to the officers up on the balcony that there was no thinning out of the bombers to suggest that tonight there would be more than one target. Tonight they were all headed for London.

Chapter Twelve

DECEMBER 29, 1940
HOME SERVICE
6.0 – Time: News 6.30 – News in Norwegian
FOR THE FORCES
6.0 – News in Dutch and French

Broadcasting column, *Sunday Times*

LONDON HAD ENTERED the world of war once more.

The six o'clock chimes of Big Ben rang out over a river again in darkness (though lifted tonight by just a sliver of new moon). Deprived of electric lighting, gas lamps or even the 'lanthorne and candlelight' of the Elizabethan Age, Londoners had rediscovered the ancient starry night sky above their city, and primeval ambivalence about the moon had returned. 'Bomber's Moon' they called it now, whenever its broad face smiled down benignly, lighting up the snaking Thames for incoming Luftwaffe. Though, as the Air Ministry knew all too well, not even the darkest night, the thickest cloud cover, shielded any of Britain's great cities now.

Citizens of the Capital of the World, now prisoners of the night as much as the cave-dwellers of pre-history, found their new dark haunted by creeping monsters too. In the blackout, simply crossing the road had become a perilous adventure, as shuttered headlamps turned the friendly London bus into a dark and deadly predator. Indeed, some correct Englishmen threw decorum to the wind and let their white shirt tails dangle outside their trousers to warn drivers of their presence.

The odd less-correct Englishman lurked too, though one of Whitehall's rare female senior civil servants had her own answer to that. She had no truck with foolishness: she ran a fearsomely efficient card index from which she could produce an engineer or a statistician for the war effort at the drop of a hat; she had been hard at work on the very first Sunday of the war, summoning specialists from across industry and academia to new roles of national importance. Her time was precious so, if accosted in the blackout, she simply shone her dimmed torch-beam on to her face, said, 'Over forty and very busy,' and strode on.

AT SIX O'CLOCK PRECISELY, simultaneously with the chimes of Big Ben on the wireless, phones began to ring in town halls across London. London Region HQ's switchboard was on the line with a Yellow warning from Fighter Command: German raiders had been detected heading in their direction.

A Yellow did not necessarily herald a full-blown attack: only if a Red followed within the next ten minutes or so would the sirens sound, giving people about five minutes more to take cover before bombs began to drop. That was the theory, at any rate. Sometimes there were warnings but no planes; sometimes planes without warning.

At the Guildhall, Mr Murphy set his team in the basement City Control Room to work on their bank of twenty phones, calling the Yellow through to the relevant City defenders: ARP, First Aid posts, Stretcher Parties, Heavy Rescue depots and key points around the Square Mile.

The same pattern was being repeated from town halls throughout the capital, while London-wide services like the LCC's Ambulance and Auxiliary Ambulance Service, the Fire Brigade and AFS, the utility companies, the Home Guard, the Metropolitan Police and the City of London Police were getting their 'action stations' command direct. The hospitals got their calls too and, on the Underground, trains running on lines beneath the Thames were stopped at the next station they came to, and huge concrete doors were closed across the tunnel entrances to hold back the flood, should high explosive blast the riverbed.

Phone calls swiftly spread news of the Yellow down the ARP chain of command. E. I. Ekpenyon explained how things worked in his borough:

> The borough . . . is divided into divisions. A division or district is subdivided into wardens' posts and each post is divided again into sectors. At the head of a division there is a District Warden and his acting deputies. At a post there is a Post Warden and deputy. In a sector there is a Senior Warden and a No. 2 warden, along with other wardens. All the heads have a certain amount of responsibility. I am a Senior Warden, responsible for my sector.

INSIDE EACH ARP brick shelter, shed and basement, the glow of gas heater and Valor lamp was well shielded from enemy view. But these warm wells of humanity, where the 'poor condemnéd English' once again sat 'Like sacrifices, by their watchful fires', inly ruminating approaching danger, were, in one sense, points of light in the darkness as vivid as the camp fires before Agincourt had been to London audiences of three-and-a-half centuries ago.

What a scene Shakespeare could have conjured out of any ARP post tonight from those, dotted every few streets across his old stamping grounds. For *Henry V* he had drawn, perhaps, on endless alehouse ear-bendings about what had and hadn't been done back in Armada Year, spinning Londoners' memories, sceptical humour and stoic heroism into his tale of a yet more distant past. But tonight, in the here and now and London, there was more than story-telling and play-acting could encompass.

In Southwark, time and experience had given substance to the defiant notice pinned to the wall when Amelia Street's Reporting Post 12 was established:

STANDING ORDER
If the Post is attacked it will resist by every
means and remain until relieved. If the garrison
cannot remain alive it will remain dead – but in
any case IT WILL REMAIN.

Even Shakespeare might have hesitated to invent Post 12's messenger boys, whose wayward and unsustainable appetite for cake and danger was recorded by their Deputy Warden. Tackling incendiaries and pitching in to rescues with gusto, they had acquired, he wrote, 'a fund of gruesome stories which would turn the hair of the oldest soldier'. And these they 'delighted in recounting . . . at meal and other inappropriate times'.

And Shakespeare's boldness in mixing comedy and tragedy, clowns and kings, might have positively trembled before Warden Blainey's latest ditty, written (to the tune of *Any Old Iron*) for Post 12's upcoming Supper and Social:

> Post Twelve up, Post Twelve up,
> Post Twelve up and at 'em.
> With tin hat complete
> We all feel a treat;
> Blooming great rubber boots a'
> Bouncing on our feet.
> HE bombs, incendiary bombs –
> We can all combat 'em;
> With our stirrup pump in hand
> And a bucket full of sand,
> POST TWELVE UP AND AT 'EM.

ERNIE PYLE HAD ARRIVED, he wrote a few days into his stay in London, 'afraid of bombs and also afraid to have anyone know I was afraid. Now I'm only afraid of bombs.' This welcome transformation had taken place when he went to get a haircut. His barber informed him that there would be sure to be a raid along soon enough. 'And I'll tell you,' he added kindly, 'if you don't get a little windy your first night, then you're not much of a man. A fellow who doesn't get his wind up at the first experience isn't a man at all. He's just an animal with no nerves in his body.'

He himself, he said, was a volunteer Air Raid Warden in his home suburb and during his first raid his 'wind up' had sent him straight into a public shelter – where he was so ashamed that he took his ARP badge off so no one knew he was supposed to be out in the thick of it. Four months on, though, he was on standby every night and on duty all night every third night, come what may. And he wasn't afraid at all.

What Ernie didn't yet know was that there were many in London who could tell the opposite story – brave men and women who had performed miracles of courage in those terrible early days but who now went on duty each night sick with fear that this might be the raid when their nerve finally snapped.

Australian Bert Snow was on duty one night with a man 'who had been battling with nervous illness for some time'. The man came close to collapse when a bomb exploded and their ambulance received a glancing blow from flying masonry. But he steeled himself to go on, to the burning gas works they had been sent to. He was off for two weeks after that and, on his return, asked to partner Bert again. 'I accepted this request as a simple and sincere honour,' Bert recalled. 'I was very pleased to drive once more with this brave man, who had overcome so much, and after that night together in another raid, he was never again seriously affected.'

There had not been anything remotely approaching the number of mental collapses expected by the authorities. *PM* editor Ralph Ingersoll had spoken to Austrian child psychologist Anna Freud who was living in the Hampstead home where her father Sigmund had died in exile and where she was now working to set up a special rest centre for children. The Blitz had been a revelation to the psychiatric community, she told Ingersoll. A meeting of London psychiatrists found that, while many of the soldiers retreating from Dunkirk had been understandably shell-shocked, no London practitioner had found a single true case among bombed civilians in the first few weeks. 'You have never seen anything like these people,' she said. 'You wouldn't believe it unless you lived here. They are so calm, and they take it all so well.'

Not everyone was fine: 'In a great city, there are always people whose lives become too difficult for them to handle, but we cannot see that they have been aggravated by the bombing.' In fact, one of her neurotic patients now drove an ambulance and had been very agitated and over-talkative after being in a very bad bombing. But less so the next day. And by the third day she was back to normal.

The British, naturally, had their own explanation for how they held up. The 'two universal solaces' for strain, according to the official Blitz instant history *Front Line*, were: 'Tea and Telling about it.'

> Those who had no more to say than the proverbial 'Couldn't have been more than fifty yards away' – the mere onlookers – were labelled Bomb Bores and frowned or joked into comparative silence. But the real sufferers were allowed, by wise helpers at the Rest Centres and Information Bureaux to
> 'Cleanse the stuff'd bosom of that perilous stuff
> That weighs upon the heart.'

So typical that Shakespeare, rather than Freud, should have sprung naturally to the London chronicler's pen. Though the focus on official 'wise helpers' underestimated how much friends, neighbours or passers-by took on the role of comforter as the situation demanded, well aware that, any day, their positions might be reversed.

The tenderness with which people watched over one another when the need arose was noticed everywhere. The intimacy of the words that crop up again and again in accounts of rescues – the ubiquitous 'mate', and 'dear' or 'love', but also, very often, 'Mother', 'Dad' and 'Son' – brought comfort to both the trapped and rescuers. And where young men on the battlefield called, in extremity, for their mothers, in this fight their mother – or someone else's – was on hand within minutes with a cup of tea and a sympathetic ear.

In extremity, you did what you could then you did what you had to. Bert Snow told profuse and shameless lies during one raid to elderly refugees in a Rest Centre, anxious about the tumult outside. It was only the noise of our guns, he declared boldly, as bombs fell terrifyingly close. On another noisy night, he managed to stop a terrified woman climbing off his stretcher by convincing her that bombs never fell on an already-bombed area: 'The enduring faith that anxious, ill and terrified people had in Civil Defence workers was very impressive.'

For Civil Defence workers themselves, 'Tea and Telling about it' was supplemented by liberal doses of Trench Humour. Great War veterans were wiser in the ways of 'shell-shock' than their commanders had been. And when the usual recourse of black comedy and extravagant obscenity was no longer enough to keep a bloke on an even keel, it was amazing what even a short break 'up the line' could do to repair a shattered soul.

Out in the provinces, some people were 'doing their bit' by giving hard-pressed ARP wardens a rest from the bombing. A letter in the files of one such scheme is worth quoting in full:

34 Devonshire Close W1
Langham 1201

Professor Burn,
Dept of Pharmacology,
Oxford

Dear Professor Burn,
    This is to confirm our telephone conversation of yesterday.

WARDEN DANES Travelling 21st
Mrs Dodds Aged about 62, Warden at Hackney. Has been very ill and is terribly down on his luck. According to the Post Warden (an extremely reliable fellow) the 'boys' have been looking after him. He should be away for a fortnight, but you may find that after a week, or ten days that he is anxious to get back to London to earn a bit of money. It would be kind of you to try and persuade him to stay the full time. He is about 6' 1" and will carry his Warden's helmet. He is travelling on the train arriving at Oxford at 11.25 and perhaps he would be met?

MR HILLIER Travelling 21st
Mrs Yates Warden, Catford. Elderly, ex-professional football player, thick-set, nicely spoken, thoroughly deserves a holiday. *(Perhaps he could be met.)*

MR GREGORY Travelling 22nd
Balliol Bermondsey ARP. Elderly, lost 2 daughters in a shelter incident, third daughter walked out a couple of weeks later suffering from apparent loss of memory. Extremely badly in need of a rest (as you can imagine). Has 8 days. Could he be met too? Should not be separated from his great friend:–

MR NEWLAND Travelling 22nd
Balliol Bermondsey ARP. Elderly. No special details except that, as you know, all Bermondsey need leave.

E BAKER Travelling 22nd
Balliol Bermondsey ARP youngish, deafness due to blast.

MR HAMILTON Travelling 22nd
Mrs Powicke till Tuesday Bermondsey ARP youngish, Irish. I heard this morning that he has been doing great work in our most recent tragedy of Sunday night, when a railway arch shelter was hit. This incident alone would entitle him to a holiday.

173

I will be very interested to hear if you are successful in finding accommodation for Mr and Mrs James Blake and their 18 months old child. It may mean, repeating myself, that the above shelter incident will result in a good few of the Bermondsey people having to have a rest, in which case I will immediately get in touch with you.

With very many thanks for all you are doing for us

Yours sincerely,

Helen Lee

Organising Secretary

The Bermondsey tragedy referred to was the second in which a railway arch at London Bridge had received a direct hit while being used as a semi-official air raid shelter. The earlier incident, at Stainer Street arch, had killed sixty-eight and injured many more. One person with a relative employed 'on the Rescue' recalled that he 'was never right for two or three months after what he saw in there . . . The bomb went right through first and then exploded inside. It was all arms and legs all over the place.'

WARTIME WARDENS were as local as old-time parish beadles and constables, and the individual ARP posts took their tang from the neighbourhood they served. The small terraced houses and flats of Finsbury on the City's northern fringed made up, relative newcomer Barbara Nixon had discovered, 'a community as closely knit together as that of any Cotswold village'.

Out-of-work actress Barbara had found among her fellow-volunteers at Post 2 'railway workers, post-office sorters, lawyers, newspapermen, garage hands' plus 'a few of no very definable profession'. Some full-timers were even harder to pin down:

> Owing to the fact that race tracks, boxing rings, and similar chancy means of livelihood closed down at the outbreak of war, there was a large percentage of bookie's touts, and even more parasitic professions, in the CD services, together with a mixed collection of workers in light industry, 'intellectuals', opera singers, street traders, dog fanciers etc. . . . However although all of us would not in the ordinary way have been called worthy citizens, we had many who were first-class wardens.

Like Southwark, Finsbury had long been a refuge from firm Corporation government: Shakespeare had sent Falstaff and a young Justice Shallow roistering in its bawdy houses; Dickens had located Fagin's pickpocketing academy hereabouts. Present-day Finsbury folk were a mixed bunch, at once local and exotic, like most of London's poorer communities. Many of its terraces' pocket-handkerchief front gardens sprouted hopeful grapevines – evidence of its long-established, settled Italian community.

Barbara had chosen ARP because she wanted an 'active' job – and she got it. In the first week of the Blitz, her 'part-time' hours totalled seventy-eight; in the second, 102. 'I was so determined,' she explained, 'to avoid the usual accusation against voluntary helpers – that they did not turn up – that I overdid it. So did most of the others.'

Wardens visited every shelter on their patch during raids to keep people informed about what was going on outside and help shelter marshals keep spirits up. Shy despite her theatre background, Barbara had found the shelterers as frightening as the bombs at first. She had stood in embarrassed silence among crowds of strangers on 'Black Saturday', while the senior warden 'BB', a Great War veteran, chatted easily with everyone, appearing not to notice the racket outside.

No bombs had fallen on their patch that day. She was terrified, she wrote, 'that I might be sick when I saw my first entrails.' Her test came in another part of London when, as ARP policy dictated, she stayed to assist the local chaps when the sirens went. 'I was not let down lightly. In the middle of the street lay the remains of a baby. It had been blown clean through the window, and had burst on striking the roadway.' However: 'To my intense relief, pitiful and horrible as it was, I was not nauseated, and found a torn piece of curtain in which to wrap it.'

After that, like thousands of wardens all over London, she had, in the common phrase, 'just got on with it'. She discovered the magical power of a tin hat to inspire confidence, and the warm welcome that greeted her whenever she popped her head round a shelter door. Raids became her passport into the community: 'Whereas before few of us had even known our next-door neighbour, within a week people called good morning to one from their bedroom windows, and we chatted in the grocer's as though we were villagers.'

Barbara had eventually signed on as a full-time warden, which required a move to Post 13 near Bunhill Fields, where she was the only woman. She felt out of place at first – but a few judicious profanities dropped into the conversation, and a taste for beer rather than port and lemon in the pub, helped to ease her acceptance into '13' society. The men had all gone to the same school, from the senior warden (a steady electrician) to one man who 'looked like a *Punch* cartoon of a burglar' (and, so far as she knew, was one). Though, Bedales and Cambridge-educated Barbara noted, the respectable tradesmen and 'those who had chosen the more rackety professions' were generally only on nodding terms, as a classics man might be with a modern languages man of the same university.

That the chaos of the first days of the Blitz had evolved, by the end of December, into some kind of workable and above all humane routine was due in no small part to the humour, lively good sense and common decency of such Londoners. 'Go anywhere you want among the civilian workers,' wrote one American, 'ARP, AFS, the auxiliary police or the women ambulance drivers, and particularly among the leading spirits of the big air raid shelters – and you will find them anxious, fretting to do the small, immediate practical thing to make life not only safe but tolerable.' The higher he went 'into official strata', the less concern he found about this 'small, immediate practical thing' and the more about the big picture: 'There must be "plans".'

Bureaucratic thinking sometimes brought vigorous protest from 'the sharp end'. In Southwark, the Reverend J. G. Markham, Senior Warden as well as vicar at St Peter's Walworth, near Post 12's patch, had been nonplussed to find Southwark Town Hall giving out Government subsistence payments for wardens in the form of bread and cheese, Oxo cubes and a small amount of tea. His growing pile of uneaten stale bread and mousetrap cheese was recycled via the Deputy Warden's hens, and he did a deal with a local shelter warden to swap 5,000 salty Oxo cubes for more tea (which, with large mugs of Bournvita and powdered glucose, was the most his wardens could face at night). Official rations, 'became stranger as time went on', he wrote – 'bags of sweets and lettuce leaves' – before the Council finally bowed to pressure and paid out the cash so posts could cater for themselves.

Barbara Nixon criticised her Town Hall too. Though, to be fair, officials seemed to take their responsibilities seriously in trying circumstances. During a memorable shelter altercation over sleeping arrangements with one large and notably forthright lady, more and more senior figures were summoned to try to calm her. Finally, Barbara recorded with subversive glee, a bowler-hatted dignitary appeared. And his dignified 'My good woman, I'm the the Mayor' was met with a robust: 'I don't care if you're the effing 'orse, I want my bleedin' bunk!'

Wardens themselves were used to abuse. Before the war, one distributor of Anderson shelters had been accused, so the story went, of 'fostering war mentality' and informed that

the mere provision of shelters was conditioning the people for a war that need never happen if the decent kindly German people were left to their own devices and not agitated by war-like preparations. The resultant clash of opinion terminated in an all-in wrestling match on the pavement.

During the Phoney War, when their role was mostly enforcing blackout restrictions on others while noticeably maintaining their own morale and volunteer levels with social gatherings, ARP was said down Borough way to mean 'Anging Round Pubs'. But wardens' status in the community had been transformed once the bombs began to fall. Nigerian E. I. Ekpenyon had suffered the extra indignity, at first, of colour prejudice even from his fellow wardens; once the Blitz began, he turned the locals' strange ideas to his – and their – advantage.

It amuses me to know that in the district where I work the people believe that because I am a man of colour I am a lucky omen. I had heard of such childlike beliefs, but I am delighted that such beliefs exist, for wherever my duties take me the people listen to my instructions and orders, and are willing to allow me to lead them. So I am able to control them, which makes my duties lighter in these troublous days.

Reverend Markham's flock in Walworth, 'a very wonderful lot of people', were every bit as much villagers as Barbara Nixon's Finsbury folk across the river. His parish included a cottage estate built by the Church Commissioners, street markets, a colony of boxers including a young Freddie Mills, and a 'miniature Hyde Park Corner' for speakers of all persuasions at the gates of his elegant Sir John Soane-designed church. It was also, he admitted, 'reputed to have a very high proportion of the burglars and other gentlemen known to the police'.

It was a very dull thief who had not tried to secure the after-dark passport that an official badge and identity card provided. The savvy Reverend rejected one would-be warden who claimed: 'I am always first on the scene of any incident. I have a small van and can be on the spot without delay.' Discreet enquiries had revealed that the said van carried jemmies and other tools of his trade.

But while he kept rogues out of his own team, the vicar could do little about a forty-strong volunteer 'fire guard' who patrolled in pairs, much impressing the authorities with their zeal. When raids started, the police returned to their stations to await emergency call-outs. In this bobby-free paradise, one 'fire guard patrol' would lob a brick through a shop window which the next, minutes later, would clear out. The vicar chased them off if he found them at their game but did not inform on them: 'My job both as a parish priest and as a warden would have been impossible, if I had been known to tell tales to the police.'

Even so, he recalled gratefully, he was 'never attacked, never threatened, not even sworn at' throughout his time as a warden, 'although I had to chase would-be looters, discipline wardens, and was a "bloody parson" possibly in the minds of many in the recent past'.

WARDENS' FIRST JOB now was unlocking the public shelters in preparation for a possible Red. Meanwhile, intrepid boy messengers sped off to thump on the doors of those volunteers down for duty tonight. Though no messenger came tonight for Barbara Nixon: she was confined to bed by – of all childish things, she complained – chickenpox.

That Reverend Markham was on duty tonight was a miracle in more ways than one. The day before Christmas Eve, as he was about to light the altar candles for a wedding service, he had noticed a strong smell of gas. Realising that the main must have been reconnected at last, he rushed down into the crypt and turned off a gas tap that had been overlooked in the recent turmoil. Having thus averted either gassing or blowing up the assembling wedding guests, he informed his wife that she would not, after all, have to cook Christmas dinner on the Primus stove with which she had prepared him a hot meal every day for the past two months: ever since their 'incident'.

The crypt of St Peter's, Walworth, designated a public shelter for 230, had regularly housed 600 to 900 people whom nothing could keep out. As with railway arches and Underground stations, memories of sheltering in the much lighter bombardment of the last war had given church crypts an exalted status in local legend. One family at least, the vicar knew, lived down in his crypt almost twenty-four hours a day rather than lose their position. Some arrived nightly by taxi.

Shelter marshals and volunteers had worked hard to keep the crypt as pleasant as possible in difficult circumstances. There was a canteen; young church club members provided music; some of the war's great unsung heroes maintained the chemical toilets; and the shelterers themselves had a whip-round to buy fans to waft the foetid air about. Reverend Markham, who developed a lifelong aversion to the smell of pine cleaning fluid during this period, ventured into the crypt as seldom as possible. He would much rather be out among the bombs with his wardens on their 'blitz bikes, brakeless, lampless' than stepping gingerly between bodies squeezed together on deck chairs, mattresses and benches.

Then, just after midnight on 28th October, two HE had pierced the roof of St Peter's and the floor beneath, exploding with full force on the stone floor of the crypt. Over seventy people had been killed and 250 seri-ously injured; hundreds more had staggered out covered from head to foot in white dust. Two of Reverend Markham's team were among the dead; the rest had rushed to help bring out the injured, aided by an RAF balloon crew from the school next door, who 'worked like Trojans' through the night.

Amid the horrors, the vicar was conscious of the speed with which his report to Southwark Town Hall of 'two hundred-plus casualties' had conjured up medical teams, stretcher parties and Heavy Rescue men from across the borough and beyond. Within half an hour, all the neces-sary services were on hand. Mousetrap cheese notwithstanding, local bureaucracy had delivered the goods when it mattered most.

The crypt of St Peter's Walworth was back in use as a wardens' post tonight. But it had taken Heavy Rescue men in face masks six weeks, working in two-hour shifts, to clear it. It had been a gruesome task: blast had literally lifted St Peter's into the air slightly for a moment and flying fragments of flesh and clothing had been trapped in the gaps between the bricks of the crypt as it settled down again.

While Reverend Markham and his helpers had continued their ARP work by night, by day they had established an area for religious services inside the shattered church. The damaged High Altar had been rolled over the spot where the bodies had lain that night, blood staining the flagstones, until the mortuary vans arrived.

As WARDENS REPORTED for duty to the crypt of St Peter's Walworth tonight, in the heart of the City, members of the No. 2 Watch at St Paul's Cathedral had just finished emergency drill and broken for tea. As soon as Crypt HQ received the Yellow from City Control at five past six, it was rung up to Advance HQ in the Whispering Gallery and the main roofs. The crypt lights were also switched on, gas curtains let down, and the north-west door unlocked to receive residents from the Deanery, Amen Court and other Cathedral houses nearby – though the 'safety' they were being offered was still a matter of some debate.

'At the time of Munich,' wrote the Dean,

> we were most anxious to find out what the authorities wanted us to do about closing the Cathedral in the event of air raids. In the 1914–18 war it had been regarded as a shelter and people caught in the streets had been encouraged to take refuge in it. Was this to be the policy again, or was the Cathedral a dan-gerous structure?

'It would be difficult to convey to the reader the feeling of perplexity which oppressed us,' he recorded. The Dean and Surveyor of the Fabric had interrogated all the official departments they could think of before they came upon 'a harassed man in a small office then in charge of the City's ARP. He said, "I don't think it matters much what you do. If there is a raid tonight we expect 30,000 casualties." After that we ceased to worry.'

In due course, a more considered judgement was given: the crypt was on no account to be used as a public shelter, by day or night. Despite the almost half a million pounds spent on repairs between the wars, there were only a few strong points in the crypt that could be made safe from falling masonry. These were put aside as sleeping quarters for the Watch and for Cathedral staff living nearby. But even these were a gamble.

The fact that it was not to be a public shelter meant there could be no official First Aid Post, so the Cathedral organised its own. Volunteers under the supervision of Canon and Mrs Cocking included a qualified hospital sister, a volunteer doctor who lived nearby and more volunteers from the British Red Cross and St John's Ambulance Brigade.

Tonight, Canon and Mrs Cocking and their helpers set up the first-aid dressing station in the crypt's barrel arch which, protected by the northwest tower, was judged to be its strongest point. Tables and a bed were arranged, water boiled for hot water bottles and a Thermos of tea prepared. One medically qualified first-aider was left below while the others trekked up the 259 steps to the Whispering Gallery, where they would be based for the rest of the night, ready to treat casualties from the roofs. Major casualties were dreaded: before the war someone had climbed up to the Golden Gallery to shoot himself and it had taken three hours to carry the body down the winding staircase. The Dean, who often manned the AHQ phone, reflected that the decision to exclude women from the Watch on the grounds that it would be too taxing for them was rather invalidated by the sterling performance of the ladies of the First Aid Unit.

ON SUCH NIGHTS, looking down from his post in the Whispering Gallery to the floor of the darkened Cathedral ninety-nine feet below, the Dean found the view 'mysterious and romantic'. Andrew Butler's architect's eye had been most struck by the effect when you stood on the floor and looked up. The dim glow, 'amber below and the blue and silver from the moon above', was, he wrote,

> just enough light to show the main lines of the design and to blot out complexities of detail and all the added frippery. The aisles and dark caverns of the

transepts fade into black velvet depths. The vaults and arches seem really to swing above you in great semibreves of rhythm. All the lines are soft and take on the quality of a big sketch in sepia, such as Wren might have done when he was conceiving it. This seems to me to be an instance when architecture reaches the level of great music – and even higher, playing in perpetual splendour.

With the great windows uncovered, lighting was restricted to the single lamp glowing red at the centre of the floor beneath the dome and a green one at the Chancel steps to the east. These allowed the Watch to orient themselves as they navigated the vast gloom by any available starlight or moonlight, and the small signalling lamps they wore clipped to their belts.

Though their purpose was grim enough, Watch members were alive to the comical picture they made: ageing gents in tin hats and rough blue overalls. Before the Blitz, Sir Colin Anderson had written a poem about it for Andrew Butler:

> We seem intruders, Early English louts,
> Shapeless, steel-helmeted and flickering lit,
> Who shock these cultured shades – whose groping flouts
> Their suave humanities.
> St Paul's is fit for an Augustan peopling, not for ours
> And yet, perhaps, our hideous masks conceal
> Minds fuller fledged, for which this dome, these towers,
> May hold content their minds could never feel.
> We who can balance brighter yesterdays with these days'
>   darknesses
> Have quickened ears to seize uncaptured chords.
> Our eyes appraise each fount of stone which mounts and
>   disappears;
> Our senses leave the column and the plinth
> To rise and thread that soaring labyrinth.

Now the clownish 'Early English louts' with their buckets and stirrup pumps readied once again: the ridiculous protecting the sublime.

MEANWHILE, the effect of the Yellow continued to galvanise the hundreds-and-thousands mix of London defenders across the capital. In ambulance stations, Cockney cabbies whose 'Knowledge' of London streets was a godsend in the blackout now worked alongside women rich enough to have learned to drive their own cars before the war. Bert Snow sometimes met intrepid young women on the streets of Poplar who had driven all the way from Westminster, through blazing, rubble-strewn streets, 'towards an area where bombs whistled and exploded with ever increasing intensity'. One nearby station 'was in the charge of a titled lady'.

One twenty-two-year-old from Kensington – in South Wales tonight, as a veteran sent down to help with their blitz – had explained her decision to drive ambulances in a letter to her mother in the country. Her first major air raid had been thundering overhead as she wrote ('One wants something to do to pass the time,' she explained). She had offered herself for night work: 'It will mean 24 hours work a day & something like 168 per week.'

No that's wrong because I shall only be training for five days & I can stand it for five days – but continual warnings during the day are going to be a trial. Anyway I feel frightfully pleased that they want me and it will be a case of training during the day & priceless experience by night. (Here comes another plane in a great hurry and such a welcome of guns for him – the same old throbbing noise.) The more I see of Londoners the more I admire their amazing calmness. True they all look a trifle white & tired, but not drawn and most cheerful & ordinary.

10.35 My God! This is hellish! Over went a plane just now & dropped about six bombs, each one swishing as it dropped. I just crouch terror-stricken with an eiderdown up round my ears, but it has gone away now, and here comes another. Oddly enough I didn't hear the bang of the bombs, so they must really have been miles away.

11.50 Well – we're still alive anyway & honestly I don't find it so alarming except when the bombs fall . . .

1.50 Fancy that. I think I now consider myself quite case-hardened. A bomb came whooshing down then & exploded about as far away as the bottom of Church Street, and I didn't bother to cover my ears for it . . .

3.30 One gets beastly cold at this time in the morning, and I think I must be getting very tired too because that last series of whooshes set me palpitating with alarm. I don't think the last one exploded either but perhaps it was incendiary . . .

5.50 The All-clear has gone & I am going to bed . . . I feel myself that having survived last night I can survive anything. Also I shan't find tonight half so alarming as I shall know just what to expect.

Many male ambulance men were pacifists, like Australian Bert Snow and Nev Coates of the Friends Ambulance Unit, which was just one of the ad hoc bodies that, like the Red Cross and St John's Ambulance, supplemented the official services. The capital's hospitals were a typically London mixture of ancient and modern, public and private, commercial and charitable. But 'for the duration' they were acting in concert.

Wartime London was divided into ten health sectors radiating out from the centre like the spokes of a wheel. Non-urgent cases were treated in a sector's outlying institutions while big central hospitals like Guy's, Bart's and St Thomas' were kept as empty as possible, acting as field hospitals during raids and shipping patients out in converted bus-ambulances. One Auxiliary Fireman remembered his long hours on a bumpy stretcher as 'the worst journey of my life'. But he remembered, too, with gratitude, the nurses who on his arrival had spent many hours patiently removing, one by one, the faceful of glass splinters he had received from a direct hit on his sub-station that killed many on his watch.

St Bartholomew's Hospital – Bart's – prided itself on being the 'Mother of English Hospitals', occupying the same Smithfield site for over eight centuries.

It was into Bart's that, in 1381, the peasants had carried Wat Tyler when he was stabbed by the Lord Mayor (though he was swiftly dragged out again and beheaded), and William Harvey, who discovered the circulation of blood, was numbered among its famous 'Bart's Men'. It had ridden the wave of the Reformation that saw its monks replaced by lay doctors, and it had escaped the flames of 1666 – though barely: Pie Corner across the street marked the limit of the Great Fire. No further off in another direction, the half-timbered gateway to St Bartholomew the Great church was a legacy of a Zeppelin raid: a bomb had sheered away the later plaster façade in the last war to reveal its Tudor heart.

This war had ended the hospital's long lucky streak: both the hospital and its new medical college in nearby Charterhouse Square had their battle scars. Almost as worrying for the treasurer, the blitzing of properties given or willed to the hospital by citizens over the past eight centuries was drastically reducing the rents that paid the bulk of its operating costs.

A First Aid Post outside the gates of Bart's now tackled light injuries during raids, while more serious casualties were treated in the basement where a canteen and rest rooms had been converted into resuscitation wards, a blood transfusion centre and operating theatres (there was a duplicate set beneath another block in case the first was bombed). The top two floors of the medical and surgical blocks on the elegant Georgian quadrangle were empty – too vulnerable – and those beneath were reserved for casualties and acute cases only. The medical school was evacuated: though some students remained to work on the wards and take turns at 'bodging' (bomb-dodging) up on the roofs during raids.

Two days ago, a perky little staff Christmas show called *Nuts and*

Crackers had offered a varied programme including a pantomime sketch complete with Ugly Sisters, a mock ballet – and 'a little inaccuracy in hitting the high notes did not materially affect the success of *Rhapsody in Blue*,' recorded the staff journal review. Within hours, performers and audience alike had been in the thick of Friday night's raid. As high explosive and firebombs fell all around, fifty new air raid casualties had kept not only Bart's underground operating theatres but two of the peacetime ones above in continuous use for several hours.

Patients were only admitted to the wards if absolutely necessary and were shipped out again to safer hospitals within twenty-four hours if at all possible. Nevertheless, this Sunday evening the wards still contained many casualties from Friday's raid. And the last thing Bart's needed was the phone call they got now – Warning Red.

Chapter Thirteen

29th Dec. 1940
18.08 Public warning heard
18.09 Control room manned – Operator informed.
18.15 Patrols 1 & 2 reported on duty
18.15   "   4 & 5   "   "

Fire Picket Log Book, LCC County Hall

ERNIE PYLE had promised people back home that he would try to describe exactly what those air raid sirens that they heard so much about sounded like. The All Clear, he decided, was 'exactly like the lonely singing of telephone wires on a bitter cold night in the prairies of the Middle West'. But the Alert, which was wailing ominously now, had a more complex musicality. 'The sound goes from a low to a high pitch, up and down every few seconds. The result is, if you aren't close to it, it sounds much like a train whistling for a crossing – except that it just keeps whistling for one crossing after another.' There were sirens every fifteen blocks or so. First you heard one – usually from the south; then they were all around you; and then they passed on, away to the north in a matter of minutes: 'It is like a series of great sound waves washing over the city.'

'To me,' wrote Ernie Pyle, 'the sirens do not sound fiendish, or even weird. I think they're sort of pretty.' But then he had not – as he would have been the first to admit – lived in England very long. More established Londoners had, over the past four months, developed their own feelings about 'Moaning Minnie'. To most, it was a signal that sent them hurrying to their own chosen place of safety; for many, it was a summons to their own chosen place of danger.

SEVERAL MILES UP, the ten Heinkels of Kampfgruppe 100 were bearing inexorably down on their target from the south-west on a path laid down by the X-Gerät. Not that pin-point precision would be required of this raid. Tonight it was not a single factory or installation that was to be obliterated. And fire was to be not merely the pathfinding prelude to destruction but its purpose. Kampfgruppe 100 was minutes away from delivering 10,470 firebombs into the heart of the British Empire. And that would be just the beginning.

At twelve minutes past six, London's anti-aircraft guns started up as the planes came within range of ack-ack batteries' detectors, and powerful searchlights began swinging across the sky, sometimes catching the silver gleam of the huge barrage balloons tethered on metal cables, floating high above the roofs of London. Ernie Pyle, fascinated by these balloons, had asked what happened if all those miles of cable became untethered. 'Plenty happens,' he discovered. 'The cable folds and wraps itself around buildings all over its particular section of town. This doesn't happen often, but when it does I would just as soon be elsewhere.'

Pursuing his task of conveying the reality of raids to Americans back home, he identified anti-aircraft fire as 'like thunder in a violent electric storm'. He had wondered how close the guns would be, but they had turned out to be all around. And, he wrote, 'When they are very close they sound as though lightning were striking within a quarter of a mile. They shake the floor and rattle the windows.' He had not been around for the start of the Blitz, so had not witnessed the absolute joy that spread across London when, after the first few terrible days and nights of listening to bombs screaming down – without, it seemed, any way of fighting back – this new noise had split the air. But he soon recognised how possessive people were about *their* gun: they told all their friends stories about it, and were quite annoyed if it was moved away.

The unacknowledged fact was that ack-ack shrapnel killed more British people on the ground than Germans in the air, but the effect of the guns on London's morale was incalculable. Like the various mysterious winkings and blinkings and bangs high above them – and like the news of raids on German cities, and the progress against the Italians in North Africa, and the gallant resistance of the Greeks – the fact that freedom was giving the Axis a taste of its own medicine kept despair at bay. 'There are millions of people in this world who fear that England may eventually lose this war,' wrote Ernie Pyle. 'Such an ending is inconceivable to the British.' On Christmas Eve, in what he called 'typical British conversation', a chambermaid had told him: 'I'll never forgive that old Hitler if he gives us a blitz on Christmas Day.'

> The attitude of the people is not one of bravado. It is no self-injection of 'Do or die for dear old Siwash'. It isn't flag-waving, or our own sometimes silly brand of patriotism. In fact, I've never seen or heard the word patriotism since coming here.
>
> No, it is none of these. It is simply a quaint old British idea that nobody is going to push them around with any lasting success.

However good ack-ack was for London's morale, its more immediate effects were swiftly borne in on two young men on the roof of Jackson Brothers in Old Street, north-east of the City. When the sirens went, fire-watcher Stanley Champion and his colleague Howard had been in their basement with their opposite numbers from papermakers Grosvenor Chater, whose factory was at the far end of the yard. In their haste to see what was going on, they forgot to grab their tin hats before they pounded up the stairs to see what they could see – a decision quickly reversed as ack-ack barked out and shrapnel began descending all around them.

In south London Leslie Paul, who had only just arrived back home from his Woodcraft Folk party when the sirens went off, found it a perilous business getting to the shelter. It seemed clear to him almost immediately that this raid was going to be something out of the ordinary.

AT THE SIREN'S cry, company fire patrols all over London went into action. Many City buildings were locked and shuttered for the holiday weekend but at Hitchcock, Williams & Co., naturally, there was no slacking. General Manager Mr Lester, who had lived there day and night since the war began, commanded the firewatchers, while Mr Hugh, instigator of *The Log,* was the Williams brother on duty tonight. At the heart of City government, Mr Munson and seventeen-year-old Mr Lott of the Remembrancer's Office were dispatched to the west and east roofs of the Guildhall. And over the river at County Hall, the Fire Picket got ready to defend the headquarters of the London County Council.

Just south of London Bridge, sixty-year-old Elizabeth Barnicot began the difficult task of shepherding her off-duty nurses to the shelter at Guy's Hospital. She had trained as a nurse here many years ago and had returned to help run the medical staff quarters. It was no easy ride: one Sunday, after working twenty-two hours without a break, she wrote to her daughter that she felt very well but 'for all sakes' she would say they must have help. The porter had his Saturday half-day, she explained, and the maids and other women staff were sent to the shelter as soon as the sirens went, but the three nursing staff were expected to just carry on – and 'the nurses won't stay put'. 'Some do and some don't,' she wrote, 'so at every warning we have to go to every room as they try to remain in them and they hate going to earth.'

The 8th December raid had been her worst experience so far: 'The stream of bombers over us and the noise of flares and then incendiary bombs, and then the real huge bombs falling was a perfectly awful nightmare.' Though, as with so many other people, she had slipped this information in among much other family gossip – of presents (Christmas crackers, and dolls, and a boot scraper for Anthony), food (Ursula's pullets were laying well) – and sendings of love.

ACROSS LONDON, Rest Centres prepared for another night in which the 'Rest' in their name would be even more of a misnomer than usual. A fortnight into the Blitz, Nev Coates of the FAU had volunteered to help out in one such Centre and found a 'spot of chaos'.

> Over 100 people, from old people to babies, living communally in the hall and classrooms, sitting and standing about, fellows and girls smoking, plenty of noise and no fresh air, and all in the gloom of a few hurricane lamps. Discipline was bad and the officials were not expecting us, didn't know where to put us, and didn't give us jobs . . .
>
> The people were of the very poorest and as the night got older the smell and stuffiness got stronger. We admitted some people during the night from a bombed house close by. One old man was pretty badly shocked and whimpering. Later in the evening he got up from his mattress on the floor and would have urinated in the corner of the room, but I caught him in time and took him to the proper place. The proper place was a cloakroom with two huge buckets, already full, so the old boy had to use a wash basin. This horrible arrangement is because the lavatories are open in the school yard, and people must not go out during an air raid . . .
>
> My impression of these homeless slum people was that they were acting like cattle, and what was worse, were being treated like cattle. The four chaps from the Pacifist Service Unit were the only ray of light in the place . . . It is rather surprising that these centres were chosen for the job at the time of the September 1938 crisis and that when the first refugees moved in the places weren't even blacked out.

But the following night the WVS had moved in to take the Deptford Centre in hand and Nev was sent on to Lambeth. 'I saw the difference immediately I got inside,' he wrote in his journal.

> The place was very well organised, and the efficient workers treated the refugees like human beings. The refugees themselves were well behaved, and one or two helped. The staff consisted of three women and two men, with a homeless policeman and his wife helping, so that I had very little to do . . . It could be that in places like Stanley Street in Deptford are in the minority. Let's hope so. The people in some of the places where I've been are very cheerful and making the best of a bad job.

Miss Hellar, the teacher evacuated with her Stoke Newington pupils in

1939, had not been able to persuade her mother to join her in the country, so had answered the LCC call for volunteers for the beleaguered London Rest Centres when the Blitz began. She now commuted from home in Winchmore Hill to working-class Clapton, where three headteachers, two younger teachers and the elderly Miss Clarke ('three generals, one non-com and two privates') cared for hundreds of homeless people every night. A nurse had volunteered to sleep there after her shift at the hospital, and taught them all to turn their shoes upside down before sleeping. She had treated many bad injuries caused when people woke quickly after a bomb fell and thrust their feet into shoes full of glass splinters.

Their twenty-four-hour shifts began at midday and, besides providing a cold supper and dealing with any new influx from each night's raid, the teachers provided refugees with a hearty breakfast before work (which for some was as early as three, four or five o'clock). Their speciality was porridge, cooked all night in a huge cauldron, with plenty of milk and a whole tin of golden syrup. They usually managed hot water for the men to shave with and, thanks to the wise generosity of the WVS, each woman was given a little bag with a 'comb, hair grips, hair pins, hankies etc.: These were greatly appreciated.'

Working residents ate lunch out, but a hot meal was sent in for the elderly, who often relished not only the food but the companionship. 'Little Eadie', rescued by firemen when her top floor flat was sliced in half by a bomb, had not wanted to be rehoused at all and had offered to pay to stay on at the Rest Centre. But there were always newly homeless people needing each place.

Temporary residents spent most waking hours chatting, playing cards, singing or even dancing. They were, recalled Miss Hellar, 'wonderfully cheerful considering that all had been bombed out and lost their homes and many had lost family and friends'. But people depended on one other to maintain that curious mass calm. During one raid, the calm broke. Miss Hellar heard the singing stop amid shouts and screams, the heavy pounding of feet and 'a horrible sound like moaning and baying from the panic stricken people'. A young woman with mental problems had gone berserk and tried to strangle a girl sitting next to her. Though she was quickly restrained by a couple of residents, others were spooked by the sudden commotion and ran upstairs in panic. They were only slowly persuaded to return to the ground floor, while the volunteer nurse conducted the girl and her parents to a securely guarded room to wait until the raid was over and an ambulance could be summoned.

THE SIREN WAS NO respecters of persons, and there was a particular dread of being caught on the toilet or in the bath. Tonight's wail caught lab technician Sidney Chave soaking in the bath in south-east London but he didn't panic. It was a nuisance, but he wasn't going to rush to get dried and dressed and run outside to their Anderson. It was a freezing cold night, and he could hear his wife Lee preparing tea downstairs. He would go down to join her and they would sit in front of the fire and eat their tea in peace – of a kind. If things got too hot upstairs, they would join baby Jillian, already asleep in the back room which they had judged to be the safest in the house.

Not far away, in West Norwood, Nell Carver, home from the CTO, took to the kitchen with her mother and elderly aunt. No cold, damp Anderson for them either. To many, though, these brilliantly simple pieces of engineering had proved little heroes of the Blitz. They were not protection against a direct hit by a high-explosive bomb – very little was – but, packed round with earth, the Anderson was remarkably effective protection against blast, which was a big killer, and shrapnel, which was another. Nell Carver's mother had been quite right about the damp though: inevitable in what was, essentially, a covered hole in the ground. The airing of bedclothes became a twenty-four-hour task if you were to ward off illness, especially in the depths of December.

The Chaves and Carvers were not that unusual. In fact, their relatively relaxed approach to shelter was far more typical of Londoners than that of the much-publicised Tube dwellers, who actually accounted for just six per cent of the capital's population. Use of the Tubes as shelters had been forbidden – they were not designed for the purpose and many afforded little real protection. But direct action by the public had soon taken care of official regulations. And the authorities, bowing to the inevitable, had set about trying to ensure that the tunnels didn't kill more than they saved.

Epidemics were a constant fear in all forms of public shelter through this winter and Sidney Chave, a laboratory technician, was currently working on a medicinal snuff to keep disease at bay. It might work, it might not – that was science. 'Boffins' all over Britain were secretly trying all sorts of things that sounded even more unlikely.

A small multinational team at Oxford University, for example, had high hopes of fungus. German Jewish refugee Ernst Chain had read an old scientific paper, written in London by Scot Alexander Fleming, and alerted Australian team leader Howard Florey to the bacteria-killing properties of *Penicillium notatum*. Ingenious Oxford technician Norman Heatley had managed to extract enough active ingredient from this mould for some lab tests, in which it had killed a deadly bacteria injected into mice.

Trials on humans would require thousands of times as much so, with money and industrial capacity in short supply, Heatley had spent Christmas Day in the lab seeding hundreds of cheap ceramic 'bed pans' with spores. He had built a Heath Robinson apparatus out of rubber tubing, parachute silk and an old bookcase discarded by the Bodleian Library with which to extract the active ingredient from the fungus. If it grew, and if the apparatus worked, the first human trial of this 'penicillin' might begin in a few weeks' time.

While about a quarter of London's population used public shelters of all kinds, and another quarter took to their Andersons, about half of all Londoners simply stayed indoors. They took to basements, like the Speeds in Brixton, or a room strengthened for the purpose, like the Chaves, or just slept as normal in their own beds, trusting to God and the law of averages to keep them safe.

One family shored up the basement of their West Hampstead home with railway sleepers and it did the job – as they discovered on the night when a near miss violently shook the house and deposited the dust of years on their heads. But at only about five feet high, it meant you kept banging your head on the gas and water pipes. And there was nothing to do, recalled the son of the house, but listen to your own breathing grow louder and more sinister in the silence between the sirens and the drone of bombers overhead.

> The candles would flicker vigorously at the reaction to our heavier breathing and shadows would dance on our faces . . . As the house shook with the vibration from the heavy anti-aircraft guns, sited on the long railway wagons only a couple of hundred yards away, the coal dust would trickle down from the heaped coal, and perhaps a spider would scuttle out of harm's way.

He was up on the roof of the Cambridge University Press building in Euston tonight, watching for firebombs, and happier to be so.

In the outer suburb of Sutton, Viola Bawtree's basement was an altogether more welcoming place: still decorated with the tinsel, glitter, ivy and fairy lights she had put up for Christmas. Viola had also pinned up some of the Victorian Christmas cards she been sent as a baby. She hadn't needed to wait for the siren's call tonight to come down. She was less intrepid than her siblings – Christmas night had been the first time since the raids came to Sutton that she had spent the evening above ground. She had forced herself to stay in the dining room to be sociable while the others played Beetle that night, but when 'the loudspeaker started comic stuff' she had gratefully slipped away to the basement.

JUST OFF LEICESTER SQUARE, the audience's laughter at the antics of Adenoid Hynkel, Dictator of Tomania, could not drown out the sound of sirens. *The Great Dictator* was briefly halted and a message flashed on the screen, directing anyone who wanted to leave to the shelter below. No one moved, and the comic business resumed.

Bill White, sitting with Marguerite in the circle of the Gaumont Haymarket, decided to stay to the end of the movie. So did Derick and Mary of Hoare's Bank, enjoying the glorious Technicolor of *The Thief of Bagdad* at Leicester Square Odeon. *Gone With the Wind*'s matinee audience at the Ritz was already setting off for home and one of the big talking points was bound to be the spectacular Burning of Atlanta. The producers had re-dressed sets from *King Kong* and Cecil B. de Mille's Jerusalem from the silent *King of Kings* and had set fire to them on a Hollywood backlot at a cost of $25,000. Three 5,000-gallon water tanks had been needed to quench the flames afterwards. It had been well worth Londoners queuing for ages on a freezing cold day like today to see a spectacle like that.

Chapter Fourteen

Time of call	18.15
Place	108, Stamford Street, SE1
Name of occupier	Unknown
Business	Private
Supposed cause of fire	Incendiary bomb
Damage or other particulars	Passage on fourth floor and contents slightly damaged by fire, heat, smoke and water.

Air Raid Fire Calls Daily Returns, 29th December 1940

PERHAPS SOUTHWARK Fire Station's clock was running a little slow. By Luftwaffe reckoning, it wasn't until seventeen minutes past six that the pilot of the first Heinkel 111 of Kampfgruppe 100 opened a bomb chute and released his first four BSK canisters. They fell through the air for a few moments then broke open, spilling out their incendiaries over a wide arc. At intervals of around three minutes, the other nine planes of the Gruppe started to drop their canisters too.

Between them, the ten aircraft of KG100 would drop incendiaries at a rate of more than 300 firebombs a minute for the next half hour: over 10,000 in total. And there were about ninety further German bombers following them into the target area. 'It is going to be a warm night,' remarked one laconic roof-spotter to journalist Ritchie Calder, as the 'Molotov Breadbaskets' disgorged their tiny burdens in seemingly endless procession.

Mr Munson, who had rushed up to the eastern Guildhall roofs as soon as the sirens went, had been scanning the sky for ten anxious minutes when he saw the first incendiaries fall in the City – or heard them, rather. High-explosive bombs were often fitted with cardboard or metal tubes so that they screamed rather than whistled as they fell, to terrify even before they destroyed. But the sound of firebombs rushing through the darkness was ominously gentle – like a heavy rain shower, according to one person; the rustling of autumn leaves blowing along the pavement, said another. The Dean of St Paul's wife, who was making up beds at that precise moment, thought that the sound was like a series of coal-scuttles being emptied on to the floor outside.

Up on the City rooftops, though, the evidence of his eyes made it all too easy for Mr Munson to resolve the sound into what it really was: hundreds and hundreds of firebombs. He heard 'for some seconds a prolonged swishing noise which gradually increased in intensity', then saw points of light flare up as the incendiaries hit surrounding buildings – and his own. Downstairs at Fire Squad HQ, Mr George received calls for assistance from his No. 1 Post and No. 2 Post almost simultaneously, and gave both Mr Munson and young Mr Lott permission to leave their posts to tackle the scattering of bombs that they could already see burning around them on the Guildhall roofs.

Malcolm Clark of the *Daily Herald* was being driven through the City when he saw an incendiary crash through the window of a radio shop nearby and flames start to shoot up inside. He and his driver both got out and clambered in through the broken window to put out the flames – just as the incendiary exploded, spraying out burning thermite and metal in all directions.

One in every ten incendiaries was now primed to explode after burning for a short while: a recent sophistication on the basic firebomb that was specifically designed to target and intimidate firewatchers. Information about this new development had been succinctly incorporated into the instructions given to members of the St Paul's Watch:

Explosive IB
Explodes half a minute to five minutes after impact – dealt with as IB with pro-
viso that cover must be taken.

The *Daily Herald* men had not taken cover but the driver had escaped injury. As for Malcolm Clark, as his colleague Ritchie Calder later record-ed, 'It was the old but true story of the wallet which averted death': a bomb splinter was deflected from his heart and ripped through his side. Ever the newsman, Clark insisted on being driven back to the office to report his adventure before heading off to hospital.

At Jackson Brothers in Old Street, firewatchers Champion and Howard, racing back down to retrieve their tin hats, heard a loud swishing noise fol-lowed by light thuds, signalling firebombs in the yard outside. Grabbing buckets of sand, they ran up and out into the yard with the Grosvenor Chater men and found several incendiaries burning on the ground by the emergency exit. Once these were successfully dealt with, they looked up to see a glow from the top floor at the far end of the yard: fire had broken out in Grosvenor Chater's stationery factory. The Jackson men were just about to go with their friends when they realised they had no time to spare for Grosvenor Chater's fire – there were flames up above in Jackson Brothers too.

Deeper into the City, incendiaries were clattering down on the Aldermanbury roofs on the western side of the Guildhall. An office messenger spotted them from a window in the Corporation Engineer's Office and managed to put some out and kick the rest over the parapet into the street below. These were then dealt with by passers-by and some of the shelterers in a basement of 18/19 Aldermanbury, who had answered their calls for help.

You didn't see these little firebombs falling but, when they struck the street, Ernie Pyle later explained to his readers, they 'bounce crazily like a football, splutter violently for the first minute, throwing white fire about thirty feet, and then simmer down in an intense molten mass and burn about ten minutes more. It is said they burn at a temperature of 2,000 degrees.' If they were in the street they were easily smothered by sand: 'Common ordinary citizens have smothered thousands of them.' But if they landed on a roof, burned a hole and dropped though, it was a different matter – as other journalists, working at the Associated Press building in Fleet Street, were currently discovering for themselves.

Looking down from the roofs of St Paul's Cathedral, the glitter of magnesium flares on the ground, seen through the bare branches of the winter trees below as they sputtered and burned out harmlessly on the pavement, had a strange and terrible beauty which seemed somehow in keeping with the Christmas season. It was the first time tonight that the incongruous splendour of the growing catastrophe had been noted – it would not be the last.

In her basement in Brixton, May Speed listened to the raiders overhead. '6.20,' she noted. 'Chug chug go the engines. Planes going over in a steady stream.' And she heard the shattering response of the anti-aircraft guns. Two fire engines raced along the road outside, and she thought of Fred, out on ARP duty. 'Planes continue to come in a steady stream . . . Looks like a brutal night again.'

At the same moment, just three minutes after the first bomb-release, the first phone rang in the City's ARP Control Centre in the Guildhall basement. Then another, and another. Soon all twenty lines were in constant use as Mr Wells of the Chamberlain's Department and the other operators under Mr Murphy's command took down details of fresh falls of incendiaries across the Square Mile and relayed the details as best they could to the emergency services – when they could find a fire station with a line free.

195

SOON, IT WAS NOT just incendiaries falling. The pathfinders of Kampf-gruppe 100 were joined over the City by the next contingents of tonight's raiders: eight Junker 88s and eleven Heinkel 111s from I/KG 28, eight more Junker 88s from I/KG 51 and nine Dornier 17s from KGr 606. Circling as ack-ack shells burst around them, they spilled out thousands of incendiaries. But high-explosive bombs of various sizes were falling too – and not exclusively over the Square Mile. In south-west London, Sidney Chave and his wife Lee decided to abandon their fireside: 'It got rather heavy, the planes were flying low and several bombs were dropped so we went under cover near Jillian in the back room.' The tea washing-up would just have to wait.

In the West End, the entire balcony of the Gaumont Haymarket cinema waggled back and forth 'slowly and majestically, for about ten seconds' as a large bomb exploded some distance away. One man had given a graphic description of a typical scene in a cinema during a raid:

> Rather a close one came down and the building swayed unpleasantly. The audi-ence let out a momentary, collective, giggled 'phew', then was suddenly quite silent, waiting to see if it was a singleton or one of a stick, then said to itself, 'quite near enough for me, thank you' and began to prepare to leave with much feeling for hats and clicking of handbags and banging of seats tipping up, and then, just as though it was one person it changed its mind, sat down again and saw the film through. Only two people left.

Sitting front row centre of the Gaumont, neither Bill White nor his companion 'mentioned the waggling', but both realised things must be hotting up outside.

In Fleet Street, the cluster of press agencies around St Bride's had never been closer to a news story. At 6.31, Whitefriars Fire Station received a report from an air raid warden of a sixty-pump fire around Shoe Lane, where an area of approximately 1,000 feet square was severely damaged by fire and collapse. At 6.32 they despatched ten pumps and a turntable ladder to St Bride's church. And at 6.33 they received another call from '20 Tudor Street, Associated Press of GB and AP of America'.

Night copy boy Fred Backhouse had gone up to help the Associated Press men, who were trying to tackle the fires started by the three incendiaries that had landed on their roof. Down below, those on St Bride's had quickly melted the lead and fallen inside. Journalists, doormen and copy boys rushed out from the Press Association, Reuters and the Press Club as soon as flames were spotted. But while some incendiaries were quickly extin-guished, another fell far beyond their reach and took hold. It soon became obvious that nothing could be done to stop the building burning, though they could still salvage some of its treasures. The brass lectern was reputed to have been man-handled out of St Bride's during the Great Fire in 1666; tonight it emerged triumphant once again.

Above the rescuers' heads, Wren's tower, with its distinctive tiered spire, modelled on the classical Temple of the Winds and echoed in a million British wedding cakes, blazed with light. And inside the tower, St Bride's famous bells, bearing their good wishes from history of 'PROSPERITY TO ENGLAND' and 'PEACE & GOOD NEIGHBOVRHOOD', sat in their burning wooden bell cages, awaiting their inevitable fate in silence.

IN OLD STREET, Champion and Howard dashed up the stairs again to tackle the fire on their upper floor. At the top of the stairs, Howard threw open a door – and was met by a wall of flame. In the matter of minutes that had elapsed while they were dealing with the incendiaries down below, firebombs had set the contents of the room ablaze. They had only a couple of buckets of water and a stirrup pump between them and this was no job to tackle alone. Stanley Champion volunteered to race back downstairs to get help from sub-station 68Z, about 200 yards away in Baltic Street School.

First, though, he had to brave Old Street, which was littered with incendiaries. Head well down to get maximum protection from his tin hat, Stanley began to dodge between the burning bombs lying a few yards apart. As he got halfway across, some started to explode, showering metal shards on the wall behind him. If he had been running before, he was even faster now, and as he gasped out his message he felt he had reached Baltic Street in record time. It was only on his return journey, as the swish of falling incendiaries mingled with sporadic explosions, that he realised that Jackson Brothers' crisis was just a tiny part of what was in store for the City tonight. As elsewhere across the capital, the firebombs' silent approach, and the relative scarcity of 'screamers', left many people on the ground unaware of just how many small fires were being started.

'All large fires start as small ones,' the Government's pre-war leaflet on *Fire Precautions in War Time* warned: 'Once a fire gets out of control you cannot tell how fast it may spread.' As the City's hundreds and thousands of small fires took hold and became bigger fires, and then joined up to make bigger fires still, the Government's warning had never been more prophetic: 'However strong the Fire Brigade may be, an outbreak of many fires all close together and beginning at the same time would be more than it could successfully deal with *unless the householder himself and his family took the first steps in defending their home.*'

The homes of most City workers were far away and they were still at home in them. There were many thousands of people out on this freezing cold night, ready to protect the City. But there were also many thousands of buildings. And tens of thousands of firebombs.

IN CLERKENWELL, at about twenty-five to seven, a senior LFB officer was called to a fifty-pump fire in City Road – but he couldn't locate it. What he did find, though, as he went along City Road was a thirty-pump job at Dingley Road, with another twenty pumps needed for a fire in Central Street. When he informed the mobilising officer at No. 66 Station Clerkenwell, he responded that he already had calls in for 400 pumps. Good water had been accessed from the hydrants in Peartree Court but he couldn't get through to district control to order on more pumps as all of 66 watchroom's phone lines were clogged with incoming calls.

'I "take off my hat" to the Watchroom staffs, men and women,' AFS man Frank Hurd had written in one of his essays. '*They* are the people to thank for getting fires attended as soon as they break out. When a big raid is in progress they are hard at it, often all night, under pretty tough conditions.' Frank was on duty again in Euston tonight when the bells went down. He wouldn't have to hang on to his engine all the way to Docklands tonight though: his 'heavy' was destined for Smithfield, the disused meat market on the fringe of the City, opposite St Bartholomew's Hospital.

Up on the west wing of the Guildhall roofs, young Mr Lott of the Remembrancer's Department could see that the incendiary he was tackling was caught in the ceiling of No. 3 Committee Room and that other members of the fire squad were down below, trying to get at it from there. He poked at it until it fell through and the men below played a hydrant on to the small fire it caused.

Mr Fitzhugh of the Chamberlain's Office had been still struggling into his overalls when the call came through that an incendiary had dropped through the roof into the lobby. He rushed out without even changing into his gumboots. But by the time he got to the Hallkeeper's door he saw that it was already being competently tackled, so reported straight to HQ where Mr George dispatched him up to the roof to help young Lott, while Mr Byford was sent to assist Mr Munson at No. 2 Post.

Mr Munson had smothered two IBs on the east wing quite easily with sand, but there was another on a ledge over one of the glass roofs of the Art Gallery. It was out of his reach and when he sprayed it with his stirrup pump, it only burnt more fiercely. But reinforcements arrived and, with persistence and some hard pumping, they managed to get it out.

Another fire had sprung up in the kitchen over the Art Gallery, so Mr Munson ran back to his post and rang down for more men to tackle it from the inside. When they broke the door down they found a firebomb burning its way through the floor of a cupboard and it was only with considerable difficulty that they managed to extinguish the flames. Then came a shout: 'The CIV Room is alight!' As the others scrambled downstairs to deal with this new emergency, Mr Munson reported in at his post and began gathering and refilling the emptied buckets and putting them back in place around the roofs for when they would be next needed.

In Old Street, Stanley Champion had arrived back at Jackson Brothers with a three-man AFS trailer pump crew. But it soon became apparent that they would not be able to get control of the inferno that the top floors of the factory had now become. As the firemen worked on regardless, Howard and Champion realised their stirrup pump could do nothing to help save the old firm now, and decided to make themselves useful at 68Z. Heavy units and taxi pumps were racing out from Baltic Street in all directions and for the next hour and more the two Jackson Brothers firewatchers would run back and forth through the blazing streets carrying information to and from the officers in charge of fires. On one return journey, when they were lucky enough to get a lift in the van hauling a trailer pump, they would hear debris hitting the roof as it bumped along.

Sub-station 68Z Baltic Street reported to No. 68 Station Redcross Street, where things had seemed pretty calm at first. The sirens had gone, and the Watchroom staff started taking calls but each one seemed to indicate only a smallish fire. The four girls who manned the phones were young – their company officer was only twenty-one – and Jean Savory and her friend grumbled that, working nights inside their heavily sandbagged station, they had never, in all these months, seen a 'proper fire' for themselves. Station Officer Waterman – 'a wonderful man, no panic or shouting, he just got on with the job and expected you to do the same' – offered to oblige. He took them out into the street and pointed out several of the small fires that they had already logged, including 'the Cripplegate

Institute going up nicely in spite of a TL [turntable ladder] at work', recalled Jean later, and the girls went back to their phones satisfied.

Messages that came in from sub-stations, wardens, police or 'by stranger' (direct from the public) were entered both on paper and on the situation boards on the wall, so that they could be quickly matched up with available pumps. When an appliance was dispatched to an incident, the relevant disc was moved from one set of hooks to another and the Occurrence Book updated. As with the girls of the Ops Room at Fighter Command, small, precise and focused actions created a clear, up-to-date picture for the officers watching the dramatic situation develop.

Though the picture did not seem out of the ordinary yet inside 68, at London Fire Brigade HQ in Lambeth, which was collating reports from stations across the capital – and, crucially, from the Observation Posts set up in the highest buildings across London – the picture that was building up was not a pretty one.

To many people on the ground, it was already clear that their own building or patch of ground was going to have a pretty hot time of it tonight. But as more and more local information was passed up along the chain of command, the bigger picture was starting to emerge. Across London, and on both sides of the river – though very much concentrated in the City – hundreds of small fires were becoming larger fires as they outstripped both the firewatchers' and the fire service's resources.

And in the heart of the City, larger blazes were starting to join together into 'conflagrations'. North of St Paul's, fire was already poised to snatch command of an area of around 135 acres – more than a fifth of a square mile – from the firefighting services. And the raid was not yet half an hour old.

ERNIE PYLE had watched himself accustom himself to Blitz life with the fascination of an anthropologist. The first time he heard plane engines overhead, it took a while to register that they were not just the traffic noises that he might hear in Washington or Los Angeles. When he did realise what they were, he found he couldn't keep his mind on his writing. In fact he wasn't really aware of just what he was doing. But when he finally went to bed, he had been amused to discover that he had been obsessively tidying things – stacking his cigarette packets in a neat pile, sorting his letters, and laying out everything on his desk in neat rows.

He wrote of lying awake for hours after the guns suddenly stopped, only to be followed by a 'single ghostly "wooo-isshhh" and thud in the darkness'. This, he confessed in a letter to a friend, 'damn near scared me to death.

My heart stopped a few seconds waiting for the explosion, but it never came.' The next morning he was told that, no, that was not an unexploded bomb – just shrapnel from the ack-ack falling to earth.

Now, as he sat in his Savoy hotel room with the satin-lined curtains drawn, the quick bitter firing of the guns outside told him that 'there was to be no monkey business this night'. That 'boom, crump, crump, crump, of heavy bombs at their work of tearing buildings apart' sounded very close at hand.

At about a quarter to seven, he and a bunch of other newsmen made their way through the corridors to the south-east corner of the sixth floor and out on to a darkened balcony that commanded a view: 'a third of the entire circle of London', from the South Bank, across the river and right across the City.

'Some day,' Ernie Pyle wirelessed back to his office in America many long hours later,

> when peace has returned to this odd world I want to come to London again and stand on a certain balcony on a moonlit night and look down upon the peaceful silver curve of the Thames with its dark bridges.
> And standing there, I want to tell somebody who has never seen it how London looked on a certain night in the holiday season of the year 1940.
> For on that night this old, old city was – even though I must bite my tongue in shame for saying it – the most beautiful sight I have ever seen.
> It was a night when London was ringed and stabbed with fire.

Ernie Pyle, who had scarcely witnessed an air raid before in his life, was now watching a sight that was almost beyond belief:

> As we stepped out onto the balcony, a vast inner excitement came over all of us – an excitement that had neither fear nor horror in it, because it was too full of awe.
> You have all seen big fires, but I doubt if you have ever seen the whole horizon of a city lined with great fires – scores of them, perhaps hundreds . . . The closest fires were near enough for us to hear the crackling flames and the yells of firemen. Little fires grew into big ones even as we watched. Big ones died down under the firemen's valor, only to break out again later.

The sound of high-explosive bombs – sometimes only a few seconds apart and sometimes with as much as a minute between them – did not, he learned from his more experienced companions, compare to the incessant din of those first September raids. But what they did hear coming down now were showers of incendiaries – hundreds, perhaps thousands. From their vantage point they saw two dozen go off in a matter of two seconds.

They flashed terrifically, then quickly simmered down to pin points of dazzling white, burning ferociously. These white pin points would go out one by one as the unseen heroes of the moment smothered them with sand. But also, as we watched, other pin points would burn on and soon a yellow flame would leap up from the white center. They had done their work – another building was on fire.

Their eyes turned, as did so many this night, to St Paul's – or where St Paul's ought to have been. For there ahead of them was the largest fire of all, with flames whipping up hundreds of feet into the air. And, above that, all they could see at first was a great cloud of pinkish-white smoke. Then gradually – so gradually that they thought they might be mistaken – the great dome began to take shape. It looked, Ernie thought, like 'some miraculous figure that appears before peace-hungry soldiers on a battle-field'.

As they surveyed the scene, the picture was, literally, awe-inspiring. The blacked-out streets were now in half-light from the glow of the fires.

Immediately above the fires the sky was red and angry, and overhead, making a ceiling in the vast heavens, there was a cloud of smoke all in pink. Up in that pink shrouding there were tiny, brilliant specks of flashing light – antiaircraft shells bursting. After the flash you could hear the sound.

Up there, too, the barrage balloons were standing out as clearly as if it were daytime, but now they were pink instead of silver. And now and then through a hole in that pink shroud there twinkled incongruously a permanent, genuine star – the old-fashioned kind that has always been there.

It was, he said, the thing he would always remember above all the other things in his life. 'The most hateful, most beautiful single scene I have ever known.'

THE LITTLE MG that was carrying Bill and Vi Regan home towards London was flagged down by the police at a checkpoint just outside West Wycombe. It was really dark now, and Bill could see the lights of London ahead, around thirty-five miles away. The police said that their driver, as military personnel returning to base, could go on through, but that the Regans ought really to think about looking for digs in Wycombe. When Bill and Vi said they wanted to get home, one of the policemen pointed significantly towards the glow in the sky. With a shock, Bill realised that the city lights that he had casually registered were actually a great fire: 'In a mere two days of village life, we had lost all memory of the war.'

Even so, they didn't want to be stuck out here for the night. So Bill lied that if he didn't get back to Heavy Rescue he'd be classed as a deserter. 'What about the lady?' asked the policeman. 'I want to go home,' said Vi. Bill waited. The two officers look at each other for a moment, then one jerked a thumb towards London, and said, 'Off you go and be careful.' They went.

As THE REGANS sped on towards London by car, senior clerk B. J. Rogers was making his way in to the City on the Metropolitan Line. Since Stanmore was towards the outer edge of the Tube network, he found that it was necessary to sleep at the office the night before in order to guarantee that he was at his desk first thing on Monday morning. Felicity Ashbee, who sometimes made the same journey in from Bentley Priory, found that it was only on those days when her shift ended at five in the morning that it was even worth taking a chance on a quick trip home. From Stanmore overground station, she would catch the first train ('if it was running'). Then, as it neared London, it slid into the underground tunnel system: 'We would come up in Trafalgar Square, to trample through shattered glass and tangled fire-hoses to see if there were any trains from Charing Cross for a dash down home. Surprisingly, there often were!'

It was never pleasant to sit in the dark during a raid, and trains were often machine-gunned by low-flying planes. Still, Mr Rogers hadn't worried unduly when he heard the sirens ululating through the night as his train pulled out of Wembley Park Station: once the train entered the comforting enclosure of the tunnel, the carriage lights would be turned on again and he would stay safely underground all the way to work. There were a couple of changes of line, through crowded tunnels full of people sheltering from the raid (generating a smell that Felicity Ashbee evocatively described as a cross between the monkey house at a zoo and a gent's urinal), and then, at Bank station, it would be up the steps to street level and fresh air, just a hundred or so yards' trot from Mr Rogers' office at the Bank of England, in the heart of the City of London.

Chapter Fifteen

6.50 Incendiary on Library Floor.

Occurrence Book: Advance HQ, St Paul's Watch

AT ST PAUL'S CATHEDRAL, lack of water had been a problem almost from the start. The Surveyor of the Fabric, working with the Dean, used mains water to extinguish the Cathedral's first firebomb of the night, which had burned through the roof above the Library Aisle corridor. It left a scar on the floor – evidence, wrote the Dean afterwards, of 'my one little positive contribution to the defeat of Hitler!' Shortly afterwards, though, the mains supply failed. So, too, did the dry riser, a vertical pipe through which they should have been able to pump up extra supplies to the roofs in case of fire.

'The Watch was now forced back on their reserves and had to rely entirely on stirrup pump and sandbags,' wrote the Dean.

> How we blessed the prescience of our commander who had insisted on having our supplies of reserve water augmented in case of an emergency like that which we now confronted! Tanks, baths and pails full of water with their complement of crowbars, shovels, and other fire-fighting equipment were now liberally installed in all the vulnerable parts of the building and were so arranged that men approaching the scene of a fire from any direction would be certain of finding the necessary appliances to hand.

The IBs were falling in thick showers, and observers on the *Daily Telegraph* roof saw a cascade glance off the Cathedral dome and fall on to its roofs below. Some penetrated but burned out harmlessly on fire-resistant levels beneath; others lodged in the roof timbers. With stirrup pumps working from above and below, each one of these took about three-quarters of an hour to put out. 'The lower squad had the additional discomfort of being drenched by the pumps of their more elevated colleagues,' the Dean recorded.

As they battled on with stirrup pump and bucket, no one in the Watch realised that the Cathedral was in even more spectacular danger until the Watchroom at Cannon Street Fire Station called through the urgent message that there were flames issuing from the dome above their heads. Down below, in offices that were themselves surrounded by flames, American journalists were rushing to cable across the Atlantic that this was the Second Great Fire of London and St Paul's itself was burning once again.

One of the shower of incendiaries had hit the dome and was stuck half-in and half-out of the lead shell. The phosphorous was burning fiercely and the lead melting around the bomb would inevitably let it fall. Inwards or outwards? If inwards, then the journalists had their story all right.

All members of the Watch had been fully occupied extinguishing fire-bombs so there was no one on dome patrol. By the time anyone got to this incendiary, flames would already have hold of the timbers and, in the great airy cavity under the dome, the fire would become an inferno. If the timbers burned, then the outer dome would collapse. And if the brick cone inside fractured, the massive 850-ton stone lantern, ball and cross that topped the Cathedral could come crashing down. Down through the inner dome to the floor where the red lamp glowed 300 feet below. And down into the crypt, where it would explode like a bomb, causing who knew what havoc. As men raced up to the Stone Gallery, there was nothing to do but pray.

'I have to confess,' wrote the Dean afterwards,

> that it is uncertain how the bomb came to fall. Was it that by some means it was dislodged or did it fall by its own weight? I incline to the latter opinion because, so far as I know, no member of the Watch claims to have had any part in producing the result. At any rate the Cathedral was saved from one of its most perilous predicaments, whether by human means or by what we call 'accident'. In either case we thank God that our great church was spared at the moment when the situation looked almost hopeless.

The teetering bomb had fallen outward, on to the external Stone Galley, where it was easily extinguished by members of the Watch.

Down below, meanwhile, the crypt was suddenly plunged into darkness. It must have been something pretty major that was hit because, at the same instant, the lights went out over at the Guildhall too. The City Control Room in the basement, which had been fielding a flood of calls, informed the utility company and worked on by emergency lights. By the dim lamps in St Paul's crypt, the man on the book at the Crypt HQ desk consulted his watch and recorded an explosion 'very close', on the Paternoster Row side of the Cathedral at nine minutes past seven. Outside, the Cathedral was already ringed by fires: off-duty members of the Watch, who saw an ominous glow in that part of the sky where they were accustomed to seeing the Cathedral, had dropped everything and were already en route for the City.

ACROSS THE RIVER, fire patrols at the LCC's home of County Hall were being kept busy too. Though the handwriting in the LCC Control Room Occurrence Book remained steady throughout, occasional crossings out and interpolations showed how difficult it was to keep up with the pace of events. There were four entries for 18.55 alone: The New Inn, when contacted about a fire seen by Fire Patrols 4 & 5, said their warden was satisfied that there was no fire there; 4 & 5 had then confirmed that there was fire on the fifth floor of the North Block and had 'suggested presence of ammunition'; 4 & 5 had 'asked for assistance'; Fireman Bonniface had reported that he had extinguished his incendiary on the Members' Terrace; and he – '& (later) "Reserve"' – had been sent to assist in the North Block. All this within the space of a minute.

At four minutes past seven, the Fire Brigade arrived at the North Block fire. At seven minutes past, Control recorded 'Heavy detonation heard' and, at almost the same moment, Mr Dowd of the Chief Engineer's office confirmed that, yes indeed, there was ammunition at the seat of the fire in the North Block.

Things were not as serious as they seemed, however. At eight minutes past seven, Patrols 4 & 5 rang in again, large as life and twice as indignant, to report that, when they had arrived: 1) they were impeded by many people, including some soldiers; 2) that the door had been 'partly hacked away' ['and damaged *not* by fire picket', added Control in the margin] 'and therefore the door could not be unlocked'; 3) that extinguishers were tried through broken panel; and 4) that Brigade now had the fire in hand.

IT WAS, recorded Nell Carver, 'very unpleasant' sitting in the kitchen in West Norwood with her mother and aunt tonight, listening to the planes coming over. And they 'dodged under the stairs several times' when the planes sounded to be right overhead. But though the Germans seemed to be flying low, she didn't hear anything dropping nearby: they were, she feared, going up to Town tonight. She was right. And in Town her dear old CTO was, like the rest of the GPO headquarters, at the very heart of the night's action.

The GPO fire guards had been coping well with the showers of incendiaries falling on their various buildings. But, at seven o'clock, burning embers and debris were blasted in through every door and window of the Wood Street telephone building by an HE, putting the automatic switchboards on the sixth floor in peril. Even automatic calls sometimes had to be completed manually, so while some of the workers went down to the

206

basement shelter to work on the old manual telephone switchboards, others soldiered on through the smoke and heat above. There was plenty for them to do: this was turning out to be a night when everyone, it seemed, needed to speak to everyone else, top priority.

At London Region HQ in Kensington, the calls coming in from LFB HQ at Lambeth, and from borough controls across the capital, made it clear that the London Fire Brigade was finally face to face with the spectre that had haunted it from its birth. Major Jackson, having only just begun his first brief holiday, had been informed and was driving back at top speed to take control of events. The Lord Mayor of London was also coming in. His predecessor had famously dismissed early news of the 1666 Fire with the words 'A woman might piss it out' – it was not a precedent to follow.

The extreme vulnerability of City tinderbox had been one of the constants of Aylmer Firebrace's working life for twenty years. And now that his worst nightmare was coming true, there was little he, personally, could do about it. He had just been moved, somewhat against his will, to the Home Office to make a start on nationalising the fire service. But he felt that he just had to get out there, on the ground – his ground – to get a picture of what was happening. As he drove through the City with his senior staff officer, he could see that an 'ugly' situation was developing in Queen Victoria Street south of St Paul's, and serious fires were developing, too, over the river in Southwark: London Bridge Station and the buildings in the Station Approach were already in flames.

The heavy shower of incendiaries falling over the roof and forecourt of London Bridge station was by no means the first test the Southern Railway had been through. Scarcely a day had gone by since the Blitz began without a raid on some part of its network. In daylight, train tracks lined with factories directed a bomber's flight path along an almost unmissable, miles-long target. And it didn't take much illumination at night to reveal the huge, distinctive footprint of a major terminus or marshalling yard to the target-hungry aviator. That was true for any railway company within bomber range, but none was more vulnerable than the Southern, which commanded the links between the Channel ports, the south coast and London.

Over one week last summer, hundreds of trains from all over the country had transferred a third of a million dazed and defeated men from Dunkirk along Southern track to relative safety. Nell Carver had seen old men stand and raise their hats as they went by. Southern Railway's cross-Channel steamers, fresh from their own historic role at Dunkirk, had then been sent to bring thousands of Channel Islanders to new homes on the mainland. And Southern trains, as busy as any in the first mass evacuation from the capital at the outbreak of war, were soon in use again for the re-evacuation of those children who had been relocated, in the easy confidence of the Phoney War, to the seaside. These alarums and excursions over, Southern Railway's job had been, like everyone else's, to maintain boring old business as usual: to deliver its freight and its commuters each morning, no matter what the previous night's blitz had thrown at it.

There was a fire squad on duty at London Bridge station tonight and other staff, police and troops around to give a hand: their incendiaries would be dealt with. But there were empty buildings and warehouses around London Bridge station with no one looking out for them. And even as the railway crews were able to report with satisfaction that all their own firebombs had been dealt with, flames issuing from nearby premises showed that the worst of the night was yet to come. Now the first priority became to ensure that all empty rolling stock, and all staff who were not actually able to help, were clear of the danger zone.

Opposite London Bridge station, noted Commander Firebrace, 'an uncontrolled fire was in progress' at Guy's Hospital. Such firefighter-speak signifies more than at first appears: Fleet Street hacks might talk glibly about any and all fires 'blazing out of control'. But when the ex-head of the London Fire Brigade, ex-fire chief of London Region and Home Office adviser on a National Fire Service says you have an uncontrolled fire on your hands, an uncontrolled fire is just what you've got.

Inside Guy's, Elizabeth Barnicot already knew that the nightmare of 8th December had been surpassed. A shower of 'bombs of every sort' had been raining down all around for the past quarter of an hour and, with fires raging around the south end of London Bridge, efforts to get a call though to the local fire station were in vain. The lines were permanently engaged.

While one man continued to try to get the Brigade on the phone, the rest of the hospital's air raid wardens tackled incendiaries as they fell. Using the hospital's own stored water supply, they extinguished many fires before they properly took hold. But ultimately it was a hopeless task: IBs were dropping constantly, it seemed, over the whole hospital and water reserves were soon exhausted. By ten past seven, when the local fire station finally took their call, a high-explosive bomb had also severely damaged the four-storey surgical block. And by the time the fire engines arrived, the crews found the nurses' home roof burning, Jesus College burning, the roofs over Elizabeth Barnicot's own balcony burning . . . fires all over.

Despite the Luftwaffe's best efforts, Fleet Street began this last Sunday of 1940 still looking much as it had in the last summer of peace (*top*), but, from his Alpine retreat, the Führer of the Third Reich was planning the most spectacular news story ever for journalists working at the Heart of Empire.

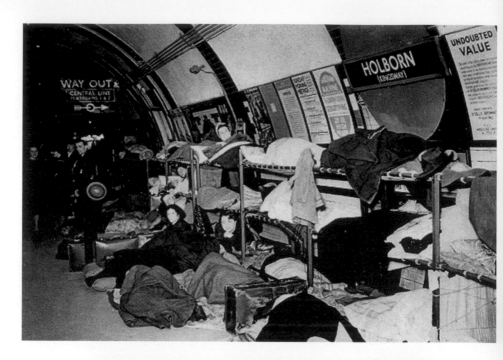

Over four months of Blitz, the extraordinary had become commonplace. Londoners now prepared to spend their nights in bizarre locations from the bowels of the Underground (*top*) to high up in St Paul's (*above*).

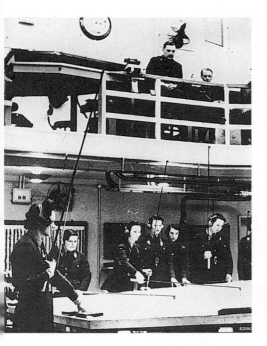

Information was key to controlling chaos. The RAF (*top left*), London Fire Brigade (*top right*) and a hundred other services collated data and fed it up the line, minute-by-minute. At the heart of London's defences, Regional HQ (*above*) was located among the museums of Kensington. At its head was Ernest Gowers (*foreground*): 'one of the greatest public servants of his day' (*The Times*).

Looking down from St Paul's as the fires took hold, the situation looked desperate (*top*). On the ground, it was more desperate still.

Artist Leonard Rosoman's memories of the horrific 'incident' he witnessed in Shoe Lane were captured in this painting, first seen in an exhibition of work by firemen-artists in 1941.

The total area of destruction was immense, though its extent was only gradually revealed to view as dangerous structures were demolished. Soldiers (*above*) help businessmen salvage what they can of their workplaces.

The BBC's lunchtime broadcast of the 'Arsenal of Democracy' speech by President Roosevelt (*top*) helped to lift spirits. Individual casualties of the night such as St Bride's (*above left*) were all too obvious when the Prime Minister and his wife visited the City on Monday afternoon (*above right*).

Though Ludgate Hill was a scene of chaos, the dome of St Paul's rose triumphantly over it, still – and Fleet Street had its story.

When Bank of England clerk B. J. Rogers reached Bank Underground station at the end of his long journey, he found it even more packed with shelterers than he would have expected for a Sunday night. The exit that he usually used appeared to be closed off so, following the voices of Underground staff calling 'This way out', he made his way through the network of long pedestrian tunnels, stairs and escalators connecting Bank and Monument stations. This would mean he had a longer walk to the office. It also, as it happened, meant that he emerged from the Underground just a stone's throw from Pudding Lane.

When he made his way up and out into the open air, Mr Rogers realised for the first time the full import of the ordered chaos below. As he wrote afterwards to his daughter, he saw to his horror that

> it was as light as day, with huge fires all around, flames rising far above the houses, the place full of smoke and sparks and great blobs of burning stuff floating about, and every now and then a bomb.

It took a minute to register this unexpected turn of events. Then: 'Well, I thought, I must get to the Bank somehow, so I started off at a trot up King William St.'

Just as he reached the junction with Lombard Street, he recognised the ominous whistle of a high-explosive bomb coming down close – very close. He 'flopped down on the pavement in terror', and was almost stunned by the concussion and crash of walls as the bomb exploded.

It was some time before he realised that he had sustained no injury – the bomb had fallen on the far side of the Lombard Street buildings, which shielded him from the explosion and blast. 'I pulled myself together,' he wrote, 'and eventually reached the Bank, passing a lot of police and wardens rushing towards the scene of the explosion.'

Inside the thick, safe, insulating walls of the Bank of England, other members of staff looked up in some astonishment as Mr Rogers stumbled in, 'covered with ashes and mud and perspiration'. Though the Bank's own firewatchers were hard at work up on the roofs, down here at ground level, behind their sturdy doors and thick, windowless walls, no one had had any idea that tonight's raid was proving to be something out of the ordinary. Soon – after a welcome 'wash and brush up' – Mr Rogers had recovered his equanimity too. And, as he settled down gratefully to some supper, he did allow himself an extra glass to celebrate his escape.

In Poplar, wardens stood in little knots watching the glow in the sky over the City. This area, focus of so many raids past, was pretty quiet so far. Well, 'quiet' was a misnomer, given the thunder of the Isle of Dogs ack-ack battery. But there had been no major incidents as yet and one of the wardens was heard to say, 'They're ignoring us, the cocky so-and-sos, ignoring us.' At Blackwall Police Station, Sergeant Grey was still seated comfortably in his office chair with his feet up on the desk when, at around ten to seven, he heard a car draw up outside and saw the man from the Home Office walk right in.

Sergeant Grey had been one of the officers called in to Scotland Yard for a round table discussion about improving interaction between police and ARP at 'incidents'. A Home Office expert had said that he would visit the station one night when there was a raid on. 'The old cynical distrust of leaders from the back row bobbed up,' confessed Sergeant Grey, and a sceptical comment had 'slipped out without trying'. But now here was the civil servant, true to his word.

At that moment, there was the unmistakable sound of an approaching stick of high-explosive bombs, 'marching, one by one' towards them from the direction of Greenwich just across the water. Sergeant Grey sat look-ing at the expert, feet still on the desk, and the expert looked at him. 'I told you I would come and see you,' said the Home Office man, and explained to the policeman what was happening tonight in the City. Then he left.

'He must have thought I was the rudest or the coolest man he would ever see,' wrote Sergeant Grey later. 'I still retained my original position as the bombs came over across the River. He could not have guessed my feet were locked together and I couldn't move them. The lace tags on my boots had caught up and I couldn't undo my feet – I was stuck.'

Two men had acquired another 'bomb story' for their collection – though their interpretations of events might differ. But on the far side of the Thames in East Greenwich, the other kind of bomb story was unfolding. A bomb had hit Glenister Road School, used as a sub-station of No. 54 Fire Station, East Greenwich. (Things could have been worse: no fatalities, one fireman slight-ly injured.) Other bombs in the stick had been more destructive, inflicting severe damage on forty-one houses in Conley Street and twenty-nine more in Commerell Street. But it was Blackwall Lane that got the worst of it.

The parachute mine had originally been devised for use at sea. But Hitler's 'secret weapon', which could make harbours fatal to ships, had been thwart-ed early in the 'Wizard War'. The ingenious 'de-gaussing' process allowed ships to sail over them without setting off the magnetic trigger. So now the mines devised to attack sailors were dropped by parachute on cities – and the effect was devastating.

St Paul's Cathedral

Lister's Timber Merchants had been totally demolished together with nine shops, Greenwich Town Social Club was badly damaged and there was a hole in the road about the size of a London bus. (This had quickly become the standard yardstick for estimating the size of craters – someone once wrote she had seen one as big as a bus garage.)

Dyson House, four storeys of LCC 'model dwellings', had been hit too and there were many dead and injured. The first priority for the first ARP warden at any major incident was to get accurate news up the line through the local Reporting Post. This could be the hardest part of the job: having to run *away* from the site, perhaps leaving the injured screaming or crying out for help. But it was a vital part of the system – the only way to ensure that the right kinds of help were summoned quickly enough to save lives. Doctors and ambulances, fire and rescue crews, stretcher parties, police, mortuary vans, even the canteen vans and tea cars of the WVS and Salvation Army, Church Army and YMCA, all waited on that first call, and on that first warden on the scene who was to be their eyes and ears.

The Reporting Post rang news of the incident through to the Fire Brigade, and details of location and approximate casualties to Borough Control, which then mobilised all the other services. This was followed up by a detailed M/1 form, which had to be filled in and biked over to Borough Control. But services would already be on their way long before it arrived at its destination.

The precise administrative process varied from borough to borough, but that recorded in minute detail by the Borough of St Pancras was fairly typical, once more giving the lie to the belief that London's Blitz was purely a matter of 'muddling through'.

A small permanent staff was bolstered by volunteers, who took turns for twenty-four-hour shifts. This meant doing their normal council job during the day (unless there was a raid), working in the Control Room all night, then back to their normal job the next day. Weekend duty, especially Sundays, was the short straw, taking you from nine o'clock on Sunday morning straight into the beginning of another working week.

In the Message Room, permanent staff – 'headphones on, message pads in front of them, pencils well sharpened all ready' – manned six 'IN' telephones while volunteers manned six 'OUT' phones. These and the dedicated Fire and Police phones were under the eye of the Message Room Supervisor, and a Log Clerk sat near the door. Meanwhile, in the middle of the Control Room was a table map of the area, round which the Controller and various other officers responsible for front-line services, from Heavy Rescue to Highways maintenance and repair, were gathered.

From the time of the warden's first call, the paper trail began.

Each message was taken down in quintuplicate by the 'IN' telephonist, checked by the Message Room Supervisor and passed to the Log Clerk who gave the incident an occurrence number (used for all subsequent messages about the same incident), entered it in the log sheet and passed it to the OC Report Centre. Here the parties to be dispatched were entered on the form and the top copy (of the five) passed to the Resources Officer to mark out the number of parties despatched on the Tally Board. This top copy was then taken back to the Message Room and the 'OUT' telephonist ordered out the necessary parties, wrote out the time of completion, initialled the form, and handed it to the records clerk to file.

The Controller or Sub-Controller in the Control Room kept his own carbon copy of each message. The other three carbons went to the Medical Officer of Health, who shared it with the Heavy Rescue Officer; to the Plotting Officer, who marked the incident on the Control Map; and to the Liaison Officer, who passed the details up the line to Group. When the M/1 form arrived direct from the ARP Reporting Post, any extra information given would be fed through the same channels as officers consulted on what further help, if any, should be sent.

The Controller and Sub-Controller, who worked alternate twenty-four-hour shifts, were also responsible for ensuring that the police and public utilities companies like gas, electricity and water were informed; that road blocks were reported to HQ, ARP and Ambulance Stations, and that all homeless people had been taken to Rest Centres. If possible, they also went out to individual sites to interview the Incident Officer to make sure all that could be done was being done for the homeless.

Out in the field, the Incident Officer – usually a senior warden, or possibly a policeman, depending on who got there first (and perhaps with a bit of argy-bargy between them) – took charge on the spot to ensure co-ordination of the various services and the passers-by who often pitched in to help. Messages would fly back and forth from incident to Reporting Post to Control as the situation became clearer and needs more defined.

Treating the walking wounded or getting them to a First Aid Post was one priority; getting the homeless away another. Before they disappeared, though, shocked and distressed people had to be questioned carefully to ensure that they had given the wardens all the information they could about who might still be trapped under the rubble and where they were likely to be. The success of Heavy Rescue's tunnelling could depend on it.

Unless fire took hold at an incident, which brought problems of its own, night rescues took place in the same profound darkness that applied everywhere. The strong lights supplied by the authorities were rarely used because local people objected: they didn't want to be a target for a second time. Falling shrapnel from the ack-ack barrage was an ever-present danger too, though wardens, police and rescue workers at least had their tin hats on, painted with each service's identifying letters for quick recognition in the dark.

As ambulances, stretcher parties and cars for 'sitting cases' took the more serious casualties off to hospital, first-aiders on the spot took care of the walking wounded so they could be conducted to Rest Centres for a cup of hot, sweet tea. But if there were many trapped, as here at Dyson House, a mobile hospital unit with a doctor and nurses would attend. Doctors were often called on to perform emergency medical procedures *in situ* and one common task for doctors was to wriggle down into a tight spot, through the tunnels created by Heavy Rescue, in order to give morphine injections. Trapped survivors might face many hours of agony, perhaps jammed up against dead or dying friends and family, before they could be brought out safely.

The full extent of this Dyson House incident would not be clear to anyone on the ground for some time. But the official record alone tells something of its unfolding story. There were eighty casualties in all, it was reported. James Chater, aged fifty-four, dead at number 20, and James Churchill, thirty-six, at number 42; Amelia Field, forty-two, was rescued from number 46 but died later in hospital. Arthur Rackstraw, twenty-five, visiting at number 50, was killed outright, as was Robert Rudrum, thirty-five, at number 51; Charles Thompson, fifty-two, at 52; John Moyle at 59; Frederick Garland, fifty-one, at number 62 and George French, sixty-one, at 71.

Frederick Newman, aged fourteen, was rescued from number 68, and Mary Horn, twenty-four, and Albert Lockey, twenty-nine, were both brought out alive from number 60, but all three died later in hospital. Also killed nearby was Home Guardsman Albert Webb, aged seventeen.

The fact that, unusually, no husband and wife died together in the Dyson House incident points to many successful rescues amid the chaos of destruction: only a dozen fatalities from Dyson House itself. Only a dozen. Only a tiny fraction of the more than twelve thousand deaths of the Blitz so far. But what worlds of pain and grief spread out like ripples from each one.

Chapter Sixteen

> 19.30 Bomb just whistled down. Planes, planes,
> planes and more planes. Still they roll on.
>
> May Speed's diary, 29th December 1940

THIS WAS, by May Speed's reckoning, their 417th raid since the Blitz began (a single night being often marked by a series of separate air raid sirens and All Clears). Planes had been going over in a steady stream for more than an hour.

May's friend Etta, who had been staying with the Speeds in Brixton since she was bombed out, considered May 'the life and soul of the party' during air raids. It was May who kept up morale, 'arranging all kinds of diversions from guessing games to "Penny Readings"'. But often, too, she could be seen straining her eyes in a bad light, writing – or 'scribbling' as they called it.

Etta had been visiting family in the countryside for the weekend and had returned this afternoon saying that she was glad to be back: 'A little of one's relations goes a long way.' May could empathise: her fraught family Christmas had erupted into a 'row royal' today, which she had poured into the diary in which she now recorded the bombers droning over and the bombs whistling and crashing about her.

Mabel Speed had impulsively signed up for munitions work at the Labour Exchange, after another big argument with Norah. But now, after hearing Bertha bemoan her life in lodgings, she was thinking better of her decision to leave home. 'Last night she said to Ethel, "If you can arrange for Norah to give up the cooking and would help me, I won't go on munitions – but let Norah think you suggested it." Oh, the petty intrigue!' It had all gone horribly wrong, of course, and this morning Norah had decided that Mabel was scheming with Ethel – and May – to get *her* out of the house. And then, 'Mabel of course flared'.

Well, the fractious family gathering was due to start dispersing tomorrow morning, starting with Bertha, who had a taxi booked for eight. And May did at least have some good news to 'scribble' today: Etta had come back from her weekend away bearing gifts. 'Real country produce, fresh cut.' Not only 'Brussels sprouts, leeks, carrots' and savoy cabbage, but eggs. And not only eggs, but onions. And not only onions, but 'whoppers'.

AT ADVANCED HQ in the Whispering Gallery of St Paul's, firebombs were reported on the South-East buttress. Members of the Watch were soon scrambling on to one of those 'good receptacles for incendiary bombs', where flames had been seen. At 7.37 the crypt phone, which had been moved into the Practice Room after the lights went out, rang. It was a message from up top to say that the South-East pocket roof fire was getting out of hand and to call the Fire Brigade. No engine had arrived when, a quarter of an hour later, the phone rang again. The Watch had managed to put it out themselves with stirrup pumps so the call to the Brigade could be cancelled.

It was just as well: all the City fire stations were at full stretch. And it was not just firebombs they had to deal with. The sound of the massive explosion noted by St Paul's at ten past seven had also rung through the Guildhall's dimly-lit Control Room. Another five minutes later and the room was again startled by an explosion, this time from the north. The ack-ack forcing the raiders high meant that any idea that they could aim for specific targets was academic. But it didn't really matter where HE bombs fell over the City tonight: every one had an excellent prospect of making a hole in a roadway and cutting vital telephone and electricity cables and gas and fracturing water mains, not to mention sewers.

From his vantage point on the Guildhall roof, Mr Fitzhugh not only heard these thunderclaps but saw the lightning that preceded them too: 'There would be a sound of something rushing through the air – then a brilliant flash which would light up the entire sky and horizon and followed within two to three seconds by the most resounding explosion.' One HE fell on Ibex House in the Minories – the 'Wine Land' given over to vintners and tea warehouses by the Tower; closer at hand to the north, another one hit Moor Lane Police Station by the *Jewish Chronicle* offices. By the time he was relieved at his post, Mr Fitzhugh reckoned that around half a dozen explosions had occurred within a quarter of a mile radius.

In the meantime, his and Mr Lott's attention was caught by shouts coming from the direction of Aldermanbury. Patrols on the roof of Bradbury Greatorex textile warehouse had spotted a fire on one of the Guildhall roofs between the North and South Courts. The Guildhall firemen rang the information down to Fire Squad HQ – and, shortly after, a further piece of information that had been bellowed to them from the warehouse roof: an incendiary had apparently landed on St Lawrence Jewry church.

In the City Control Room, the fact that the Guildhall above him had been hit by a dozen firebombs was the least of Mr Murphy's problems. Those incendiaries were the business of the building's own fire squad. His concern was the hundreds, thousands, of empty buildings across the City that had no firewatchers at all. The warren of City streets was home, as it had always been, to quite modest premises as well as large ones: shops, offices, workshops and small factories – family businesses like the Speeds'. But owners no longer lived over the shop as they had in the old days and most weren't due to return until tomorrow morning. Their premises had been left, in many cases, locked and shuttered against burglars, with no means of entry and no spare keys lodged with the local ARP post.

Thankfully, many of the bigger office blocks and warehouses had – like Hitchcock, Williams & Co. – teams of firewatchers hard at work on their roofs. In fact, all companies with more than thirty employees were supposed to provide fire guards. Just as all companies were supposed to have cleared their loft space of combustible material. But some had done neither. Some had placed their trust in their expensive pre-war sprinkler systems to protect their premises from fire. And as fire spread across the City, these sprinklers, activated by the heat, were suddenly springing into action, one by one, spraying precious water randomly and uselessly over deserted offices and factory floors.

Mr Murphy got his first, graphic intimations of the scale of the situation that was developing around him with a grim report that came in from the Guildhall Fire Squad HQ. Post No. 1 had rung down to say that, to the north, the entire block bounded by Bassishaw House, Fore Street, Aldermanbury and Bassinghall Street – about an acre in all – was one single mass of flame.

Turning to the fires in the east, Mr Fitzhugh saw the steeple and weathercock of St Stephen's, Coleman Street, suddenly collapse and disappear into the flames below. Its steeple had been St Stephen's glory: like so many of the churches that Wren built in narrow City streets, it had not been much to look at from ground level. Almost its only distinction for passers-by had been a relief carving over the gateway to the churchyard. About five feet by two and a half, it showed a Last Judgement: God in majesty, Satan falling and angels leaning out over clouds of glory to help pull the awakening dead up into heaven. It was a plaster replica of a much older plaque that had been removed to the vestry for safe-keeping. It was believed to have survived from the pre-Fire church in 1666; it would not survive this time.

IN THE WEST END of London, Charlie Chaplin had made his final plea for peace and understanding at the end of *The Great Dictator,* the National Anthem played and journalist W. L. White had emerged from the cinema with Marguerite into what he described as 'the weirdest city I had ever seen'.

> London looked like a production in technicolor of the burning of Rome by Cecil B. DeMille. The whole sky was pink, and in splotches around us on the horizon it was bright orange. It was so garish as to be a little bit overdramatized and in bad taste.

Marguerite had to stop off at her office to proof-read an article but when they got there it was deserted. They finally located the other journalists, correcting proofs in the basement, among the printing presses and great rolls of paper waiting to produce the morning editions. Marguerite checked over her article then they left to find somewhere to eat.

There were still people on the streets, some of them breaking into a trot when a bomb was heard whistling down. 'Because of this crazy Cecil DeMille pink over everything, you could see the faces of the people, see which ones were scared and just how scared,' wrote Bill White. 'A few of them weren't liking it at all.' From within the narrow streets of Covent Garden it wasn't clear quite how big a raid this was, so Bill and Marguerite went down to the riverside by Waterloo Bridge to see if there was anything on the south side of the river too.

> The Thames was the same kind of baby ribbon pink as the sky, except for the yellow flames from a barge that had caught fire, and high yellow flames in two patches from what might be warehouses.

Most fires seemed to be on this side of the river: they hailed any vehicle they saw approaching in the hopes that it might be a taxi, but as they came up close most turned out to be fire engines heading in the direction of the City.

Suddenly, Bill and Marguerite were surrounded by a shower of incendiaries, bouncing and rattling around all up and down the street. As each one struck the roadway it 'burst into a ball of greenish white flame about the size of a cat and the color of a mercury vapor lamp', lending a strange greenish-white tinge to the pink light around them. Up above, they could hear the shouts of the roof-spotters, and the pounding of ARP wardens' feet approaching.

One particular firebomb, making a glass panel set into the pavement melt and bubble, seemed to infuriate Marguerite particularly. A hearty kick sent it spinning into the gutter, then she grabbed for her foot and began hopping around. The leather of her shoe was burnt right through. But she said she only expected a small blister on her foot and, anyway, it was worth it. Having vented her anger somewhat, she helped Bill rather more effectively, using the contents of sandbags standing against a nearby bank building to smother more incendiaries.

Up above, an orange-yellow glow was developing behind the darkened windows of some of the top-storey offices. As he watched the light flicker and grow, Bill recalled the boast of a Nazi newspaperman he had met in Berlin the year before. In London, the German had said, there were large areas – the docks and the older parts of the City – which 'could be burnt off like weed patches from the air any time they decided to do it'. He told Marguerite and she said, in that case, this could turn out to be a big story that could last all night. And in that case, said Bill, they had better get something to eat before they set off to cover it. It was Sunday night and they drew a blank looking for a restaurant that was open, finally opting for the one that they knew would be – the Savoy.

Unlike so many of his journalistic colleagues, Bill White had no particular affection for the Savoy hotel. Its style was in marked contrast to his own, the 'saddest hotel in the world', where his fellow-guests were

> Czech colonels and Norwegian university professors and Polish admirals and Dutch artillery officers and cabinet ministers from the Baltic states now occupied by Russia. Here are the 'free French' who follow General de Gaulle, and the 'free Belgians' who continued fighting after Leopold surrendered. With a sprinkling of sad-eyed Central European Jews, businessmen or intellectuals sitting silently with their sad-eyed wives.
>
> Here is the Europe of Yesterday, or at least that part of it which could still get across the English Channel to the only country still fighting for a free Europe.
>
> They are at this hotel somewhat because it is made of sweet, lovely concrete and mostly because it is the only place in London where you can be respectable on three dollars a day.

You didn't stay at the Savoy if you needed to get by on three dollars a day.

In his younger days, Bill White – 'W. L.' – had ruffled feathers back home in Emporia, Kansas, by returning from Harvard complete with English accent and monocle. But his tastes had changed since those callow days. As they walked into the underground dining room tonight and looked round at the Savoy's well-fed diners, he and Marguerite 'agreed on how easy it is to get very fond of the British people, who on the whole are so brave, and so truly courteous, and friendly, and tolerant, if only you stay out of the Savoy'.

They did see one Free French officer. Marguerite knew him and said he was a rare example of a Frenchman who got out with more than the clothes on his back. Otherwise, wrote Bill, 'the people at the tables were well-dressed. Many of them were in uniform. They all had placid serene Munich-looking faces.'

For what it was worth, the brains behind the 'placid serene Munich-looking faces' probably shared Bill White's sentiments – certainly about their fellow-diners, and possibly about themselves too. Almost daily, Ernie Pyle had encountered Englishmen in hotel dining rooms 'express a little shame' at eating such a meal when so many others couldn't, and 'a little revulsion' at the sight of hundreds of well-fed diners like themselves. It was a feeling Ernie himself sort of shared.

NEV COATES had been in the Hermitage shelter in Wapping last night dressed as Santa Claus; now he was back there in his normal guise as a Friends Ambulance Unit volunteer. He and his friend Robin du Boulay had been forced to crouch close in to a wall in Reardon Street on their way here as a stick of bombs came down, then again in Wapping High Street. Another stick of bombs had fallen in front of them as they neared the shelter and they had found some of the 400 shelterers gathered in groups at the bottom of the stairs, with an 'air of anticipation and subdued excitement'.

There had been more excitement since. Some shelterers were called up to help deal with a sudden shower of incendiaries and had returned with news that a nearby shelter had been evacuated because the building next door was on fire. Then two women were brought in, suffering badly from shock, and were given a hot drink and allowed to rest until they were well enough to get to their usual bunks.

At half past seven, three HEs had come down, one of them hitting the end of the Hermitage. The bomb shook the old building and raised dust. But it held up. 'Some of the folks were frightened,' wrote Nev, 'but there was no panic, except for one young lady who flung her arms round my neck.'

Some men were brought in, bleeding: they had been out dealing with incendiaries and helping to rescue some terrified horses from a burning stable. Several had shrapnel wounds; one was unconscious. Nev and

Robin got to work on them in the first-aid area while someone else went to the Warden's Post to call for an ambulance.

Dealing with all the injuries took half an hour, and then Nev was informed that the ambulance had finally arrived. He went out into the main shelter to ask for volunteers to help with the stretchers – and found it empty, apart from two men waiting at the bottom of the stairs. 'Where's everybody?' asked Nev. 'Had to get out,' he was told, 'The bloody building's on fire.'

Chapter Seventeen

Post 2 In: 19.57 Out 19.58
Keyworth shelters have been hit
send RP & AMB Lancaster Street

Reporting Post 2, message sent, express, to Southwark Control

THE KEYWORTH STREET shelters were on a patch of open ground near the Elephant & Castle. Keyworth Street had actually been Dantzic Street until relatively recently: it was renamed after a young Great War hero, Leonard Keyworth VC, who had died of wounds in France in 1915. It was actually quite an interesting story if you had the time . . . but no one had time for stories tonight.

And forget street names anyway: for the rest of the night and well into tomorrow, this would be 'Incident 43A' for the workers at Southwark Control and all the many emergency services depots they were calling.

Post 2's request was passed on to local Rescue Party and Ambulance Stations within minutes. But Control's further request, at a quarter past eight, asking West Square School Rescue Service Depot for a Light Rescue Squad to 'clear debris in front of ambulance station to allow ambulances clear exit', showed this was not going to be a simple job. There were thirty people currently believed to be trapped under the debris, several dead, and yet another water main had been broken by high explosive.

IN THE HEART of the City, Mr Munson called down to Fire Squad HQ from the Guildhall roofs to report the incendiary burning in the north-west corner of the tower of St Lawrence Jewry church – again. This was the second time of telling, and ten minutes later, worried that no one had come to tackle it, he called it through again. But HQ said they had already passed the message to City Control and, beyond keep reminding them, there was nothing they could do – the squad's priority had to be the Guildhall itself. At around eight o'clock, when he was relieved by Mr Guggiari the boilerman, Mr Munson pointed out where the firebomb had fallen, though it seemed, by now, to have largely burned itself out. It certainly didn't look as if the tower itself had taken fire, though small flames could still be seen, flickering intermittently above the parapet.

To the north-east, with all the pumps from 68Z Baltic Street now out on jobs, Champion and Howard of Jackson Brothers found themselves without a useful role once more and decided to walk along Old Street and just lend a hand wherever it was needed. Sutton's the carriers was burning 'like matchwood' and they found firemen struggling to get the blaze under control. The stables in the courtyard were on fire too. They could see people leading terrified carthorses, one by one, through the fires and out into the relative darkness of Ironmonger Row where, away from the flames, they were tied up to the railings of St Luke's church. They decided to pitch in.

Stanley Champion's first attempt at a rescue was a nightmare: his horse was very jumpy from the off, and was soon slipping about on a road awash with water from the firemen's hoses. There was a sudden explosion and the horse that Stanley had been desperately hanging on to became frantic. His arms were almost pulled out of their sockets as it broke away from him and plunged down the street. Fortunately, someone else managed to catch hold of it and calm it sufficiently to lead it away to safety.

Stanley turned round and went back in through the gateway, which was now well alight. He was no sooner inside than someone shouted that it could collapse at any moment. The only way out now would be by an exit that was largely blocked by carts and vans, leaving a gangway of just a few feet for man and beast to squeeze through.

Luckily for them both, Stanley was given a gentler horse this time. It was just as well. As hoofs clattered and skittered on the roadway, he found himself more than once squashed perilously between the animal's flank and the wall. A single kick of fear now, he knew, would mean serious injury or worse. But they made it through eventually, out into the safety of Ironmonger Row.

He turned to try again but was met by the welcome news that all the horses were out and safe. In the scrum he had lost track of his fellow fire-watcher, so he decided that he might as well go back to Jackson Brothers as anywhere, to see if there was anything to be done there. On his way back to the factory, he had to duck for cover several times as HEs and landmines exploded around him.

As sub-stations emptied of men and machines, Watchroom staffs called the information in to their main stations and thence to Lambeth HQ, where officers had to decide when and whether to start sending appliances from outlying stations. Watchrooms had to get calls out on phones that were ringing more or less constantly. But even when they did get through, it wasn't a simple case for HQ of ordering all hands to the pump and all pumps to the City.

By eight o'clock, 300 of London Region's 2,000 pumps were already in action, and most were in the few square miles at its heart. There was still a desperate lack of pumps in the worst affected areas: one officer, reporting to burning Cheapside between half past seven and eight, found that the only pump available was a single 'heavy' from Holloway, with no water left in its on-board tank.

But there was a fine line between sending in much-needed support, and wasting men and machines on unmanageable fires. In any conflagration, there was a point at which a fire officer had to take the decision to withdraw his men and machines to the periphery, letting the centre burn itself out with its own ferocity while the fire service concentrated on stopping further spread.

Plus, who knew when appliances ordered in to the City from further afield would be needed back on their own patch? Once the huge fires at the centre of the attack really got going, Luftwaffe pilots would be wasting incendiaries to stoke them further. And they were not going to waste a thing. There was scarcely a fire station across the capital that wouldn't get its own spattering of fires and explosive to keep it busy tonight.

Not every firebomb required a fire engine to put it out. Despite the lack of fire guards in some properties, wardens and firewatchers all over London were dealing with hundreds, thousands, of incendiaries and small fires before they got out of hand. South of the River, the wardens operating from the emptied crypt of St Peter's Walworth made good use of the sandbags and stirrup pumps and small fire-axes that were all that they had to work with. Reverend Markham admitted his memory was a little hazy about dates, and no night in the Blitz would ever loom as large in Walworth as their own church's bombing in October, but tonight was, he remained pretty sure, that memorable occasion when they dealt with ninety-five small fires between them within their own few streets.

But this continuing first sortie of the night to London had more than 22,000 firebombs and 127 tonnes of high explosive to distribute. And as more incendiaries came down accompanied by the whistle of high explosive, some of London's guardians were injured or killed before they even had a chance to tackle the firebombs.

In Westminster, a high explosive blew up a tramcar, killing three, and penetrated to Westminster Tube below. Two IBs on Buckingham Palace were swiftly dealt with by its firewatchers. But many fires grew dangerously large before anyone knew they had even started.

An AFS trailer pump was dispatched to nearby Victoria Street where the sixth floor of a darkened office block had been spotted well alight. The street was scattered with debris and, just as their pump bumped up to the kerb, another mixed bag of incendiaries and HE came raining down.

> 'Look out boys.'
> Bundling off the tender, we fling ourselves face downwards in the deserted road. A series of explosions close at hand is followed by the confused rattle of collapsing bricks and tinkling glass. Shrapnel strikes the wing of the pump like a vicious afterthought. Then, just as we are getting up, the sky splits open with a blinding flash, torn into strips of whistling metal.
> 'Stay where you are!' someone shouts. 'Here's another packet – the bastards!'
> Incendiaries fall in the road and lie burning in patches of greenish magnesium fire, sending off a white smoke. In the shocked after-silence tiles and bricks can be heard rattling down again.
> 'Where did that lot fall?'
> 'Over by Victoria I think.'
> An ambulance drives past like a ghost-car insistently ringing its little high-pitched bell.
> 'Someone's copped it.'
> 'F– that.'

Two of the crew uncoupled their pump and backed it into the kerb, while another, chatting about tonight's raid as he helped to manhandle a length of unwieldy suction to the hydrant, suddenly found himself under the furious eye of the pump-man who was prising open the hydrant cover in the pavement. 'Come on, there! Lend a hand for f–'s sake! What the hell do you think you are doing? Think we've come on a picnic?'

Phil Henderson, who had been a poet and literary critic in pre-war life, knew he could be a little distrait in an emergency. Nevertheless, he was 'Unreasonably annoyed – tempers tend to wear rather thin during a blitz' as he got down to help the pump-man couple up the suction.

> 'All right, no need to shout. Who do you think you are, anyway?'
> The pump-man looks up at me furiously from under his tin hat in the act of tightening the suction lugs.
> 'We're at a fire, in case you don't know. You want to wake your ideas up a bit mate!'
> Meanwhile No. 1 is having a violent argument with the caretaker of the offices.
> 'Can't let you in here,' shouts the caretaker. 'What do you want?'
> 'Your house is on fire! There's a raid on!' bellows No. 1.

'What? Air raid, do you say?'

'Come on, all shove together,' says No. 1 grimly.

The door gave way and the caretaker was pushed aside, continuing to shout from the bottom of the stairs at the retreating backs of the firemen as they dragged hose up the stairwell: 'How do I know who you are? Breaking in at this time of night! I'm in charge here. Come on out of it!'

He was, it turned out, deaf, and had been, Phil wrote, 'Asleep in the basement like a good fire-watcher', totally unaware of tonight's blitz.

Standing in position halfway up the stairs, where it was his job to manage the hose for the men with the branch up top, Phil heard the 'subdued gurgle' of the water making its way upwards from the hydrant, rounding the limp hose. 'Look out up there!' he shouted to the men above. 'WATER! Here it comes!'

As the water brought the writhing and swaying hose to life, Phil had to hang over the banisters to control it – and was caught in the silver mist of spray that shot out from innumerable tiny punctures in the hose and spurted fanwise from faulty couplings. He tried to tighten one of the couplings with his spanner, but the water shot up his sleeve and into his face, and he felt it trickle down his neck into the small of his back. The December night was cold and the water colder. And he wasn't even near enough to the fire to warm himself by it. He relieved his feelings in fine old Anglo-Saxon.

BACK IN THE CITY, Mr Lott and Mr Munson were downstairs with the rest of the Fire Guard, gulping down a welcome cup of tea. They had successfully tackled every incendiary that had come on to the Guildhall roofs in the past hour and a half, and there had been no more reported by the roof-spotters, though Mr Guggiari had been calling down periodically with progress reports on the tower of nearby St Lawrence Jewry, where the flickering incendiary looked to be catching hold. There was still no sign of a fire engine coming to tackle it.

Suddenly, from the roof, Mr Guggiari heard a clatter and clang – the bells of St Lawrence Jewry next door crashed to a noisy death on the floor of the tower. He rang down again: the church was now burning furiously inside, he said, and flames were starting to break out through the roof. Even though the church was not, strictly speaking, the responsibility of Mr George's small fire squad, it soon could be. Only the narrow Church Passage separated St Lawrence from the south-west corner of the Guildhall complex. Mr George needed to make some urgent calls. In the meantime, he sent most of the rest of the squad out to do what they could until the Fire Brigade arrived.

A fireman who was passing by the church had also heard the bells of St Lawrence Jewry fall. But he heard something else too. Noel Mander was a church organ builder who had joined the AFS when war broke out but then left to join the army. 'I came home on Christmas leave,' he recalled, 'and the City was burning. They came around from my old fire station to my house, and said could I possibly come and help; they wanted every man. We found ourselves in Gresham Street. Utter chaos prevailed. To the left and right of us buildings were burning, most of them securely locked and entry was impossible.'

Then, as they passed the church, he heard, beyond the crash of bells, an unearthly shriek which only he, perhaps, could recognise tonight for what it was: 'The organ was alight and the hot air blowing through the pipes made that magnificent instrument shriek in its death agony.' The last requiem of St Lawrence Jewry.

The Guildhall fire squad, emerging into the Yard, ran into the teeth of a gale. The light north-easterly wind that Mr Munson had noticed while he was filling up his water buckets on the roof only a short time ago was now blowing at sixty or perhaps seventy miles an hour. And though none of them was aware of it yet, this was no sudden freak of the changeable British weather: this was the beginnings of a firestorm.

The Guildhall was now surrounded by acres of flaming buildings and the fires were devouring oxygen at a prodigious rate. The passage of air being sucked into the partial vacuum created at ground level as hot air rose was producing this mighty wind. The wind in turn made every fire that it found burn ever more fiercely – and carried red-hot debris in its path to start new fires wherever it went.

As well as the fire in St Lawrence's tower, the fire squad could see that their own Port Health and Justice Room roofs were in imminent danger from burning fragments. This was not like earlier: just one incendiary here or there. Young Lott saw the cinders falling on the roof like rain. Each man grabbed a bucket and stirrup pump and went up top to tackle the fires as they started. The atmosphere was full of smoke and, as they worked, thousands of red-hot sparks stung the backs of their necks and burnt their overalls.

Battling against the intense heat and smoke was hard, exhausting work – and not only for the men pumping and up and down furiously on the stirrup pumps. Every time a bucket was emptied, the only way to fill it was to run down, dip it into the Fire Brigade water reservoir in the Yard and carry the slopping pail all the way back up again. Where the hell was the Fire Brigade?

By the time Mr George came out to join his squad, the hundred-foot tower of St Lawrence Jewry was ablaze from top to bottom and a north-easterly gale was driving sparks and burning brands forcefully across the roofs of the Justice Room, the Remembrancer's Office and on to the wooden roof of the medieval Great Hall itself.

He could see that the body of the church was burning now too, but it was impossible to get inside to do anything about it because the heavy wooden door was locked and no one knew where the key was kept. There was a new red steel fire escape ladder, only recently delivered and still in its waterproof canvas cover, beside the church. They decided to move it away from the wall so the firemen could use it to direct their hoses on to the roofs from above – when they finally arrived. Mr Munson managed to pull off the cover, which had started to smoulder, but no one knew how to work the ladder and one of the stays jammed. In the end, there was nothing for it but brute force: working together, they manhandled it, an agonising foot or two at a time, away from the wall of St Lawrence's.

APPROACHING THE CITY from the south, Mr Walden gazed in horrified awe at the familiar dome of St Paul's, silhouetted and reddened by the flames all around it. Like so many others, he found it was impossible for the eye not to be impressed by the terrible beauty of this night – even as the heart reached out towards familiar scenes and old friends who must now be in danger.

If the flames were so close to the Cathedral, he knew that Hitchcock, Williams & Co., its firewatchers and the eighty-plus people who sheltered in its basement must be in their greatest peril of the Blitz so far. His journey along Cannon Street from the station was a nightmare as he negotiated the snaking hoses of the fire crews. He passed several large raging fires, and smoke and sparks filled the air from one large block in Queen Victoria Street in particular. From time to time, the menacing roar of the attacking planes overhead and the constant hiss of falling incendiaries became too much to bear, and Mr Walden would duck into a doorway and take shelter for a while before pressing on. He knew he had to see what lay before him in St Paul's Churchyard.

There was naught for his comfort in the sight that greeted him. Several fires had taken hold on the roof of Pawson & Leaf. Even nearer to home,

Debenham & Co. was almost gutted. It would have been possible to read a book, he thought – to use the old Blitz cliché – by the light of the blazing warehouses of Paternoster Row, Ivy Lane, Warwick Lane, Warwick Square, London House Yard . . . 'I shall not easily forget seeing the faces of some of our fire fighters in the glare,' he wrote later, 'with every detail defined at a considerable distance.' In his despair, he noted how many of the burning buildings were those that provided no firewatching squad of their own.

His company's own squads, veterans of so many high-spirited but dedicated dummy runs, had performed magnificently, he learned when he finally arrived at the firm. They had put out all the incendiaries that fell on their own roof, and some had gone out into the street to deal with incendiaries there too. But with blazing buildings all around and a strong wind blowing, it seemed only a matter of time before the fire got its fangs into Hitchcock, Williams at last.

FIRE CREWS had finally arrived at the Guildhall Yard to tackle St Lawrence Jewry. They began to play their hoses on to the church from the Yard and, fighting to keep their branches steady in the teeth of the gale, down from the roof of the Port Health building too. It was no use.

At No. 2 Post, Mr Guggiari saw a lump of burning debris had started a fire in the gutter of the main Guildhall roof. He grabbed a bucket of water and managed to put it out, but at that moment young Lott, watching from the Port Health roof, saw St Lawrence's steeple begin to give way, then crash in, taking most of the roof with it. There was a sudden uprush of sparks and a huge cloud of embers was swept by the gale across the top of the Guildhall and straight towards Mr Guggiari.

Mr Guggiari turned and saw a shower of debris coming towards him, then saw that there was now fire on the bottom flushing of a dormer window on the main roof, 'just above the staircase on the right of the porch, and to the left of No. 2 Post'.

> I extinguished that with a stirrup-pump. I kept on pouring water over lumps of debris on the concrete roof-passage. I saw a flicker of light from the top corner of the same dormer window. I started to put that out with a stirrup-pump and rang down to HQ for assistance.

Exhausted, Mr Guggiari continued to pump away until help arrived in the shape of two members of the fire guard and a fireman, hauling a length of hose up on to the roof. The fireman braced himself, branch in hand, and the water began to come through – but the stream fell short of the fire. He sent Mr Guggiari down to the Yard to tell the trailer pump man down by the water dam to stop the pump and put in another length. When this was done, the fireman on the roof signalled 'water on' and Mr Guggiari decided it was time he went down to see from the inside what was happening to the Great Hall.

Meanwhile, on the east wing, with the whole of the Port Health roof thoroughly soaked, the Guildhall men who had been working there formed up again and went back down to the Yard – where they arrived just in time to hear someone shouting: 'The Guildhall is alight!' They looked up and saw that smoke, though as yet no flame, was issuing from beneath the slates just under the centre of the great oak roof on the south side of the medieval Great Hall.

THE RAF PILOT who had driven them down in the MG wished Bill and Vi Regan luck as he waved them off at Southall station – and their luck held long enough for the ticket collector to be looking the other way as they airily flashed their rail tickets at the barrier. They had a lot of changing on and off trains to do before they got to Aldgate Underground. But, thought Bill, 'That was all right. We were going in the right direction.' There was no Tube station near their house – the low, flat land of the Isle of Dogs couldn't take underground tunnels. Getting home, or to the Heavy Rescue depot where Bill was due to start work tomorrow, would mean going up to street level at Aldgate Station and then catching a bus.

Tube life was a new experience for the Regans: 'We had heard about people taking shelter in the Underground and amusing themselves with a sing-song before bedding down for the night, but these weren't singing: perhaps they were having an off night.'

At Aldgate, an air raid warden was sitting on a chair behind a miniature blast-wall of sandbags by the exit. 'Hey you, you can't go out there,' he said. 'Why not?' said Bill, 'We've got tickets.'

So he says, 'Oh you're a clever Dick are you? You know there's a bloody big raid on.' I said, 'Yep, seen one and you've seen the lot, but it's alright mate, we're in the same business.' After a little more chat, he said, 'Where are you going?' Vi piped up, 'We're going home' he says, 'Where's that?' and when Vi said, 'The Isle of Dogs' he rolled his eyes upwards. 'You're both barmy, or else you're taking the micky.' I said, 'No straight up mate. Any buses going past here for Poplar?' He was most impolite and told us to 'P – off, you give me a headache.' We went off giggling like two little kids.

The nearest bus stop was a couple of hundred yards away from the station and they saw one bus go by before they got there, so they took shelter in a shop doorway to wait for another. 'We had stopped our silly giggling, and were beginning to realise what was happening . . . All the City seemed to be burning, like the first few raids on the Island, and I'm not enjoying it: it's not background noise any more.'

It was not just the growl of planes overhead or the sound of explosions that had altered their mood. 'What's that awful screaming noise?' Vi asked her husband. But then she answered her own question: 'It sounds like horses.' Bill knew the area. 'That must be from the stables behind the Minories, where the brewery dray horses are kept,' he told her. Bill also knew his wife: 'And don't get any bright ideas,' he warned her, 'we're waiting for a bus.'

As he said this, he saw two buses approaching from Commercial Street in the firelight. He dodged out from the protection of the doorway to hail them but they shot past without stopping. 'Beginning to get angry' now, he promised Vi that the next one would stop or it would have to mow him down. And, he instructed, 'If it stops, don't hang about, get on it, if it doesn't stop you'll have to walk home.' Fortunately, the next bus slowed down as he jumped in front of it, waving his arms 'like an irritated traffic copper'. 'Blackwall Tunnel only, mate,' called the driver. 'That's far enough for me, old mate,' said Bill.

Inside, the conductor refused to take their fares: 'Have this one on me.' Bill told him about the previous two buses, and the conductor said that they had probably forgotten to put the cat out. They were moving slowly forward when Vi suddenly asked for the bus to stop and the conductor automatically pulled the cord.

Vi's eye had been caught by the beautiful lights of a chandelier flare that was sinking slowly on its parachutes behind them. 'Can I get off for a minute?' she asked. 'Here, you're not letting her go and pick that up are you?' the conductor asked Bill. 'Not likely,' said Bill holding on to Vi's hand. 'She thinks it looks pretty.'

They all just sat there for a moment in the bus. 'I have hold of her hand,' wrote Bill afterwards, 'and she just sits looking at it as it slowly burned on the road behind. And Vi says to no one in particular: "Doesn't it look so beautiful? I'd love to have it."'

'Never mind, darling,' said the conductor, as he came to and dinged the bell twice to get them moving again. 'It was too big to hang in the front room.'

In Old Street, Stanley Champion was not surprised to find Jackson Brothers in a worse state than ever. But he was astonished to find that the paper merchants at the other end of the yard was still intact – for now, at least. Amazingly, Grosvenor Chater's men had managed to get almost all their early incendiary fires out before they could get a proper hold. Another, which had burned its way down from the roof to the ground floor, had been dealt with by the AFS.

The building was still in distinct danger, though – the air was alive with sparks and burning embers whipped up by the intensely hot wind from the burning buildings all around. The Grosvenor Chater men were trying to extinguish them as they landed. Now, with Stanley to help out, they were able to take a floor apiece.

Every time another huge lump of wall came crashing down from the all-but-destroyed building next door, another shower of sparks came in through the broken windows. But burning debris proved not to be as difficult to put out as the white-hot incendiaries: with buckets of water at the ready, they found they were able to douse them quite easily, so long as they were quick.

Then, suddenly, the sound of machine-guns filled the air above Stanley Champion's head. He called to the others to keep low. This must be the next phase of the raid, he thought: having set the City alight, the raiders were now returning to shoot at the people fighting the fires.

Chapter Eighteen

> . . . and at about 2100 hrs, the sound of machine-gun
> fire . . .
>
> Report No. 1 by Major C P Stacey to the Director, Historical Section
> (G.S.), Canadian National Defence Headquarters, Ottawa

STANDING IN THE STREET by Queensway Tube Station in west London, the Canadian General Staff's new Historical Officer had been watching history happen before his eyes for the past two and half hours. Wave after wave of bombers had been grinding overhead and, though he couldn't see them, he could trace their progress across the night sky by the burst of ack-ack shells attempting to bring them down. The focus of tonight's raid was a couple of miles to the east of him, where he had seen a forest of barrage balloons quickly illumined by large fires. And then the ack-ack had stopped . . .

As the Major correctly surmised, the sound of machine-guns did not indicate, as Stanley Champion had thought, the Luftwaffe coming in to kill firefighters. It was the RAF night fighters at work, sent up in the hopes of locating and destroying the enemy by the light of the fires. That was why the ack-ack had stopped so suddenly. In the City, journalist Ritchie Calder felt it cease rather than heard it – 'with the curtness of a conductor flicking his baton'. He got the impression that the bombers were being chased away by the machine-gun fire. 'We cheered. There seemed no doubt that the sudden appearance of the night-fighters had surprised them into flight, but we did not delude ourselves that that would be the end of them. We expected them back.'

Twenty-six-year-old Squadron Leader Peter Townsend was a pioneer of the still-fledgeling night-fighter squadrons. In his history of their operations, he later recorded that during Friday night's raid a dense haze had reduced horizontal visibility to zero, and the grounded RAF pilots had watched helplessly as the vapour trails of the Luftwaffe bombers streamed up the Thames estuary towards London. Tonight, at least, they were able to share the sky with them. But the 'layers' system, in which 'cat's-eye' fighters stacked one above the other every 500 feet, was hopelessly inadequate to penetrate the darkness.

From below, however, things looked more hopeful than they did to the RAF pilots. From his vantage point on the Guildhall roofs, Mr Fitzhugh looked up when he heard the bursts of machine-gun fire and saw planes silhouetted against the flames: it looked to him as if the RAF had the advantage.

As the most modern technology in the world flung itself around the skies over the centuries-old Guildhall, it was clear that any distinctions that had ever existed between the City's past, present and future had become purely notional tonight. At No. 68 Station Redcross Street, a desperate call came in to the mobilising officer from the LFB man who had taken charge of the St Lawrence Jewry fire – which was in the process of becoming, it appeared, the Guildhall fire too. He desperately needed more men and more machines, he called in on his field telephone: 'We are burning history here, for the sake of a few pumps!' 'We are *making* history here,' replied the beleaguered Station Officer Waterman tersely from the '68' end of the line – but all the same he ordered on two more appliances to do what they could to help.

Londoners battling the flames tonight told each other that there had been nothing like it since 1666, in tones that implied they had been here then, too. And anyone trying to describe what he saw around him on 29th December could, thought one long-time historian of London, borrow wholesale from Samuel Pepys's diary entry for 2nd September:

> . . . saw the fire grow; and as it grew darker, appeared more and more, and in corners and upon steeples, and between churches and houses, as far as we could see up the hill of the City in a most horrid, malicious, bloody flame, not like an ordinary fire.

But where Pepys, once the 1666 fire had done its worst, had looked out from the tower of All Hallows in the east of the City on to 'the saddest sight of desolation' he had ever seen, tonight All Hallows was itself in flames.

Here, as elsewhere across the City, centuries of history were peeling off the stone walls in layers, spinning ancient sacred sites back into their history. At All Hallows Barking, the work of Toc H and the Great War that had given birth to it passed away in a moment, swiftly followed by Victorian prosperity and expensive woodwork. It was fortunate that the old wooden font in which William Penn had been baptised, when America was still barely English, had been sent off to Philadelphia back in 1697. For tonight its magnificently carved stone replacement was cracking and crumbling in the intense heat. The Jacobean pulpit was burning, too, perhaps with a wisp of words rising amid the smoke:

> . . . When wasteful war shall statues overturn,
> And broils root out the work of masonry . . .

Now Dissenters and Church of England alike disappeared into nothingness and England became Catholic again. The nuns of Barking Abbey who gave the church its name returned – and left again as Fire drove Time back before it. Back beyond the limits of parish register and brass plaque and stone effigy. Back beyond the Conquest and into ages of unsuspected antiquity. Norman construction collapsed to reveal hidden remains of the first church that Saxon piety had built here, using remnants of old Londinium – some of them still bearing the scorch-marks of Boudicca's fire – left behind by the retreating Romans. Beyond whom there was nothing; nothing but grass, and wildflowers, a shadowy Druid or two, and the ever-flowing Thames.

Not that everything of All Hallows had gone yet – the destruction, as so often, was proving patchy. Notable parishioners like William Thynne, for one – Henry VIII's Clerk of the Kitchen and a notable editor of Chaucer – lay safe beneath his brass and an asbestos mat. Here, as elsewhere, the church bells crashed down and smashed, but the tower they had hung in stood firm. If enough of the fabric survived the perilous present one might even dream of a future for All Hallows, in which this great fire of 1940 would be just another part of its long history, for any busy Londoner who had time to stop and listen . . .

No living Londoner could know all that was being lost, or gained, here tonight, because no Londoner could ever comprehend even a fraction of what London was, is, or might become. In a darkened church in the northeast of the City, untouched so far by fire or bomb, someone who had tried to capture London on paper sat, writing at his desk, as he had sat these 300 years and more. This carved stone memorial was a rich monument to the labours of City tailor John Stow, who had almost bankrupted himself with his passion for uncovering London stories. Even now, the Lord Mayor of London regularly honoured him with a new quill pen on his birthday. And John Stow was absolutely the man to come to if you wanted to hear stories of the old City churches that were burning tonight.

When Stow tramped the streets of London updating his guidebook, *Hamlet* was still a big new box-office hit. The Square Mile had more than twice as many churches then – almost a hundred. Far too many for a saint each, hence the nicknames: St Benet Fink and St Benet Sherehog; St Clement Eastcheap and St Clement Danes; St Michael le Querne and St Michael Paternoster Royal. Stow's own dim church of St Andrew Undershaft, he would tell you, got its name from the tall maypole next door, confiscated after the 1517 May Day festivities got out of hand. Whereas St Andrew-by-the-Wardrobe, currently blazing away now at the bottom of St Andrew's Hill, got its name from a thirteenth-century royal warehouse nearby. And at the bottom of St Andrew's Hill, the vicar was now braving the flames to rescue not just church plate and linen but its even more precious parish registers of births, marriages and deaths going back to when John Stow was a young man.

There had been Marys by the dozen among the churches too: Mary Abchurch, Mary At Hill, Mary Bothaw, Mary Colechurch, Mary Aldermary. And, not far from the Cockney-creating St Mary-le-Bow, there was St Mary Aldermanbury, beside the Guildhall. And as Aldermanbury burned tonight, St Mary's was burning with it.

John Stow might have been surprised to find two of his more non-descript contemporaries celebrated here: a churchwarden and a vestryman who earned their living as actors – and were responsible for getting the complete works of one of their late colleagues into print. Without John Heminges and Henry Condell, declared an obelisk in the churchyard, surrounded by roaring flames, the Shakespeare we knew would be so much the poorer: no *As You Like It*, no *Julius Caesar*, no *Antony and Cleopatra*. And no final playwright-prophecy of the day when, towers, temples and gorgeous palaces – even 'the great Globe itself' – would dissolve and, 'like this insubstantial pageant faded, Leave not a rack behind.'

There were so many stories John Stow could have told, if there was time, about all these bruised and burning churches tonight. St Anne & St Agnes – known as St Anne-in-the-Willows in greener times – St Alban, St Augustine, St Bride's, St Dunstan-in-the-East, St Vedast-alias-Foster, St Mary Abchurch, St Giles Cripplegate . . . No time, no time. No time even to tell them over and to say what had been there before what was there now – and would soon be there no longer.

At least in 1666 the Fire had moved slowly enough for people to get a sense of what they were losing. From the early hours of Sunday morning in Pudding Lane, it had taken until Monday evening before the flames had started to catch hold of St Paul's; Tuesday night before Samuel Pepys took the precaution of burying his wine and Parmesan cheese in his back garden in Seething Lane by the Tower; Wednesday before the flames in Fleet Street had reached the Temple – and Charles II had ordered the blowing up of houses in Cripplegate to stop the fire in its tracks and so save Bart's Hospital from destruction.

At least in 1666 not all the horrors had happened at once, as they seemed to be doing tonight. But then in 1666 there had been no night-time raiders spilling out more and more fires from the sky . . .

In Kingsway, Deputy Chief of the Air Staff Arthur Harris was still at work when news of what was happening overhead drew him up to the Air Ministry roof. He was so struck by what he saw there that he went down and fetched Air Marshal Portal to see it too. They watched as streams of bombers poured firebombs and oil bombs and high explosive into the growing conflagration at the very heart of London's history. A conflagration that was destroying so much that had been loved and cherished. A conflagration which, if the bombers did return tonight to bomb the firefighters, could assume yet more unimaginable proportions. Now the man they called 'Bomber' Harris spoke to his chief with something like anger in his voice: 'Well, they have sown the wind . . .'

HAVING WAVED GOODBYE to the bus at Cotton Street, Bill and Vi Regan set off on foot. But when they reached the Marshal Keate pub, just off Poplar High Street, Bill realised this wasn't going to be a simple walk home.

> I suppose they thought the City was done, and now were dropping them before they got to the centre of London, and we could hear them coming much lower than the barrage balloons are usually moored . . . After a few minutes standing in the pub doorway, we moved on and tried to ignore what was going on.

'We talked to each other,' he wrote later, 'but I can't remember what we talked about.'

They walked on for a bit but then everything around them 'seemed to be alive with explosions' and they had to huddle together on the pavement in the lee of a wall. Bill now realised why the bombers had been able to come in so low: 'The barrage balloons were down . . . above the usual noise we could hear fighters, and bursts of machine-gun fire, and the zoom away, and roar in for another burst.' He asked Vi, 'Shall we go?' And, as they stood up, he brushed the dust from her back, thinking: 'What the hell are we worrying about a little dust on our backs for?'

They had just got across Managers Street when they heard – over the lighter sound of a night fighter in hot pursuit, its machine-gun chattering away – the drone of a bomber. It seemed to be headed straight for them. 'And then a sound of falling bombs, unmistakable, three of them, and it was taking a long time to happen':

The first one exploded somewhere close, hours later the next one, closer, the third one was whistling straight for us and I was pushing Vi back against the wall, and it was taking a long time, and this thing was still coming at us, and I wondered if it was going to take a very long time to die, then the whistling stopped, then a terrific thump as it hit the ground, and everything seem to expand, then contract with deliberation, and stillness seemed to be all around.

'Bill,' said Vi. 'The last one didn't go off.'

'No,' Bill said. 'It's probably a dud. I wonder if they get their money back, or a replacement?'

'I never asked Vi what she was thinking while it was happening,' he wrote afterwards 'I wanted to know, but I thought it would be invading her privacy, and why was I already trying to be flippant?'

An unexploded bomb was something for the ARP boys, not a Rescue bloke, and so they set off again, holding hands. 'We could hear a racket still going on, but didn't seem to be of any importance. We had had our moment, nothing else was going to bother us in future.' In the middle of the next bridge they stopped and had a good look around them, still holding hands. Then walked on, unhurriedly, along East Ferry Road and strolled into the Heavy Rescue depot in Glengall Road.

'Consternation!' wrote Bill. 'A woman in the men's sleeping quarters.' The boys had received no call-outs so far and everyone was lounging around in the boiler-house, sitting on their bunks or playing cards. Bill introduced Vi around, then nipped across to the office shelter, where his boss told him he really needn't have bothered trying to get back to the depot 'under what he called the prevailing conditions'.

On his return to the boiler-house, Bill found 'Joe Marks had won a couple of blankets, and a bunk, for Vi'. George Jillings had been to the cook-house and made tea, and gave them a mug each. Then 'everyone settled down and waited for daylight'. Bill decided:

Whatever may happen in the next few days, must wait, until I get down on paper, the way we got home from Lidstone; and if our Joan and little Vi get to read this, which I very much hope they do, some day in the future, they will know their dear mother much better than a normal life could ever tell them.

Tonight, though, they would have only had to ask the other blokes at the depot: 'Everyone thinks Vi is wonderful,' Bill recorded at the end of his account of their adventure: 'No one even thinks about me.'

BILL AND VI might have felt invulnerable as they strolled down East Ferry Road after their 'moment' but the dangers around them had been very real. One fireman from nearby Fire Station No. 35 had already been injured earlier this evening at Glengall Grove School, and at 9.25 p.m. the 35 watchroom registered a call 'by stranger' to the Globe Rope Works in East Ferry Road. Rope-making was one of the many traditional dockland trades that had a hungry appetite for fire, and Hawkins & Tipsons had been set ablaze by a shower of incendiaries. Station Officer John Hill, forty-six, was an experienced fireman – but when you took a crew out in a raid like this there were never any guarantees. Before the night was out, he would be one of five firemen rushed from the scene to Poplar Hospital. Before the next day was out, his wife Mary would be a widow.

AT REDCROSS STREET, Jean Savory and her colleagues at No. 68 Station were continuing to take calls at a fearsome rate. Their appeals for assistance from further afield had finally been heeded, and a senior officer arriving there found 'appliances were approaching from all angles'. As the 'No. 1' men reported in with their details – station coming from, type of appliance, number of men in crew and name of man in charge – they were allocated a fire. To lessen the chaos in the narrow City streets, jobs were given out on the basis of which way each vehicle happened to be pointing at the time. There were plenty of fires to go around: it was later estimated that the Luftwaffe started 1,500 fires tonight.

Although, paradoxically, as time went on the number of fires was actually going down even as it was rising. Not because of the firemen's and firewatchers' many welcome successes, but because tens of hundreds of small fires were growing and combining to produce a single mass of flame. When the pathfinders of Kampfgruppe 100 had swung away from the target area just before seven o'clock, heading for home, they reported seeing fifty-four fires, seventeen of them very large, on both sides of the river. Now the City seemed to be in the grip of three huge blazes which had exhausted all the London Fire Brigade's precise gradations of small, medium, serious and even major. These were 'conflagrations'. There was a conflagration engulfing 'Wine Land' with All Hallows Barking at its heart, where the Regans had heard the screaming dray horses. A second, even larger, raged south and east of St Paul's, running along Cheapside and Cannon Street and Queen Victoria Street, where Mr Walden had come through. The largest of all was north of St Paul's, covering most of the north-west of the City and up into Finsbury, Islington and beyond. And these last two, within a matter of yards of the north and south sides of the Cathedral, were now threatening to become one.

Just north of the Cathedral, six million new books were burning along Paternoster Row, and the textile warehouses between Paternoster Row and St Paul's Churchyard looked set to follow. At Lambeth Fire Brigade HQ, one firewoman saw her officer go white as he took a phone call. 'That was the Prime Minister,' he told her. 'He told me that St Paul's must be saved at all costs.' The message was sent to City Control in the Guildhall basement, who conveyed it to the St Paul's Watch. 'We were grateful for this voice from outside assuring us that the thoughts of many were with us that night,' wrote the Dean afterwards, 'though it would not be true to say that the Watch was spurred to greater efforts, for it was already extended to the limit of human endurance.'

AT THE GUILDHALL, members of the fire squad were helping the AFS men flatten out the hose from the trailer pump and run it indoors to the Great Hall while Mr George ran on ahead to assess the situation. Inside the Hall, everything was still in comparative darkness but there were flames licking at the centre of the south roof. The firemen came in and stood ready, their branch directed towards the spot, and the water started coming.

The flow was poor; young Lott was told to run back to the pump-man and ask him for all the water pressure they could have, but he returned minutes later with the message that they already had it. There were a lot of pumps taking water from a lot of hydrants tonight.

Then came the moment that London Fire Region's Aylmer Firebrace called the Blitz firefighter's 'continual bugbear'. One minute the AFS men were standing, branch in hand, braced against a blast of water; the next, the water gave, in the words of the fire chief, 'the impression of retreating resignedly back into its hose'. And the flow dried up completely.

Fire is the firefighter's business but water is his life. It is, in Firebrace's words, 'the fireman's ammunition'. When it runs out, flames which have been held at bay or even forced into retreat come swaggering back, full of bravado, like stone-throwing youths who realise a soldier's gun has jammed.

The AFS men inside the Great Hall were now in an all-too-familiar quandary. The problem might be purely local: a hose burned through, back along its length, by an incendiary; squashed flat or blocked by a sudden fall of masonry; burst by a racing vehicle whose wheels hadn't kept to the ramps which protected hoses across vulnerable junctions. It was possible, though, that the trailer pump itself had been hit: in one bizarre incident elsewhere in the City tonight, a crew was forced to turn its hose on its own TP after it burst into flames – and by some miracle the water kept pumping long enough to put the fire out.

The first thing the firemen in the Great Hall had to do now was check that their hose was intact and their pump wasn't on fire – or blown to pieces – out in the Yard. But this wasn't simply a matter of putting the hose on the floor and going to find out. If the water came back on again with the hose unattended, the heavy metal branch would whip and swirl round the room like a crazy thing, breaking limbs and cracking skulls. So young Lott was given the responsibility of holding the branch for a while, like a real fireman, while the situation was investigated.

It turned out that both hose and pump were intact, which meant that the problem must be further back and therefore more severe. The water main that they were tapping into had probably been fractured by one of the HE explosions, water bubbling up into the air somewhere or seeping uselessly into the earth.

The Victorians who designed London's water supply had been more concerned to have pipes accessible for repair than about burying them deep beyond the range of high explosive. At just three to ten feet below the roadway, water mains were frequent casualties in air raids – an average of seventy breaks a night across London's 6,000 miles of main, which had to be located and isolated by a turncock to keep the water supply going.

Half a million pounds had been spent before the war to try to prepare the capital for the fight ahead. New pumping stations built at Charing Cross and Blackfriars Bridge helped to fill three huge new 'dirty water mains' which fed rain, river and lake water to special hydrants which couldn't be worked by a little TP, only by a heavy. But these mains could be broken too.

The Metropolitan Water Board had doubled its staffing levels ready for war but, even so, until they located the right stopcock and shut off the leak, firemen were often condemned to stand, waterless, as buildings burned before them. The Brigade's local water officer would be calling in the turncocks now and racing to tap into one of the alternative sources of supply in the meantime. If he could find more water to refill the Guildhall Yard dam, then the gush might resume at any moment. There was nothing for the firemen to do but go back to their branch, hang on, wait and hope.

When there was a fire, the first duty of a water officer, it was drummed into him, was *to remain on his own ground*. And he should know his ground like the back of his hand. Not only every hydrant into clean or dirty water main, but every river, canal and dock basin, steel artificial dam or canvas version which could be brought in on a lorry and filled. London was built on an artesian basin, which provided plentiful supplies of clean water for the capital's many breweries: Whitbread's, up in the Barbican area, had vast water tanks which 68 Station's water officer knew all about. But there were other, smaller wells around the City, like Hoare's Bank in Fleet Street and nearby Bouverie House. Swimming pools were designated as emergency water supplies too – and new children's paddling pools had been built in many London parks before the war (a neat idea that Commander Firebrace had brought home after a trip to Sweden). Not that there were parks and pools close at hand in the crowded City. But then there was no telling how far water might have to come tonight.

'Of all the monotonous jobs,' AFS man Frank Hurd had noted in one of his essays, 'I think series pumping is the worst.'

> The idea is to relay water from a considerable distance either direct or, as in this case, to a point adjacent to the fire. Pumps are spaced about 1,000' apart, starting from the water supply & water is pumped thro' this 'chain', each pump passing the water on. The pumps are used to maintain pressure, as over long distances, the 'lifting' pump is not sufficient to force the water thro'.

Frank's first experience of this thankless task – which mostly involved keeping an eye on your pump, and guarding your hose from being burst by speeding traffic, in order to feed water to a fire you probably couldn't even see – had been over the Black Saturday weekend. Stuck out in the open at a crossroads in the East End as bombs and shrapnel rained down, with only his fire engine for cover, he must have thought that this was about as bad as it got. But the waterless men at the Guildhall tonight were not to be envied either.

The officer in charge of the fire at Guildhall made another call back to '68', reporting that the appliances he'd asked for had arrived but that now the mains were dry. What should he do?

'Line up the men and tell them to . . .' – the exasperated Station Officer Waterman glanced at the upturned faces of the young Watchroom girls – 'spit on it!'

Meanwhile the Guildhall's own fire squad was not ready to give up on the Great Hall yet. They still had their buckets and stirrup pumps, which they hoped might be of some use provided they could get up close enough. Someone went to get the telescopic ladder that the electricians used for changing the light bulbs. But, as with the escape by the church, no one was familiar with how the ladder worked, and as the already-exhausted men

241

struggled with the unwieldy apparatus in the gloom its ropes got caught up. Out in the Yard, by the blazing St Lawrence Jewry, the big red metal escape was tall enough to do the job. And there were firemen about now who knew how to use it. But the blast wall that had been built in front of the entrance to the Guildhall made the approach too narrow to get the thing through.

Mr Fitzhugh, running into the Great Hall, was surprised to see that there were small flames licking the inside of the roof, though he wasn't too alarmed at first. It looked as if things were under control: Mr Arnold was setting up an expanding ladder to reach the flames and there were members of the fire squad, the Hallkeeper's night staff, LFB and AFS, all on hand. Then the firemen who were standing, branches at the ready, aimed toward the flames, told him that they had been standing like this, without water, for the past fifteen minutes.

Mr Munson finally gave up hope of the electricians' ladder and went back up on the roof to see what a stirrup pump from above could do. But he realised that the roof must now be well alight beneath him: 'With each strong gust of wind the flames appeared to be drawn right through the slates momentarily and then disappeared as the gust passed.' It was like bellows on a coal fire.

Across the river, the firemen tackling the many blazes at Guy's Hospital found, like their colleagues at the Guildhall, that their hoses were emptying one by one as the demands on the mains outstripped supply. The hospital's own water tanks were empty by now too, and so was the swimming pool. However, they were only a matter of a few hundred yards from the River Thames. River water was never used directly on a fire but could be pumped into a canvas dam, to be accessed by heavies: that way you avoided too much mud and debris in the pumps. At high tide, a heavy duty pump could be positioned near the river and a length of hose simply dropped in. At low tide, the firefighters relied on the fireboats and heavy pumping units fitted on dumb barges, put in position by tugs, to get the water out from the centre of the river.

Thirty-one fire boats were at work tonight, but ten times as many wouldn't have been enough. Some were fighting wharf fires direct. One working in St Katharine's Dock had struck a sunken wreck. Others trying to come up from below Tower Bridge had to be halted after a time bomb fell into the Thames. One fire boat came downriver from Barnes, where the Thames was much narrower, with only four lengths of hose. When firemen went down to connect hoses with another boat that had been ordered to the north end of Southwark Bridge, they found it had gone to the south side by mistake and had already been put to work. And there were only three tugs to manoeuvre the Fire Service's five dumb barges.

Even the Thames itself seemed to be conspiring against them tonight. It was low tide. Worse than that, it was very low even for a 'spring' tide – one of those nights in the year when the sun and moon's gravitational pull work in unison to drag the waters as far away from the riverbanks as they can get. In order to maintain the pressure from the centre of the river, the firemen would have to get their own pumps as near to the fire-boats as possible. Where they could, crews on both banks of the river manhandled trailer pumps down the river steps to the very edge of the mud, into which they waded waist-high with their heavy hoses to make the connection. Some even tried suspending TPs on ropes over the bridges – anything was worth trying in order to get at the water without which they were impotent.

At Guy's, the May Pond entrance was burning and the front way out of the Hospital was blocked by a raging fire in Downs Brothers, a large surgical instrument shop. On the Borough side, there was a petrol station ablaze and a fire behind Nuffield House. There was a constant tinkle of broken glass as windows cracked in the heat and fell out on to Newcomb Street, where flames from burning houses licked the hospital walls. Put simply: the hospital was surrounded by fire; there was no water; and without water there could be no escape. A policeman who had managed to beat a path in through the flames told the acting Matron and Superintendent that there was no way that any ambulances could get in to evacuate the remaining patients. But they should ready them to leave so that if and when the hoses started to work again everyone would be ready to move immediately.

In LEADENHALL, worldwide insurers Lloyd's of London, hosts to the FAU shelter, maintained a fire squad of about fifty, who were managing to keep on top of their own share of problems. From their roof, though, they had a clear view of what others were suffering: 'The air was filled with burning embers from the cloth warehouses round St Paul's and heavy with the drone of enemy bombers, which seemed to come in without any hindrance, drop a load into the middle of the great fires and depart.'

From their vantage point high up on the roofs of the Cathedral, the Dean and his team had been able to track the rapid progress of the flames from building to building around the Churchyard. 'We noted that some could have been saved had there been easy access to them,' he wrote, 'but the owners had locked up and gone home as in the days of peace!' The high wind, he noted, carried the flames and blazing pieces of wood over very long distances.

Hitchcock, Williams' conscientious fire guard, led as ever by Mr Lester, had fought valiantly. But, hemmed in on all sides by the blazing cloth warehouses of St Paul's Churchyard, and the burning books of Paternoster Row behind, they didn't stand a chance. Even if the building had to go, however, the business could still be saved, and staff hurried to secure as many of the most important ledgers and papers as possible. It was now imperative that their four basement shelters be evacuated. But where to? With fire and falling masonry all around it was too dangerous to go far, but the crypt of St Paul's lay just across the Churchyard, so permission was sought for entry. The drill would, naturally, be ladies first. Mr Lester had a quiet word with Mr Walden, entrusting to him the task of conducting the female members of staff. 'They quietly collected their necessities and blankets,' Mr Walden recorded:

> And with one or two excusable exceptions, the calm manner of their journey despite the sight of flames and sparks which greeted them upon coming out of doors to ground level, is worthy of very special mention. The men followed shortly afterwards.

Fortunately, the electricity men had been hard at work in the City and lights had just come back on in the crypt. The Cathedral staff prepared to receive their guests, even though the question of how much protection they really had to offer shelterers had never been satisfactorily resolved. The Watch were used to taking their chances, but Mr Linge had come down one night to find the gatekeeper facing over forty men, women and children, who had fled their Friday Street shelter when it was surrounded by fire. The gatekeeper had tried to persuade them that there were not enough safe places to take them all but it was no use.

> They were very frightened and distressed and one soon realised that their coming to the Cathedral was an act of faith. Some chairs were hastily found for them at the west end of the Crypt. The expression of relief from their ordeal was ample reward for any trouble we had taken.

The Dean, reading Mr Linge's report of the incident later, wondered if that was the same night that he had found some emergency guests had recovered from their distress sufficiently to be playing cards. He wondered whether he ought to stop them: 'What absurd thoughts one has in times of strain!'

Now, with around a hundred firewatchers, first-aiders and other workers on their way from Hitchcock, Williams – and others coming in from nearby shelters through streets blazing on all sides – and no feasible prospect of evacuating them to a place of genuine safety, the whole night would have to become an act of faith.

Inevitably, kettles were put on. But it was perhaps a reflection of the seriousness of tonight's situation that the refugees were greeted with cocoa rather than tea. Mr Walden was grateful for the cocoa, and the turmoil of his feelings was much relieved by the quiet atmosphere of the crypt, which made it seem miles away from the chaos outside. A younger colleague Gordon Papps, a firewatcher who lived in the now-burning premises, found the silence more eerie than anything.

Typical Londoners, many in the crypt tonight had never visited the Cathedral before. One young lady took the opportunity to quiz a clergyman about the funeral carriage of the Duke of Wellington, one of the more extravagant reminders of the great and good buried here. The crypt of St Paul's provided a wealth of memento mori for those settling down to a night of fitful sleep. Some shelterers made themselves as comfortable as possible in pews but the majority settled for the cold stone floor, only a matter of feet above the defunct Londoners whose numbers they might join before sunrise.

This didn't escape their notice. 'My own blanket,' recorded Mr Walden, 'covered a flat gravestone, the inscription of which recorded the death in 1787 of Elias Jenkins, a former verger of the Cathedral.' The enterprising Gordon Papps, meanwhile, had secured himself a fur coat from the stock that was about to go up in flames and he was sleeping on that. And, in a move that Mr Walden might have found more than a little presumptuous, he had settled down to sleep on the grave of co-founder of the firm and YMCA paterfamilias Sir George Williams.

Chapter Nineteen

SUNDAY Home Service
9.25 Bach's Christmas Oratorio, parts 3 and 4.

BBC Radio Times Christmas Edition, 1940

IN CHALK FARM, Isabelle Granger had been disappointed in her hopes of a blissful evening of Bach. When she should have been listening to the shepherds lauding the 'ruler of the sky' in exultation at the angels' message of peace on earth, she was standing in a freezing, unnatural daylight created not by an angelic host but by the burning City, a few miles off. And the sound around her was the crackle of machine-guns as the RAF attempted to clear the sky of Nazi bombers.

The BBC faded out when raids became heavy, and this was one of the nastiest raids she could remember. Mercifully, Freidl was away tonight, so they were spared his gas-tap obsession. But the incessant din had even put a stop to her knitting as angry-sounding planes flew low over them for hour after hour. They had not heard many bombs fall close by, however, so at about nine she and Lilibet had decided to go outside with their friend Margery, who was staying overnight in Freidl's absence.

Outside the sky was aglow: 'the night had turned into a wild surmise of leaping flames: it was awe-inspiring, horrible, wonderfully beautiful'. But though it was, she wrote to Harrison Brown afterwards, 'horrible & tragic',

> nothing like this is intolerable in this war when we understand its mentality. I hate being bombed & am frightened often & resentful of its interference with my normal life. But if it's the way to show most people what Hitler & the Appeasers stood for, then let the bombs drop & shriek out louder than we've been able to: it's a language everyone understands & if it will restore a sense of values to everyone, every bomb is worth while. I must say people are not bitter; the Lion tamer, the ARP wardens in the street, the grocer, don't like it, but they haven't mixed up Germany with Hitler. None of my friends are having trouble about being Germans or Austrians & the worst fury comes from Lilibet & Irina who feel that reprisals are the only way to teach their fellow-countrymen what it's like & to stop this terrible business.

In Brixton, things had been dropping all around the Speed household.

'Etta says her aunt, a very good woman, prays for us,' May noted in her diary. 'Pleasant thought. "And," she said to Etta, "He has kept you safe."' Then, at twenty-five past nine exactly, she recorded: 'Heavy biff and repercussion. With falling glass.' Something had hit the house. She put down her diary, got out of bed and ran upstairs in the dark to investigate.

As she reached the top landing, she received a sudden blow to the face. Feeling around in the dark, she realised that she had walked into something. 'Some silly fool has left the cupboard door open,' she told herself – then it dawned on her that it must have been blown open by blast. Inside the cupboard half the plaster was down, and when she looked up there was an eighteen-inch-square hole in the roof, through which she could see a patch of brilliant light. When she looked down again, she could now see in the glow that the landing was scattered with coping.

She thought that the glare up above might be coming from fires outside. But equally, she realised, it might indicate an incendiary burning in their loft – to which there was no access. Calling downstairs for the stirrup pump, she ran back as far as the ground floor where she found Norah waiting, water bucket in hand. This she thrust into May's hands, leaving her to lumber back up the stairs carrying both the bucket of water and the pump, while Etta Evans loyally trailed behind with a bucket of sand.

HAVING VACATED the burning Hermitage in Wapping once the ambulance had taken their patients away, Nev and Robin of the FAU had been called to the First Aid Post at Matilda House flats, where they pitched in, helping to treat cuts, bruises and shock – there had also been two fatalities. Then it was time to locate their 'scattered Hermitage family', who had been conducted through the streets to shelter in two Colonial wharves on either side of Wapping High Street: the smaller, riverside, shelter was usually reserved for employees; the larger one wasn't usually open at all and was in complete darkness.

Hoping to rustle up more supplies from the FAU, they made for the nearest ARP Post but found it out of action and abandoned so pressed on to St Peter's School, which was locked. They forced the door and, fortunately, the phone inside was still working. Nev rang in for blankets, first-aid equipment and as many men as could be spared, and said he'd be back in half an hour with an update.

It was now ten minutes to ten and firemen were fighting an almost hopeless battle against the fast-spreading fires. The roof of the small Colonial building was already on fire by the time Nev and Robin reached it, and wardens were moving shelterers across the road to the larger one. Nev went back to St Peter's to report and ask for a mobile canteen to be sent.

Almost at that moment, like the cavalry, the pacifists arrived: an open truck 'with ten men ranged in the back like stormtroopers with their tin hats and packs'. Two stayed at the school in case it was needed as an emergency rest centre later on, while Nev took the others with him, dropping two each off at the St John's, Orient and Morocco shelters. The last pair would go with him to the Colonial, which was now sheltering 500 people.

IN THE HEART of the City, the police and Fire Brigade warned the fire guard of Wood Street telephone exchange that it was time to evacuate. Four staff stayed behind with a trailer pump crew, ready to do what they could – although they had no water to do it with. At the CTO nearby, any staff who were sleeping in the Refuges and had not already been woken by the explosions were now roused by the wardens. The basements were starting to flood. Also, the church of Greyfriars opposite was well alight and there was a possibility that the spire could come crashing down and trap them. Staff were evacuated first to 'C' shelter, then to 'R', and finally, for the first time since the Blitz began, to the subterranean fastness of the Post Office Railway.

IN THE STRAND, sustained by their Savoy dinner, Bill White and Marguerite decided that it was high time they began covering the story unfolding outside. There were still no fires close to the hotel but, about a quarter to half a mile away, a bank of smoke rose up, Bill judged, several thousand feet high and they could see the light of huge fires reflected on its underside. It would be worth getting a taxi if they could find one, but they still found fire engines were more common on the streets than cabs. One did come from the direction of the fire and stopped for them. But the driver seemed really frightened and told them the whole City was alight, out of control, and that nothing would take him back there, not even two quid – though he did wait to see if the two quid was offered. It wasn't.

They decided they would probably have to settle for proceeding on foot but, around ten, they found a young cabbie who said he was interested in seeing for himself what was happening anyway, and that he would carry them for whatever they thought it was worth. He said that he had heard that the flames were moving on to St Paul's and that the Guildhall was going too. They told him to drive to where the glow was brightest.

MAY SPEED was mightily relieved when, just after ten o'clock, Fred popped back to check up on them all and she could consult him about the hole in the roof. He had maintained a discreet silence this evening, he said, when someone at the Post had said, 'Now every Warden has had something done to his house.' And here it was, true after all. He went upstairs to look at the hole and was able to reassure his sisters that there was no incendiary burning in the loft.

Fred said that a bomb had hit the Billiard Hall in Brixton Road and another had hit 30 Holland Grove: it was probably this that had thrown up the debris that had made a hole in their roof. He was still on duty and had to go back so May accompanied him as far as the front door. Outside, she could see that the streets were littered with rubble and, as he left, Fred warned her not to expect a gas supply in the morning.

IN WAPPING, Nev Coates could see in the bright glare that the main streets were beginning to pack with fire engines and that the rapid spread of the fires had now all but surrounded the larger Colonial wharf too. Now, for the hundreds of Hermitage folk inside, 'epic move number 3 began'.

> Some were reluctant to go, but eventually everyone joined in the long quarter-of-a-mile trek, using alleys and back lanes to avoid the fires. A ghostly pilgrimage of people, picking their way in the smoke between hosepipes, splashing in the running gutters, carrying their bedding and babies, old men being carried on chairs, families huddled closely together, looking grim and scared, but very brave. Everyone helping each other, and not the slightest sign of panic.
>
> The bombing had miraculously stopped – some said the fighters were up, others heard the machine gun fire.

The displaced were now crammed into the already crowded St John's, Orient and Morocco shelters. But at least the mobile canteen had found its way through, and 300 LCC blankets arrived in a van for those who had to spend tonight on cold concrete. 'Again those who still could, gave help to the exhausted and shocked, our little prostitute being an angel helping with kids and cheering folks up.' When the shelterers were settled, the FAU men worked on, supplying scores of firemen with refreshment. Nev watched one of his colleagues:

> grimy, tin hat awry, cheerful as ever, scrambling up ladders, hands full – 'A cup of tea – some cake?' 'Gawd bless yer, mite.' 'Tea and cake?' 'Just the job, I've been fighting this effing fire for five hours.'

FEW PEOPLE had got anything to eat at the Guildhall this evening: calls were still flooding in to the City Control Room in the basement and there had been no time for supper. Mr Murphy decided that it was time he found out just what the situation was like up above them. Earlier, he had received the message that a small fire on the roof was being dealt with. Then another that both the ordinary and hydraulic water supplies had broken down. He went up to the Lady Mayoress's Gallery overlooking the Great Hall: he should be able to judge for himself how things were going from there.

It hadn't taken long for the wind to whip the 'small flames' that Mr Fitzhugh had seen into something more formidable. Looking down into the Hall, Mr Murphy found 'a lofty, murky cavern, illuminated in its upper portions by the flames which were now consuming the fleche [the small spire in the centre of the roof-ridge] and by the light of the fires outside pouring through the east and west windows'. Indeed, so strong was the light coming in through the west window that he could no longer make out any of its coloured figures – only the stone tracery standing in sharp relief against the glare.

The accustomed silence of the great dark hall had been replaced by a deafening cacophony: 'The roar of the flames and the crackle of the burning woodwork drowned even the voices of the figures of the firemen, just visible on the floor below, who continued to play their hose, through which water occasionally trickled, despite the danger of falling beams and embers.' Though he couldn't hear what was being said, he saw that a runner had suddenly arrived with a message that sent several members of the fire squad dashing out of the Hall.

The Guildhall Library's Newspaper Room was on fire. The seat of the blaze seemed to be a ventilator in the ceiling, so Messrs Arnold, Byford and Fitzhugh rushed upstairs to Post No. 2, where filled buckets again stood at the ready. They could see smoke and flame issuing from the ventilator in the centre of the roof: an incendiary was lodged inside but hadn't exploded, and they reckoned they could still put it out if it was doused thoroughly. For the next ten minutes, in relays, they edged inch by inch along the arch of the roof, balancing a bucket of water in either hand, till they could reach the ventilator and pour the water down it.

It was now about eleven o'clock and it was time for Mr Murphy to think about getting his Control Room staff out of the basement, where they were in grave danger of being cut off. He would have a tricky job of it: the nearest exit was on the west of the building but that was too

250

dangerous – fires had now worked their way up and down Aldermanbury.

Up on the roofs, the three fire squad men were finally satisfied that their fire in the Newspaper Room ventilator was out, and looked about them. They could see that the whole of the Great Hall roof was catching light and they couldn't do much about that with buckets and stirrup pumps, so they decided to make the best escape they could downstairs through the now-searing heat. From the roof of the Library corridor to the Council Chamber they ran the gauntlet of flaming embers, then descended by an iron staircase to the Works Department. Through all his adventures so far Mr Fitzhugh had still been wearing his ordinary shoes, so Mr Arnold gave him the key to the store of No. 4 Shelter where the gumboots were kept and he went off with Mr Kimber and young Lott, to change into them.

It was without much hope that the others went back into the Hall one last time to see if there was anything they could do. The situation was as bad as they had feared though, ironically, everything that they had been hoping for such a short time ago was finally in place. Water had started to flow again through the firemen's hoses; Mr Guggiari and the others, who had been struggling all this time to erect the electricians' ladder, had finally got it in place. But it was too little and too late. The firemen warned them that the roof might fall in and that it was time to clear out. By the time Mr Fitzhugh rushed up in his gumboots, it was too dangerous to enter.

But even if the Great Hall was lost, the fire squad was not giving up on the rest of the building without a fight. Mr Kimber and Mr Lott damped down a heap of debris they found burning in the Works Department yard and young Lott was detailed to keep an eye on the situation. But, hard as he worked, each time he went away, the fire had sprung back into life again when he came back to check. Finally, Mr Munson and Mr Hitchcock came back with him and together they damped the whole area down thoroughly. This was now imperative as the yard was being constantly blasted with burning cinders raining down from the next door warehouse. Bradbury Greatorex – the textile firm whose firewatchers had yelled the first warning to No. 1 Post back at the beginning of the raid – was now well alight itself.

The Lady Mayoress's Gallery, from which Mr Murphy had looked down into the burning Hall such a short time ago, was ablaze too. The squad kept the flames at bay there for a while – until a fall of masonry and the crackle of the wooden floor outside the Hallkeeper's Office drew them out and they could see that flames were licking the lobby door.

Most of the fire squad were gathered outside the Hallkeeper's Office door, where they had dealt so efficiently with that first incendiary – how many hours ago was it? – when a loud crash sent them running into the Council Chamber. A flaming block of wood had fallen from its roof. Young Lott joined Mr Sharp in treading out cinders, but it was no good: the fire was already burning above their heads in the lobby and slowly edging down towards the Committee Rooms. Lott tried the hydrant outside No. 3 Committee Room, but there was not a drop of water in it. The whole roof looked like giving way and it would clearly soon be as doomed as the Hall.

As THEIR TAXI headed towards the main fires, Bill White and Marguerite now and then passed a pump 'puffing away at a hydrant', or the cab would suddenly bump over a fire hose leading off to some distant fire (occasioning, no doubt, some choice expletives at a distant branch). They stopped at a rope barrier slung across the road and it was here that they got their first whiff of the fire – but it was not, thought Bill, the strong rancid stench that they had become accustomed to in raids: 'I remember noticing even then that for some reason it was vaguely pleasant and harmonized with the orange glow which penetrated everything so that we could see each other's faces even in the car.'

Bill and Marguerite showed their press cards and the taxi was allowed through the police line but the streets ahead were blocked by fire engines. They asked the cabbie to park so they could get out and investigate.

At the Associated Press building, which they both knew well, the roof had fallen in and the firemen were attempting to stop the fire from spreading by soaking a lower floor, though only three feeble streams of water were hissing from the branches and hitting the red-hot roof timbers with a frying noise. They were told that nearby St Bride's was burning too and they went to look.

As they turned the corner, the sight before them was heartbreakingly beautiful, like a Christmas card picture, with light streaming from the church windows just as they had before the war. But as they approached as near to the open doors as the heat would allow, they could see that the roof of St Bride's had already fallen in and that pieces of stone, 'about the size of your hand and sometimes as big as your head', were peeling from the walls in a steady rain, 'clicking and knocking and rattling down on the stone floor'.

They noticed, too, that curious smell – almost like incense, Marguerite suggested. The burning of seasoned oak that had been put in place a quarter of a millennium ago, plus 'the ancient records of venerable British business firms whose columns of figures supported the empire', combined, wrote Bill afterwards, into a haunting perfume that ought to be bottled: 'Surely no attar of roses could ever be so expensive as this scent which you could only get by burning the City of London.'

ERNIE PYLE was also out and about. He had borrowed a tin hat and left the Savoy with his friends from the balcony – though he had pretty soon split off from the group to wander alone. He saw plenty of those bouncing football incendiaries that were so easily smothered if you got to them in time. But as he walked along Fleet Street, he also saw an undetected firebomb finally reveal its unsuspected presence as a dark five-storey building suddenly leapt into flames.

He found he didn't need to show his Press card anywhere: no one seemed very interested in stopping a man in a tin hat wandering where he liked – so he did. A little foolishly, sometimes, he realised after he had walked the length of a 'street that was afire both sides, past walls that would soon be ready to fall'. All around him,

> Hundreds of small motor pumps, carried in two-wheeled trailers behind cars, stood in the streets. The engines made such a whir you couldn't have heard a plane overhead. Firemen by the hundreds were working calmly, shouting orders to each other, smoking cigarettes, and paying no attention to pedestrians.

He walked ten blocks, picking his way over the muddle of hosepipes, never fearful but only concerned that he shouldn't get in the firemen's way. It was the strangest thing:

> Somehow I didn't have a feeling that this was war . . . Even when I came upon two buildings that had been blown to dust by heavy bombs less than an hour before, there was still a feeling that it was all perfectly 'natural'.

Ritchie Calder, too, out on behalf of the *Daily Herald*, found a strange equilibrium on the streets. Though for him,

> Only that private self with whom I took urgent consultation knows what reluctance, misgiving and honest-to-goodness wind-up had to be overcome before I ventured out. It did not last long, because what courage I lacked I borrowed from the wardens, from the civilians whom I found scrambling into burning buildings to drag out valuables or to douche incendiaries, and from the Auxiliary Firemen who were singing as they fought the fires, regardless of the imminence of 'Jerry' overhead.

As a group of AFS men investigated one of the Fleet Street hydrants, Calder heard the firemen's 'theme song'– *Our John's a fireman bold . . .* – floating towards him and felt 'rather like a child who has been taken comfortingly by the hand and told that there is no reason to be afraid of the bogey-man upstairs'. It was time, he decided, to go back upstairs himself and see if the bogeyman was still about.

What he saw, from the top of a building that had regularly given him shelter in the past, was that the rooftops of Fleet Street had become a 'stockade of flames'. The Middle Temple library and part of the *Daily Telegraph* building were both burning furiously. Looking towards St Bride's, he saw its spire as a 'macabre Christmas tree festooned in fire' with its inner pillars burning like candles. Churches were burning like torches elsewhere too – even St Paul's, it seemed, as the fires appeared to lap around its dome: 'As one ventured to the edge of the roof the flames reached out like fondling arms from nearby buildings.' It felt, he wrote,

> like a Smithfield Martyr must have felt as faggots were lit around him. Or that one was living a nightmare marooned on a rock as a burning tide rose.

Above the City, dense clouds of smoke were lit up by the fires from below, 'as the smoke of a railway-engine is from a firebox. But such a firebox, incandescent clouds as angry as Judgement Day.'

Calder's horror was all the more intense because he knew this area so well. It was not sentimental attachment to familiar haunts that worried him but what was inside these buildings that could, at any change in the wind, become next in the fire's path: 'a paper warehouse, or a varnish works, or a celluloid store, or a photographer's wholesaler stocked with film – food for the insatiable appetite of the flames.'

Aylmer Firebrace believed that, in the end, the only way to learn about fires was by fighting fires. Ritchie Calder could do nothing from his rooftop perch to hold back the tide of flame but, as he watched this sight, unseen since 1666, he received an intensive education in how the fire monster operated. He even discerned a 'kind of routine' in the way it devoured London:

> Flames licked round the walls as though they were sampling a fresh tit-bit; then thrust through the windows and attacked the stores hungrily. Beams caught alight. The roofs slowly sagged as though they were gelatine, and then crashed with a roar. A container would explode and add fresh fuel to the flames. Floors would be eaten through and collapse in succession and then, with each new gift of stores, the fires would leap up.

At 37 Fleet Street, Hoare's Bank was experiencing what was recorded in the company diary as 'for us at the bank . . . quite the most exciting night of the war'. Derick and Mary had emerged from *The Thief of Bagdad* into a Technicolor adventure of their own, with a bus ride from a lit-up Trafalgar Square along the Strand, past the Savoy and into work. The bank had received four incendiaries from among the showers that were heard falling 'in quantities' at around 6.30. One, which fell on the roof of the plunge pool, was tackled from the window of the Master of the Temple's house next door. Another failed to go off, while the third exploded but did no serious harm. The fourth, though, had set fire to the roof of the bank's museum and this was still being dealt with when Derick and Mary arrived.

When Derick went up on to the roof with an AFS man he counted twelve fires circling the bank, including one in an adjoining building at the back, one in the Temple next door and one immediately opposite on the far side of Fleet Street. The bank's own fire squad fought alongside the AFS to put out the fire in the adjoining building, until the Fire Brigade decided to stop both Hoare's hose and the one of their own that had been connected to the Fleet Street main, in order to help relieve the demand and maintain decent water pressure on the rest of them.

Hoare's own private well could, in theory, deliver 600 gallons of water per hour to its tanks, but the belt on their deep well pump kept slipping. When Bertram Hoare, who was not due on duty tonight, rang in and heard about the pump he said he would come at once. At about this time 'an HE landed unpleasantly close', blowing out two windows.

The Hoare's team had, like Stanley Champion in Old Street, got something of the wind-up at the sound of machine-guns around nine. But worse was to follow. The firemen could get no water at all through their one remaining fire-hose into the main. It was down to Hoare's Bank's stirrup pumps now, and buckets of water from the filled sinks and baths that had been laid up, as at St Paul's Cathedral, all over the building in preparation for such an eventuality. But they had to try again to get the deep well pump operating.

'To those who have had practical experience of fire-fighting in a heavy raid,' wrote Bertram Hoare later, ' . . . it is clear that much expensive fire equipment is not necessary. It is, however, essential that there should be a determined fire party and a staunch watcher on the roof.' His diary entry for tonight recorded what being a 'determined fire party' meant:

Mary took up a forward position on the warehouse roof as near as possible to the fire next door, holding the nozzle while Bertram pumped until he was relieved by Albert Turner & this continued until the main supply of water came on again.

Bertram & Derick then went to the roof to see what could be done from our hose reel working from our well. It was found to be only long enough to reach a fire on our own top floor but we hope to increase its length for the future.

Looking down from his rooftop, Ritchie Calder saw that 'Johnson's London, those narrow back courts which are the hinterland of Fleet Street, was a flaming acre' – and painter and art teacher turned Auxiliary Fireman Leonard Rosoman was down in the heart of it. The alleyway that ran from Dr Johnson's House in Gough Square to Shoe Lane was too narrow to appear on any but the most detailed maps (though it was Wine Office Court to those who knew it). And Frank Hurd's warnings about 'an eighty foot high wall collapsing into a twenty foot road' in the City would have been all too relevant here tonight.

Leonard Rosoman, in his early twenties, had been standing at his gushing branch at the rear of the *Daily Express* building for many hours already. So it was a relief when the leader of his four-man crew asked him to come and help haul a hose up on to the roof of a nearby building, where it might do more good. A fellow crew member, Sidney Holder, relieved him at the branch and Leonard followed No. 1 into the building. As he remembered it, they had only just got inside when there was 'the most God-awful noise' and, very slowly it seemed, the wall he had left just moments before started to fall, filling the whole alleyway with blazing hot bricks.

Another team of firemen, who had been working to keep flames away from Dr Johnson's house and had lost their way among the smoky alleyways, were horrified witnesses. 'I thought when I saw them that they were too near,' said one of the approaching crew. 'Just at that moment a wall, which looked as if it was bulging dangerously, crashed down on them. As we looked round all we could see was a heap of debris with a hose leading towards it.'

For a time, Leonard and his crew leader were imprisoned in their building. When they were brought out they saw that the pump man, some distance away, was still alive but that Sidney had been buried under a huge weight of bricks.

When they finally found him, there was no describing what they found – but his fireman's steel helmet was flattened, recalled Leonard, 'like a plate'. It would be some weeks before Leonard would be in any fit state, mentally, to return to duty.

There was some confusion about whether more firemen had been caught by the collapse. This was the dilemma the Heavy Rescue faced in every raid and, after an LCC enquiry into the operation of the Rescue service in the very early days of the Blitz, it had been decided that only a senior officer should have to bear the terrible responsibility of pulling a team off a job.

With heavy heart, City depot chief Harry Anderson now did just that. More 'incidents' could happen at any time:

Walls and coping stones were crashing down, filling the narrow streets with debris. Firemen were shouting warnings to each other – 'Watch that wall!' or 'Look out over there!' There were some hoses working but many water mains had been hit and the pumps were taking what water there was from emergency dams.

There would be many other calls on his men's strength and skills before morning:

It was obvious that it would take hours of work by several gangs to make any impression on that enormous pile of rubble and the men would be in constant danger from the other collapsing buildings as they worked. I could not imagine that any of those firemen could possibly be alive under that pile of bricks and mortar so I told the leader to call off his men.

He felt he should inform Control in the Guildhall about his decision and, as he could find no phones working anywhere, he set off to walk, a fifteen-minute journey that tonight would take an hour as he made endless detours round the blocked and cratered streets.

COMMANDER FIREBRACE had also decided he must get out of his car and walk. After an increasingly perilous journey through City streets piled high with debris, he and his staff officer had abandoned their vehicle in Cannon Street. He wanted to get to No. 68 Station Redcross Street, at the heart of the huge conflagration developing to the north of St Paul's, and the only way to do it was on foot.

At Redcross Street, there were no more complaints about not having seen a 'proper fire'. The situation board was completely full, and the girls were now writing addresses on the wall beside it as new fires were rung in, even though the station had no more pumps to send out. Jean Savory saw senior officers arrive and heard them asking questions like: 'What time is high tide at London Bridge?' (The dismal answer was just after half past three tomorrow morning.) During their conference, Commander Firebrace arrived with the latest eye-witness accounts of the chaos outside: 'How black – or, more realistically, how red – is the situation, only those who have recently been in the open realise,' he wrote afterwards.

One by one telephone lines fail; the heat from the fires penetrates to the control room and the atmosphere is stifling. Earlier in the evening, after a bomb falls near, the station lights fail – a few unshaded electric hand lamps now supply bright pin-point lights in sharp contrast to the few oil lamps and some perspiring candles.

The firewomen on duty show no sign of alarm, though they must know, from the messages passing, as well as from the anxious tones of officers, that the situation is approaching the desperate,

Jean Savory certainly learned all she needed to from the calls she was taking from 68's sub-stations – or not taking. Each sub-station had a dedicated phone in the Control Room. Y Station in St Bartholomew's Close, Smithfield, rang through to say they were surrounded by fire and evacuating to a place of safety. There was a call from 68Z Baltic Street to say that the asphalt in the school playground had burst into flames so they were leaving. Although, rather than getting right out of the area, two of the Z firewomen had made their way through the burning streets to help the Redcross Street girls. Calls from X Station, at the Wool Exchange in Basinghall Street next to the Guildhall, had suddenly stopped altogether. That left only U and V, two LCC schools in Central Street and Chequer Street, but the Redcross Street girls were still kept busy taking their calls.

Then the Z phone – silent since Baltic Street was abandoned – suddenly rang. Outwardly calm, Jean felt a jolt: 'we were afraid to answer it, expecting to hear a ghostly voice.' It was Z's gate patrol man. He had not been around when the station was evacuated and was assumed to have found himself a place of safety. 'The whole place is going up in smoke and I must be the only person in the world,' he told Redcross Street. 'Have you any orders for me?'

The calmness of the Redcross Street watchroom concealed a high adrenaline level, as was betrayed when the door was flung open to reveal a red-eyed warden, sweaty and black-faced. 'Your bloody roof's alight!' he yelled before disappearing back into the night – too soon, Commander Firebrace guessed, to hear 'the undismayed, if undisciplined, cry of "Whoopee!" from a firewoman, to be suitably echoed by the remainder'.

It was clear to Commander Firebrace that it was time Redcross Street itself was abandoned. But that would have to be an LFB, not a Home Office, decision so he and Mr Sullivan set about making their own exit from the danger zone. It wouldn't be easy. The scene outside was even more appalling than it had been when they arrived:

> The high wind which accompanies conflagrations is now stronger than ever, and the air is filled with a fierce driving rain of red-hot sparks and burning brands. The clouds overhead are a rose-pink from the reflected glow of the fires, and fortunately it is light enough to pick our way eastward down Fore Street. Here fires are blazing on both sides of the road; burnt-out and abandoned fire appliances lie smouldering in the roadway, their rubber tyres completely melted.

Scrambling and jumping, they used the larger chunks of masonry as stepping stones to negotiate piles of rubble three and four feet high, blocking their passage to the edge of the stricken area.

The LFB officers had come to the same conclusion as Commander Firebrace about 68 and, a few minutes after he left, they gave the command to evacuate. The plan was to regroup at U Station in Central Street and continue running the section from there, but getting to U, which was north of Old Street, was going to be an obstacle race even worse than that which was facing the Commander.

The roads were blocked with debris and their tarred wooden cobbles were blazing. 'An off-duty sub-officer arrived,' Jean Savory recalled:

> found a lorry and, like a knight in shining armour, drove us away. It was not easy. Outside, the whole world was on fire and we were in the middle . . . Our driver spent more time reversing than going forward but, somehow, we found Bunhill Fields and the driver decided to cut through the Honourable Artillery Company's Barracks, where fire pumps were working on a section of the building. The last message we had had from them was, 'Fire spreading to the ammunition store.' But we were not in the mood to tarry.

They finally made it to Central Street, and continued to work from there for the rest of the night.

AFTER HIS DINNER, B. J. Rogers had gone up on the roof with some Bank of England officials to get a better picture of the chaos he had come through.

> Here an appalling sight met our eyes. The whole of London seemed alight! We were hemmed in by a wall of flame in every direction. It was not just big fires just here and there, but a continuous sheet of flame all round us. And so close! The building next door to our dining club was alight and of course the churches and Guildhall are only a few yards away from us. We could see St Lawrence Jewry already burnt out, glowing like an incandescent coal fire, while the Guildhall was burning furiously. In the distance was St Paul's, standing out black in a ring

of fire . . . The other side of the river, in Southwark, was well alight, also the East End and the Docks area. Altogether a wonderful and terrifying sight, and we rather got the wind up, as it looked absolutely out of control, and we thought if it did reach us, how were we going to get away?

The Bank had received its fair share of incendiaries, he learned from the firewatchers, and one 'nasty little fire' had taken hold but, so far, everything was under control on their own premises. He decided to try to get some sleep but, descending into the Treasury, which was 'full of smoke and intolerably hot', he decided it would be wiser not to undress before lying down on his bunk. As he dozed fitfully to the accompaniment of 'lumps of burning stuff falling in the Bullion Yard outside and being stamped out by the night watchmen', he heard a rattle of machine-gun fire and awaited, with dread, the drone of the heavy bombers returning to finish the job.

FOR ELIZABETH BARNICOT, still in the thick of things at Guy's Hospital, the huge task ahead had driven away all thoughts of fear for a time. But as the fires raged on there was nothing to do but wait. Having done all she could do to get the patients and staff ready for evacuation, the perils of their situation hit Elizabeth afresh. She went back down to the basement and said to one of the Sisters there that it was time to pray as hard as she could, because: 'There is no hope now excepting from God.'

Whether the Sister complied or not, there was just a short while later a sudden flurry of activity and they were told to get ready to leave. The Thames tide had turned some time ago and, though high tide was still a long way off, desperate efforts on the foreshore meant that river water was again gushing through the LFB hoses. The firemen's first priority now was to clear a path through the Guy's fire so that staff and patients could be evacuated. The ambulances that had been waiting outside for this moment drove in quickly through the flames and patients were rushed off to other hospitals. Then it was the turn of the maids and the nurses.

The only staff who would be staying on with the firefighters were the acting Matron and Superintendent and the air raid wardens. Elizabeth Barnicot was part of the final evacuation, made up of ward sisters and medical students. With, miraculously, not a single casualty throughout the hospital, their spirits were remarkably high as they trooped through Borough with their bundles and suitcases. They were then driven off in a 'Black Maria', she informed her daughters Ann and Ursula with some relish in her letters afterwards – and 'the students sang'.

Meanwhile, the battle at nearby London Bridge Station continued. And, over at Waterloo Station, those fighting a fire on the roof were not helped by the choking smoke coming from a blazing rubber factory nearby. A time bomb had also gone off, blocking several tracks, and an ack-ack shell had damaged overhead cables, cutting off the station's phones, which meant that the points controlling the trains in and out had to be worked by hand. Though, ironically some coal trucks had provided a protective screen for London & South-West's Necropolis train, which plied the route between the station and 'the most peaceful railway station in the kingdom' at Brookwood Cemetery.

A DOZEN TIMES through the night, Leslie Paul and a neighbour had been to the shelter door in Forest Hill to see what was happening and to argue about the source of the different fires. They watched 'great red suns break and vanish' in the distance as high-explosive bombs detonated, and soon the trees behind the shelter were silhouetted against 'a bloody and orange sky – as in a wild sunset'. They were joined now by another neighbour, who had driven home through town and who brought news of fires at Charing Cross and Lambeth and of seeing 'a train burning like a torch at Peckham'. This obviously prompted an exchange of bomb stories. Leslie Paul noted down one piece of stray 'shelter talk' for his collection: 'When the oil bomb fell in the shelter they had nothing on – they were sleeping in bunks. They got terribly burned and walked barefoot along the streets through broken glass. Burns hanging down like balloons from their arms . . .'

Chapter Twenty

Organ Music

THE SHADOW: Who knows what evil lurks in the hearts of
    men? The Shadow Knows! Ha ha ha ha ha . . .

ANNOUNCER: 'Blue Coal' requires less attention, gives you greater
    heating comfort at less cost. What's more, an
    order of 'Blue Coal' entitles you to the full benefit of
    extra home heating service. So phone your friendly 'Blue Coal'
    dealer tomorrow, won't you? Start the New Year
    the easy, economical 'Blue Coal' way.

The Shadow: The Ghost on the Stair
5.30pm EST Mutual Network USA, 29th December 1940

AS THE CHILDREN of tea-time America petitioned to have the lights
turned out at the first bars of 'Omphale's Spinning Wheel' so that the
sepulchral laughter of the mysterious crime-fighting 'Shadow' could make
their flesh creep even more thrillingly, many of their parents had other
things on their minds.

The adult audience had already heard on this afternoon's radio news
that, at this very moment – at another time and place, in a world far, far
away – London was burning. And they were waiting to hear the
President's broadcast from his White House fireside, later this evening,
about what he thought the future held in store for America.

So, too, was London. In Fleet Street, the news pages were – not unnaturally, given what was happening outside their doors – in a constant
state of flux. But at *The Times*, off Ludgate Hill, they already had on hand
a story from their New York correspondent, giving the results of the most
recent American Gallup Poll.

A sub-editor had added the hopeful headline 'Aid for Britain at Risk at
War – 60 per cent Gallup Vote in Support', though the text itself was less
reassuring. While three out of five Americans questioned did indeed say it
was worth taking the risk of antagonising Hitler to help the British keep
fighting, when asked whether they would actually vote to join the war at
Britain's side given the chance, fewer than one of those five said yes. In fact,
that yes vote had fallen from 17 per cent in October to just 12 per cent now.

This was due to Britain's recent military successes in North Africa, explained Dr Gallup, and to Americans' belief that aid alone might turn the tide. To which a frustrated British Prime Minister might well respond tonight, 'What aid is that, then?'

Which is not to say that Americans had not been generous. Like the peoples of the Empire, they had been moved by Britons' plight: around half of the 300 organisations in the US collecting money for foreign aid were collecting for Britain. About 90 per cent of that aid came through the American Red Cross. And the ladies of the WVS were kept busy sorting and distributing American 'Bundles for Britain': second-hand clothes for people who had lost everything in the bombing. But, most welcome as these were, wars are not won with old clothes and bandages. There had been no US Spitfire Funds to help keep Britain fighting nor, more importantly, any US Government commitment – whether as gifts, loans or credit guarantees – to keep Britain's war effort going when its dollar and gold reserves ran out, which was going to be sooner rather than later. Tonight's events in London would have to share the front pages with whatever the President of the United States had to say.

AT THE PRECISE moment that, in America, The Shadow began his chilling tale of *The Ghost On The Stair*, in the City of London Mr Murphy left Captain Daw and a small number of his staff behind to man the Control Room in the Guildhall basement while he led the rest of his team up and out of the threatened building. Mr Murphy had tried in vain to extinguish a bank of sandbags covered with wood and tarpaulin by the Control Room entrance, fighting a losing battle against a constant stream of embers coming from the Council Chamber only a few feet away. As he had watched the Chamber burn, a mass of flames inside the now windowless round building, he saw it as a vast cauldron – in which the erect figure of George III still stood, defying the raging flames.

With the Aldermanbury exit blocked, he had to pilot his staff right across to the other side of the complex and out of the Valuation & Ratings entrance in Basinghall Street to the east. They emerged to find the northern end of the street blocked by debris, but they eventually made their way through to the safety of the public shelter at 8 Basinghall Street. (By the time Harry Anderson of the Heavy Rescue finally reached the Guildhall to report the *Daily Express* incident to City Control, he found it abandoned and was told that staff were working on from Secondary Control in the basement of the City Police HQ in Old Jewry.)

Mr Murphy could hardly believe that it was almost midnight. The street was as light, he noted with precision, 'as at 7.30 p.m. on bright August evenings'. And one of the firewatchers on duty in a modern office block off Basinghall Street noted the 'quite fantastic' contrast between those parts of streets that were glaringly lit by fire and those still in shadow. His own building had not caught light yet but 'all round everywhere was a mass of flames, and one really felt rather like a sprig of holly on top of a Christmas pudding with the brandy blazing all the way round'. Firemen at the top of their towering escapes looked tiny silhouetted against the flames: 'There was very little water available, and with the hoses playing on the fire at the Guildhall it just looked like little boys peeing on an enormous bonfire. That's what it did actually look like.'

The gales were now sweeping fire through the building with terrifying speed. Flames were belching from the top storey of Coopers Hall, and attacking the Engineer's Office block from the south and east. The fire was so fierce that there was little smoke to be seen from the ground – except in the Port Health Department Building, where black clouds showed that the firemen on the roofs were at last having some success with the small fires below.

The fire squad had returned to their HQ, where Mr George took roll call. Mr Murphy hoped that the north-west corner offices might be saved but, in case they weren't, he had suggested the fire squad get as many important documents as possible to safety, taking books and records from the Town Clerk's Office down into the strongroom. While they were doing this, the offices around them started to burn.

It became clear that they could do nothing to stop the fire spreading so Mr George had sent a messenger to the Control Room to ask Captain Daw if they should evacuate. The Captain said two fire squad members should stay on but the rest should get out now. Mr George went up into his office to collect a couple of bags and then they went out, through the Alderman's Court Room, into the Recreation Room, out into the Valuation & Rating Staircase and down into Church Passage, where they emerged to find Basinghall Street full of firemen's hoses. At the ARP basement shelter at 8 Basinghall Street, Fitzhugh and Mr Hurford finally had their smarting eyes bathed by a first-aider.

IN OLD STREET, Stanley Champion's eyes were smarting too – and his throat. When it seemed that Grosvenor Chater had come through its own fires intact and that the other fires still raging were no longer a danger to their building, the desperately weary fire guards had gone down to the front office to try to get a little sleep. But Stanley could not settle. He went back out into the street, where he watched as the firemen played hundreds of streams of water on the fires. They might have been conquering the fire, but it meant that the air was if anything even thicker now, the water producing clouds of choking smoke that caught his throat and sparks that whirled into his face.

He stood with his back against the wall, watching a blazing five-storey building opposite. Several times he moved back as the heat became more intense, and then he finally gave up and went back into Grosvenor Chater – where he found that Howard had come back too, after helping the firemen finish up at Sutton's.

THERE HAD BEEN no sound of aeroplanes coming over for some time now, though few of the weary firefighters at work by their puffing trailer pumps in the roaring heart of the fires would have heard them if they had. A little further out, though, Leslie Paul in Forest Hill and Major Stacey in Queensway both noted the sound of a single plane or a few planes flying overhead just after half past eleven, and the boom of the ack-ack attempting to bring the enemy down. At the Speed household, where they had all returned to bed after their night's excitement, May also noted sporadic gunfire. Then, at around quarter to midnight, another sound came wailing through the air in waves over the capital. They all heard it – and it even penetrated the consciousness of one firefighter hard at work on a fire in Southwark.

He heard it but he didn't believe it. It *sounded* like the All Clear. What could that possibly mean? Were the raiders returning, or was it something worse? Worse even than a gas attack – which he knew would be signalled by ARP wardens whirling hand-rattles? Even when he realised it really *was* the All Clear, he wondered whether it might be some sort of Fifth Column ruse to deceive the defence workers.

But no. Out at Bentley Priory, Fighter Command's map covering the south-east of England was clear now of planes, and had been for some time. Although the people fighting the fires on the ground couldn't be expected to have registered this, there had been no fresh fall of firebombs or high explosive for the past two hours. The people on the ground were still quite busy enough dealing with the aftermath of the previous three and a quarter hours, when central London had been battered by more than 400 high-explosive bombs, totalling 127 tonnes – and had received 22,068 small, lethal incendiaries. No wonder the wailing of the All Clear had sounded disorientatingly inappropriate,

Of course this was not meant to be the end of the raid. But its second sortie, which would have bombed the firefighters in the heart of the inferno so that nothing could stop it spreading, would not now take place. In northern France and Belgium, the last Luftwaffe pilots coming in through the bad weather were greeted by the welcome news that the weather had closed in too much to take off again any time soon. The prospects for a second sortie had dwindled to nothing. One Junker 88 from II/KG51, with its landing gear damaged, had crash landed at Bretigny with one fatality. One RAF gunner from 141 Squadron had also been killed and one plane written off. But, even though the limited air battle was long over, there was a war still going on in the City of London.

EVEN ON THIS battlefield, though, there were strange incongruities, with the war looking won on one part and lost on another.

At Grosvenor Chater, the Jackson Brothers firewatchers had finally settled down to get some rest. Their feet were cold and soaked so they wrapped them in brown paper before they lay down: Howard on the wide office counter and Stanley Champion on a wooden seat. It was hardly the lap of luxury, but: 'This time,' he recorded in his diary afterwards, 'we did sleep.'

Sleep would not come to Mr Walden in the crypt of St Paul's Cathedral, as Hitchcock, Williams & Co. burnt on. 'To define in praise the work of our fire fighters would be to limit the extent of their great services,' he wrote afterwards. 'Three times the Police instructed them to leave as the building was becoming dangerous: but they refused to go, and eventually Mr Lester had personally to order and almost drag them away. Even then they asked to stay and continue the unequal struggle.'

This had been more than a workplace to some. It had become a second home, filled with memories of old friends and colleagues, old times, old jokes – occasions when they had decked the buildings with bunting as the City's and the nation's high days and holidays had drawn people to celebrate at the Cathedral over the decades. 'Many of us could neither rest nor remain in the Crypt,' wrote Mr Walden, 'but came out at intervals to stand and stare fascinated – and dejected – at the scene confronting us but a few yards away; we were even warmed by the heat of the blaze.' Amid the knot of Hitchcock, Williams staff drifting in and out, Mr Walden felt that: 'The quiet, philosophic bearing of Mr Hugh Williams and the

Manager as they stood and watched the burning warehouse were an example to us all.'

A FEW HUNDRED YARDS away to the north-west, though, stoical resignation was not yet an option. 'Bodgers' at St Bartholomew's had a grand-stand view of the peril their hospital was in. London was now an 'awesome sight' viewed from the bridges connecting the wards to the nurses' home. Whipped up by the strong winds, the edge of a huge conflagration was now speeding along Newgate Street towards them, as it had in 1666. Though then the fire's pace had been slow enough to contemplate making a fire-break with explosive – not an option now. The flames had already reached as far as the General Post Office in King Edward Street and it seemed as if they must soon envelop the hospital itself.

Earlier this evening, an HE had destroyed the upper floors of one of the Hospital's old college buildings in Giltspur Street, and the new Chemistry Block in Charterhouse Square was now in the process of burning to the ground. There had been no major casualties among the staff so far but the gas supply had been cut off and an electrical circuit damaged. In the wards above ground, where there were severely injured patients, the nurses had simply pulled down the blackout when the lights failed and worked on by the light of the burning city.

The Casualty Receiving Station in the basement had received over 120 civilian casualties so far tonight – though it had been able to notify sector HQ of fewer than half of these before the phone connection went down. Most were now either on their way home or to other hospitals, but some forty of the most serious cases had been admitted on to the wards or were in the operating theatres.

The City of London Police's Assistant Commissioner arrived with a message from the Fire Service: they were doing everything they could to stop the fire's approach but Bart's should get ready to evacuate in case they failed. There was a total of 225 patients currently within the hospital who would have to be evacuated. Of these, 102 were in the wards above ground level. And since the electrical failure had put the lifts out of action, each one would have to be carried bodily downstairs on a stretcher. The process would take, it was estimated, at least three hours; the Fire Service could only promise the hospital half an hour's notice.

The decision was taken that those who could be moved should be, straight away. The long, bumpy ride on a converted Green Line bus ambulance was a trial for those who were fit and well, let alone for the sick. For the very poorly it might well prove fatal. Those judged too ill to travel at all would just have to stay. They would be moved as far as possible from the approaching flames, ready for a second evacuation which would take place only if absolutely necessary.

As the Emergency Medical Service buses began to draw up in Smithfield, the first patients were stretchered out to them. Hospital porters, medical students and any member of the Clerk of Works' staff who was free to help took turns to ferry the injured downstairs and out on to the buses for their journey. When the poorly sprung buses started to move, every bump could be felt – and the only passable road in and out of the hospital was also in constant use by the firemen still attempting to keep the flames at bay. It was not a good night.

ERNIE PYLE had returned to the Savoy and found it still intact.

> Although bombs are liable to fall anywhere, it happened that none came within six blocks of where we stood watching the early part of the fantastic show Sunday night. There were fires all around us but we seemed to be on an island of immunity.

The All Clear had sounded just as he stepped into the hotel. When he got back up to the warmth of his comfortable room, he wrote, 'I discovered that my feet were soaked and my coat drenched with spray from leaky hoses.' He turned out the light and drew back the curtains. The room was flooded with the fire's light, making it difficult to sleep. But he did sleep.

Bill White's night, meanwhile, was only just beginning. It is only a hundred yards or so walk up Ludgate Hill from St Bride's to St Paul's. But his cab, making its way into the heart of the inferno, had been forced to take a long, slow detour, sandwiched between the fire engines, hose carts and hook and ladder wagons also making for the biggest fires. The driver finally found an alleyway where he could turn off and park to let Bill and Marguerite out. They wanted to see what was happening to the Cathedral. Their press passes would let them through to places where ordinary members of the public would be turned back and the cabbie asked if he could go with them, explaining that he had never seen anything like it before and might not again. As they got out, they noticed for the first time that there was a high wind. Bill held his felt hat tight to stop it flying from his head.

In St Paul's Churchyard, they could see, high up above them, tiny figures on the Stone Gallery just below the dome – members of the Watch were still on patrol, watching for any burning debris swept on to the roofs below.

Three fireman were working from the top of ladders raised four or five storeys high, pouring water on to a row of buildings to one side of the Churchyard. They played their hoses on to high, dark window gaps in which ominous lights appeared from time to time: fires were clearly already burning at the back of the buildings. The intention, Bill could see, was to stop the fires endangering St Paul's. On the far side of the Churchyard, though, tall buildings were already being consumed by 'high twisting flames'.

The trio left the Churchyard for a burning street of small, shabby shops and offices where two buildings were already in flames and more were smouldering. Looking into the half-lit window of a little jeweller's at its display of cheap wedding rings and pigskin picture frames, Bill realised that the light inside came from an incendiary, which must have worked its way down through the roof and floors below and had now started a fire in the top left-hand corner of the room:

> a tiny, white inquisitive tongue of flame sticks out, lights the room like a dim electric bulb. As we watch, another bit of plaster falls, and another white tongue follows it . . . until the entire back wall is a flickering mass and the silver- and gold-plated stuff in the show-cases glitters in the wavering light.

Inside the showcases, sudden small bursts of pure white light appeared and disappeared. Is this how precious stones explode, Bill wondered? Then, as light filled the shop and he could see more pure white flashes on the counter, he realised that they must be the cheap celluloid brush and comb sets sold in this kind of shop. As they watched the showcases crack, the wedding rings in the window melt and the picture frames curl, it was a sadder sight even, Bill thought, than watching St Bride's burn: 'Because no prosperous and pious people will get a spiritual uplift out of rebuilding this little jewelry shop with loving care exactly as it was.' On this historic night, it was not just the grand and celebrated past of London but the intimate, hidden, unchronicled working-class present that was being swept away and destroyed for ever.

Chapter Twenty-one

THE SHADOW: The weed of crime bears bitter fruit. Crime
   does not pay. The Shadow knows! Ha ha ha ha ha ...
   Organ Music

ANNOUNCER: Next week, same time, same station, the Blue
   Coal Dealers of America bring you an adventure of *The Shadow*
   unequalled for sheer terror and stirring dramatic action. So be
   sure to listen and be sure to phone your friendly 'Blue Coal'
   dealer for greater heating comfort at less cost.
   This is Ken Roberts saying: 'Keep the Home Fires Burning with
   "Blue Coal".'

The Shadow: The Ghost on the Stair
Mutual Network USA, 29th December 1940

HALF AN HOUR had gone by and, at six o'clock on the East Coast of the
United States, parents could switch the lights back on, ready to begin their
children's bedtime routine and get the smaller ones to sleep before
America settled down to hear the President's Fireside Chat. In London it
was midnight. And in the basement of Bridge House in Blackfriars, the
children of caretaker Gus Weir had slept right through the All Clear.

Although tonight's raid had been noisy, it had not sounded as bad as
some of the others they had been through – fewer bangs. The Weir boys
had settled down to sleep at bedtime as usual. So, later on, had their mother – wondering as she fell asleep about the strange 'popping sounds' that
she could hear outside. Now, she was suddenly and dramatically woken –
the room was full of firemen, and they were saying that they all had to get
out quickly as the building was on fire and might collapse at any minute.

Mrs Weir hurriedly helped the boys to dress as quickly as possible and
they went up to ground-floor level, where they found Gus waiting anxiously for them – he had been up above conferring with the firemen when
the decision was taken to evacuate.

Emerging sleepily from his shelter into the bright, sudden orange glare,
nine-year-old Ron was terrified. Everywhere he could see firemen were running back and forth, pulling tenders, dragging hoses in streets awash with

water and debris from burning buildings. His mother kept trying to reassure him, but Ron could feel her distress and he wasn't convinced. He could see that the north side of their building was well alight – and so was the J. Lyons cafeteria next door. The popping sound that Mrs Weir had heard earlier had been the sound of wood burning.

The family were shepherded across the hose-strewn road to the imposing modern Unilever House, where they joined many more of the night's refugees, sheltering in the second-level basement. Ron was given tea and kindness and a bed, and eventually, exhausted by his terror, he drifted off to sleep again.

Unilever House was secondary control for No. 62 Station if the Whitefriars building should go down, as well as home to the appliances of 62 X. Its basements also housed an official First Aid Post and, as Sunday 29th rolled over into Monday 30th December 1940, carbons were transferred and new pages of the official record of injuries treated steadily filled up – in triplicate, of course (one for Post records, one for the Medical Officer of Health and one for the Ministry of Pensions).

SERIAL NO.	FULL NAME (SURNAME FIRST)	AGE	ADDRESS	NATURE OF INJURY	DISPOSAL
[29th]					
285	Klust	34	AFS 62Y	Rupture (Hernia)	8 hrs rest
286	Owen	29	AFS 62 U annexe	Blast Exhaustion ..	”
287	Behuer	32	City of London RP	” ”	6 hrs rest
288	Bogard	54	”	” ”	Treatment
289	Asby F	29	AFS Unilever	Blow from fire branch	Rest
290	Padder	28	76 U LFB	Lac glass Finger	Dressed
291	Jamison R	30	62 U Local	” Rt Index	”
292	Daniels T G	39	AFS 62	Lac Rt Thumb, Burns	”
294	Greasey F M	33	LFB 62 U	Rt Eye, smoke	”
295	Sudbury P	59	C of L SP	Fumes, Exhaustion	”
296	Wright	27	34 Z Unit AFS	Foreign body, rt eye	Removed
297	Hutchinson	47	RP C of London Sch	Fumes Exhaustion	Rest
~~298~~	~~Sub Off Abbot R G~~	~~49~~	~~Islington~~		
299	Taylor F	31	12 Nevilles Court EC4	Eye injuries, Leg injury	Barts
[30th]					
300	Owston W	34	Wolsey Wood St	Smoke F B in eyes	Rest
301	Tralaw W	37	”	”	”

Though its modern construction and vigilant firewatchers kept Unilever House safe enough, in the tangle of street behind it, where St Bride's and the Associated Press building still burned, a crisis point had been reached. The spaces for each day weren't very big in seventeen-year-old Frank

Backhouse's little Boots diary, but he managed to squeeze in most of his salient points of this historic night when he filled it in afterwards:

29 SUNDAY - 1st after Christmas (364-2)
I arrived at office 4 o/c. WARNING 6 o/c. PV and Mrs PV there. At 6.10 Incendiaries dropped. Three on our roof. PV and I helped AP staff in TRYING to get them out. IN VAIN. Others roughly 10,000 dropped during. Huge Fire-raising raid City London. Hundreds fires started. Ward Lock, Sam Jones Tanners burnt down. Guildhall. Newgate St. St Brides Church. TERRIBLE NITE. CP & AP went to PA building. At 12 o/c Michaels, Jones, Folks of APGB & myself were taken to Waldorf Hotel. We had good nite.

IT WAS at midnight precisely, after a long and arduous journey conducted largely in total darkness, that Peter Maynard's train finally arrived, several hours late, in St Pancras Station. Eighteen-year-old Peter, a trainee with Burmah Shell Oil, had been visiting his parents in Derbyshire and was due back at work in the City tomorrow. His train had been stopped for a long time at Bedford, from where he had been able to see the glow of London burning, forty miles away. He, like other young workers with no London base, now lived in the basement of headquarters at Britannic House, a large, modern Lutyens-designed office building in Finsbury Circus. If his train had arrived on time, it would have been a couple of stops on the Tube to Moorgate. But the Tube had stopped running. He went outside and tried, in vain, to find a taxi that would take him the mile or more to the office. The All Clear had been sounded, he was told, but there were fires still raging all over the City.

'A NICE TIDY JOB if I may say so,' said a fireman with singed eyebrows and a blistered nose to the Daily Herald's Ritchie Calder. He was regarding the remains of the isolated fire that his crew had just finished dealing with very satisfactorily. His only regret was that there had been no 'red appliance boys' around to watch, he told the journalist. He was an ex-motor-salesman, AFS trained – one of the 'taxi brigade' – and the old rivalry with the 'red stuff' was clearly still alive and well. Then, to Calder's astonishment, he added, 'Many fires about tonight, old boy?'

But that was typical, Ritchie Calder discovered as he wandered the City streets after the All Clear. While they were tackling their own 'private do', firemen had no eyes for any fire but their own. Even when bombs had been dropping all around them, their focus on the job in hand could be total.

But when one fire was dealt with, it was time to go and find another. Once, that is, the flaccid hose was loaded back on the pump ready for use, which was no mean feat in itself. The rubber hose was heavy, its canvas covering soaking wet, icy cold – and probably scintillating with the tiny shards of glass that shattering windows spread everywhere, and which bit into your hands in a hundred places as you struggled to roll up its unwieldy fifty-foot length while it buckled and twisted itself into perverse shapes or unwound itself again at your feet. One Auxiliary Fireman who 'wrestled like Laocoön with a serpentine hose-pipe' asked Ritchie Calder whether it was gone midnight yet. Told that it was, he confided: 'Then it's me birfday. Blimey, what a party!' As Calder watched the birthday boy disappear, with his coiled hose, up an alleyway that looked like a furnace door, he didn't have the nerve to wish him many happy returns.

AT MIDNIGHT, the remaining men fighting for the Wood Street Telephone Exchange had been ordered out. The last man had barely made it when a wall collapsed, blocking the street. At the Speeds' house in Brixton, Fred came home again, this time with the news that there might be a time bomb in Theobald's Garage. Hoping that at least there would be no return visit by the raiders, May settled down to sleep at last. And above the Underground platform shelter where May Speed and Etta had admired the decorations on Christmas morning, London Bridge main line station was still blazing away at the Southwark end of London Bridge.

But at least now Thames water was coming through into the Fire Brigade dams. Elsewhere the station's own fire squad were hard at work with their more modest reserves. A burning factory wall suddenly collapsed on the line, starting a small fire on the railway bridge. It was only a small fire but it could set the railway bridge timbers alight if it wasn't tackled. So they got a stirrup pump, filled a bucket from the water tank of one of the engines standing in the station, and put it out.

AT ST PANCRAS, Peter Maynard had quickly realised that if he wanted to get home to Britannic House tonight he would have to walk. When he turned into the broad City Road, which ran right through the heart of tonight's most extensive conflagration, he saw that ahead of him tall buildings were blazing furiously on both sides of the street. A fierce gale was blowing now. To the east of the City of London, Australian ambulance driver Bert Snow saw millions of small glowing embers hurtling along tonight, borne by the wind along Whitechapel High Road and filling the whole width of the street. But as Peter Maynard battled against the storm in City Road to the north of it, as he wrote to his parents next morning, 'great hunks of burning wood' were flying horizontally across his path, carried effortlessly by the ferocious gale.

The road underfoot was partly flooded – a water main had obviously been broken somewhere – but the firefighters he passed seemed to be bat-tling on with charged hoses. With all the hydrants dry, fires were being fought with the waters of the Thames, he was told: many of the gallons spraying out of the hoses in City Road had been pumped through the streets, hose by hose, engine by engine, a mile and a half from the river.

IN WESTMINSTER, Phil Henderson's crew, back in the warmth of the fire station just before midnight, had been gently steaming in their wet uni-forms, drinking tea and joking with the girls. Crowded into the recreation room and overflowing into the kitchen and stairs, sitting on the floor, the tables, the chairs, it felt as if they had all come to a party.

> The raid was forgotten in a general feeling of relief and the light-heartedness of danger endured. In spite of tiredness and discomfort, at such moments one is happy and irresponsible; everyone is your friend, for you have all been 'on the job' together. Cigarettes and sandwiches are exchanged and the experiences of the night are already material for stories that will be re-told and re-enacted time and again in the mess. For it is chiefly the ludicrous elements that one chooses to remember. Meanwhile do not think of what may be happening at home, do not begin wondering whether your wife is spending the night in a damp, crowded shelter, or whether, on returning home next day, you will find your house in ruins. Those are the sort of things that only happen to other people . . .

But their own adventures were by no means over yet. The bells went down again – and this time everyone was ordered out to the City.

> The roads are choked with pumps, strange intestinal coils of hose and huge turntable ladders backing and manoeuvring into position. Isolated groups of men in yellow anti-gas capes and gas-shields hanging from their tin hats to keep the water from running down their necks, looking like Bedouin Arabs, others like porpoises in their glistening oily black mackintoshes, stand directing jets of water through shattered shop fronts and gaping windows on to the chaos of flaming debris within.

One of the Westminster crews, making for the Barbican, turned into Chiswell Street and found the whole road in flames. The crew jumped from the tender and ran but 'they ran into a collapsing wall of fire, scald-ed and blinded by fire. They fainted while fighting their way out.' They were rescued by some soldiers on leave and seven were taken to hospital, 'four so badly burned as to be hardly recognisable'. But Phil would not know about this until much later, and as he drove on through the warm, sticky spray of water rebounding off the burning buildings tonight, his mind was strangely caught by a stray line of Wordsworth: 'The sounding cataract haunted me like a passion . . .'

His trailer pump ground to a halt by the empty lunatic asylum in City Road where a jumble of pumps, hose, petrol and water lorries were being ordered in various directions by LFB officers in black coxcomb helmets and brass epaulettes: 'Men are stumbling out of the fires, vomiting with smoke, groping their way like the blind, as the wind carries swarms of golden sparks and shining plumes of flame from one house to another.' The whole sky was 'lit with the glow of a fatal sunset' and there was no cheery singing of firemen here. Nor the sweet incense smell of burning Wren churches – only a 'sour, sickening stench'.

His crew was ordered on to Bunhill Row in Finsbury, where they were sent to support men at the top of a modern factory which was literally sandwiched by fire: six floors up, the roof was well alight but there was a fire in the basement too. Slowly – coughing, eyes stinging – they groped their way up to the top landing, directed upwards by confused shouts and thin torch-beams piercing the smoke. They found themselves in a long storeroom running the whole length of the top floor which was stocked with bales of paper – it must have been a feast for the first incendiary that burned its way through the roof.

At first, though, they could see nothing for the smoke 'pouring down-stairs in thick, oily drifts and meeting the steam and vapour rising from the basement'. They could hear coughing, though, far off, and they eventually located two men, barely keeping their feet at their branch but unable to let it go: 'The strangled noises wrung from them by the biting yellowish smoke are scarcely human.' Then suddenly Phil, too, was caught by the smoke and doubled up, retching and coughing.

From below the heat is steadily rising.

'Come on, mates,' someone shouts. 'Drop that f–in' branch and get out, or we'll be roasted.'

But the men on the branch can only reel about, vomiting their guts up with long-drawn-out, incoherent growls like enraged beasts. We snatch the branch out of their hands and wedge it, hissing furiously, beneath a heavy bale of paper and lead them, slipping and stumbling, down the waterfall of the stairs.

Minutes after they emerged, there was a roar behind them, the roof fell in and a gigantic burst of flame rushed skywards. Amid the roar they could hear heavy objects falling: 'exploding tins of printers' ink, the clang of falling girders, the rending clash of subsiding floors'. The LFB sub-officer who had ordered them in now came running up wild-eyed: were all the men out?

'It's all right, Sub. Don't you worry. We got 'em out.'

The other side of the street was soon burning too, as the collapsing factory floors flung flaming debris up and in all directions (elsewhere in Bunhill Row, Post 13's hut lost its roof): 'We stand at the end of an avenue of fire, curiously detached and isolated before a monstrous conflagration that leaps and towers above us into its own livid day.'

Two or three radial branches were pouring water into the heart of the fires, which were also being tackled from a water tower in a side street. There was nothing more Phil and his crew could do. They took off their saturated neckcloths and laid them on top of their tin hats, where the intense heat quickly dried them. Someone told them that a canteen van was round the corner: 'With hands and faces grimy and blackened as miners, we line up for our mugs of cocoa. A tin of biscuits is passed round; each man dives in and grabs a handful.' And, in another of those little miracles of unmuddled Blitz thinking that maintained order amid chaos, 'for every mug returned there is a slab of chocolate'. Sitting on the kerb, Phil reached in his pocket for a cigarette . . . and drew out a handful of damp yellow pulp.

In a City Road ablaze almost all along its length, Edward Morgan, thirty-three-year-old Station Officer of No. 73 Euston, was officer-in-charge of the fire at a shop at numbers 51 and 53. The building was already well alight from the bottom to the top when a small figure was spotted stumbling out of the fire close to the wall, beneath the flames pouring out of the ground-floor windows. When the firemen got to her they realised it was an old lady, wearing a gas mask. She told the firemen that her husband was on his way out behind her but that two women who had been sheltering with them in the cellar were too frightened to leave and were still there.

Officer Morgan was a good man to have around in a crisis. He had already won a British Empire Medal for his actions at an incident in September, in which the previous Station Officer had died. Taking Sub-Officer Hill with him, he ran towards the building and broke in through the front door. They were greeted by a blast of intense heat: it was impossible to get through that way. Outside, in the wall beneath the shop window, was a grille fitted with thick glass panels giving on to the basement, which LCC building regulations insisted on for exactly this sort of emergency. The firemen took it out and the two officers dropped through the opening into the smoke-filled basement below.

STAGGERING ALONG City Road, fighting against wind, fumes and smoke, it took Peter Maynard a very long time to get to Britannic House. It was about one in the morning when he arrived, so exhausted that he could barely make his way across Finsbury Circus. He was greeted at the door by the Assistant Manager and May, the maid, both of whom had been there all night. And they told him all about the building's lucky escape: '. . . one of the most miraculous escapes of any building in history I should think,' wrote Peter to his parents the next morning.

Like so many of the buildings that had been protected by its own fire-watchers, the danger had not been the firebombs that fell on its own roof – only eight incendiaries had fallen directly on to Britannic House during the first half-hour of the raid, and they had all been swiftly dealt with – but by the firestorm created in the deserted premises all around. 'We were doomed to catch alight at 11.0 last night because the wind was driving flames right across the road,' Peter wrote. But at 11.15, the wind direction had 'changed completely and we were saved'.

The change of wind direction may have had an effect on the fate of the Guildhall too. In the Basinghall Street shelter, the exhausted and defeated fire guard were supposed to be trying to get some rest, but they couldn't sleep. Some went out to watch the firemen fight the fire that had got hold in the Port Health Department, scene of their earlier labours. 'We couldn't do anything to help as we didn't have any water in our hydrants to work with,' wrote young Mr Lott afterwards, 'but I am sure we could have done a great deal of useful work as we know the roofs a lot better than the firemen there. All we could do was to watch other buildings share the same ordeal.'

Well, not quite. The western, Aldermanbury, side of the Guildhall complex was, amazingly, still intact for now and the Pension Book had been playing on the mind of Mr Wells from the Control Room. He had been working on it when the sirens first went and it was there still. Mr Fitzhugh reckoned they ought to have another go at rescuing some more files. Mr Arnold thought it would be 'somewhat unsafe', Fitzhugh recalled later, but agreed to go with them just the same. So Mr Wells got the keys to the Aldermanbury entrance from the Beadle and they all made their way through the darkened corridors to the Justice Room.

There was a small fire in a window in the Pensions Fund office, so Fitzhugh and Arnold manned the stirrup pump between them to put it out while Mr Wells carried almost all the superannuation records from the Chamberlain's Office into the strong room and locked them in. Then Mr Fitzhugh went down into the basement in search of Mr Wells's Pension Book, but the smoke-filled Control Room defeated him. If Mr Wells knew exactly where he'd left it, he told him when he came back, then it was worth having another try. He did, and they found it in an adjoining shelter.

It was about a quarter to two when they got back to 8 Basinghall Street. They were now thoroughly wet through, and it was a freezing cold night when you were away from the fires, so they borrowed some protective clothing and went in search of a hot drink. In Cheapside, it seemed that every building on both sides of the street was blazing and Mr Fitzhugh noticed that the top floor of the GPO building behind was burning fiercely. Though St Mary-le-Bow, Cheapside, was still safe for now – and, amid the flames, Wordsworth's plane tree could still be seen, standing in the open churchyard left by the last Great Fire. The Guildhall men finally got their coffee at London Bridge. Cafés were used to opening early here for the fishmongers of Billingsgate, though the Market itself didn't operate on Monday mornings – this morning. Which, all things considered, was just as well.

Back at the Guildhall, Stanley Baron of the *News Chronicle* was watching a scene of beautiful devastation from the shelter of an archway. An AFS man high above on a water tower poured the now-plentiful water inside, silhouetted against 'an aura changing from white to lemon and sulphur, even to green . . . Every now and again a hanging timber gave a last flare and fell.' Three firemen stumbled out towards him over rubble and 'Sparks kicked up from still smouldering timber made as it were a phosphorescent outline of their feet as they walked.' And they confirmed to him that, yes, the giants Gog and Magog were among tonight's casualties.

IT WAS THREE O'CLOCK on Monday morning when Home Guard Volunteer E. T. Wistow of the 5th Battalion 'R' Zone London got back to his post – the end of a wearing weekend, if not the end of his duties.

He and fellow-Volunteer E. T. Smith had been on duty when a serious fire had broken out in their building during Friday night's raid. They had helped put that out then spent much of Saturday and Sunday repairing the damage. As they tackled the shower of incendiaries raining down on them on Sunday night, an ominous sense of déjà-vu must have overtaken them. But then, with massive suddenness, their firewatching duties had come to an abrupt end.

With two huge explosions, a pair of HE bombs had hit the building. There was a terrible crash as the roof fell in and both men plunged down, through the building, with the debris. Miraculously, as the noise died away, they found that they were both alive, though both wounded and suffering from severe shock. Scrambling over the pile of rubble, they realised that the exit to the basement air raid shelter was blocked – and that there must be people trapped inside.

Setting to work, they were able, between them, to clear a passage through the debris and get the people out. Under the now-brilliant night sky they led them through the streets to a more secure shelter at which point, with the rescue services on hand, Wistow had finally let himself be driven off in an ambulance. But Smith refused to go and worked on. Now Wistow, after his hospital treatment, was reporting back for duty.

IN ALL OF Fleet Street's two centuries of making newspapers, never had the night's biggest story come closer to hand. And never in news photography's rather shorter history had an historic opportunity so obligingly presented itself to the waiting lens. Though, as colour film was not only expensive and rare but positively discouraged by the censor, the one thing that would escape capture was its astonishing beauty. Standing by St Paul's Cathedral, Stanley Baron of the *News Chronicle*, for example, he noted the 'pale apple-green light running along the cornices of the Churchyard office blocks and storehouses' and, later, how 'for long minutes together the cathedral was merely a dim shape seen through sparks that aped a red snowstorm'.

> Then with the momentary clearing of the smoke pall the dome, ball and shining cross would be throwing back every colour the flames cast upon them, orange, blood-red, green, yellow and tender amber – a strangely flowering glory.

Photographer Herbert Mason could not capture all this on his black-and-white film but he had been having a memorable night too. He had left Fleet Street for St Paul's with his camera, walking up a Ludgate Hill 'carpeted in hose-pipes, a scampering rat here and there, a reeling bird in the flames'. He had seen firemen fighting on doggedly despite the 'pathetically little' water coming from their hoses. And had seen how, when a fresh supply suddenly came through, 'a hose running riot would lash out and knock firemen from their feet'. On the far side of the Churchyard, Cheapside was 'a mass of flames, leaping from one side of the road to another'.

Having seen and photographed all that he needed at ground level, he went back to the office and up to the roof of the *Daily Mail* building. And there, in the small hours of the morning, as he watched the wider panorama, he recalled: 'The smoke parted like the curtain of a theatre and there before me was this wonderful vista, more like a dream, not frightening.' Against the flames, Wren's famous dome of St Paul's stood silhouetted and, almost miraculously, unscathed. Mason saw the light gleam on the golden cross above and, at the perfect instant, clicked the shutter.

RITCHIE CALDER was upstairs too, in the Fleet Street office that he sometimes used, and he wound a piece of paper into the machine on the desk in front of him. 'The typewriter is treading flakes of soot into the paper as this chapter is being written,' he tapped out. 'Every now and then, like the opening of an oven door, as the wind changes, a gasp of hot breath comes in through the seventh-floor window, a breath foul with the reek of burning London . . .'

HAVING LEFT the doomed jewellers by St Paul's, Bill White and his companions had walked on to a small square, where they saw a stream of people emerging from a basement shelter. Some of them, he learned, had only arrived there a short time ago. The building above their own shelter had caught alight and the ARP wardens had moved them to safety. Then, as the fire spread, that shelter too had been threatened and the fire had driven them here. Now the wardens were moving them on again, helping them to carry their shabby bedding on to who knows where.

Watching these cleaners and caretakers who were the City's population these days standing patiently in line, Bill White found no hysteria, nor even grumbling.

> The wardens were good sturdy Londoners, tired with work and responsibility, but with those steady British nerves we had been watching all evening. And, always, that unfailing, even, kindly, British politeness with which these people can smooth over the rough edges of even the worst crisis. Again we agreed that if you only stayed out of the Savoy it was so easy to see they were a fine, brave, kindly and noble people. After all, it isn't hard to stay out of the Savoy.

Chapter Twenty-two

My Friends:

   This is not a fireside chat on war. It is a talk on national
security, because the nub of the whole purpose of your
President is to keep you now, and your children later, and
your grandchildren much later, out of a last-ditch war for
the preservation of American independence and all of the
things that American independence means to you and to me
and to ours . . .

President Roosevelt's Fireside Chat*, 29th December 1940

THE PRESIDENT gave the assembled company a nod and a slight smile as he
was wheeled to the desk clustered with microphones for the various radio
networks that would carry his words out across America and the world. He
opened the folder, took out the manuscript and began to speak . . .

   In Washington DC, at nine-thirty in the evening Eastern Seaboard
Time (three-thirty in the morning London time), the President of the
United States began his 'Chat' to the nation. Eighteen months ago, he had
sat in this same room with King George VI and Queen Elizabeth on their
pre-war visit. Tonight, there had been quite a mixed crowd waiting for
the President, including his mother, members of staff – and Clark Gable,
with his wife Carole Lombard. Truth outstripped fiction now: Rhett
Butler's Scarlett O'Hara was now en route, via Lisbon, to blitzed London
with her new husband Laurence Olivier, and they were all now part of a
larger drama than a cinema screen could encompass.

   The attention and anxiety with which this broadcast was monitored in
official British circles could not be overestimated. The text of speeches
being beamed across the Atlantic in both directions in these days would
take their place among the most famous words in the English language.
But it was the subtext of those speeches that would help determine the
future of the world.

   The British war effort was short of almost everything now. But the one
resource its Prime Minister could spend without fear of bankruptcy was
words. Britain and America had been called 'two countries divided by a

*Appendix B, p.351

281

common language' but it was perhaps truer to say they were now two empires unnaturally yoked together by it. And half-American Churchill had been doing everything that written and spoken word could do to bind 'the English-speaking peoples' together in the defence of the liberal democracy and freedom – or at least the promise of liberal democracy and freedom – that their two empires embodied.

'Hitler knows,' the Prime Minister had said in his 'Finest Hour' speech,

> that he will have to break us in this island or lose the war. If we can stand up to him, all Europe may be freed and the life of the world may move forward into broad, sunlit uplands. But if we fail, then the whole world, including the United States, including all that we have known and cared for, will sink into the abyss of a new dark age.

FEW KNEW THEN how this reference to America was related to Roosevelt's last Fireside Chat, 'On National Defense', which had come almost exactly seven months ago, barely two weeks into Churchill's premiership and in what then seemed to be the dying days of the European War.

In Britain, that last Sunday in May had been a national day of prayer, led by the King and Queen in Westminster Abbey, while the new Prime Minister spent the day in a flurry of Cabinet meetings and talks with foreign delegations. That evening, after a dinner at which he ate and drank almost nothing, Churchill had risen looking desperately sad, saying he felt physically sick. British troops at Calais had surrendered and a last, desperate attempt to rescue as many men as possible from the beaches of Dunkirk had begun . . .

Across the Atlantic, Roosevelt had been approaching the end of his second term of office and, with France crumbling and Britain, it seemed, soon to follow, he had needed to prepare Americans for a Nazi Europe – and whatever might follow. And what might follow, according to a secret report prepared by his London embassy a year before, was totalitarian control of world commerce that would 'penetrate into every American home' and take unemployment back up to the pre-New Deal levels that had threatened to tear his nation apart when he first came to office.

> Today the United States, with a population of 130 millions and its vast wealth and resources, holds the balance of power in the world. The defeat of the British Empire would mean the disappearance of this predominant role. Vast as are American resources they might well be less than those of a totalitarian world in arms . . . In short, America, alone in a jealous and hostile world, would find that the effort and cost of maintaining 'splendid isolation' would be such as to bring about the destruction of all those values which the isolation policy had been designed to preserve.

The President had every reason on 26th May 1940 to believe that he was speaking for liberal democracy's last roll of the dice. 'For more than three centuries,' he had told his fellow citizens that night

> We Americans have been building on this continent a free society, a society in which the promise of the human spirit may find fulfillment. Commingled here are the blood and genius of all the peoples of the world who have sought this promise.
>
> We have built well. We are continuing our efforts to bring the blessings of a free society, of a free and productive economic system, to every family in the land. This is the promise of America.
>
> It is this that we must continue to build — this that we must continue to defend.
>
> It is the task of our generation, yours and mine. But we build and defend not for our generation alone. We defend the foundations laid down by our fathers. We build a life for generations yet unborn. We defend and we build a way of life, not for America alone, but for all mankind. Ours is a high duty, a noble task.

This Fireside Chat, inspiring to its intended audience, might have left a British listener feeling a little bereft. For, while the President spoke of Norway, Holland, Luxembourg, France (twice) and Belgium (twice), Europe as a whole, Canada, Mexico and North, Central and South America, but there was no mention of Britain or the British in his speech. And as he prepared his nation for their noble and historic task, just how little the distant British Isles – as opposed to its Royal Navy – featured in the President's thinking was revealed in a conversation that he'd had the day before with Canadian plenipotentiary H. L. Keenleyside.

The United States was strong in economic resources but militarily weak. Its standing army had been ranked just eighteenth in the world by its own Chief of Staff in 1938; compared to the growing European air forces, America's was barely off the starting blocks and, crucially, was untried in combat; and while the US did have a world-class navy, it was a one-ocean navy and that ocean was the Pacific. For more than a century it had relied on the informal protection of a friendly Royal Navy to negate any Atlantic threat. And among the top navies of Germany, Italy, France, Great Britain and Japan, it might soon have no friend at all.

If Britain surrendered now, the President and his Secretary of State told Keenleyside on 25th May, it was vital that whatever remained of the British fleet should not be left in the hands of a collaborationist British government. Canadian Premier Mackenzie King must get his fellow Commonwealth heads to urge Churchill to send the Navy, in that event, to Canada, the Caribbean, South Africa and Singapore. But, they said,

Mackenzie King must claim it as his own idea: Churchill must not know the suggestion came from America.

The Canadian Prime Minister, however, had no intention of deceiving the British Prime Minister and gave London the gist of the conversation. Churchill – who had already been waiting a fortnight for the President's response to his urgent appeal to buy, borrow or have some mothballed Great War US destroyers – was bitterly hurt and disappointed.

Still, he could not afford to write off the United States as friend or ally. His job now was – and would continue to be – to convince America, and one American in particular, that neither could the US afford to write off the united British Empire, the still-mighty Royal Navy, the newly laurelled RAF or the indomitable British people. On 4th June, with invasion imminent but more men saved off the Dunkirk beaches than he could possibly have hoped for, the Prime Minister's message to the House of Commons had shimmered with meaning for the wider world.

> I have myself full confidence that if all do their duty and if the best arrangements are made, as they are being made, we shall prove ourselves once again able to defend our island home, ride out the storms of war, outlive the menace of tyranny, if necessary, for years, if necessary, alone . . . We shall not flag nor fail. We shall go on to the end. We shall fight in France and on the seas and oceans; we shall fight with growing confidence and growing strength in the air. We shall defend our island whatever the cost may be; we shall fight on the beaches. We shall fight on the landing grounds. We shall fight in the fields, and in the streets, we shall fight in the hills. We shall never surrender and even if, which I do not for the moment believe, this island or a large part of it were subjugated and starving, then our empire beyond the seas, armed and guarded by the British Fleet, will carry on the struggle until in God's good time the New World with all its power and might, sets forth to the liberation and rescue of the Old.

The actions of the President of the United States in the intervening months had been, one might say, at the least, open to interpretation.

AFTER SEVERAL MONTHS of tough negotiation between the two governments, President Roosevelt had discovered that he was not, after all, required to consult a hostile Congress over the supply of the fifty old US destroyers to Britain if he judged that it aided America's own defence. At the end of September he had therefore effected the 'Destroyers for Bases' deal by Executive Order. And, at the end of December, some disquiet was being expressed in both Whitehall and Buckingham Palace about what George VI's official biographer described as 'less than the requisite amount of tact and discretion' being displayed by the US authorities in their dealings with local administrations in the colonies and dominions concerned. There were suggestions of more military forces being stationed than seemed strictly necessary for bases and, in addition, a US Economic Mission had visited some of the islands concerned, where 'the assiduity of their enquiries awakened acute anxiety'.

The exchange OF fifty old US destroyers for military bases had been a sensible expedient for both sides but it was a political manoeuvre that could hardly be repeated ad infinitum. In this weekend's *Sunday Times*, the proprietor of the *Chicago Daily Times* had given his own analysis of American public opinion and surmised that

> the great majority of our people believe that, in addition to preparations for our own defence, we should manufacture and deliver to you all the armaments and war supplies that you can effectively use and transport. I doubt if many among us expect that we shall ever be paid their cost, either in gold which we do not need, or in kind.

But readers' warm feelings towards him at that point might have been cooled somewhat by the next sentence: 'Most of those whose opinion I can learn still feel that our recognition of your need for armaments and our help in providing them should be met with an offer to transfer your Caribbean insular possessions in exchange.'

The much-needed ships that the bases bought had not even proved to be as seaworthy as had been hoped, according to high-level gossip. 'The American destroyers aren't much good,' a young man had written to his mother, after a visit to Chequers three weeks ago,

> or won't be till the Spring as they are badly built. They roll 70° and there was apparently a scandal about them in America & the naval under secretary & designer were sacked & the ships never put into commission.

Churchill had been much more circumspect in phrasing his personal and secret cable to the President on Boxing Day, in which he detailed just how much refitting some of the destroyers still required. It was only this, he wrote – and not, as rumoured, lack of suitable crews – that meant only nine of the fifty were currently in service with the Royal Navy. He did not want the American people, he wrote, to ascribe the delay to British dilatoriness, which might prevent them wishing to send anything else.

Despite its careful composition, the British Embassy in Washington had thought it wiser not to rush to deliver the Prime Minister's cable to the White House. Certainly not before the President had made clear in tonight's Fireside Chat just what getting 'rid of the silly, foolish old dollar sign' would mean for the relationship between the United States and a Britain under siege.

DOLLARS WERE NOW at the very heart of Britain's problems. And only President Roosevelt could solve them, as the British ambassador had made very plain when he returned to the US after his discreet withdrawal during the presidential election campaign.

On first acquaintance, FDR had found Lord Lothian altogether too Old World for his tastes. 'I wish the British would stop this "We who are about to die, salute thee" attitude,' he had written impatiently to his old Harvard history teacher in the immediate run-up to war. In their meeting Lothian had, he wrote,

> started the conversation by saying he had completely abandoned his former belief that Hitler could be dealt with as a semi-reasonable human being, and went on to say that the British for a thousand years had been the guardians of Anglo-Saxon civilization – that the scepter or the sword or something like that had dropped from their palsied fingers – that the USA must snatch it up – that FDR alone could save the world – etc, etc.
>
> I got mad clear through and told him that just so long as he or Britishers like him took that attitude of complete despair, the British would not be worth saving anyway.
>
> What the British need today is good stiff grog, inducing not only the desire to save civilization but the continued belief that they can do it. In such an event they will have a lot more support from their American cousins – don't you think so?

'I think you are a bit hard on "the average Britisher",' replied his teacher mildly:

> Some of his itinerant exports over here are intolerable – I see shoals of them and know where of I speak – but the bulk of the stay-at-homes are of better quality. The fact is I think that a lot of those who come over here for the first time don't quite know how to behave with us, and hit the wrong note at the outset.

But Lord Lothian's time spent in America since had obviously enhanced his capacity to 'talk turkey' to Americans and, when he was met at the airport by US newsmen at the end of November 1940, he declared: 'Well, boys, Britain's broke; it's your money we want' – refusing to elaborate but happy to repeat the phrase for the newsreel cameras.

FDR was furious. He wasn't sure that he believed him – and he certainly didn't appreciate such plain speaking if it was true. Their next meeting had been frosty.

It had also been their last. On the 11th December came Lord Lothian's final speech as British ambassador:

> Hitlerism is a tragedy for Germany. Its doctrine is not true. All history proves it wrong. The Sermon on the Mount is in the long run much stronger than all Hitler's propaganda or Goering's gun and bombs. The core of the Allied creed is liberty, justice and truth, and that, we believe, will unfailingly prevail if we have resolution and the courage to resist to the end.

It may have been a return to the 'We who are about to die, salute thee' strain. But then Lord Lothian had done perhaps the one thing he could do that stopped it being so much phoney-baloney – he died. As a devout Christian Scientist, he had refused treatment for a serious infection and was already on his deathbed when his speech was read for him by an Embassy official.

THIS NEWS REACHED President Roosevelt while he was on a Caribbean cruise, arriving shortly after a letter from Winston Churchill. Although the Prime Minister had gently rebuked his Ambassador for his over-frankness about Britain's financial situation, he had relied on Lothian's input, before his departure for America, to the early drafts of this long, agonised-over appeal to the President.

In it, Churchill sketched out the prospects for 1941. He did it 'with candour and confidence', he wrote, since it seemed to him that the vast majority of Americans believed that the safety of the United States 'as well as the future of our two democracies and the kind of civilization for which they stand are bound up with the survival and independence of the British Commonwealth of Nations'.

He laid out the war situation at length, point by point, finally arriving at the question of Finance at point 17. Explaining how low Britain's coffers were, he wrote:

> You may be certain that we shall prove ourselves ready to suffer and sacrifice to the utmost for the Cause, and that we glory in being its champions. The rest we leave with confidence to you and to your people, being sure that ways and means will be found which future generations on both sides of the Atlantic will approve and admire.

'If as I believe,' he concluded, 'you are convinced, Mr President, that the defeat of the Nazi and Fascist tyranny is a matter of high consequence to the people of the United States and to the Western Hemisphere, you will regard this letter not as an appeal for aid, but as a statement of the minimum action necessary to achieve our common purpose.'

Nor were these appeals all that President Roosevelt had to think about on his cruise. The US Chief of Naval Operations had last winter expressed the view to the Secretary of State that, if it should come to war against Japan or others,

> if Britain wins decisively against Germany we could win everywhere; but that if she loses . . . while we might not lose everywhere, we might, possibly, not win anywhere.

On 12th November 1940, shortly after the election, he amplified those remarks; giving, over twenty-six closely argued pages, the options that he saw lying before the President. None of them made pleasant reading in the White House. And in Whitehall, some parts of his analysis would have tasted, at best, bitter-sweet.

> It is my opinion that the British are over-optimistic as to their chances for ultimate success. It is not at all sure that the British Isles can hold out, and it may be that they do not realize the danger that will exist should they lose in other regions.
>
> Should Britain lose the war, the military consequences to the United States would be serious.
>
> If we are to prevent the disruption of the British Empire, we must support its vital needs.

On his return from his voyage, President Roosevelt had called a press conference and talked, in his friendly, casual way, about the 'silly, foolish old dollar sign' and about lending one's neighbour a fire hose . . .

As BILL WHITE and his companions turned the corner in London, they were suddenly confronted by the backs of a double rank of firemen who, to judge by the insignia on their collars, had been drafted into the City from London's outer boroughs. Flames poured out of the street ahead of them like an 'upside down Niagara'. Even though their press passes still held good, the firemen were clearly dubious about letting them nearer the fire, especially Marguerite, and they warned them to look sharp for falling bricks up ahead.

The shops in this street were tall and narrow and the fire was working its way steadily towards them at the rate of one twenty-five-foot shop front every two minutes. One by one, wrote Bill, each shop was 'transformed into a five-story chimney' as the roof and wooden floors collapsed. Beyond the current fires, Bill could see the burnt-out shells of shops that had already been through their agony. Sometimes there would be a 'clicking rumble' and one would sag and collapse, sending an avalanche of red-hot bricks spilling across the street.

The fire was roaring 'like a thousand great chimneys, as loud as the roar of air behind the propellers of a loaded bomber about to take off', augmented by the steady tinkle of broken glass falling from the shattered windows on to the pavements below 'in a steady musical drizzle'. And as the flames rushed skyward, at street level a torrent of icy air was sucked into the fire to replenish what was being lost, making the fire burn all the brighter. Bill White kept a tight grip on his hat.

Ahead, the tall column of sparks curved over and Bill could see at the end of the street a church in a darkened square: 'And this was the most beautiful thing I have ever seen,' he wrote,' because it was a slow fall of fiery snowflakes – enormous ones coming gently and gracefully down in lovely curving spirals.'

Marguerite was entranced: 'It's Wagnerian! It's a blizzard of fire! I want to run through it.' It was crazy but she was not to be dissuaded, so Bill told the cabbie to go back to the car and they would join him in a while.

'I'm coming with you,' said the driver. 'This is my town and this will never happen again, and I don't want to miss any of it.'

And so they made their insane dash together, one each side of Marguerite, holding her arms, running down the street and over occasional spills of hot bricks, past shop doorways that blasted out heat like furnaces and were filled with a bluish-red fire that it hurt to look at. Hot brands as big as a thumbnail were starting to fall down on to their coats and they had to squint against the heat. This was ceasing to be fun.

> All at once there was a crackling, clicking sound behind us which swelled into a crackling roar. We glanced back to see that the entire five-story front of the building we had just passed had collapsed in an avalanche of red-hot bricks and flaming timbers into the street.

The debris was several feet high: there was no retreating now. The only thing to do was run on, into the little square, where acrid smoke made their eyes stream and their throats gag. The sparks that had looked so beautiful from afar were now showering down on them. Bill, afraid they would set fire to Marguerite's hair, clapped his own felt hat on her head – and felt the sting as they hit his bald spot. Both Marguerite and the cab driver now had their eyes tight shut and Bill could only just hold one eye open with his finger and thumb. Putting his arms round both their waists, he managed to guide his blinded companions across the square, telling them when to step up as they reached a kerb, and then out into a dark street where there was no fire.

Their appetite for experiencing more of this amazing night had petered out. They made their way back to where the cab was parked, miraculously still safe. It was four o'clock in the morning. Marguerite said she had to start work at seven-thirty. They drove her home in silence. Looking behind them after fifteen minutes, the City appeared in the back window as a tall orange column with that same pink aura on the horizon that had greeted them when they left the cinema.

'Wasn't it beautiful and weren't the people nice?' said Marguerite.

'I never knew nicer people.'

'Nice, and clean, and brave, and steady, and beautiful people,' said Marguerite, 'and now I want to go to sleep.'

FOR OTHERS, the fight went on. In City Road, Station Officer Morgan and Sub-Officer Hill had, with difficulty, located the two missing women in a back room of the hot and smoke-filled basement. They brought them to the front, underneath the small opening in the shop front, where there were men waiting to haul them up. As they took them out, one by one, the back of the building where the women had huddled collapsed with a crash. Sub-Officer Hill was helped out next. An exhausted Morgan, badly affected by smoke, was unable to haul himself up. They threw him down a line which he secured around himself, and gradually he was heaved up to a point where he could be grabbed, and dragged out into the open air to await an ambulance.

He was one of the lucky firemen working the City Road fires. At the far end, up by Moorfields Hospital, five firemen had died when a wall collapsed in Dingley Place; two more had died in the ambulance near to St Bartholomew's Hospital.

CHORALE

Chapter Twenty-three

Home Service MONDAY
7.0 a.m Big Ben; NEWS
and summary of today's programmes
for the Forces

BBC Radio Times Christmas Edition, 1940

FOR ANYONE within a forty-mile radius of London last night, it was obvious that there was more to report than the BBC was telling this morning.
May Speed, on the front steps of her house at seven, could see a large fire
'still glowing fitfully against black clouds and a rain-filled sky'.

The borough cleaners were already out in Brixton, trying to clean up the
mess in the streets before dawn. At eight-thirty, Bertha's taxi arrived to
take her to the station for her journey back to Glasgow, 'as full of discon-
tents as she arrived', but she was not going to have an easy time of it: the
driver brought news that the City was blocked to traffic – and that fifteen
horses had been killed at a brewery in Moorgate.

Today, even the laconic Frank Jackson, back in his office in Lambeth
and making his daily report to County Hall, could not be confined to a
single small sheet of paper if he was to tell Eric Salmon his story.

Dear Salmon,
   Fire situation in London - 24 hours to 06 hours,
   30th December, 1940.
   A bad night with the whole Brigade heavily engaged. The areas most affected
were the City, particularly Moorgate Street and City Road area and around St
Paul's and the London Bridge and Borough High Street areas on the south side
of the River.
   Details of the total number of fires in the 'B' and 'F' Districts are not yet complete but, so far, about 700 fires have been reported of which ten were major
fires, twenty-eight serious and 101 medium. There were in addition a number of
conflagrations, particulars of which are not yet to hand, but practically the
whole of the 'City Danger Zone' has been burned out.
   All available pumps and fire boats in London, together with 500 pumps from
the Region and the down-river boats were brought into use. For relief purposes,
pumps from outside the London Fire Region are being employed.
   Damage to the mains and to the dirty water main from the City Road Basin
led to a serious shortage of water and the difficulties were aggravated by the low

state of the tide before midnight. The events of the night demonstrated the total inadequacy of our present water unit and turntable ladder strength.

I regret to say that one regular station officer and eleven auxiliaries were killed.

Redcross Street Fire Station had to be evacuated; all except one of the sub-stations on Redcross Street's ground had also to be evacuated and four other sub-stations. No. 65 'U' Sub-Station, Billingsgate, was destroyed and No. 48 'Z' Sub-Station, Grove Lane School, was severely damaged by HE bombs, in each case without casualties.

The situation, however, was in hand by six o'clock this morning.

Yours sincerely,

F. W. Jackson

One might almost suspect, from that final sentence, that the unflappable 'Gentleman' Jackson had finally snapped, but what he said was indeed true. Though the massive, ungovernable blazes of last night were by no means wholly conquered, the situation was 'in hand' and the remaining fires were contained.

Ernie Pyle, waking at around six in his Savoy hotel room, was surprised to find 'the great light in the sky' was gone: 'London again was almost as dark as it had been every night for a year and a half. So well do the firemen of London do their work.'

As any fire chief would admit, at the heart of huge conflagrations, where temperatures could reach 1,000 degrees centigrade and more, fire did its own work, burning itself out relatively quickly by its own ferocity. But the very real triumph of the LFB and AFS last night and this morning had been in not allowing the large fires to spread further than they did. And that was not to mention the contribution of thousands of wardens and fire guards and ordinary passers-by all over London who had prevented so many more small fires getting a hold at all.

The City area consumed by the fire was less than it had been in 1666 – but not by much. Later, after all the reports came in, the LCC's Eric Salmon conveyed Major Jackson's final judgement on the City Fire to the City Corporation: 'Owing to narrow streets and inflammable buildings, it was not possible to extinguish most of the fires at an early stage or to stop a certain amount of spread of fire. But a great deal was done, otherwise an area two or three times larger would have been destroyed.'

At half past six Stanley Champion, waking from his less comfortable bed in the front office of Grosvenor Chater, was as astonished as Ernie Pyle when he looked outside to find that the fires all seemed to be pretty much under control. At the end of the yard, only the shell of Jackson

Brothers was standing now, with a mass of smouldering rubble and timber piled up inside. Elsewhere, in all directions, the roads were covered in a mass of hoses, pumps and firefighting equipment, as weary firemen clung doggedly on, aiming their branches into still-burning buildings.

Looking out from the roof of the Bank of England at about seven, B. J. Rogers could appreciate the full scale of the firefighters' achievement. Against the darkness, great fires still burned: 'but now they were localised, dotted about here and there, and not the terrible menace of the night before'.

Ritchie Calder was still at his typewriter in Fleet Street.

> While I am writing, the fires are still burning. The AFS men are down there in the fire-maze of Johnson's London. There is a warning shout, a crash and a rumble of falling masonry. Another building has collapsed.

Outside his door, there was the 'familiar flop' of the morning papers. He went and picked them up. There, with the others, was the *Daily Telegraph* as usual. He looked out of the window. There was the *Daily Telegraph* building, still smoking. London was Carrying On.

IN WAPPING, Nev Coates's stamina training with the FAU was paying off. Having returned to his hostel in the wee small hours, he had managed three hours' solid sleep before returning to the job at eight. He had promised the family of an Italian internee, whose shop and house had been burnt out last night, that he would get them all to a rest centre. He was also aware – because he had attended to him last night at Matilda House – that the eldest girl Bruna's fiancé had died, but she didn't know it yet.

He was too late: when he arrived, Bruna and three other older children had been sent to St Peter's school which was now operating as a rest centre, while the three youngest had been taken elsewhere with their mother. Nev collected them all together at St Peter's and arranged for them to go on to a Catholic rest centre at a church in Lukin Street. But by then Bruna had heard the news about her fiancé and was in a state of collapse.

She was desperate to see the body and Nev told the supervisor at St Peter's that he thought it best: 'I knew that there wasn't a mark on the boy.' He managed to borrow a small truck to take her and a priest, her fiancé's sister and a friend to the mortuary, and then brought the whole family to Lukin Street 'where they were very kindly received'. Later, he returned to the Hermitage, and found the Christmas decorations still hanging from the ceiling, contrasting strangely with the tree decorations, tinsel, paper and the odd bottle that were floating in eighteen inches of black water on the floor.

GUY'S HOSPITAL, so menaced by the lack of water last night, was also swimming in it this morning. Elizabeth Barnicot had, as she informed her daughter, enjoyed a 'wonderful time' in her rest centre in Westminster overnight.

> Tea when we got there, mattresses on the floor and we slept like logs from 2.00 till 6.00. We washed in the infants' cloakroom each with a clean towel and had breakfast at 6.30 ['huge mugs of sweetened tea bread and butter and cold sausage' she told her other daughter] sitting in the main hall all decorated for Xmas with Xmas trees. We found that Guy's was still standing so back we went walking and tramming and got back at 8.00 to find the most awful smell and havoc but we all set to work.

Jesus College was half burnt down. Downs Brothers was gutted and so was the whole of Newcombe Street. But though Nuffield House had lost its windows it had escaped serious harm and, once patched up, became Elizabeth's centre of operations for the task of housing dozens and feeding hundreds over the days ahead.

Like all survivors, she soon had her share of miraculous bomb stories to pass on – an explosion in the road by the massage building had burst up through a ward floor but 'No one was hurt, the baby in the cot just over the shop was in the bathroom, etc., etc., etc.'. The surrounding devastation was a constant reminder of just how narrow her own escape had been. 'It is just a mass of ruins round here,' she wrote to her daughter. 'I marvel that we are still here – we were literally surrounded by burning building.'

Nearby, parts of London Bridge Station were still on fire. But, though the offices of seven departments had been utterly destroyed, some services were running, with a few trains from Charing Cross and Cannon Street operating into a single platform. In all, five London rail termini had been hit in the night, and sixteen Underground stations were still closed. But by a combination of train, bus and foot and the occasional car (to the frustration of the firemen wielding any hose they ran over), a remarkable number of people seemed to be getting to work.

Sidney Chave's route in to the lab today included several diversions for new bomb craters: 'I could see the glow of a fire burning at Peckham. There was another still burning next to Waterloo Hospital . . . Traffic blocks were everywhere. Poor old London.'

As a devastated rail network struggled to offer commuters business as usual, one man, travelling in to London after a weekend in Brighton, recorded:

We stopped at all stations after Purley and people crowded into the already full train and girls began to faint. At Streatham Common the stationmaster against much opposition packed another 20 into the coach and tempers got very hot . . . There were no porters either at Brighton or Victoria.

The trouble on the railways is only to be expected after last night's raid. London Bridge Station is closed and no Underground trains are running east of the Temple.

Colclough, who lives in the Temple, said that the Temple fire engine had been called away early in the evening to the City, whereupon 14 incendiary bombs fell on the Temple. The Temple Church was ringed with fires but seems to have been saved.

The porter of our flats told us that the Home Guard had received orders to stand by, possibly in expectation of a troubled night (but nothing occurred).

He himself was a civil engineer, employed on the half-finished Waterloo Bridge. Construction had been put on hold 'for the duration' but everything had to be maintained so it could be completed at record speed if any of the existing bridges were hit. Miraculously, though, they seemed to have all survived again last night, pretty much intact.

All over London, people were continuing to get in to work as best they could. One young lad from Upper Tooting, who had a near miss last night – a bomb had fallen nearby and put out all the lights for an hour and a half – had to get to work at Marshall & Snelgrove department store in Oxford Street. He had a long wait for a bus and didn't get in until twenty past nine; and 'One chap,' he recorded with awe, 'arrived at 11.'

Frank Backhouse's working day, by contrast, began in most civilised fashion. Awaking to the unaccustomed luxury of the Waldorf Hotel at the Aldwych, he left at around half past eight for the short stroll along the devastation that was Fleet Street. Frank met up with the rest of the Canadian Press exiles for a post-mortem on the night's adventures in their new home with the Press Association. The Associated Press building was beyond rescue.

Most of the worst damage along Fleet Street was hidden from view in the back alleys, where Dr Johnson's house was among the casualties: in the attic where he had produced his famous *Dictionary*, the roof was a mass of charred timbers. St Bride's, too, was one mass of black and smoking ruin within its calcined walls, though Christopher Wren's much-loved spire still soared above them. Wren would have been pleased that his faith in the apparently delicate design of his tallest spire, 'that madrigal in stone', had been vindicated. Legend had it that this had been the first of the churches he rebuilt after the 1666 Fire; local legend also had it that,

297

in practical fashion, he had built the pub next door first so that the builders would have somewhere to refresh themselves while they were working on it.

It would be a long time before anyone could even start to think about whether reconstruction or repair might be possible now. Though when they did, they would have Wren's original architect's plans to work from and even (London being London) the original builders' account ledgers to refer to. It would be some time, too, before (as at Tubby Clayton's All Hallows, in a similarly woeful state on the far side of the City) the archaeological treasure trove that lay beneath the blackened timbers and lumps of stonework would be revealed. This morning, what had been lost of eighteenth- and nineteenth-century London was more sadly apparent than the much more ancient City that lay awaiting rediscovery.

In the safe at St Lawrence Jewry church, though still too hot to open at present, there had been a grievous loss. While the church plate had survived intact, the church registers had suffered badly. Ironically, the most recent, paper ones had got away with a scorching on the edges. But the older ones were written on vellum: thin calfskin. And the heat had welded the pages into a solid mass, burying St Lawrence's ancient parishioners for a second time.

NELL CARVER was due to start work at the Central Telegraph Office at nine, just before sunrise. The lack of trains from West Norwood seemed ominous but she had managed to catch a number 68 bus. The conductor had more information to offer than the BBC – the whole City was still in flames from last night, he said. But Nell knew 'people so often exaggerate', so she wasn't very worried – yet.

'I wasn't prepared for the horrible sights which met my eyes as I got out in Holborn,' she recorded in her diary that night. 'Most of the station was gone & the rest still blazing away. Several other buildings in Newgate Street were on fire & the smell of smoke was strong.' She picked her way with difficulty over a mixture of broken glass and water.

When she got to King Edward Building she knew, the moment she got inside, that there something was very wrong. 'All the rooms & corridors were simply crammed with people – nowhere for them to go. They looked very upset & the noise and confusion made my heart sink – it was so reminiscent of Sept. 11th.'

Once again, she faced that same devastating sense of loss. 'We have often groused about our office,' she admitted. 'Most of us, in fact, at one time or another, but today many people were in tears – realising that we had seen the last of the old building & that one chapter in our daily lives was closed.' As a certain amount of duplicate equipment was installed in King Edward Building, CTO staff would later take pride in the fact that communications had never been wholly broken off by the raid, not even for a minute. But, with no phones operating yet, Nell had to sit and hear 'the whole wretched story, over & over again'.

DAWN BROKE. 'The coming of daylight is always a blessing,' Ernie Pyle stabbed out on his trusty Corona 3, on the desk in his Savoy hotel room. 'Things have a way of looking overly grotesque at night.'

> Today I can go out onto our balcony, where we stood watching London burn, and London will look just as it did the afternoon before the raiders came. True, property was destroyed – much property, valuable both materially and senti-mentally. And lives were lost. But London is big and its lives are many. You feel a little abashed to realize the next morning that London is still here. The skyline looks just the same. The streets are jammed with human beings.
>   Life is going on – where last night you felt that this must be the end of everything.

When Ernie said the skyline looked just the same, of course, what he mostly meant was that St Paul's was still there. And so long as the Cathedral still dominated the horizon, its dome unshattered, then some-how the world that was England remained intact.

Up close, the parlous state of St Paul's Churchyard made the survival of the Cathedral – once more displaying its brightly lit Christmas trees and charitable wishes by the West Doors – seem even more miraculous than it had among the fires last night. B. J. Rogers was one of many drawn here irresistibly before the day was out (to the occasional frustration of the fire-men). 'No traffic was allowed, as all the streets are covered with miles of hoses and engines playing on all the various fires,' he wrote to his daugh-ter. The shops on the south side of the Churchyard were, he wrote, 'very bad'. While, to the north,

> Paternoster Row has practically ceased to exist. I could look right through into Newgate Street, which is terribly burnt out, the GPO, St Martin-le-Grand, badly burnt out on the top storey. Ludgate Hill was still burning, and all the district west of Moorgate is absolutely laid waste. Moorgate St Station is no more, and all those huge warehouses, full of 'soft goods' are burnt out.

This was where the Speeds' New Union Street factory was, and Fred came looking for it today. He wasn't allowed through: it was in the heart

299

of the most perilous zone, where walls could come crashing down at any time. The City would soon be resounding to daylight explosions again as the Army came in to help the demolition squads bring down the skeletons of local landmarks, one by one. 'Some of the men were aliens,' the Ministry of Information later recorded of the Pioneer Corps, with the clumsy good intentions for which it was famous:

> deeply content with this chance to oppose their muscle and will to that of the enemy who had done his best to wreck their lives. Some were coloured, good workers and very powerful, who did prodigies of strength and endurance – a lively lot who made friends everywhere and entertained passers-by on the banjo.

There was nothing, as yet, to be seen of this rather improbable scenario this morning. But it was clear that the accustomed processes of Carrying On witnessed on so many mornings past was not going to fail on this one.

Ritchie Calder stood with *Time*'s Walter Graebner watching a demolition squad pull down a gable end which was all that was left of one building.

> Against it, poised like the trigger of a rat-trap, leaned an enormous girder, and up this girder an overalled figure was climbing, dragging a heavy cable. The metal was slippery. His every movement teased the toppling wall and threatened to bring it crashing on top of him. Yet he never hesitated until he reached what had been the fourth floor. Then, balancing himself even more dangerously and swaying like a tightrope walker, he made repeated attempts to lasso the ragged top of the gable end by slinging the loose end of the rope round it. Time and again he tried, lurching with every miss, until at last he succeeded. Grabbing the loose end, he coiled it round him, and with the impudence of a perky schoolboy he squatted down on the red girder and tobogganed to ground on the seat of his pants.

As soon as he was down and away, the rest of the crew pulled on the rope, the wall wavered and fell, and the girder was buried in tons of bricks. Walter Graebner turned to Ritchie Calder and said indignantly, 'Now, what so-and-so would give a guy an order to take a risk like that?'

'Well,' said Ritchie, 'he did not do it for his Fuehrer; he didn't even do it for Churchill, and he didn't do it on the orders of his superior officer, because there is not one around.'

'Then,' said the American, 'I guess he just did it because he thought he ought to . . .'

Ritchie Calder decided that these words encapsulated the central issue of the war, what they were fighting for.

> I have seen that phrase glorified. Impossible risks were taken and impossible situations saved by the initiative and self-sacrifice of ordinary people 'because they

thought they ought to'. It was not a case merely of doing their duty; it was something more. It was the way they exceeded their duty . . . they chose to 'because they thought they ought to'.

JOURNALISTS HAD SPECIAL dispensation to wander. But it would be some days yet before the Speeds would get a permit to explore this wilderness, after a trail for a compensation form that took them from the Guildhall to cordoned-off King Street, where they found only the WVS helping those in immediate need, to a long queue in Basinghall Street, which was the wrong place too, and then on again to the City Remembrancer's office, 'which was right – but they had no forms!'.

And when they were finally allowed in to explore,

> So complete is the destruction that you have to stand still to take bearings. 'This was Fore Street, this was Aldermanbury.' A canteen presented by the people of Malaya was going round & the soldiers, firemen & demolition squads were served with hot drinks. They needed them.

When they got to the factory, there was nothing left.

> The air raid shelter which had been in the centre of the basement had withstood the fire, but in all that mess around & on top of it, I could not distinguish one single object, not even a button. Amazing when you think of the heaviness of Ethel's mahogany showcase & the mahogany counter which ran all along one wall. They had disappeared as completely as a match stick.

> Fred did find the safe, though, and some firemen offered to force it open with axe and crowbar. The charred ledgers fell to dust as they were lifted out and all the paper money was gone too, leaving just twenty-five shillings in coins – and so discoloured that it was hard to tell half-crowns from pennies. Ethel gave a pound of it to the fireman, 'which left her 5/- salved from her entire business, but opening the safe had been no light task'.

> Suddenly there was a shout from the street above: 'All out, all out, we are going to pull down this wall now,' and they hurriedly left the demolition squads to it. Wandering over to gutted and roofless St Giles Cripplegate, May found that John Speed's bust at least had survived 'triumphantly without even a singed whisker – Says much for the hardihood of our tribe!' And John Milton, who had been propped up in a corner since August, had acquired a tin hat.

'THE WHOLE OF THE CITY is full of smoke and paper etc. is still falling this morning,' Peter Maynard wrote to his parents from Britannic House in Finsbury Circus on the morning of 30th December:

The streets are full of business men with nothing to do. Imagine coming to one's office in the morning and finding it a gutted skeleton or still burning. Hundreds of people have done that this morning. They have had to dynamite to prevent the fires from spreading. All our telephones are out of action. Hardly any work being done this morning. The whole of Moorgate is closed . . . I have tried to get to see if Ernest's office is OK. I doubt it. I will have another try at lunch.

Bill White went out with *Life* photographer Bill Vandivert to explore the streets that had been so awesomely beautiful last night. 'By the dull winter daylight it was a shambles,' he wrote,

almost deserted except for the occasional firemen playing hoses on heaps of rubbish. But once we ran into half a dozen neatly dressed businessmen in wellbrushed bowler hats, the directors of a famous London bank. They had trudged through the rubble to peer, over a shattered wall, at a safe which contained the company's records. It had crashed through to the basement and now lay on its side – a steel island in a pool of charcoal-stained water.

They met a young man, too, who had been bombed out twice before moving to premises here. 'Today he got permission to pass the lines and climb through several blocks of rubbish to see if anything was left of it. Nothing was.'

Presently we happened onto a couple of elderly men, partners in some firm which had been completely destroyed. They were asking their way, because some of the streets they couldn't recognize. When they discovered we were American reporters, they began talking as people often do when they realize they may be quoted.
'We will carry on,' one of them said, 'no doubt about it, in spite of things like this. Our spirit isn't broken. After all, what else is there to do? Carry on! That's what we should do!'
They said these things half to themselves, half to us, because they knew we were reporters. We turned off at a side street and left them climbing over rubbish toward their little business, which both we and they knew they would not find.

Hitchcock, Williams & Co. was, like so many other burnt-out businesses, already busy arranging new premises while it waited to see what could be salvaged from the old ones. And, of course, new accommodation for the live-in staff. All across the Square Mile, by tomorrow, the ropes that blocked off the devastation would be festooned with notes about where postmen and visitors could now find the firms that they were seeking: Business As Slightly Unusual.
Over by the Tower, the merchants of 'Wine Land' were as attached to their own few bibulous streets, clustered around Falstaff's Eastcheap, as

any stubborn East Ender. And now they took in their neighbours just as readily. The next edition of *Wine & Spirit Trade Record* (whose own offices had received 'relatively slight damage – broken windows, doors inside the rooms blown off hinges, and so forth') carried a list of some sixty businesses that had been burnt or blasted out. A few gave new addresses outside London but most had relocated just a little further down the same street or round the corner in the next one, moving from St Dunstan's Hill to Water Lane, or Water Lane to Great Tower Street, or Great Tower Street to Mark Lane, or Mark Lane to St Mary-at-Hill, and thus back full circle, almost, to St Dunstan's again.

There was a faintly fruity, Dickensian aroma to the messages from these wine merchants, whose premises Dickens himself must have passed often on his walking jaunts around the City:

> MESSRS DENT, URWICK AND YEATMAN regret to announce that their offices which they have occupied at 34, Great Tower Street for well over a hundred years were demolished by enemy action on the 29th December. For the time being therefore, through kindness of friends in the Trade, they have established a temporary address at 40, Eastcheap EC, where all communications should be addressed. In consequence of the raid all records, and a considerable amount of duty-paid stock, have been lost. Messrs Dent, Urwick and Yeatman would be very grateful if any friends would send them any transactions or accounts outstanding in order to help them over this difficult time.

Elsewhere Messrs Farrow and Jackson Ltd, in a similar fix, assured readers that: 'If suppliers will forward statements of any accounts outstanding, together with copies of relative invoices, these statements will be promptly met.'

It was business as usual too, though, for some equally Dickensian trades, as the same issue of *Wine & Spirit Trade Record* revealed. Like its predecessor in 1666, this fire had destroyed Halls of the ancient City Livery Companies, including that of the Bakers Company in Harp Lane. But as an official had – perhaps unwisely – informed a *Daily Mail* reporter, its cellars, containing the priceless wine stocks of two other Livery companies as well as its own, remained happily intact. 'The cellar,' he added, 'was beneath the hall, the floor of which was still smouldering after the fire.' On consideration, the Bakers Company decided that it was wisest to let the wine cool before attempting to remove it and ordered that the cellar door be sealed in the meantime. 'This was to have been done the next day,' the *Record* recorded, 'but before it could be effected the beadle reported that the bulk of the wines had gone.'

LESLIE PAUL, due to give an LCC lecture to his regulars in Bullivant's Wharf shelter in Poplar later today, set off via Camberwell Green and the Elephant & Castle. With no buses running to the City, he switched to the Underground, getting off at Bank where he hoped to get a bus to Aldgate. But when he emerged above ground he realised that only emergency vehicles were lumbering across the hose-strewn roads. He started east on foot, walking about three-quarters of a mile before finding a bus beyond Aldgate in the Commercial Road. As he walked, he tried to take in the magnitude of what had happened.

There was still a mass of fires around Aldgate and firemen were directing their hoses into two flaming restaurants; he counted at least three more fires before he got to Gardiner's Corner, and flames and rolling clouds of smoke were still issuing from the Minories. The Mazawattee Tea warehouse by the Tower was gutted. The network of streets around Petticoat Lane's Aldgate end was now a mass of smoking ruins smouldering against a dark winter sky. Burning buildings continued periodically up into Commercial Road.

He had bought a newspaper and, as he read about the destruction that had been wrought in the City, he felt close to tears.

> I was more than usually in a rage about the vandalism and barbarity of it all. I daresay we are doing and will do some evil things ourselves, but it is all so monstrous and so terrible that I walk about wanting to wring the necks of Germans. I am angry.

He was struck, though, by 'the persistence of our lives'.

> In a warehouse in Houndsditch a window dresser solemnly arranging a show of models of infants in various kinds of green knitted woollen goods under a brilliant light. A boy bouncing a ball indifferent to a smouldering building behind him. The same pretzel seller by Gardiner's. Children with cases going back to granny in the country or remote suburbs after Christmas at home.
>
> I noticed, too, many children today – sightseeing in Aldgate, clambering on trucks and ruins, playing in the bombed streets, walking holding mother's hand.

All around were the firemen, who seemed to have performed overnight miracles to get things under control so quickly. Though grimy and sweaty, they were 'calmly and ordinarily working away with hoses and pumps as though it was a drill'.

> Having lectured to them for a year I know many by sight, and by name, and all by temperament. They are unemployed builders, clerks, barbers, little Jewish tradesmen and tailors, earning three pounds five per week in their wartime job.

Heroes seems a trite, banal compliment to them. They labour like Hercules at a task like Sisyphus'.

The men of the Guildhall Fire Guard (for even Mr Lott could no longer, in fairness, be regarded as a boy after last night), now on their way home, might not be aware that Sisyphus has been condemned to push up a hill each day a boulder which rolled to the bottom again each night. But they would have greeted him with fellow feeling in the cold light of Monday morning. In fact, much had been saved at the Guildhall. But what had been saved, not unnaturally, seemed insufficient compensation for what had been lost.

US Military Attaché General Lee, who had shocked his English friend Ted Villiers by finding the battering of The Temple rather comical, felt no such impulse about the Guildhall. He and his wife had once been received by the Lord Mayor in all his finery at the Guildhall, and he now experienced for himself that strange attachment to the past that one could feel when one's personal life had been ceremonially wound into the long skein of British history.

He was not the only one so affected. 'Old London is irreplaceable,' wrote the *New York Times*: 'The district known as "The City" is more than the heart and nerve center of a world-wide empire. It is what every son of the English race sees and thinks of when he speaks of London. So solidly is it built in the memory and tradition and literature of England that many who have never seen it know it well – the medieval courts, Gray's Inn, St Swithin's Lane, the pointed spires of ancient chapels, the haunts of Johnson and Pepys, Sterne, and Dickens.'

General Lee was a practical American military man, not a professional wordsmith. But in his diary he wrote a romantic requiem for old Gog and Magog and for all the other remnants of the past that had been kept at the Guildhall. And, in terms that might have warmed Winston Churchill's heart, he mourned both the building and the role it had played in nurturing individual freedom against autocratic power.

Nor were the Guildhall's trials over yet. The Librarian arrived to find a smouldering among the bookshelves which, he informed the Corporation afterwards, could have proved disastrous were it not for his staff's quick action with a stirrup pump, using water from the sink in his own lavatory. And some of the Library's more precious books, damaged by water from firemen's hoses, were to spend many weeks slowly drying before coal fires at Zaehnsdorf bookbinders. In the strongroom, too, the files that had been rescued with such effort last night might have taken fire at last in the superheated atmosphere inside, had not a quick-thinking official arranged for its walls to be cooled by firemen's hoses.

However, for the fire squad of last night, the Guildhall was someone else's responsibility at last. 'The members of the Chamberlain's Office assembled at No. 8 Basinghall Street at 10 a.m.,' concluded Mr Fitzhugh's account of the night for the subsequent enquiry:

> (Mr Michelmore having been warned by telephone of the position.) Mr George, the Commander of the Fire Squad, gave me permission to go home (which applied to the whole Squad).
>
> I returned home at about 11 a.m., still wearing a sodden overall, helmet and gum-boots, as my clothes had perished in the Fire.

In Old Street, despite their exhaustion, the Jackson Brothers firewatchers had worked on alongside the arriving workers, to salvage what few cloths and garments had survived under the rubble. Howard cut his hand badly on some glass while trying to force open a door and was sent to get it stitched. At half past eleven Mr Austen told Stanley Champion to go home too. He was all in, but still had a hard job ahead of him just getting home. A landmine had brought down dozens of buildings in Chiswell Street. And as Stanley clambered over a several-foot-high pile of rubble, some of it still burning and smouldering beneath his feet, he noticed a postman retrieving letters from a post box burnt black by the fire. When he finally got home to Romford, his Mum told him that his friend Arthur's workplace had also been burnt out, and that Arthur had gone up to London to make enquiries about Stanley and see if he was safe.

At lunch time, Nell Carver followed some postmen up on to the roof of the King Edward Building.

> The sight from up there was dreadful, more like the Great Fire of London. Greyfriars Church was just a shell, you could see downwards right into it as no roof was left – only the spire remained. Paternoster Row in ruins, part of St Paul's Churchyard, & most of Newgate Street also were gone. TS was still burning but it was very difficult to distinguish one place from another – the whole City looked to be either burnt out or still on fire.

Their lovely new CTO dining room was gone, of course, with all its equipment, but the King Edward Buffet was still serving lunches – goodness knows how.

Firewoman Jean Savory had gone back to Redcross Street to see if anything remained of the Fire Station and was astounded, after last night's inferno, to find it still intact. But that was about all that was.

Looking around the immediate streets, I wondered if a fire station was justified in such a devastated area. Great heaps of debris were all that remained of the tall office blocks that comprised Jewin Street and all the roads across to Aldersgate Street. St Giles's Church, just across the road from the fire station, was a burnt-out shell; the fire station and Whitbread's Brewery seemed to be the only buildings standing intact as far as the eye could see. It seemed incredible that the fire station had escaped damage; the flames had licked its very walls.

Since it had not needed rebuilding after the Great Fire, St Giles did not feature among the precious 'Wren churches' whose loss the later editions of the papers were talking about today. In fact the shorthand version of losses put out by the Ministry of Information could only give the sketchiest outline of what had been destroyed and what had been lost.

THE MOOD WAS lifted at lunch time by the BBC's rebroadcast of last night's Fireside Chat from America, which had already been extensively reported in the morning papers alongside the first details of the London Fire. 'Hitler will not win, Roosevelt says,' declared the *Daily Express*; 'Roosevelt says U.S. must be Great Arsenal of Democracy,' reported the *News Chronicle*; 'Axis Losing but Crisis for U.S.,' claimed the *Daily Mail*.

'Everybody is enormously cheered by President Roosevelt's stirring speech,' recorded one woman. 'Although it is hardly possible for the speech to enhance the President's reputation here, it has impressed his personality afresh upon the public mind.'

Leslie Paul, a long-time admirer, found the speech made all the more impact since he heard it 'with the rolling of atmospherics and the crackle and thunder of the spaces beyond the stars, which gave it the unearthliness of an oracle and gave its message point'. It was, he wrote, 'a smashing reply to Hitler'.

By the time he got to Bullivant's Wharf, late and weary, Leslie Paul didn't have the heart to deliver his planned lecture – which was on the subject of 'Travel'. Instead, he just let the men talk. He knew many of them from the LCC discussion group he ran before the war. Charlie Russell was relieved to see him, as he thought he might have been bombed. But when Leslie Paul said that, for all the damage, casualties were reported to have been relatively light, he responded fiercely.

'That's what I object to,' he argued. 'That's the Churchill mind. Everything's all right if the casualties aren't as much as you expect. It's inhuman, to talk that way. That's Churchill's sadistic way of thinking.'

Charlie was a staunch pacifist. He'd had a brick through his window for his views before now, and had replied with a placard thanking local citizens for their contribution to the war effort.

Another of Leslie Paul's old chaps told him again about the respite break he'd enjoyed in Ilkley, Yorkshire – just as he told him about it every week: 'I don't think he has ever had a country holiday before.' This was one East Ender who had not been in any hurry to get home to London.

> Good day to yer, they say, good day mister. So nice they are. Not like here. And it was so lovely . . . and wherever you look they was moors . . . And it didn't matter what the chap was, even if he was rich and a kind of squire, good day mister he'd say.

Before Christmas, Hitler had told Goebbels that his revenge raids on the English would 'make their eyes pop'. But Leslie Paul, who had walked all through the still-burning City and into the long-devastated East End today, had seen 'not one alarmed or frightened face anywhere and heard no expressions of defeatism or despair, until I met my old men'. And even then, he wrote, the strongest reaction he found was 'when one of them murmured diffidently, "I don't know. I think we'll 'ave to cut all this caper. It's too much."'

In Sutton, the City fire had set the sky aglow last night; today Viola Bawtree was unaware of the disaster for Toc H at All Hallows Barking, but she had already heard about the gutting of Guildhall, the saving of St Paul's and 'a Wren church badly damaged'. Hitler's handiwork did not dominate this day's diary entry though. Viola had been on yet another Velveeta hunt.

> Tried Stevenson & Rush, International, Hudsons, Home Gardens, Kinghams, no luck. Then at lower Sainsburys saw a pile of round cheese boxes labelled 'for regular customers only' & further on another pile not labelled & at last after all these months got one.

Viola Bawtree had learned to be thankful for small mercies. 'There were only about eight in the pile,' she noted, '& I don't suppose they'd have let me have two.'

DURING THEIR TRAVELS through the bombed area, Bill White and Bill Vandivert met a three-man trailer pump crew, playing a hose into a smouldering basement. 'Funny, running on to you chaps from so many miles away,' the youngest said to them.

> 'Tell me,' said the middle-aged one. 'What does America think of all this?'
> So we said something about America's sympathies being all with England.

'How soon do you think America will be in this?' asked the oldest fireman. We had to say we didn't know.

'Do you think by spring?' he asked. We had to say we didn't know. 'Maybe at least by summer?'

We had to say we didn't know.

Bill White would have loved to have been able give an answer. But in all honesty he had none to give.

'How long do you think this war will last?' asked the middle-aged fireman. He was very tired, having had almost no sleep since the big raid Sunday night, and his face showed it. We had to say we didn't know. The youngest fireman said he thought it might last four or five years.

'It can't last that long,' said the oldest fireman. 'This sort of thing didn't happen in the last war. This one is going much faster than the other. I don't see how anyone can stand it for more than a year or two.' He told us he had been in the army all four years of the last war.

As they walked through the ruins, they were constantly asked if the rumour was true that the King was coming. George VI had 'no vivid personality', wrote Bill White: 'but the English people, after a disaster, are most eager to see him. His appearance is for them a symbol that the rest of the nation is in touch with them, appreciates their bravery and will help.'

So all day in that shattered city with jagged soot-stained walls, people asked us if we had seen the King and what we thought America would do. We hadn't seen the King and we didn't know about America.

The City didn't get the King this afternoon, but it did get the Prime Minister. Mr and Mrs Churchill spent two hours in the Square Mile, gathering a cheering crowd as they visited the Guildhall and ruined churches. In a deep shelter, to cries of 'Good luck', Churchill responded 'Good luck to you'; and when a woman asked, 'When will the war be over?' he replied, 'When we've beaten 'em.'

WHEN NELL CARVER left the ruins of the CTO building at four o'clock this afternoon for the long struggle home, she noted that the streets were still strewn with hundreds of hoses, more than she had ever seen before. Night copy boy Frank Backhouse, meanwhile, was already struggling back in to the City after a brief visit home – and for once he was late for work, not arriving until five.

If this was the movies – if this was *Gone With the Wind* – it would be enough to say 'Tomorrow is another day', and the music would swell up and the credits roll. But this was real life. This was London. And tomorrow was a day that had to be lived through just like today – even though it might prove to be even worse. Despair was no longer simply 'a stage in courage': despair and courage had been welded together into a single entity for which even the abundantly wordy English language had no name.

For some, of course, there would be no tomorrow. As Leslie Paul had said, although the loss of property had been immense, the death toll in this raid had been relatively light. But perhaps, as Charlie Russell had said, there was something inhuman in having to learn to be grateful for fewer deaths than expected.

In Southwark, Incident 43A was officially brought to a close at twenty-two minutes to five, with one man left behind to guard body parts until they could be collected, a quarter of an hour later. This had been an average sort of incident to judge by the winding-up report.

Re Keyworth Street Shelters Incident
    HE on 2 shelters in Keyworth Street 30 people believed to be trapped 4 casualties sent to hospital 6 dead removed to 98 Lancaster Street. Personal property stored at 48 Ontario Street and left in charge of Warden Post 2
    Burst water main attended to by MWB. Excellent work performed by Rescue Parties & Pioneer Corps
    signed A E Knight F S Bridges O/Cs Incident

Though, of course, every incident had its own features that made it memorable amid the routine. And in the case of Incident 43A, rescuers who had worked all night and had pulled out corpse after corpse from the rubble had been rewarded at half past five this morning, after more than nine hours' digging, with the emergence of eight-year-old Frederick Feldon, quite unharmed – though bereaved now of three members of his family.

Altogether, something in the region of 200 people had been killed or fatally injured in last night's raid on London – it was impossible to say exactly how many yet: some people would take a long time to die. But if you knew one of them, then even one was enough. And today, in the Royal Free Hospital in Gray's Inn Road, Frank Hurd – the Auxiliary Fireman who had written down his adventures in the East End and Euston and the City for posterity, had been snapped for the papers drinking tea, and had thanked God that Londoners could laugh at the absurdities of the Blitz – died of his injuries, sustained last night in Smithfield Market. He was twenty-four years old.

MAY AND ETHEL SPEED had been clearing up the top landing today. May had 'salved' some bulbs from the cupboard, though there had been casualties: 'And of those remaining, if any survive, well – like Londoners, "they can take it".'

They soon discovered that the culprit that had done for their roof last night wasn't a bomb or even shrapnel but 'a chunk of clayey turf' that 'must have been hurled through the roof with terrific force to make so big a hole'.

The garden was strewn with bricks and roof tiles. 'We've been lucky,' May concluded. 'If it had been some of the brick bats in the garden things could have been very much worse.' The lady next door but one was even more sanguine about the hole in her own roof: 'I feel like a war hero now,' she told May and Ethel cheerfully. 'I'm so glad – we can take it.' 'Hope she feels the same if the whole house came down,' said Fred with a grin, when they told him after he came home.

'The flames have died down now,' May concluded Monday's entry in her diary. 'There is no glimmer in the night sky. Heavy rain clouds and a wind. One newspaper seller today had chalked up "Pompeii".'

THE BLACKOUT had resumed. And, across London, thousands of guardians were on duty again tonight. In Wapping, Nev Coates and a team of chaps from the FAU borrowed some chemical toilets from less well-used shelters to supplement those in the now-crowded Orient, and hung screens round them that had been salvaged from the flooded Hermitage. Though some of their regulars, Nev knew, had decided to stay at home tonight and just take their chances.

As far as everyone among the exhausted civil defence networks was concerned – and every Londoner who was making his or her own arrangements for shelter tonight – there was no reason to suppose Monday night would not be a repeat of Sunday night. It was even likely: the heavy provincial blitzes had usually come in blocks of two or three nights on the trot. And of course, before London's 'lull' the raids had come night after night after night.

But those who were manning – or womanning – the occurrence books across London had no 'Reds' to record. The sirens didn't wail. The weather was getting worse. Snow was on the way. But while no one was in a position to be certain about anything, a quiet night was a quiet night. And you made the most of it till it turned unquiet.

'I suppose you've heard about the fire last night,' Australian Win Marshall wrote in her daily letter to her fiancé Teddy, just before midnight.

It is still burning tonight and there is a glow in the sky . . . night was turned into day by the ferocity of the fire. I'm sorry to say that the damage is quite extensive, and there were thousands of incendiaries dropped. However our night fighters went up and the All Clear sounded at 11p.m. . . . Those RAF boys are very brave. It cheers one's heart to think that we can do something at night to combat this German peril and evil.

She had been on WVS duty last night but there had not been anything in their West End patch, she wrote, nor had they been called out to help elsewhere. She would be on duty again tomorrow night but tonight she had been out to the Chaplin film.

In the end he gave an impassioned speech to the presumably German people, appealing to their better natures. He asked, not for cleverness, but for kindness and humanity. It makes me very sad to think of the hate in the world – so much can be done by understanding and tolerance.

Despite the state of the world and the lateness of the hour, she wrote,

I don't feel tired . . . and am inclined to secret dreams . . . I am ever one to be purely idealistic about l'amour but have never before found anyone who felt and thought the same way . . . Ce soir je t'aime trop bien!

Win

Chapter Twenty-four

31st December 1940

We are deeply grateful for all you said yesterday. We welcome especially the outline of your plans for giving us the aid, without which Hitlerism cannot be extirpated from Europe and Asia. We can readily guess why you have not been able to give a precise account of how your proposals will be worked out. Meanwhile, some things make me anxious . . .

Winston S. Churchill to President Roosevelt, Premier Papers, 4/17/1

THE PRIME MINISTER was still hard at work into the early hours of Tuesday morning: finalising the text of his deeply pondered and carefully phrased cable to the President of the United States. It had been through a number of drafts already and had not been an easy composition.

If this was the movies – if this was *The Great Dictator* – the story could have ended with Roosevelt's fine-sounding speech, full of hope and courage and determination for the future. But this was real life. This was London. And in real life London some things still made Winston Churchill anxious.

Before he went walking through the City ruins with his wife Clementine on Monday afternoon, he had told a Cabinet meeting that he was encouraged that Roosevelt's speech had committed America implacably against the Three-Power Pact. The President's talk about keeping the US out of a 'last-ditch' war might, he thought, prove significant.

Nevertheless, despite the British newspapers' universally positive interpretation of the President's words, it was still difficult to discern the financial framework underpinning the inspiring rhetoric, or quite how it related to the expectations raised by his press conference of a fortnight ago. The President had said in his Fireside Chat that America must be the 'Arsenal of Democracy', which sounded wonderful. But like 'All aid short of war', which remained the same rose-coloured conundrum it had been over these past months, it was open to interpretation.

Churchill's first attempt at his cable in response had begun brightly, conflating the pre-Christmas press conference and Sunday night's speech in a single burst of optimism: 'There are great hopes here that you are going to invite the United States to give us substantial aid in the spirit of your declaration about the firehose . . .' he dictated. But these bold words never made it across the Atlantic.

In truth, the Prime Minister still had no real indication whether the President was proposing that the US give or lend Britain all or any of what it would need to survive. Nor, if he did, whether Congress would allow it. Nor, if Hitler made a move on Britain in the spring, or if Britain's military situation weakened, US defence experts might find a better use for their 'Arsenal of Democracy' than to send its stockpiles across the Atlantic. Winston Churchill still hoped for the best from Franklin Roosevelt, but the relationship between the two leaders was still young and tentative and it had suffered a bruising beginning.

AT THE HEART of the Prime Minister's anxieties in the wee small hours of this morning was a United States ship that was steaming, in great secrecy, to collect $18 million of British gold in part-payment for existing British arms orders with US companies. It was not the gold itself so much as US insistence on collecting it that played on Churchill's mind. For the President must know only too well that Britain had spent its way to the edge of bankruptcy in fighting this war, and that $18 million was a drop in the ocean compared to what Britain would require from America if she was to fight on. It did not augur well.

The Capetown gold, Churchill dictated to his secretary, was a 'last reserve, from which alone we might buy a few months' food'. And if, as seemed likely, this operation came to be known, it 'would wear the aspect of a sheriff collecting the last assets of a helpless debtor'. Not surprisingly, perhaps, neither of these phrases survived in the cable as finally sent. Nor did the Prime Minister's hint that the surrender of the gold must be contingent on at least some clue as to what, if anything, the President – let alone Congress – was ready to commit towards Britain's defence when Britain's financial resources were gone.

'Remember, Mr President,' he dictated – and this was one heartfelt sentence that did make it into the final draft – 'we do not know what you have in mind, or exactly what the United States is going to do, and we are fighting for our lives.'

IF THIS WAS the movies – if this was *The Thief of Bagdad* – then perhaps a magical 'all-seeing eye' could have probed the intentions and motives of friends and enemies around the world and cast some light on the road ahead. But this was real life. This was London. And in real-life London, Churchill consistently confronted the 'dense and baffling . . . veil of the Unknown'. Sometimes – not in this case, obviously, but sometimes – the Prime Minister signed off memos and letters with a trademark 'KBO' ('Keep Buggering On'). Sometimes it was the only thing to do.

'They burned a large part of the City of London last night,' he concluded his cable to the President,

> and the scenes of widespread destruction here and in our provincial centres are shocking, but when I visited the still burning ruins to-day the spirit of Londoners was as high as in the first days of the indiscriminate bombing in September, four months ago.
>
> I thank you for testifying before all the world that the future safety and greatness of the American Union are intimately concerned with the upholding and the effective arming of that indomitable spirit.
>
> All my heartiest good wishes to you in the New Year of storm that is opening upon us.

When it got to Washington, the British Embassy removed the paragraph referring to the bombing of September, lest it awaken ugly memories.

CHURCHILL WOULD HAVE slept the sounder, when he finally went off to bed, if he had known that, in Washington, messages of support for the frank tone of the President's 'Arsenal of Democracy' speech were pouring in from the American public, at the rate of a hundred to one.

And sounder still if he had been aware of the existence of an unregarded document in an in-tray in Moscow: a slip of paper which, among all the upheavals and adventures of the past thirty-six hours, was perhaps the most significant portent for the future that had been produced by anyone on 29th December 1940.

For the information it contained, picked up among high-ranking intelligence contacts in Berlin, had been essentially correct. Adolf Hitler had indeed decided that Britain's final subjugation must wait for a while.

Of course his Luftwaffe would go on bombing Britain for now, and his U-boats would tighten their stranglehold around her Atlantic convoys. But the Russians' poor showing in Finland had convinced him it would not take long to knock them out; he might even delay his attack a little in order to go to Mussolini's support in Greece and still have time to put the USSR out of the picture by next winter. And then we would see what had happened to that ridiculous British will to resist. On 18th December 1940

Hitler had issued his twenty-first operational directive of the war: 'The German Armed Forces must be prepared, even before the conclusion of the war against England, to crush Soviet Russia in a rapid campaign ("Operation Barbarossa").'

FULLER ACCOUNTS of last night's devastation would appear in the Tuesday papers that were already rolling off the presses in Fleet Street. But none would convey the epic 'story' of this night like the cropped-in picture of St Paul's on the front page of the *Daily Mail*.

The back page of the paper carried the other 'angle' on the night's story: the same scene, but taken from the far side of the river. And if the front page of the *Mail* was a message for the future, then the back page was a message from the past. For it showed something of the huge scale of the fires that had stretched right across the Square Mile that night – and recalled nothing so much as the pictures painted, almost three hundred years before, of the Great Fire of London.

It is impossible to say who had first used the words 'Second Great Fire of London' on Sunday night but, over the course of Monday, the phrase had captured Fleet Street. And thus the many individual horrors of the night – like the eighty horses killed by an HE bomb on a Moorgate brewery, an incident picked up by many papers alongside the destruction at the Guildhall, the 'two hospitals' hit, and this or that anonymous 'famous Wren church' – became part of a greater story. And it was already transforming into a story in which it was London itself, not Hitler's Luftwaffe, that had triumphed. Which might, indeed, even count as another 'own goal' for Hitler, a Home Front Dunkirk.

For everyone knew that a Great Fire of London was something that the British knew how to *do*: had done before; could do again. Something that carried a message from the past of persistence, pride and renewal quite as much as destruction and despair. And it was certainly no cue to give up or give in. This night had been no Turning Point, and that would be its glory. If London had collapsed it might have been a turning point. But London had Carried On.

MUCH THOUGH Londoners owed to the exhausted members of the St Paul's Watch, some of them back on duty again tonight, tending the Christmas tree and refilling the sand buckets, it is debatable whether even the destruction of Wren's Cathedral could have quite destroyed this feeling. But the fact that St Paul's did stand, apparently undamaged and unchanged, whenever you looked towards it (and thanks to Herbert Mason's photograph, the whole of the free world would soon be looking towards it) seemed a glorious blessing. And, to many, it was a gift from both God and man equally, working in friendly co-operation.

The Dean and Chapter made their own thanks to God but also recorded that

> Great praise was due to the Surveyor of the Fabric for the excellence of the air raid precautions taken for the safety of the Cathedral and especially with the smoothness with which the arrangements had worked on the night of 29th December 1940. It was decided that the record should also be made of the efficiency of the Watch and permanent staff on this alarming occasion.

Home Secretary Herbert Morrison was more concerned with the inefficiency displayed by other fire squads – and the general lack of them. The British had been 'slacking', he told them brusquely in a tea-time broadcast at six o'clock on New Year's Eve. Never again should any part of any city be so unprotected. Henceforth everyone, men and women, would be trained as fire guards and would have to serve their turn.

AT THE CTO, communications might have been severely limited in the wake of the Great Fire but the feline jungle telegraph seemed to have worked effortlessly, producing an influx of cats. 'They enjoy themselves with us,' wrote Nell Carver, 'as we pet them up so. It does look strange but somehow comforting to see them. Nobody minds & they stroll in & out as they please.' She did not subscribe to the more mournful assessments of the destruction of the office:

> I've heard several people say that the old TS is gone for ever, & its spirit also etc. but that is quite absurd. TS is more an atmosphere than a place & we are all spared to make a new one – so let's not look back too much.

In the days that followed, touring the City with her friend Edith, she found – not least perhaps because she was looking for it – a similarly indomitable spirit. They headed first, as did so many, for St Paul's. They found its Chapter House gone, and the lovely old Lloyd's Bank building on the corner where they had often admired the staircase.

'Hitchcock, Williams, Fullers & Stoneham's on Ludgate Hill and all of Ivy Lane are no more,' she noted.

> It's a terrible clearance of so many of our cherished landmarks. This would be very depressing if it were not for the cheerfulness & pluck of the City folk. In Cheapside, Bread St, Wood Street & Newgate St, a string of cards has been hung

317

out stating where the unfortunate owners have moved to (they appear to have already all found accommodation – if only half a room) & every now & then you come across girls & men loaded up with their salvaged goods. Some alas have nothing to save – it's all gone into dust. There is not the slightest feeling of defeat in the air or on the faces of the clerks & shopkeepers – only a stern & grim determination to hold on to the end – Hitler's end.

Isabelle Granger, too, found the City inspirational when she and Elisabeth went to view the damage: 'It's gruesome, but the people are quite amazingly good tempered, gay: I love living here, now – its like getting a personal dig at Hitler every time a bomb drops & leaves me alive to spite him by living.'

PERHAPS LONDON could take it, but not every Londoner could. Leslie Paul received a call to help arrange one man's evacuation, and another to help a friend move across London from Eltham to Mill Hill, where she felt she would be safer: 'She says she can't stop trembling and her nerves are all shot to pieces.' On the whole, though, he wrote in his diary on New Year's Eve, 'We're veterans of war now, and don't trouble so much to rush to shelters . . . The difference between being a veteran and an apprentice is that you feel it less important that you should wake up alive in the morning.'

Half an hour before midnight he went out on the balcony and looked toward the City, where he could just discern a glimmer of still-burning fires. 'There's only one year that can be worse than 1940 – that's 1941,' he closed his last diary entry of the year. 'We are bombing the New Year in. I'm going to bed. To hell with the New Year.'

OTHERS STAYED UP to welcome it in, and record their hopes for the future. For Sidney Chave, it was: 'Enough to say that we are confident. Confident, that with the help of God, 1941 will see us well on the way to beating the pagan, Jew-baiting Hun.'

Canadian Yvonne Green, unable to be with her soldier husband, had invited round a small gathering of friends 'in honour of the death of this particularly ruddy year'. And then Leonard managed to telephone, 'which was the next best thing to seeing him', so they had 'a pleasant if not riotous time performing the suitable obsequies'.

Some people made a livelier evening. 'Piccadilly blacked out and St Paul's surrounded by smouldering ruins. But never can every restaurant and club have been more completely packed, never can crowds have been more spontaneously gay,' wrote the Bloomsbury social worker.

> Last year we were sober because the threat of the future was a threat still, and
> we knew the year was bringing us dread ordeals and hazards. 1941 will bring
> them too, but we have gazed right into the furnace, and recaptured our belief in
> ourselves.

She herself saw in the New Year at Meurice, once Quaglino's. There
was a band playing 'Oh Johnny, how you can love', and a Transatlantic
cabaret, with Canadian and American singers.

> As midnight struck we sang Auld Lang Syne with joined hands and waved our
> paper hats and danced a highland reel on two inches of space. Would that Hitler
> could have seen us. I think he'd have found it disheartening.

In Wapping, the dog-tired shelterers in the Orient were asleep before
eleven o'clock. But at St John's Nev Coates witnessed: 'Young people in
huge circles, jumping up and down in a strange, spontaneous dance, arms
around the one on each side, singing to drown the drumming of the
piano.'

> Then hands on shoulders, 'Fall in and follow me,' to trudge around the shelter,
> around beds, a long squirming line, into the dark corners, circles again, concen-
> tric, then 'Knees up, Mother Brown,' the inner circle being kicked – wilder, nois-
> ier, dusty, sweaty, then almost breathlessly subsided into 'Auld Lang Syne' at
> midnight and finished with 'There'll Always be an England'.

There was 'Auld Lang Syne' in Brixton, too. May Speed began her first
diary entry of 1941 by recording that 'No air raid sirens disturbed the
birth of the new year' but that she had been woken, instead, by joyous
singing in the street. 'People it seemed had made a spontaneous demon-
stration.' 'Auld Lang Syne' was followed by a very energetic 'Knees Up
Mother Brown', and finally 'God Save The King'. 'After that there was
silence.'

IN FLEET STREET, the presses were roaring once again. And in Covent
Garden, at the *Daily Herald* works in Long Acre, the paper was offering
to fulfil its earlier promise to address the 'Riddles of 1941':

> Will Hitler invade Britain?
> Will America enter the war?
> What next in the air?
> Can we smash the U-boat campaign?
> Can we take the offensive in 1941?

319

What will happen in the Balkans?
What are Stalin's plans?
Will our blockade win?
What will happen to Europe's neutrals?
What will happen in the Far East?
How will the world pay for the war?
Where do we go when we win?

Well, it was 1941 now. And there was really only one way to find out.

CODA

IT WAS A QUARTER to ten on a chilly January morning. And in Westminster, the deep-throated bell known the world over as Big Ben tolled out across London skies that were cold and clear and grey. As the last chime died away, Big Ben fell silent and would remain silent until midnight.

It was stilled – as it had never been stilled during daylight by all the efforts of the Luftwaffe through almost six years of war – because today, Saturday 30th January 1965, Britain was burying its war leader, Winston Churchill.

For three days his old body had lain in the ancient Westminster Hall, great ceremonial chamber of the nation, while its people queued in their hundreds of thousands in the freezing cold outside, waiting to file past his coffin. Now it would be carried past huge, silent crowds, on a gun carriage, through the streets of London.

From the Parliament buildings he loved, along Whitehall from Cromwell to Charles I, passing his wartime home of Downing Street on the way. To Nelson's Trafalgar Square and then taking that old highway of history along Strand, Fleet Street and Ludgate Hill to St Paul's Cathedral, for a national service of thanksgiving and remembrance. 'St Paul's must be saved at all costs,' he had commanded one night long ago – a night when commands meant nothing and faith, and courage, and luck, and superhuman effort meant everything. A night that gave substance to the popular wartime slogan: 'It All Depends On Me'. Though whether you added, as the Dean of St Paul's did, 'And I Depend On God' was up to you. It was, after all, a free country.

After the short memorial service, at which men and women of all nations sang 'He who would true valour see', 'Fight the good fight', 'O God our help in ages past' and 'The Battle Hymn of the Republic' – Churchill's old body would be carried on through the City to the Tower of London. And at Tower Pier, it would be placed on a motor-launch that would take it a short way back up the Thames to Waterloo, for the train to Oxfordshire and the small country churchyard where he had asked to be buried.

It was all as he had planned it to be: an historic journey for an historic figure. But he had not planned the one thing that everyone would remember most from this day – for as the launch bearing his coffin passed the Thamesside wharves, every dockers' crane had dipped, in silent homage.

It was homage to a man, but also to a time. A time when history had come here, to this city that Josef Goebbels had called 'Churchill's monster', and the world had watched it burn its heart out. History had moved on now, and the world had moved on too. But the much-changed modern world was taking time out today, to look back, and to wonder.

Churchill the historian had been fascinated by the 'what ifs' of history. But by no act of the imagination could he have foreseen exactly how the 'what is' of history would unfold from those last, dark days of 1940 to this day of sad celebration. How it would take every ounce of the combined strengths of the British Empire, the United States of America, the Soviet Union and the rest of the 'United Nations', working together in unlikely unison, to wipe the terrors of the Nazi regime from the face of the earth, and how men and women of every race and every nation would pay the ultimate sacrifice in that cause. Though Churchill the historian would not have been so jejune as to imagine that even this great and wonderful victory would presage the end of history.

Every event, every personality, of the Second World War and its aftermath had been argued about, and would continue to be argued about, for as long as people remember that the War happened at all. But the significance of this man, at this moment, was that he had looked early, and looked deep, into the very heart of the Nazi vision and had found from somewhere a faith that this was not, after all, to be the future of the world. And, by the power of his oratory, he had reassured the world over many dark years that this insane faith might be, in some deep, unfathomable sense, justified. And had demonstrated for all time that, even when things seem darkest of all and there is little rational cause for hope, there might yet be a reason to 'Keep Buggering On'.

But it was more than that. For he also shared with the world his conviction that, even if he turned out to be wrong – and he had been wrong before, many times and about many things – if this Nazi world of dictators and brute force and scorn for the rule of law and basic humanity did turn out to be the only world the future had to offer, then it was a world that he, and they, wanted no part of. 'Keep Buggering On' might involve dying for freedom. And that can sound like the most difficult thing there is to do – until you are faced with the prospect of living on without it.

Yet to consider even a fraction of the price that was paid, even in one city, even on one night*, for freedom is to shame those who take it for granted. And to shame, too, any tin-pot Churchillian who would lightly or recklessly hazard the future of peoples on the bloody and uncertain outcomes of war.

Winston Churchill had led a nation and an empire along the edge of a precipice and he knew it: it was no coward soul that had learned to value 'jaw-jaw' above 'war-war' after a lifetime's acquaintance with both.

Of those who saw London burn on 29th December 1940, many would not live to see the peace they hazarded their lives for. Frank Hurd did not see 1941; within a fortnight, fifty-six of the shelterers Mr Rogers had walked past in Bank Tube died when the station received a direct hit. Leslie Paul's Bullivant's Wharf suffered carnage too, in an incident for which Sergeant Grey's actions won him a British Empire Medal. Yvonne Green – 'Papoose' to her mother and 'Canada' to her AFS colleagues – was killed firewatching in April 1941 while helping to guard Chelsea Old Church. And the following month, four of warden Barbara Nixon's old colleagues from Finsbury's Post 2 died in the final raid of this first great phase of the Blitz on London.

Australian Win Marshall married her beloved Teddy, but saw VE Day as a war widow, after he parachuted into France on Special Operations, never having seen their baby daughter. And American Ernie Pyle, who came to England expecting a 'holocaust of souls' but found himself instead in a tale by Dickens, was killed by a Japanese sniper's bullet on the island of Ie Shima in the Pacific in April 1945, less than one week after the death of his President.

In his wartime role, Churchill acknowledged, 'It was the nation and the race dwelling all round the globe that had the lion heart: I had the luck to be called upon to give the roar.' He had not been called upon himself, as he might have been, to face death, pistol in hand, as his world crumbled around him. Against unimaginable odds – as viewed from any rational perspective at the end of 1940 – that would turn out to be Adolf Hitler's fate instead. But Churchill did, perhaps, reserve the greatest speech of his life for that moment when, naked and defeated, he had faced the collapse of all his hopes.

The war in Europe was over, the war in the Far East still raging, when

*see Appendix A, p. 329

Britain held its first General Election since 1935. The Prime Minister was in his bath when the head of his Map Room brought the first intimation that the electorate had rejected his bid to take them into the peace, and had instead elected a landslide Labour Government. Churchill turned grey and the officer thought he would faint. Then Churchill spoke: 'They are perfectly entitled to vote as they please. This is democracy. This is what we've been fighting for.'

AND SO LONDON had begun to rebuild, slowly, its future on the ruins of its past. The Corporation of London laid out the various options for putting a new face on the City in a book whose frontispiece map – and who could be surprised? – was of the devastated London that Wren had faced in 1666, together with an explanation of, and justification for, the piecemeal way the Corporation had gone about the job last time around. Hitler had made a fundamental mistake in thinking that he was destroying something by attacking this City. For the long story of the Square Mile had proved that you cannot destroy history – you can only make more.

Every Londoner has a unique history, though not every one gets told. Their lives weave in and out, from every nation and to every nation, and sometimes no one sees the going of them, and sometimes a record remains behind. Bill and Vi Regan, for instance, got their girls home at last and lived to see them married, and their grandchildren, great-grandchildren and even a great-great grandchild flourish.

Isabelle Granger continued her internationalism and good works after the war, joining the National Council for the Unmarried Mother and her Child and becoming its General Secretary from 1946 to 1961. Laboratory technician Sidney Chave became a distinguished specialist in public health, specialising in the effects of environment on mental health. May Speed, in spite of all her domestic frustrations, managed to get four novels published, under her given name of Florence, while Nell Carver poured her literary talents into editing a news bulletin for retired CTO staff when she came to the end of her own working life. And, in a move that might have astonished his younger self, Woodcraft Folk founder Leslie Paul spent five years on the General Synod of the Church of England.

And some survivors of 29th December 1940, at the time of writing, survive still. I know, for I have spoken to them. In their seventies, eighties and nineties now, and poorly some of them, though others are hale and hearty. Some with clear recollections of that momentous night; others, confronted by the evidence left behind by their younger selves, wondering how they could have forgotten so much among all that has happened since. One, tracked down in Ecuador, called to say that he kept a copy of Herbert Mason's photograph pinned up above his desk, St Paul's looking just as it had done that night from the roof of his own office block in Finsbury Circus.

All of them have been, to me, tremendously kind, and patient, in explaining details of their far-off world to clarify the written record. Few have not told me a funny story or two from those far-off days; few have not also said that they were terrible times, and regretted the loss of some lovely woman or good bloke who had been less lucky than themselves. None have seen themselves as special, or as heroes. Like everyone else, they tend to say that they 'just got on with it'.

It is impossible not to reach, one last time, for Shakespeare, who understood everything, and London most of all, and say simply, in conclusion: 'We that are young, Shall never see so much, nor live so long.'

APPENDIX A: One Night's Blitz

Died as a Result of Enemy Action

commemorated in perpetuity in the civilian war dead
register by the commonwealth graves commission

IN GREATER LONDON AREA ON 29TH DECEMBER 1940
UNLESS OTHERWISE STATED

Municipal Borough of Battersea

DORIS LOVELL
Daughter of William G T and Elizabeth Jane Lovell
of 16A Swanage Rd, Wandsworth.
Injured 29th December at 16A Swanage Rd;
died next day at St James' Hospital. Age 13

Municipal Borough of Beckenham, Kent

HAZEL JEAN BURGESS
of St Christopher's School, Lennard Rd.
Daughter of Mrs J L Burgess of 24 Abbot's Way.
At St Christopher's School. Age 11

Metropolitan Borough of Bermondsey

EDWIN WALTER AMBRIDGE
Fireman, AFS, of 6 Abernethy Rd, Lewisham.
Husband of Lilian Maud Ambridge.
Injured at Crucifix Lane 30 December;
died same day at St Olave's Hospital. Age 27

GRACE LILIAN ARCHER
of 38A Grinstead Rd, Deptford.
Daughter of Mr T B Fryer of 13E Sutton Model Estates
and the late M Fryer; wife of John W Archer.
Injured 29th December at 38A Grinstead Rd;
died next day at St Olave's Hospital. Age 34

BENJAMIN CHARLES CARTER
of 279 Devon Mansions, Tooley St.
Husband of Violet Louise Carter.
At Devon Mansions. Age 61

VIOLET LOUISE CARTER
of 279 Devon Mansions, Tooley St.
Wife of Benjamin Charles Carter.
At Devon Mansions. Age 56

LILLIE BRIDGETT RATCLIFFE
of 17 Brunswick Court. Widow of James Ratcliffe.
At 17 Brunswick Court. Age 62

JAMES DANIEL TOBIN
of 51 Richardson St. Son of William and Louisa Tobin.
Injured at Richardson St;
died same day at St Olave's Hospital. Age 18

ISABEL WHITE
of 299 Devon Mansions, Tooley St. Wife of E J White.
Injured at 299 Devon Mansions;
died same day at St Olave's Hospital. Age 53

CHARLOTTE WOOFF
of 221 Lynton Rd. Wife of Frank Wyndham Wooff.
At 221 Lynton Rd. Age 57

FRANK WYNDHAM WOOFF
of 221 Lynton Rd. Husband of Charlotte Wooff.
At 221 Lynton Rd. Age 66

Metropolitan Borough of Camberwell

NORA ALICE ASPIN
of 45 Verney Rd.
Daughter of Mr and Mrs William Aspin.
opposite Turk's Head, Old Kent Rd. Age 16

JULIA MAY BAKER
of 44 Loncroft Rd. Daughter of W E Baker.
At Loncroft Rd. Age 16

THOMAS JOHN BARNETT
of 19 Sandover Rd. Son of T and L Barnett.
At Loncroft Rd. Age 20

ANNIE BEVIS
of 38 Sandover Rd. Wife of Percy Henry Bevis.
At 38 Sandover Rd. Age 72

PERCY HENRY BEVIS
of 38 Sandover Rd. Husband of Annie Bevis.
At 38 Sandover Rd. Age 68

ALICE BISHOP
of 89 Peckham Park Rd. Wife of John William Bishop.
At 89 Peckham Park Rd on 30 December. Age 43

JOHN WILLIAM BISHOP
of 89 Peckham Park Rd. Husband of Alice Bishop.
At 89 Peckham Park Rd on 30 December. Age 51

LILIAN BRAUND
of 10 Calmington Rd.
At 15 Calmington Rd on 31st December.
Aged between 60 and 65

SAMUEL ERNEST BRAUND
of 10 Calmington Rd.
At 15 Calmington Rd on 31st December.
Aged between 60 and 65

WILLIAM CHARLES BROOKS
of 18 George Lane, Lewisham.
Husband of Susan Brooks.
At 709 Old Kent Rd. Age 62

IVY FLORENCE CLARK
of 43 Barlow St, East St, Southwark.
Daughter of George W and Louisa Clark.
Near Dalwood St, Southampton Way. Age 26

LOUIS FREDERICK COOPER
of 95 Southampton Way. Son of W and E Cooper.
At junction of Loncroft Rd and Kempshead Rd. Age 19

CHARLES THOMAS DARLINGTON
Air Raid Warden of 62 Shenley Rd.
Outside Town Hall, Peckham Rd. Age 44

LUIGI DEL NEVO
of 26 De Crespigny Park.
Husband of Blanche Del Nevo.
At 26 De Crespigny Park. Age 40

MAUREEN DEL NEVO
of 26 De Crespigny Park.
Daughter of Luigi and Blanche Del Nevo.
At 26 De Crespigny Park. Age 5

WILLIAM HENRY DIRK
of 60 Vestry Rd.
Outside Town Hall, Peckham Rd. Age 49

JOHN JOSEPH EAST
of 34 Loncroft Rd.
Injured 29th December at 34 Loncroft Rd;
died next day at Dulwich Hospital. Age 69

HENRY CHARLES FISHER
Home Guard of 14 Cancel St, Walworth. Husband of C Fisher.
At 38 Sandover Rd. Age 45

ERNEST STANHOPE FOLLETT
ARP Ambulance Driver
of 278 Rosendale Rd, Lambeth.
Husband of Esme Follett.
Outside Town Hall, Peckham Rd. Age 35

BEATRICE ANNIE FRENCH
Daughter of Mr and Mrs T H French,
of 27 Verney Rd.
opposite Turk's Head, Old Kent Rd. Age 17

GEORGE ALBERT GRAY
Constable, Police War Reserve
of 16 Brunswick Park. Son of George William Gray
of 16 Hartside Terrace, Chevington Drift, Morpeth,
Northumberland; husband of Catherine Gray.
Outside Town Hall, Peckham Rd. Age 27

JOHN JAMES WATSON IVISON
of 23 The Gardens, East Dulwich.
Husband of Emily Ivison.
Near Dalwood St, Southampton Way. Age 58

DOROTHY EMILY JACKSON
of 10 Rosemary Gdns. Wife of Edward Jackson.
At 10 Rosemary Gdns. Age 41

EDWARD JACKSON
of 10 Rosemary Gdns.
Husband of Dorothy Emily Jackson.
At 10 Rosemary Gdns. Age 50

JOAN PEGGY JEFFERIES
of 27 Loncroft Rd.
At Loncroft Rd. Age 16

SAMUEL THOMAS JEFFERIES
Son of T Jefferies of 27 Loncroft Rd and of
Violet Rose Jefferies.
Injured 29th December at Loncroft Rd;
died two days later at Dulwich Hospital. Age 13

VIOLET ROSE JEFFERIES
Wife of T Jefferies of 27 Loncroft Rd.
At Loncroft Rd. Age 43

JAMES KING
Son of William Henry and Mary King of 24 Riddell St.
Near Dalwood St, Southampton Way. Age 20

WALTER KING
ARP demolition worker.
Son of William Henry and Mary King of 24 Riddell St.
Near Dalwood St, Southampton Way. Age 30

JAMES LAMBERT
of 39 Grenard Rd.
At Southampton Way. Age 18

DOROTHY MAY LANE
of 28 Whitworth House, Falmouth Rd.
Daughter of W T G Lane.
At 27 Loncroft Rd. Age 17

EDWARD MARRINER
of 38 Loncroft Rd. Son of Mr and Mrs J Marriner.
At Loncroft Rd. Age 13

JULES MICHEL
of 24 De Crespigny Park.
At 24 De Crespigny Park. Age 50

RICHARD HENRY NABBS
of 29 Loncroft Rd. Husband of Emily J Nabbs.
At Loncroft Rd Shelter. Age 32

WILLIAM ALFRED NEWCOMBE
Air Raid Warden of 2 Shenley Rd.
At Peckham Rd. Age 45

JOHN OWENS
Husband of Rose Owens of 46 Peckham Rd.
Outside Town Hall, Peckham Rd. Age 66

GEORGE WILLIAM PEACE
of 136 Bellenden Rd, Rye Lane.
At 136 Bellenden Rd on 30th December. Age 76

EMILY SOPHIA EVA PENFORD
Daughter of G J Penford
of 23 Whitworth House, Falmouth Rd.
At 27 Loncroft Rd. Age 14

ELLEN ALICE PILKINGTON
Daughter of George and Ellen Pilkington of
28 Leeds House, Sumner Rd.
At Loncroft Rd. Age 15

HENRY GLADSTONE POLLARD
Home Guard
Husband of Eliza M Pollard of 93 Henslowe Rd.
At Southampton Way. Age 53

ARTHUR PROBERT
of 29 Loncroft Rd. Son of Nellie Probert of
50 Elmwood Rd, Herne Hill and of the late
William Phillip Probert; husband of Mary Probert.
At 29 Loncroft Rd. Age 41

EDWARD PROBERT
Son of Nellie Probert of 50 Elmwood Rd, Herne Hill,
and of the late William Phillip Probert;
husband of Grace Probert of 8 Dovercourt Rd.
At 29 Loncroft Rd. Age 45

FRANK PROBERT
of 26 Loncroft Rd. Son of Nellie Probert of
50 Elmwood Rd, Herne Hill and of the late
William Phillip Probert; husband of Alice Probert.
At 29 Loncroft Rd. Age 36

JOHN RICHARD REGARDSOE
of 32 Loncroft Rd. Son of William Regardsoe.
At Loncroft Rd. Age 20 months

WILLIAM REGARDSOE
Shelter Marshal of 32 Loncroft Rd.
At Loncroft Rd. Age 34

DORIS LILY SAFFERY
of 84 Grove Lane. Daughter of Albert Edward
and Lily Morley of 21 Hengrave Rd, Honor Oak;
wife of Donald Eustace Saffery.
At 84 Grove Lane. Age 33

KATE RUTH STANLEY
of 245 Southampton Way. Daughter of Thomas
and Mary Poulter of Little Waltham, Chelmsford,
Essex; wife of George Swithin Stanley.
At 245 Southampton Way. Age 60

EILEEN PATRICIA TALBOT
Daughter of Robert and Ada Talbot,
of 84 Astbury Rd, Queen's Rd.
At Loncroft Rd. Age 18

DORIS IRENE THOMAS
of 55 Pomeroy St, New Cross.
Daughter of J and M C Thomas.
At Loncroft Rd. Age 17

EDWARD HENRY THORP
of 89 Goodrich Rd. Husband of Mary Thorp.
Injured 29th December at 89 Goodrich Rd;
died next day at Dulwich Hospital. Age 64

FRANCIS WILLIAM WINCH
of 153A Rye Lane.
Injured 29th December at 153A Rye Lane;
died next day at Dulwich Hospital. Age 71

AMELIA MARION WRIGHT
of 26 De Crespigny Park.
Wife of Martin Henry Wright.
At 26 De Crespigny Park. Age 37

MARTIN HENRY WRIGHT
Fireman, AFS
of 26 De Crespigny Park.
Husband of Amelia Marion Wright.
At 26 De Crespigny Park. Age 36

MARTIN ROBIN WRIGHT
of 26 De Crespigny Park.
Son of Martin Henry and Amelia Marion Wright.
At 26 De Crespigny Park. Age 2

City of London

JAMES DALY
Fireman, AFS
Husband of Emily Daly of Oakhills,
Fulling Mill Lane, Welwyn, Hertfordshire.
Injured 29th December at City Rd; died two days
later at St Bartholomew's Hospital. Age 31

GODFREY JOHN WILLIAM EMMERSON
Home Guard; Boy Scout
of 55 Great Tower St. Son of Herbert William
and Catherine Anne Emmerson.
At 55 Great Tower St. Age 16

SIDNEY ALFRED HOLDER
Fireman, AFS
of 49 Cool Oak Lane, Hendon, Middlesex.
Injured at Wine Office Court; died same day
near St Bartholomew's Hospital. Age 33

ROBERT LESLIE KERR-LINDSAY
Fireman, AFS
Son of Mrs J E Kerr-Lindsay of
22 Camden St, Camden Town.
Injured 29th December at City Rd; died two days
later at St Bartholomew's Hospital. Age 33

FRANK WILLIAM LE ROSSIGNOL
of 19 Hyde Walk, Love Lane, Morden, Surrey.
Husband of V M Le Rossignol.
Injured at Phoenix Insurance Co., King William St;
died same day near St Bartholomew's Hospital. Age 41

JAMES PORTER
Husband of D E Porter of 11 Milton Road,
West Hendon, Middlesex.
Injured at Faraday Buildings; died same day
near St Bartholomew's Hospital. Age 42

ALFRED SAMUEL REYNOLDS
Son of Rose Agnes Reynolds of 102 Grange St, Hoxton
and of the late Edward Daniel Reynolds.
Injured at City Rd, Moorfields;
died same day at St Bartholomew's Hospital. Age 16

FRANCIS THOMAS SHERBORNE
of 72 Heathfield, South Twickenham, Middlesex.
Near St Bartholomew's Hospital. Age 44

Metropolitan Borough of Deptford

THOMAS HENRY COOPER
of 1 Reaston St. Son of T J Cooper of
63 Congreve Rd, Well Hall, Eltham, Kent;
husband of Clara Emily Cooper.
At 1 Reaston St. Age 58

Metropolitan Borough of Finsbury

LESLIE VICTOR ARMS
of 14 Lampeter St, Islington.
At 238/240 City Rd. Age 15

EDWARD JOHN BATYIE
Firewatcher of 22 David St, Stratford.
At Epworth St. Age 65

HERBERT THOMAS BLUNDELL
Fireman, AFS. Husband of Mrs Blundell of
163 Hemingford Rd, Barnsbury.
At Dingley Place. Age 34

GEORGE BUCKTHORPE
Son of Mr and Mrs A Buckthorpe of
68 Grange St, Shoreditch.
At Dingley Place. Age 15

BENJAMIN EDWARD CHINNERY
Fireman, AFS
of 18 Goldington Crescent, St Pancras.
Son of Nellie Chinnery of 24 Howard Rd,
Broadstairs, Kent; husband of Emma Susan Chinnery.
At Dingley Place, City Rd. Age 33

WILLIAM COOK
Husband of Mrs Cook of
296 Mortlake Rd, Ilford, Essex.
At 146 Goswell Rd. Age 38

LEONARD JAMES FREEMAN
Fireman, AFS
Son of Mr Freeman of 101 King's Cross Rd.
At 238/240 City Rd. Age 27

HENRY WALTER HALLIDAY
Acting Sub-Officer, London Fire Brigade
Husband of Clara G Halliday of
58 Packington St, Islington.
At City Rd. Age 48

HENRY CHARLES HILLIER
Husband of Lilian Ann Hillier of
3 Grosvenor Rd, Finchley North.
At 146/8 Goswell Rd. Age 31

ALEXANDER HOWARD JACKSON
(otherwise Stanley John Brown)
of 48 Chatham Place, Hackney. Son of Mr and Mrs
J Brown of Woodstock, St Albans, Hertfordshire.
At 146/8 Goswell Rd. Age 29

JAMES PORTER
Husband of D E Porter of 11 Milton Rd,
West Hendon, Middlesex.
Injured at Faraday Buildings; died same day
near St Bartholomew's Hospital. Age 42

ALFRED SAMUEL REYNOLDS
Son of Rose Agnes Reynolds of 102 Grange St,
Hoxton and of the late Edward Daniel Reynolds.
Injured at City Rd, Moorfields; died same
day at St Bartholomew's Hospital. Age 16

HERBERT CLARENCE JAMES SAUNDERS
Fireman, AFS
Adopted son of Mr and Mrs E Dodshon of
107 College Place, NW1.
Injured at City Rd; died same day at
St Mark's Hospital. Age 45

SIDNEY RALPH WHITEHEAD
Husband of Ada C Whitehead of
13 Cecilia Rd, Hackney.
At 146/8 Goswell Rd. Age 35

Metropolitan Borough of Fulham

CHARLES ALBERT CAUDLE
Son of C Caudle and of Maud Caudle.
At 11 Mooltan St. Age 24

MAUD CAUDLE
Wife of C Caudle.
At 11 Mooltan St. Age 47

LOUISA ELIZABETH HARRIS
of 6 Silvio St. Wife of William Harris.
Injured 29th December at 6 Silvio St;
died two days later at Western Hospital. Age 52

WILLIAM HARRIS
of 6 Silvio St. Husband of Louisa Elizabeth Harris.
At 6 Silvio St. Age 64

WILLIAM SAMUEL HAYLOCK
of 6 Silvio St. Husband of Justina A Haylock.
At 6 Silvio St. Age 67

FLORENCE HEWITT
Daughter of Maud Caudle (formerly Hewitt).
At 11 Mooltan St. Age 27

HETTY MARGARET HOWARD
of 2 Aynhoe Rd.
At 11 Mooltan St. Age 20

FLORENCE ANN SULLIVAN
At 3 Mooltan St. Age 53

JOHN SULLIVAN
At 3 Mooltan St. Age 55

JAMES CHATER
of 20 Dyson House, Blackwall Lane.
At 20 Dyson House. Age 54

JAMES LEWIS CHURCHILL
of 42 Dyson House, Blackwall Lane.
Son of Harry Graham Churchill of 27 Kirkside Rd;
husband of Alma Gertrude Churchill.
At 42 Dyson House. Age 36

ALICE AMELIA FIELD
of 46 Dyson House, Blackwall Lane.
Daughter of G and H Field.
Injured 29th December at 46 Dyson House;
died next day at St Alfege's Hospital. Age 42

WALTER GEORGE FRENCH
of 71 Dyson House, Blackwall Lane.
Husband of Marian E French.
At 71 Dyson House, Blackwall Lane. Age 61

FREDERICK JOHN GARLAND
Husband of Ellen C Garland.
At 62 Dyson House, Blackwall Lane. Age 51

MARY ANN HORN
of 60 Dyson House, Blackwall Lane.
Daughter of Isaac Alfred and Elizabeth Ann Horn.
Injured at 60 Dyson House;
died same day at St Alfege's Hospital. Age 24

ALBERT CHARLES LOCKEY
of 60 Dyson House, Blackwall Lane.
Son of Harry and Margaret Lockey of 48 Hertley Close,
Honor Oak; husband of Elizabeth Ann Lockey.
Injured at 60 Dyson House;
died same day at St Alfege's Hospital. Age 29

JOHN EDWARD MOYLE
59 Dyson House, Blackwall Lane.
Husband of Alice Moyle.
At 59 Dyson House.

FREDERICK THOMAS NEWMAN
of 68 Dyson House, Blackwall Lane.
Son of Mr and Mrs F T Newman.
Injured at 68 Dyson House; died same day
at St Alfege's Hospital. Age 14

RICHARD EDWARD JAMES PLUMB
Husband of Ada Clara Plumb of
33 King Arthur St, Peckham.
Injured 29th December at 39 King Arthur St;
died two days later at Miller Hospital. Age 64

ARTHUR WILLIAM RACKSTRAW
of 9 Circus St. Son of William Thomas and
Ruth Rackstraw; husband of Hilda Violet Rackstraw.
At 50 Dyson House, Blackwall Lane. Age 25

ROBERT CHANEY RUDRUM
of 51 Dyson House, Blackwall Lane.
Son of Henry Chaney Rudrum of 38 Roan St;
husband of Jane Rudrum.
At 51 Dyson House, Blackwall Lane. Age 35

PEGGY SAWYER
of 129 Charlton Church Lane.
Daughter of Edward and Florence Sawyer.
Injured at 22 Conley St;
died same day At St Alfege's Hospital. Age 11

ELIZABETH JANE SAYERS
of 5 Reaston St, New Cross. Wife of W H Sayers.
Injured at 5 Reaston St;
died same day at Miller Hospital. Age 64

CHARLES THOMPSON
of 52 Dyson House, Blackwall Lane.
At St Alfege's Hospital. Age 52

ALBERT EDMUND WEBB
Home Guard. Son of Albert Ernest and
Annie Marie Webb of 191 Maryon Rd.
At Blackwall Lane. Age 17

Metropolitan Borough of Hammersmith

EDWARD JOHN PATTENDEN
Leading Fireman, AFS
Husband of G Pattenden of 31 Porten Houses,
Porten Rd, Kensington.
Injured at Wood Lane; died
same day at Hammersmith Hospital. Age 34

Metropolitan Borough of Holborn

FRANCIS GERVAS EDWIN TAYLOR
Constable, Police War Reserve. of 36 Coram St.
Outside Imperial Hotel, Russell Square. Age 29

Municipal Borough of Kingston upon Thames, Surrey

JOHN TERENCE FOLKERD
of 164 Elm Rd. Son of Gilbert Thomas Folkerd.
At 164 Elm Rd. Age 12

ROSE ELIZABETH FOLKERD
of 164 Elm Rd. Daughter of W Pepperrell and of
Susan Pepperrell; wife of Gilbert Thomas Folkerd.
At 164 Elm Rd. Age 31

GILBERT KIRK
of 162 Elm Rd. Son of Douglas and Rose Nicol Kirk.
At 162 Elm Rd. Age 12 months

ROSE NICOL KIRK
of 162 Elm Rd. Wife of Douglas Kirk.
At 162 Elm Rd. Age 26

EDITH DUNCAN NICOL
of 162 Elm Rd. Daughter of Mrs Spence
(formerly Duncan) of 25 Claremont St, Aberdeen
and of the late William Hardy Duncan.
At 132 Elm Rd. Age 28

GILLIAN GLADYS PEPPERRELL
of 164 Elm Rd. Daughter of Rose Elizabeth Folkerd.
At 164 Elm Rd. Age 6

SUSAN PEPPERRELL
of 164 Elm Rd. Wife of W Pepperrell.
At 164 Elm Rd. Age 53

DAISY VIOLET PICKETT
of 160 Elm Rd.
At 160 Elm Rd. Age 16

OLIVE JOAN PICKETT
of 160 Elm Rd.
At 160 Elm Rd. Age 21

IRENE WINIFRED TYLOR
of 158 Elm Rd. Wife of George Patrick Tylor.
Injured 29th December at 158 Elm Rd;
died next day at Kingston County Hospital. Age 33

EDITH FLORENCE WARWICK
of 160A Elm Rd. Wife of E Warwick.
At 160A Elm Rd. Age 71

ERNEST HELMSLEY WARWICK
of 160A Elm Rd.
Son of May Florence Victoria Warwick.
At 160A Elm Rd. Age 4

MAY FLORENCE VICTORIA WARWICK
of 160A Elm Rd. Daughter of E Warwick,
and of Edith Florence Warwick.
At 160A Elm Rd. Age 36

EDITH HILDA WHELAN
of 158 Elm Rd. Wife of Phillip Henry Whelan.
At 158 Elm Rd. Age 38

MARJORY WHELAN
of 158 Elm Rd. Daughter of
Phillip Henry and Edith Hilda Whelan.
At 158 Elm Rd. Age 4

PHILLIP HENRY WHELAN
of 158 Elm Rd. Husband of Edith Hilda Whelan.
At 158 Elm Rd. Age 40

Metropolitan Borough of Lambeth

ELSIE FLORENCE ADLINGTON
of 65 Cheltenham Rd, Camberwell.
Wife of H J Adlington.
At Lambeth Hospital on 30th December. Age 31

CHARLES HENRY BAKER
of 33 Sandover Rd, Camberwell.
Husband of Elizabeth Baker.
Injured 29th December at 33 Sandover Rd;
died next day at King's College Hospital. Age 57

ELSIE MAUD BELL
of 84 Grove Lane, Camberwell.
Daughter of Clara Marie Wood (formerly Bell)
of 8 Mackie Avenue, Hassocks, Sussex.
Injured 29th December at 84 Grove Lane;
died next day at King's College Hospital. Age 38

CAROLINE STEVENS BROSSELARD
of 63 Russell Gdns, Stangate St.
Widow of Louis Edmond Brosselard.
At 63 Russell Gdns. Age 62

ALICE SARAH GILSON
of 3 Herne Place. Wife of Charles Gilson.
At 3 Herne Place. Age 74

CHARLES GILSON
of 3 Herne Place. Husband of Alice Sarah Gilson.
At 3 Herne Place. Age 83

WILLIAM ERNEST GOULDING
of 12 Shenton St, Peckham.
At King's College Hospital. Age 69

HENRIETTA MAY HARDING
of 3 Berwyn Rd, Herne Hill.
Daughter of the late James Winkworth Harding.
At 3 Berwyn Rd on 30th December. Age 61

ANNA PESCADOR
Spanish National
of 24 De Crespigny Park, Denmark Hill, Camberwell.
Daughter of Elise Michel (formerly Pescador).
Injured 29th December at 24 De Crespigny Park;
died two days later at King's College Hospital. Age 32

FREDERICK ARTHUR SEYMOUR
of 64 Russell Gdns.
At 64 Russell Gdns. Age 58

341

ELIZA ANN WILLIAMS
of 3 Berwyn Rd. Daughter of the late Robert and
Jane Jennison, of Union St, EC1;
wife of Henry Williams.
At 3 Berwyn Rd on 30th December. Age 82

KATE ANNIE WILLIAMS
of 53 Russell Gdns, Stangate St.
Widow of Alfred Williams.
Injured 29th December at Russell Gdns;
died next day at St Thomas's Hospital. Age 66

GERALD WOOD
Sergeant, Home Guard
Son of Richard and Ada Wood; husband of
Dorothy Ethel Wood of 59 Nutfield Rd.
Injured 29th December at Peckham Rd;
died next day at King's College Hospital. Age 42

ARNOLD JEDDAH YATES
of 77A Dulwich Rd. Husband of Beatrice Pauline Yates.
At 77A Dulwich Rd. Age 43

BEATRICE PAULINE YATES
of 77A Dulwich Rd. Wife of Arnold Jeddah Yates.
At 77A Dulwich Rd. Age 41

COLIN YATES
of 77A Dulwich Rd.
Son of Arnold Jeddah and Beatrice Pauline Yates.
At 77A Dulwich Rd. Age 6

MILES YATES
of 77A Dulwich Rd.
Son of Arnold Jeddah and Beatrice Pauline Yates.
At 77A Dulwich Rd. Age 4

PATRICIA YATES
of 77A Dulwich Rd.
Daughter of Arnold Jeddah and Beatrice Pauline Yates.
At 77A Dulwich Rd. Age 8

Metropolitan Borough of Lewisham

HENRY LESLIE COTTELL
Senior Air Raid Warden
Husband of Ann Helen Cottell of
41 Manor Lane Terrace, Lee.
Injured at Lee High Rd; died
same day at Lewisham Hospital. Age 52

CECILIA EMILY SMITH
of 258 Malyons Rd. Daughter of
John Henry Stevenson of 61 Barlborough St,
New Cross; wife of Walter Smith.
At 258 Malyons Rd. Age 71

ROBERT HENRY STEVENSON
of 258 Malyons Rd.
At 258 Malyons Rd. Age 73

Metropolitan Borough of Poplar

GLADYS CRAWLEY
of 93 East Ferry Rd, Cubitt Town.
Widow of Edward Crawley.
At 93 East Ferry Rd. Age 38

JOHN WILLIAM HILL
Station Officer, London Fire Brigade
Son of John and Ada Hill of 62 Ashford Ave,
Hayes, Middlesex; husband of Mary Hill of
14 Bedford Rd, East Ham, Essex.
Injured 29th December at Hawkins and Tipsons
Rope Works, East Ferry Rd;
died next day at Poplar Hospital. Age 46

ROBERT THOMAS PALMER
of 396 Manchester Rd.
At East Ferry Rd. Age 40

Metropolitan Borough of St Pancras

M J COHEN
of 51 Gloucester Crescent.
At National Temperance Hospital
on 30th December. Age 55

FRANK WILLIAM HURD
Fireman, AFS
Son of Francis Joseph and Edith Helen Hurd
of 18 Thane Villas, Islington.
Injured 29th December 1940 at Smithfield Market;
died next day at Royal Free Hospital. Age 24

ARTHUR GEORGE WATERMAN
Fireman, AFS
Son of Mr and Mrs G H Waterman of
5 Garden Cottages, East St, Epsom, Surrey.
Injured 29th December at the Guildhall, City of London;
died next day at Royal Free Hospital. Age 37

Metropolitan Borough of Shoreditch

ANNIE EDITH ADAMS
Daughter of Robert William and Annie Lilian Adams
of 17 Ivy St, Hoxton.
At Drysdale House, Drysdale St. Age 14

ANNIE LILIAN ADAMS
Daughter of Thomas and Mary Ann Burtles of
Drysdale House; wife of
Robert William Adams of 17 Ivy St, Hoxton.
At Drysdale House, Drysdale St. Age 34

JENNY BURTLES
of 27 Drysdale House, Drysdale St.
Daughter of Thomas Douglas and Mary Ann Burtles.
At 27 Drysdale House. Age 21

MARGARET BURTLES
of 3 the Barracks, Peter's Green, Luton, Bedfordshire.
Wife of Robert Burtles.
At 27 Drysdale House, Drysdale St. Age 34

SYLVIA BURTLES
of 3 the Barracks, Peter's Green, Luton, Bedfordshire.
Daughter of Robert Burtles and of Margaret Burtles.
At 27 Drysdale House. Age 6 months.

ERNEST VERNON GREGORY
of 23 Drysdale House, Drysdale St.
At Drysdale House. Age 56

ERNEST VERNON JOHN ALBERT GREGORY
Air Raid Warden of 23 Drysdale House, Drysdale St.
Husband of Selina Gregory.
At 23 Drysdale House. Age 34

LYDIA HELSEY (OTHERWISE SKINNER)
of 39 Drysdale House, Drysdale St. Wife of W Helsey.
At 39 Drysdale House. Age 63

ROSE HELSEY (OTHERWISE SKINNER)
of 39 Drysdale House, Drysdale St.
Daughter of W Helsey and of Lydia Helsey.
At 39 Drysdale House. Age 17

GEORGE HUGHES
London Heavy Rescue Service
of 24 Drysdale House, Drysdale St.
At Drysdale House. Age 45

EDWIN JOHN LONSDALE
of 21 Drysdale House, Drysdale St.
Son of Edwin John and Sophia Jane Lonsdale.
At Drysdale House. Age 19

HENRY SAUNDERS SIMMONDS
of 35 Drysdale House, Drysdale St.
At 35 Drysdale House. Age 73

JANE SPINKS
of 26 Drysdale House, Drysdale St.
Injured 29th December at Drysdale House;
died next day at St Leonard's Hospital. Age 35

MARGARET ROSE SPINKS
of 26 Drysdale House, Drysdale St.
At Drysdale House. Age 2

SAMUEL CHARLES WEBSTER
of 38 Drysdale House, Drysdale St.
Husband of J L Webster.
At 38 Drysdale House. Age 52

Metropolitan Borough of Southwark

EDITH CORDERY
of 184 John Ruskin St.
Wife of Edward Henry Cordery.
At 184 John Ruskin St. Age 57

RICHARD COWAN
of 7 Margaret Gdns, New Kent Rd.
Husband of W D Cowan.
At 75 Southwark St. Age 43

CHARLES ALBERT EMERY
of 153 Chatham St.
At Harding and Sons, Long Lane
on 30th December. Age 58

ETHEL FELDON
of 40 Keyworth St.
Daughter of Frederick William and
Ethel Annie Feldon.
At Keyworth St Shelter. Age 15

ETHEL ANNIE FELDON
of 40 Keyworth St. Wife of Frederick William Feldon.
At Keyworth St Shelter. Age 52

FREDERICK WILLIAM FELDON
of 40 Keyworth St. Husband of Ethel Annie Feldon.
At Keyworth St Shelter. Age 53

MAGGIE FRANCES FOSTER
Wife of James William Foster.
At 102 London Rd. Age 54

JAMES WILLIAM FOSTER
Husband of Maggie Frances Foster.
At 102 London Rd. Age 53

MARY ANN GLOVER
of 96 Lancaster St. Widow of P Glover.
At Keyworth St Shelter. Age 51

ELLEN FLORA MORRIS
of 48 Ontario St.
At Keyworth St Shelter. Age 65

WALTER BENTLEY PRICE
of Trinity Square.
At Waygood Otis Factory, Falmouth Rd
on 31st December. Age 44

EDITH STEAD
of 166 Southwark Bridge Rd.
Daughter of Samuel Stead of 43 Spring Gardens,
Drighlington, Bradford, Yorkshire.
At Keyworth St Shelter. Age 28

JOHN FREDERICK STEWART
of 13 Marsland Rd. Son of J T and A Stewart of
38 Azenby Rd, Peckham; husband of L R Stewart.
At 15 Marsland Rd. Age 28

CAROLINE ELLEN STILL
Daughter of F Still of 269 Southwark Bridge Rd,
and of Caroline Maud Still.
At Keyworth St Shelter. Age 17

CAROLINE MAUD STILL
Wife of F Still of 269 Southwark Bridge Rd.
At Keyworth St Shelter. Age 49

ALFRED WILLIAM SWAIN
Son of W J Swain of 89 Lancaster St.
At Keyworth St Shelter. Age 19

GEORGE FREDERICK SWAIN
Son of W J Swain of 89 Lancaster St.
At Keyworth St Shelter. Age 17

ROBERT WEBBER
of 100 Borough Rd. Husband of Sarah Maria Webber.
At Keyworth St Shelter. Age 50

SARAH MARIA WEBBER
of 100 Borough Rd. Wife of Robert J Webber.
At Keyworth St Shelter. Age 52

Metropolitan Borough of Stepney

SOLOMON SCHNITMAN COHEN
Russian National
of 50 Vallance Rd. Husband of Sarah S Cohen.
Injured 29th December 1940 at 50 Vallance Rd;
died next day at London Hospital. Age 72

ROSE CROOK
of 44 Vallance Rd.
At 44 Vallance Rd. Age 55

ALBERT FRANCIS EADON
Son of A G and A Eadon of 47 Matilda House,
Thomas Moore St, Wapping.
At St Katherine's Way. Age 16

RONALD LESLIE EYRES
Son of Frederick George and Emily Eyres of
Colville House, Lark Row, Bethnal Green.
At Thomas Moore St. Killed in the course
of volunteer rescue work. Age 18

WILLIAM FOOT
of 5 Smith's Place.
At 67 Garden St. Age 64

SUSAN FOUNTAIN
of 2 Smith's Place, Garden St. Wife of S C Fountain.
At 2 Smith's Place. Age 65

HYMAN MEDNICK
Russian National. Husband of Sarah Mednick of
7 Lolesworth Bldgs, Thrawl St.
At 42/4 Vallance Rd. Age 58

Municipal Borough of Tottenham, Middlesex

JOHN WILLIAM ARTHUR ANDREWS
of 95 Asplins Rd. Husband of Mabel Andrews.
Injured at 95 Asplins Rd; died same
day at Prince of Wales General Hospital. Age 32

FREDERICK CHARLES ESCOTT
Husband of L Escott of 89 Asplins Rd.
At Prince of Wales General Hospital. Age 69

Metropolitan Borough of Wandsworth

HUBERT ARTHUR STANLEY BUSH
Air Raid Warden
Husband of Jessie Bush of 19 Longstone Rd.
At Longstone Rd. Age 49

ALEXANDER ALBERT COLLINS
Air Raid Warden
Husband of Blanch Ellen Collins of 109 Moyser Rd.
At Longstone Rd. Age 53

ELIZABETH JANE LOVELL
of 16A Swanage Rd. Wife of William G T Lovell.
At 16A Swanage Rd. Age 35

ALBERT READ
of 18 Swanage Rd.
At 18 Swanage Rd. Age 72

JOHN ARTHUR SKINNER
of 14A Swanage Rd. Son of Rosina
and of the late John Robert Skinner.
At 14A Swanage Rd. Age 65

ROSINA SKINNER
of 14A Swanage Rd. Widow of John Robert Skinner.
At 14A Swanage Rd. Age 89

ROSE ANN SKINNER
of 14A Swanage Rd. Daughter of Rosina
and of the late John Robert Skinner.
At 14A Swanage Rd. Age 60

MARY ELIZABETH VAN WIJK
(otherwise Whalley) of 18A Swanage Rd.
At 18A Swanage Rd. Age 73

ARCHIBALD GEORGE WHITE
of 200 Crowborough Rd. Husband of Louisa White.
At 200 Crowborough Rd. Age 46

LOUISA WHITE
of 200 Crowborough Rd.
Wife of Archibald George White.
At 200 Crowborough Rd. Age 69

City of Westminster

GODWIN AUGUSTUS BAINBRIDGE
Husband of L M Bainbridge, of Hillcrest, Carlingford
Drive, Westcliff-on-Sea, Essex.
Injured at Horse Guards Ave, Embankment;
died same day at Charing Cross Hospital. Age 54

EILEEN MARGARET BONNER
of 10 Rugby St, Holborn.
Daughter of the late Mr H S Bonner.
At Royal Egyptian Embassy, South Audley St. Age 24

EDWARD FINDLEY
Firewatcher
of 20 Moreland Buildings, Millbank.
At Victoria Embankment. Age 54

MOYLAN ANNA JONES
of 75 South Audley St.
Daughter of the late A M Jones.
At 75 South Audley St. Age 55

JOHN KIERNAN
of 79 Marsden St, St Pancras.
At Victoria Embankment. Age 64

MILLICENT PANKHURST
of 16 Upper Brook St.
At 16 Upper Brook St. Age 45

THOMAS QUINN
of 29 Lanfranc St, Lambeth.
At Victoria Embankment,
Charing Cross Underground. Age 63

CARLO SIGNINI
of 22 Stangate Buildings,
Westminster Bridge Rd, Lambeth.
At Victoria Embankment. Age 62

GEORGE WILLIAMS
of 16 Upper Brook St. Husband of E Williams.
At 16 Upper Brook St. Age 63

Metropolitan Borough of Woolwich

BENJAMIN HOSEGOOD
of School House, Haimo Rd.
Husband of Agnes M Hosegood.
At School House, Haimo Rd. Age 63

WILLIAM JOSEPH JOHNSON
Volunteer 16th City of London
Battalion, Home Guard
Son of Andrew William and
Emily Johnson of Neasden. Age 17

OUTSIDE LONDON

County Borough of Bristol, Somerset

EDGAR DOWLING
Air Raid Warden
Husband of Lily May Dowling of
11 Kerry Rd, Knowle.
At Ilminster Ave School. Age 49

FREDERICK GEORGE JENKINS
ARP Messenger
Son of Mrs. Elizabeth Jenkins of 8 Carisbrook Rd,
Filwood Park, Knowle.
At Wardens' Post, Ilminster Ave School. Age 17

Municipal Borough of Chelmsford, Essex

ERNEST GEORGE WARREN
of Moor Hill Cottages, Newney Green, Writtle.
Injured 29th December at Newney Green;
died two days later at St John's Hospital. Age 62

Municipal Borough of Crewe, Cheshire

ELLIS BROUGH
Son of Enoch Brough of 4 Brook St, Brown Lees,
Staffordshire and of the late Elizabeth Brough;
husband of Elsie Brough of 42 Station Rd, Biddulph,
Stoke-on-Trent, Staffordshire.
At Rolls-Royce Works. Age 43

GILBERT DAVIS
of 181 Bradfield Rd. Son of William Gardner Davis
of 4 Grassfield Ave, Lower Broughton, Salford,
Lancashire; husband of Elsie Davis.
At Rolls-Royce Works. Age 23

CHARLES HARROP
Son of Mr and Mrs Charles Harrop of 13 Penryn Rd,
Winnington, Northwich; husband of
C M Harrop of 11 Vicarage Rd, Haslington.
At Rolls-Royce Works. Age 37

JOHN BROOKS HATTON
Son of Mrs W Hatton of 165 High St, Winsford.
At Rolls-Royce Works. Age 19

MURIEL FANNY HIGGINS
Daughter of Michael J Higgins of 17 Timbrell Ave.
At Rolls-Royce Works. Age 24

KATHLEEN MINNIE LAFFORD
of 1 Kings Rd, Nantwich.
At Rolls-Royce Works. Age 21

WILLIAM DUNCAN LASCELLES
of 18 Nutfield Ave.
At Rolls-Royce Works. Age 29

REGINALD LEE
Son of Albert Lee of 3 Dean St, Ashton-under-Lyne,
Lancashire and of the late Dora Lee;
husband of Nellie Lee of 21 Spring Bank St, Stalybridge.
At Rolls-Royce Works. Age 36

WILLIAM NAYLOR
Husband of Winifred Naylor of 17 Selworthy Drive.
At Rolls-Royce Works. Age 48

JOHN THOMAS NICKLIN
of 20 High St, Fenton, Stoke-on-Trent, Staffordshire.
Son of Mrs A Nicklin.
At Rolls-Royce Works. Age 20

CYRIL NUNNERLEY
Son of Florance Nunnerley of 116 Claughton Ave,
and of the late Levi Nunnerley.
At Rolls-Royce Works. Age 18

ELSIE POTTS
Daughter of Mr and Mrs Potts of 96 High St,
Halmer End, Newcastle-under-Lyme, Staffordshire.
At Rolls-Royce Works. Age 21

IRENE SNELSON
of 25 Chestnut Grove. Daughter of the
late Bertie Samuel and Mary Jane Snelson.
At Rolls-Royce Works. Age 24

WILLIAM HENRY WILLIAMS
Son of Mr L Williams of 5 Wood St.
At Rolls-Royce Works. Age 19

Rural District of Malling, Kent

CHARLES WILLIAM POULSON
of 2 Salisbury Rd, Dover.
At Preston Hall Emergency Hospital, Aylesford. Age 57

Deaths of servicemen of other nations are not included, as in the case of at least
four men from a coach full of Polish soldiers, killed at a major incident outside
Southwark Town Hall (*South London Press*, 4.1.41).

APPENDIX B: The 'Arsenal of Democracy'

FRANKLIN DELANO ROOSEVELT:
FIRESIDE CHAT, 29TH DECEMBER 1940

My friends:

This is not a fireside chat on war. It is a talk on national security; because the nub of the whole purpose of your President is to keep you now, and your children later, and your grandchildren much later, out of a last-ditch war for the preservation of American independence, and all of the things that American independence means to you and to me and to ours.

Tonight, in the presence of a world crisis, my mind goes back eight years to a night in the midst of a domestic crisis. It was a time when the wheels of American industry were grinding to a full stop, when the whole banking system of our country had ceased to function. I well remember that while I sat in my study in the White House, preparing to talk with the people of the United States, I had before my eyes the picture of all those Americans with whom I was talking. I saw the workmen in the mills, the mines, the factories, the girl behind the counter, the small shopkeeper, the farmer doing his Spring plowing, the widows and the old men wondering about their life's savings. I tried to convey to the great mass of American people what the banking crisis meant to them in their daily lives.

Tonight, I want to do the same thing, with the same people, in this new crisis which faces America. We met the issue of 1933 with courage and realism. We face this new crisis, this new threat to the security of our nation, with the same courage and realism. Never before since Jamestown and Plymouth Rock has our American civilization been in such danger as now. For on September 27th, 1940 – this year – by an agreement signed in Berlin, three powerful nations, two in Europe and one in Asia, joined themselves together in the threat that if the United States of America interfered with or blocked the expansion program of these three nations – a program aimed at world control – they would unite in ultimate action against the United States.

The Nazi masters of Germany have made it clear that they intend not only to dominate all life and thought in their own country, but also to enslave the whole of Europe, and then to use the resources of Europe to dominate the rest of the world. It was only three weeks ago that their leader stated this: 'There are two worlds that stand opposed to each other.' And then in defiant reply to his opponents he said this: 'Others are correct when they say: "With this world we cannot ever reconcile ourselves."' 'I can beat any other power in the world.' So said the leader of the Nazis.

In other words, the Axis not merely admits but the Axis proclaims that there can be no ultimate peace between their philosophy – their philosophy of government – and our philosophy of government. In view of the nature of this undeniable threat, it can be asserted, properly and categorically, that the United States has no right or reason to encourage talk of peace until the day shall come when there is a clear intention on the part of the aggressor nations to abandon all thought of dominating or conquering the world.

At this moment the forces of the states that are leagued against all peoples who live in freedom are being held away from our shores. The Germans and the Italians are being blocked on the other side of the Atlantic by the British and by the Greeks, and by thousands of soldiers and sailors who were able to escape from subjugated countries. In Asia the Japanese are being engaged by the Chinese nation in another great defense. In the Pacific Ocean is our fleet.

Some of our people like to believe that wars in Europe and in Asia are of no concern to us. But it is a matter of most vital concern to us that European and Asiatic war-makers should not gain control of the oceans which lead to this hemisphere. One hundred and seventeen years ago the Monroe Doctrine was conceived by our government as a measure of defense in the face of a threat against this hemisphere by an alliance in Continental Europe. Thereafter, we stood guard in the Atlantic, with the British as neighbors. There was no treaty. There was no 'unwritten agreement'. And yet there was the feeling, proven correct by history, that we as neighbors could settle any disputes in peaceful fashion. And the fact is that during the whole of this time the Western Hemisphere has remained free from aggression from Europe or from Asia.

Does anyone seriously believe that we need to fear attack anywhere in the Americas while a free Britain remains our most powerful naval neighbor in the Atlantic? And does anyone seriously believe, on the other hand, that we could rest easy if the Axis powers were our neighbors there? If Great Britain goes down, the Axis powers will control the continents of Europe, Asia, Africa, Austral-Asia, and the high seas. And they will be in a position to bring enormous military and naval resources against this hemisphere. It is no exaggeration to say that all of us in all the Americas would be living at the point of a gun – a gun loaded with explosive bullets, economic as well as military. We should enter upon a new and terrible era in which the whole world, our hemisphere included, would be run by threats of brute force. And to survive in such a world, we would have to convert ourselves permanently into a militaristic power on the basis of war economy.

Some of us like to believe that even if Britain falls, we are still safe, because of the broad expanse of the Atlantic and of the Pacific. But the width of those oceans is not what it was in the days of clipper ships. At one point between Africa and Brazil the distance is less than it is from Washington to Denver, Colorado, five hours for the latest type of bomber. And at the north end of the Pacific Ocean, America and Asia almost touch each other. Why, even today we have planes that could fly from the British Isles to New England and back again without refueling. And remember that the range of the modern bomber is ever being increased.

During the past week many people in all parts of the nation have told me what they wanted me to say tonight. Almost all of them expressed a courageous desire to hear the plain truth about the gravity of the situation. One telegram, however, expressed the attitude of the small minority who want to see no evil and hear no evil, even though they know in their hearts that evil exists. That telegram begged me not to tell again of the ease with which our American cities could be bombed by any hostile power which had gained bases in this Western Hemisphere. The gist of that telegram was: 'Please, Mr President, don't frighten us by telling us the facts.' Frankly and definitely there is danger ahead – danger against which we must prepare. But we well know that we cannot escape danger, or the fear of danger, by crawling into bed and pulling the covers over our heads.

Some nations of Europe were bound by solemn non-intervention pacts with Germany. Other nations were assured by Germany that they need never fear invasion. Non-intervention pact or not, the fact remains that they were attacked, overrun, thrown into modern slavery at an hour's notice – or even without any notice at all. As an exiled leader of one of these nations said to me the other day, 'The notice was a minus quantity. It was given to my government two hours after German troops had poured into my country in a hundred places.' The fate of these nations tells us what it means to live at the point of a Nazi gun.

The Nazis have justified such actions by various pious frauds. One of these frauds is the claim that they are occupying a nation for the purpose of 'restoring order'. Another is that they are occupying or controlling a nation on the excuse that they are 'protecting it' against the aggression of somebody else. For example, Germany has said that she was occupying Belgium to save the Belgians from the British. Would she then hesitate to say to any South American country: 'We are occupying you to protect you from aggression by the United States'? Belgium today is being used as an invasion base against Britain, now fighting for its life. And any South American country, in Nazi hands, would always constitute a jumping off place for German attack on any one of the other republics of this hemisphere.

Analyze for yourselves the future of two other places even nearer to Germany if the Nazis won. Could Ireland hold out? Would Irish freedom be permitted as an amazing pet exception in an unfree world? Or the islands of the Azores, which still fly the flag of Portugal after five centuries? You and I think of Hawaii as an outpost of defense in the Pacific. And yet the Azores are closer to our shores in the Atlantic than Hawaii is on the other side.

There are those who say that the Axis powers would never have any desire to attack the Western Hemisphere. That is the same dangerous form of wishful thinking which has destroyed the powers of resistance of so many conquered peoples. The plain facts are that the Nazis have proclaimed, time and again, that all other races are their inferiors and therefore subject to their orders. And most important of all, the vast resources and wealth of this American hemisphere constitute the most tempting loot in all of the round world.

Let us no longer blind ourselves to the undeniable fact that the evil forces which have crushed and undermined and corrupted so many others are already within

353

our own gates. Your government knows much about them and every day is ferreting them out. Their secret emissaries are active in our own and in neighboring countries. They seek to stir up suspicion and dissension, to cause internal strife. They try to turn capital against labor, and vice versa. They try to reawaken long slumbering racial and religious enmities which should have no place in this country. They are active in every group that promotes intolerance. They exploit for their own ends our own natural abhorrence of war. These trouble-breeders have but one purpose. It is to divide our people, to divide them into hostile groups and to destroy our unity and shatter our will to defend ourselves.

There are also American citizens, many of them in high places, who, unwittingly in most cases, are aiding and abetting the work of these agents. I do not charge these American citizens with being foreign agents. But I do charge them with doing exactly the kind of work that the dictators want done in the United States. These people not only believe that we can save our own skins by shutting our eyes to the fate of other nations. Some of them go much further than that. They say that we can and should become the friends and even the partners of the Axis powers. Some of them even suggest that we should imitate the methods of the dictatorships. But Americans never can and never will do that.

The experience of the past two years has proven beyond doubt that no nation can appease the Nazis. No man can tame a tiger into a kitten by stroking it. There can be no appeasement with ruthlessness. There can be no reasoning with an incendiary bomb. We know now that a nation can have peace with the Nazis only at the price of total surrender. Even the people of Italy have been forced to become accomplices of the Nazis; but at this moment they do not know how soon they will be embraced to death by their allies.

The American appeasers ignore the warning to be found in the fate of Austria, Czechoslovakia, Poland, Norway, Belgium, the Netherlands, Denmark, and France. They tell you that the Axis powers are going to win anyway; that all of this bloodshed in the world could be saved, that the United States might just as well throw its influence into the scale of a dictated peace and get the best out of it that we can. They call it a 'negotiated peace'. Nonsense! Is it a negotiated peace if a gang of outlaws surrounds your community and on threat of extermination makes you pay tribute to save your own skins? For such a dictated peace would be no peace at all. It would be only another armistice, leading to the most gigantic armament race and the most devastating trade wars in all history. And in these contests the Americas would offer the only real resistance to the Axis power. With all their vaunted efficiency, with all their parade of pious purpose in this war, there are still in their background the concentration camp and the servants of God in chains.

The history of recent years proves that the shootings and the chains and the concentration camps are not simply the transient tools but the very altars of modern dictatorships. They may talk of a 'new order' in the world, but what they have in mind is only a revival of the oldest and the worst tyranny. In that there is no liberty, no religion, no hope. The proposed 'new order' is the very opposite of a United States of Europe or a United States of Asia. It is not a government based upon the consent of the governed. It is not a union of ordinary, self-respecting men and women to protect themselves and their freedom and their dignity from oppression. It is an unholy alliance of power and pelf to dominate and to enslave the human race.

The British people and their allies today are conducting an active war against this unholy alliance. Our own future security is greatly dependent on the outcome of that fight. Our ability to 'keep out of war' is going to be affected by that outcome. Thinking in terms of today and tomorrow, I make the direct statement to the American people that there is far less chance of the United States getting into war if we do all we can now to support the nations defending themselves against attack by the Axis than if we acquiesce in their defeat, submit tamely to an Axis victory, and wait our turn to be the object of attack in another war later on.

If we are to be completely honest with ourselves, we must admit that there is risk in any course we may take. But I deeply believe that the great majority of our people agree that the course that I advocate involves the least risk now and the greatest hope for world peace in the future.

The people of Europe who are defending themselves do not ask us to do their fighting. They ask us for the implements of war, the planes, the tanks, the guns, the freighters which will enable them to fight for their liberty and for our security. Emphatically, we must get these weapons to them, get them to them in sufficient volume and quickly enough so that we and our children will be saved the agony and suffering of war which others have had to endure.

Let not the defeatists tell us that it is too late. It will never be earlier. Tomorrow will be later than today.

Certain facts are self-evident.

In a military sense Great Britain and the British Empire are today the spearhead of resistance to world conquest. And they are putting up a fight which will live forever in the story of human gallantry. There is no demand for sending an American expeditionary force outside our own borders. There is no intention by any member of your government to send such a force. You can therefore, nail, nail any talk about sending armies to Europe as deliberate untruth. Our national policy is not directed toward war. Its sole purpose is to keep war away from our country and away from our people.

Democracy's fight against world conquest is being greatly aided, and must be more greatly aided, by the rearmament of the United States and by sending every ounce and every ton of munitions and supplies that we can possibly spare to help the defenders who are in the front lines. And it is no more un-neutral for us to do that than it is for Sweden, Russia, and other nations near Germany to send steel and ore and oil and other war materials into Germany every day in the week.

We are planning our own defense with the utmost urgency, and in its vast scale we must integrate the war needs of Britain and the other free nations which are resisting aggression. This is not a matter of sentiment or of controversial personal opinion. It is a matter of realistic, practical military policy, based on the advice of our military experts who are in close touch with existing warfare. These military and naval experts and the members of the Congress and the Administration have a single-minded purpose: the defense of the United States.

This nation is making a great effort to produce everything that is necessary in this emergency, and with all possible speed. And this great effort requires great sacrifice. I would ask no one to defend a democracy which in turn would not defend every one in the nation against want and privation. The strength of this nation shall not be diluted by the failure of the government to protect the economic well-being of its citizens. If our capacity to produce is limited by machines, it must ever be remembered that these machines are operated by the skill and the stamina of the workers.

As the government is determined to protect the rights of the workers, so the nation has a right to expect that the men who man the machines will discharge their full responsibilities to the urgent needs of defense. The worker possesses the same human dignity and is entitled to the same security of position as the engineer or the manager or the owner. For the workers provide the human power that turns out the destroyers, and the planes, and the tanks. The nation expects our defense industries to continue operation without interruption by strikes or lockouts. It expects and insists that management and workers will reconcile their differences by voluntary or legal means, to continue to produce the supplies that are so sorely needed. And on the economic side of our great defense program, we are, as you know, bending every effort to maintain stability of prices and with that the stability of the cost of living.

Nine days ago I announced the setting up of a more effective organization to direct our gigantic efforts to increase the production of munitions. The appropriation of vast sums of money and a well-coordinated executive direction of our defense efforts are not in themselves enough. Guns, planes, ships and many other things have to be built in the factories and the arsenals of America. They have to be produced by workers and managers and engineers with the aid of machines which in turn have to be built by hundreds of thousands of workers throughout the land. In this great work there has been splendid cooperation between the government and industry and labor. And I am very thankful.

American industrial genius, unmatched throughout all the world in the solution of production problems, has been called upon to bring its resources and its talents into action. Manufacturers of watches, of farm implements, of Linotypes and cash registers and automobiles, and sewing machines and lawn mowers and locomotives, are now making fuses and bomb packing crates and telescope mounts and shells and pistols and tanks.

But all of our present efforts are not enough. We must have more ships, more guns, more planes – more of everything. And this can be accomplished only if we discard the notion of 'business as usual'. This job cannot be done merely by superimposing on the existing productive facilities the added requirements of the nation for defense. Our defense efforts must not be blocked by those who fear the future consequences of surplus plant capacity. The possible consequences of failure of our defense efforts now are much more to be feared. And after the present needs of our defense are past, a proper handling of the country's peacetime needs will require all of the new productive capacity, if not still more. No pessimistic policy about the future of America shall delay the immediate expansion of those industries essential to defense. We need them.

I want to make it clear that it is the purpose of the nation to build now with all possible speed every machine, every arsenal, every factory that we need to manufacture our defense material. We have the men, the skill, the wealth, and above all, the will. I am confident that if and when production of consumer or luxury goods in certain industries requires the use of machines and raw materials that are essential for defense purposes, then such production must yield, and will gladly yield, to our primary and compelling purpose.

So I appeal to the owners of plants, to the managers, to the workers, to our own government employees to put every ounce of effort into producing these munitions swiftly and without stint. With this appeal I give you the pledge that all of us who are officers of your government will devote ourselves to the same whole-hearted extent to the great task that lies ahead.

As planes and ships and guns and shells are produced, your government, with its defense experts, can then determine how best to use them to defend this hemisphere. The decision as to how much shall be sent abroad and how much shall remain at home must be made on the basis of our overall military necessities.

We must be the great arsenal of democracy.

For us this is an emergency as serious as war itself. We must apply ourselves to our task with the same resolution, the same sense of urgency, the same spirit of patriotism and sacrifice as we would show were we at war.

We have furnished the British great material support and we will furnish far more in the future. There will be no 'bottlenecks' in our determination to aid Great Britain. No dictator, no combination of dictators, will weaken that determination by threats of how they will construe that determination. The British have received invaluable military support from the heroic Greek Army and from the forces of all the governments in exile. Their strength is growing. It is the strength of men and women who value their freedom more highly than they value their lives.

I believe that the Axis powers are not going to win this war. I base that belief on the latest and best of information.

We have no excuse for defeatism. We have every good reason for hope – hope for peace, yes, and hope for the defense of our civilization and for the building of a better civilization in the future. I have the profound conviction that the American people are now determined to put forth a mightier effort than they have ever yet made to increase our production of all the implements of defense, to meet the threat to our democratic faith.

As President of the United States, I call for that national effort. I call for it in the name of this nation which we love and honor and which we are privileged and proud to serve. I call upon our people with absolute confidence that our common cause will greatly succeed.

Appendix C: What Remains Behind

While many London boroughs 'caught a packet' during the night of 29th/30th December 1940, and many older terraces sprout the occasional modern interloper as a consequence, it was naturally the losses in the City that drew the most attention at the time. Though the human cost on this night was greater elsewhere.

Today, visitors to the modern City can easily remain unaware of the scale of devastation caused within the Square Mile over this one night*. One reason is the post-war discovery that London *could* support skyscrapers (physically, if not always emotionally) after all. But the other is the long, slow process of rebuilding, restoration and repair of historic City buildings over a quarter-century (and sometimes much more) following the end of the Second World War.

The number of churches that were wholly lost on this night may now appear to be small. But a picture book like Hanslip Fletcher's *Bombed London* (Cassell, 1947) shows how, in many cases, only the bare, burnt walls, or parts of walls, remained standing for many years before serious repair work could begin.

Open-air church services were commonplace within these 'bare ruined choirs' in the City for more than a decade, during which time the archaeologists got to work, analysing and extending the histories of the ancient sacred spaces.

Churches that were gutted on this night but are now fully restored are: All Hallows Barking; St Andrew by the Wardrobe; St Bride's; St Giles Cripplegate; St Lawrence Jewry and St-Vedast-alias-Foster. St Augustine Watling Street was gutted on this night and destroyed later in the Blitz. Also gutted on the 29th were the remains of St Alphage London Wall and St Alban Wood Street – of which only the tower now remains (in private hands). St Anne & St Agnes and St Mary Abchurch were both damaged but restored. St Dunstan-in-the-East was also damaged, then gutted in a subsequent raid.

This beautiful secret garden (if you can find it) and the rose-bedecked ruin of Christ Church in Newgate Street (also gutted on 29th December 1940) now give the only clue to the degree of damage to City churches and to the way so many of them looked for so many years.

Total losses to the City from this one raid were St Stephen's Coleman Street (though the plaster copy, over the gateway, of the old Last Judgement survived) and St Mary Aldermanbury, which was not demolished but emigrated in 1965 to the campus of Westminster College, Fulton, Missouri, where it flourishes as a tribute to

*These details are based principally on William Kent's The Lost Treasures of London and An Encyclopedia of London, William Thomson Hill's Buried London and the list of air raid damage in the City compiled by K. A. Scholey (1995) and lodged with the Corporation of London Records Office.

Winston Churchill. (Much of the lesser City rubble is said to have been used as ballast for cargo ships plying the perilous Atlantic during the war, and some may have been subsequently used in building work in the New York docks.) The obelisk commemorating Shakespeare's fellows Heminges and Condell remains in St Mary Aldermary's pleasant churchyard in the City, at the back of the Guildhall.

Though much of the Aldermanbury side of the Guildhall has been rebuilt in modern style (including the Guildhall Library entrance), the medieval Great Hall actually looks now much as it did on the Sunday morning before the Second Great Fire of London. The vanished 'famous but uncouth' statues (as *The Times* called them) of Gog and Magog have been replaced by modern but, happily, equally uncouth versions.

It had already been possible, thanks to an ingenious temporary roof arrangement, to hold the 1941 Election of the new Lord Mayor in the Great Hall on Michaelmas Day, just as it had taken place every year for centuries. During the 1950s, damaged statuary (including a decapitated Neptune on the Nelson memorial) was repaired and the great wooden roof replaced during the rebuilding. This was led by great London architect Sir Giles Gilbert Scott (already designer of London's red telephone boxes, its new Waterloo Bridge, Battersea Power Station and the Bankside Power Station that is now the Tate Modern). The Art Gallery, which the Fire Squad managed to save on 29th December, was lost in a later raid but was rebuilt and reopened in 1999, with the remains of a newly discovered Roman amphitheatre on show in the basement.

Many Livery Company Halls were, not surprisingly, clustered around the Guildhall. Badly damaged or destroyed on this night were those of the Bakers, Harp Lane; Barbers, Monkwell Street; Brewers, Addle Street; Broderers, Gutter Lane; Coachmakers, Noble Street; Coopers, Basinghall Street; Girdlers, Basinghall Avenue; Goldsmiths, Gresham Street; Haberdashers, Staining Lane; Saddlers, Cheapside; Wax Chandlers and the halls of the Parish Clerks, Silver Street and Curriers, Wood Street. The east wing of the Stationers Hall in Ave Maria Lane was also destroyed.

Along Fleet Street, the Middle Temple library was severely damaged. The fire damage to Dr Johnson's House was largely confined to the Dictionary Attic, which was subsequently restored. But in nearby Neville's Court, houses that were built in 1664 and had been spared in the last Great Fire, were consumed by this one. (To prove, that even the smallest City street or alleyway leaves behind its own literary memorial, you can find Neville's Court living still, in various recesses of the internet, in Chapter 2 of R. Austin Freeman's 1911 detective romance *The Eye of Osiris* aka *The Vanishing Man* – and in the archetypal, semi-magical City-tale form: 'I walked on briskly up Fetter Lane until a narrow, arched opening, bearing the superscription "Nevill's Court," arrested my steps, and here I turned to encounter one of those surprises that lie in wait for the wanderer in London byways . . . ') Another link with the literary past lost this night was the Coopers Arms pub on the corner of Silver Street and Monkwell Street in Cripplegate: the one pub in London that could honestly and indisputably claim that 'Shakespeare drank here' (at least, he stayed in the house that occupied the spot before the 1666 Great Fire).

A less obvious loss, at the time, was the famous London skyline, dominated by St Paul's dome and the spires of City churches. By the time Sir Winston Churchill was being carried on a gun carriage to St Paul's, the modernist City was already beginning to rise around the Cathedral on sites cleared by the Luftwaffe. And on part of that largest area of continuous devastation of the Blitz north of St Paul's, the huge Barbican Estate, designed to bring a live-in population back to the City, had just begun construction, with a restored St Giles Cripplegate at its heart.

Illustrations

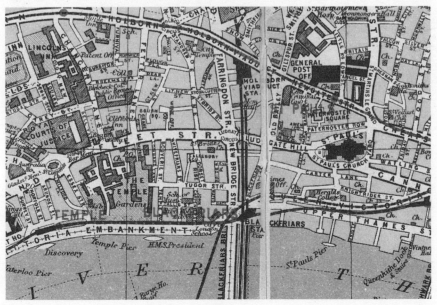

Adolf Hitler: The Hitler cult made much of the Führer's attachment to his Alpine home, and he was often pictured there, amid scenery as grandiose as his dreams for the future of the Reich. From Hitler in seinen Bergen by Heinrich Hoffmann (Berlin: 'Zeitgeschichte' Verlag und Vertriebs-Gesellschaft, 1935).

In the Underground: Tube shelterers were a very tiny, if very visible, minority of Blitz Londoners. The authorities, unable to prevent them entering the Underground system, were by December providing three-tier bunks to sleep on as well as rudimentary sanitary facilities. Volunteers helped to provide first aid, food and some social services. www.popperfoto.com (PN230159280)

St Paul's Watch: Waiting for the call on the steps to the Whispering Gallery. Advanced HQ kept in touch with the Crypt HQ and the Fire Brigade by telephone – which was on many nights manned by the Dean himself. Plans of the Cathedral "decks" can be seen on the wall.

The 'Ops' Room: At Fighter Command HQ in Stanmore, WAAFs cluster around a table map, using long magnetic wands to move 'aircraft' into positions dictated to them through their headphones by the Tellers in the Filter Room, workplace of Felicity Ashbee. Officers on the balcony tailor the RAF's response to the picture they see developing below. © THE IMPERIAL WAR MUSEUM, LONDON (C 1869)

Women Auxiliary Fire Service: Before computers, the successful monitoring and administration of an air raid required a million tiny physical operations by hundreds and thousands of human agents. Similarly to the WAAFs at Stanmore, at LFB HQ in Lambeth these WAFS show the distribution of firefighting resources by moving pins on a map of London, which officers will then use to decide when and how to send in reinforcements. © THE IMPERIAL WAR MUSEUM, LONDON (HU 36128)

London Region HQ: At the pinnacle of the capital's Civil Defence pyramid was the Senior Regional Commissioner for London Ernest Gowers, who suggested that Meredith Frampton's official portrait of him should also include two representative members of his staff. Like the Prime Minister, Gowers believed in short, old words and later edited the second edition of *Fowler's Modern English Usage*. His own post-war Civil Service guide to writing clear English, *The Complete Plain Words*, went on to become a bestseller. © THE IMPERIAL WAR MUSEUM, LONDON (LD 2905)

Second Great Fire of London: The St Paul's Watch was joined aloft tonight by a Daily Mirror photographer, whose image of the approaching fires (top) makes an interesting counterpoise to Herbert Mason's viewpoint. On the ground, shops and cafés in narrow alleys surrounding the Cathedral, like Ave Maria Lane (bottom left), stood no chance of survival, though firemen took their stand wherever there was a chance of holding the fire at bay (bottom right). © ALL DAILY MIRROR

Falling wall: Leonard Rosoman's A House Collapsing on Two Firemen, Shoe Lane, London, EC4, was prompted by his traumatic memories of the 29th December incident in Wine Office Court (just off Shoe Lane) in which thirty-three-year-old Sidney Holder died. © THE IMPERIAL WAR MUSEUM, LONDON (LD 1353)

Aftermath: Everything between St Paul's and the smaller, copper dome of the Old Bailey that echoed it (top) was clearly doomed this morning – and much else besides. When the Speed family finally got to their destroyed factory in the heart of the blitzed area, they opened their safe to find all of their vital company records burnt to ashes – but some businesses were luckier (bottom). © BOTH DAILY MAIL/SOLO

Franklin D. Roosevelt: The President's famous 'Fireside Chats' were so named because they went to listeners' firesides; not from his. The Diplomatic Reception Room, a former furnace room, was on the ground floor of the White House and convenient for wheelchair access. Behind the President's chair, the model ship is indicative of his love for, and appreciation of the sea. This was something that Churchill, as a 'former naval person' himself, saw as a useful bond between them. © FRANKLIN D. ROOSEVELT PRESIDENTIAL LIBRARY AND MUSEUM

St Bride's: The day after, and water is still being poured on to the red-hot ruins of the gutted church, sending up clouds of smoke. It would take another fifteen years of planning and fund-raising before restoration of the church could commence – under the supervision of W. Godfrey Allen former head of the St Paul's Watch. Queen Elizabeth II attended the rededication of St Bride's on 19th December 1957. © CENTRAL PRESS/GETTY IMAGES (3279839)

Winston Churchill: the Prime Minister doffs his hat in response to salutes from the crowd in heavily bombed Moorgate as he tours the City with his wife Clemmie, Parliamentary Private Secretary Brendan Bracken (far right) and officials on 30th December 1940. © GETTY IMAGES (GEORGE W. HALES/FOX PHOTOS) (3346307)

Ludgate Hill: Beyond the railway bridge, four firemen at a branch fight one of the City's continuing fires. In the foreground, the bike and motorbike of messengers taking information to and from the incident's Fire Officer. Note, too, the white paint on kerbstones, traffic island and lamp-post – which would remain vital in the years of blackouts yet to come.

Acknowledgements

Coming to the end of a story such as this, the list of thanks due is necessarily a long one – though still far too short to do justice to the contributions of others to 'my' book. They are due first, of course, to London itself and to all its inhabitants and friends who, in 1940, did 'their bit' (a phrase whose true meaning, I confess, I had never before understood). My particular gratitude goes to all those who have kindly allowed me to quote from their letters, diaries and memoirs, and to those who have let me to do so on behalf of those no longer with us. And, while most of the book has been expressly compiled from records made at the time or relatively soon after, I owe a great deal to ex-Auxiliary Firemen Thomas Carter and Leonard Rosoman for sharing their memories of their unique experiences with me in person.

I am grateful, too, for permission to quote from the archives of the following, and would like to thank all those archivists, librarians and other staff who have been so patient and so helpful to me in my research, far above and beyond the call of duty. The British Library and Newspaper Library Colindale; Corporation of London Records Office; C. Hoare & Co.; Imperial War Museum; London Fire Brigade; London Library; London Metropolitan Archive; National Archive; Guildhall Library, Guildhall Library Prints & Maps Section and Guildhall Library Manuscripts Section; The Royal Archives Windsor; St Bartholomew's Hospital; St Paul's Cathedral Library (by kind permission of the Dean and Chapter) and Southwark Local History Library.

I would like to express special thanks to the families of Ritchie Calder, Gareth Jones, Eric Sevareid, E. B. White and William L. White for permission to quote from their works; to the Scripps Howard Foundation, honourable guardians of the memory of Ernie Pyle; to A. M. Heath on behalf of the Estate of George Orwell and A. P. Watt Ltd on behalf of The Literary Executors of the Estate H. G. Wells for permission to quote from their works; to Cyril Demarne for *The London Blitz. A Fireman's Tale* and *Our Girls*; to Winston G. Ramsay for extracts from *The Blitz Then and Now* and to Sutton Publishing for Colin Perry's *Boy in the Blitz*. Excerpts from 'Freedom' from *One Man's Meat*, text copyright ©1940 by E. B. White. Copyright renewed. Reprinted by permission of Tilbury House, Publishers, Gardiner, Maine. Acknowledgements are also due to Penguin Group for permission to quote from Fred Taylor's translation of *The Goebbels Diaries*. Extracts from Churchill's books and speeches are reproduced with permission of Curtis Brown Ltd, London on behalf of The Estate of Sir Winston Churchill Copyright Winston S. Churchill. My deep appreciation goes to the Commonwealth War Graves Commission for help in confirming, and permission to use, information from their Debt of Honour Register. Every effort has been made to trace copyright holders. Where I have been unable to do so, I apologise and hope that they are content that my sincere gratitude for their part in helping me relate these historic events be acknowledged here.

Researching any book is a journey and I have met with great kindness from a number of writers and academics along this road. I am particularly grateful for the generous assistance and advice of Sally Holloway, Cyril Demarne, Winston G. Ramsey, Richard Langworth of the Churchill Centre, Adam Greenland of the Port of London Authority Hydrographic Department, Dr Geoffrey Parnell, Keeper of Tower History at the Royal Armouries, Tower of London, and, in America, Dr Karen Manners Smith of Emporia State University, Kansas, Dr James H. Williams of Middle Tennessee State University and Lise Namikas of Louisiana State University. I count myself extraordinarily fortunate that Dr Angus Calder and Sir Martin Gilbert generously agreed to read through my manuscript and make suggestions – although all errors remain, of course, my own.

The turning of a story into a book is a journey too, on which Sarah Gristwood has been, as ever, my wise and generous friend and guide in the world of books from the outset. Since which time have been added (in chronological order): best of agents Celia Hayley; Julian Loose of Faber and Faber, who saw what I saw from the very beginning and then made it happen, for which I will be eternally grateful; early helpmate and moral compass Brenda Buckle; Robert O'Hara, whose expert combing of RAF records in the National Archive was invaluable; all at Faber including Charles Boyle, Vanessa Winch, Alison Worthington, Henry Volans and exemplary copy editor Wendy Toole; and, last but by no means least, Alena Melichar. I was, in addition, fortunate enough to meet with a group of people interested in taking this story on to television. The enthusiasm, energy and insights of Julian Ware, Louise Osmond, Alex Kiehl and all at Darlow Smithson and Channel 4 have come as a delightful and unexpected bonus.

Coming back, finally, closer to home and to the friends and family who have supported and encouraged me through the whole, long process, this roll call of thanks could easily double in length. But instead I will just say that, having lived my life in parallel – the present alongside the past – for these past few years, I have found many modern teachers, too, to demonstrate in very practical ways that patience, humour, good fellowship, 'pluck' and generosity of spirit have not yet disappeared from the earth. You all know who you are, I hope, and how much you mean. My friends will know why I mention by name Judy Cramond and Ivan Kyncl; my family will know why I mention particularly my Mum and Dad. But to all the 'unknown warriors', my sincere thanks.

Select Bibliography

Unpublished Sources

I would like to pay special tribute here to Heather Creaton's invaluable *Sources for the History of London 1939–45* (British Records Association, 1998), a wonderful guide for anyone researching London's wartime experiences.

CoL: Corporation of London Records Office. Principally, War 1939–1945 and Corporation reports on the City Fire 29th/30th December 1940.
IWM: Imperial War Museum Documents Collection at http://www.iwmcollections.org.uk/qryDocuments.asp

Allan, Mrs M. E. 95/8/7 & Con shelf
Ashbee, F. 97/34/1
Backhouse, F. 90/16/1
Barnicot, Mrs E. J. 98/10/1
Bawtree, Miss V. 91/5/1
Bosanquet, Miss N. 81/33/1
Bowman, Mrs W. C. 85/45/1
Broadway, Mrs H. 95/13/1
Carver, N. V. 90/16/1
Champion, S. G. 77/178/1
Chave, Dr S. P. W. 79/27/1
Coates, R. N. 98/10/1
Gibbons, Lt A. P. 86/36/1
Granger, Miss I. H. 94/45/2 & Con shelf
Green, Mrs Y. 99/9/1
Grey, H. F. 81/10/1
Griffiths, Mrs M. L. C. 86/5/1
Heller, Miss E. 92/49/1
Hurd, F. W. 80/30/1
King, G. W. 85/49/1
Markham, Rev. J. G. 91/5/1

Marshall, Miss W. B. Con shelf
Maynard, Capt. H. A. NSPending
Newbery, C. A. 97/28/1
Paul, Dr L. A. 02/57/1
Regan, W. B. Con shelf & 88/10/1
Ridgway, R. 67/347/1
Rogers, B. J. P129
Rollinson, Mrs F. 99/66/1
Snow, H. W. P394
Speed, Miss F. M. 86/45/2
Wareham, C. P. 96/31/1
Warner, Miss P. 95/14/1
Weir, R. A. 88/49/1
Wilkins, G. 84/44/1
Williams, H. T. 02/4/1
Woodcock, S. M. S. 87/36/1
Wrigley, W. R. 76/10/1
Misc 143 (2228) Miscellaneous 2228
Misc 147 (2305) Misc.2305
Misc 180 (2706) Miscellaneous 2706

In addition, the Imperial War Museum holds an eight-minute London Fire Brigade Film Unit record of that night LFB 50.
LFB: London Fire Brigade. In addition to the Fire Brigade records held at the London Metropolitan Archive (below): *London Fire Region Deaths on Duty During the Second World War* compiled by W. F. Hickin 11.3.2000.
LMA: London Metropolitan Archive. Principally London County Council documents from sectors LCC/HG (Home Guard), LCC/CL/CD (Civil Defence), LCC/FB/STA (Fire Brigade), LCC/FB/WAR (Wartime Fire Brigade), LCC/FB/WAR/LFR (London Fire Region), LCC/PH/WAR (Public Health) and Photographic City File 4.

NA: National Archive AIR16/654, AIR22/111 and AIR41/17.
PMGL: Prints & Maps Section, Guildhall Library at
    http://collage.cityoflondon.gov.uk/
The Royal Archives, Windsor: Royal Christmas Broadcasts.
St Bartholomew's Hospital Archives: HA 16/50; HA 16/53–7; *St Barts Hospital
    Journal* Vol. II; *League News* 1939–44.
St Paul's Cathedral: documents from within the Cathedral Library (including
    research notes kindly shared by Sally Holloway) and from Boxes CF 2–5 & CF
    17 held at the Manuscripts Section, Guildhall Library, Corporation of London.
Southwark Local History Library: P.940.544.SOU *The Story of Reporting Post
    12*; bound volume of *London's Awake*; Southwark Civil Defence Second
    World War Incident Reports 5676–84.

Internet Sources

Avoiding the many bizarre websites maintained by those who seem intent on
re-fighting the Second World War to a different conclusion, there are many
excellent online resources which place rare documents, university departmental
offerings and learned journals as well as contemporary pictorial reference and
sound recordings within the researcher's reach. Those used are cited in the Notes,
but I would commend in particular:

British Library copies of the League of Coloured Peoples' *The Keys* and *News
    Letter* at http://www.movingherc.org.uk
The Franklin D. Roosevelt Digital Archives at http://www.fdrlibrary.marist.edu/
Canada's DHH Historical Resource Centre at
    http://www.forces.gc.ca/hr/dhh/engraph/home_e.asp
and National Archives at http://www.collectionscanada.ca/
Commonwealth War Graves Commission's Debt of Honour Register at
    http://www.cwgc.org/cwgcinternet/search.aspx
German Propaganda Archive at http://www.calvin.edu/academic/cas/gpa/
British Pathé's online newsreel archive (free registration) at http://www.british-
    pathe.com/
Getty Images picture archive (free registration) at http://editorial.gettyimages.com
In addition, Spartacus at http://www.spartacus.schoolnet.co.uk/ offers pathways to
    a wide library of printed sources on many aspects of the conflict and personalities
    involved.

Published Sources
(all published in London unless otherwise stated)

*Analytic Index to the Series of Records known as the Remembrancia Preserved
    among the Archives of the City of London AD 1579–1664* (Corporation of
    London, 1878)
Destruction of an Army, The First Campaign in Libya: Sept 1940–Feb 1941
    (HMSO 1941)
Fire Precautions in War Time (Lord Privy Seal's Office, August 1939)
Forward March! Vol. 2 (Chicago: Disabled Veterans of the World War, 1937)
Front Line 1940–1941 (HMSO, 1942)
Germany, The Olympic Year 1936 (Berlin: Volk und Reich Verlag, 1936)

Harper's Magazine Vol. 181 June–Nov 1940 (New York: Harper & Bros, 1940), pp. 441–4.

Keesing's Contemporary Archives Vol. IV 1940–43 (Bristol: Keesing's Publications, 1943)

Lloyd's Under Fire (Lloyd's, no date)

London, A Pictorial and Descriptive Guide (Ward Lock, 1936)

London in Paintings (Guildhall Art Gallery, 1999)

London's Awake weekly Nos 21–5 (London Regional Office, Ministry of Information, 1940–41)

Londoners Remember Living Through the Blitz (Age Exchange, 1991)

Low, The Twentieth Century's Greatest Cartoonist (BBC, 2002)

The New Yorker Book of War Pieces (Bloomsbury, 1989)

Newspaper Press Directory (C. Mitchell & Co. Ltd, 1940)

Over There, Instructions for American Servicemen in Britain 1942 (Oxford: Bodleian, 1994)

Reconstruction in the City of London (Batsford, 1944)

Reporting World War II Part 1 (New York: Penguin, 1995)

Addison, Paul, *The Road to 1945* (Pimlico, 1994)

Alanbrooke, Field Marshal Lord, *War Diaries 1939–1945*, eds Alex Danchev and Daniel Todman (Weidenfeld & Nicolson, 2001)

Alldritt, Keith, *The Greatest of Friends* (Robert Hale, 1995)

Arapoff, Cyril, *London in the Thirties* (Nishen, 1988)

Baddeley, Sir John James, Bt JP, *The Guildhall of the City of London* (Corporation of London, 1952)

Beaman, Katharine Bentley, *Green Sleeves: The Story of WVS/WRVS* (Seeley Service, 1977)

Bielenberg, Christabel, *The Past is Myself* (Chatto & Windus, 1968)

Brittain, Vera, *England's Hour* (Futura, 1981)

Brown, Mike, *Put That Light Out! Britain's Civil Defence Services at War 1939–45* (Stroud: Alan Sutton, 1999)

Burns, James MacGregor, *Roosevelt: The Lion and the Fox* (Secker & Warburg, 1957)

Butler, A. S. G., *Recording Ruin* (Macmillan, 1942)

Calder, Angus, *The Myth of the Blitz* (Pimlico, 2001)

– *The People's War* (Pimlico, 1997)

Calder, Ritchie, *Carry On London* (English Universities Press, 1941)

– *The Lesson of London* (Secker & Warburg, 1941)

Cannadine, David, *In Churchill's Shadow* (Penguin, 2002)

Carr, William, *Arms, Autarky and Aggression* (Edward Arnold, 1972)

Carsten, F. L., *The Rise of Fascism* (Methuen, 1967)

Charman, Terry, *The German Home Front 1939–45* (Barrie & Jenkins, 1989)

Chater, Michael, *Family Business, A History of Grosvenor Chater 1690–1977* (Grosvenor Chater, 1977)

Churchill, Winston, *The River War: An Historical Account of The Reconquest of the Soudan* (Longmans, Green, 1899)

– *Into Battle* (Cassell, 1941)

Churchill, Winston S. *The Second World War Volume II: Their Finest Hour* (Reprint Society, 1952)
– *The Second World War Volume III: The Grand Alliance* (Cassell, 1950)
– *The Secret Session Speeches* (Cassell, 1946)
– *The Unrelenting Struggle* (Cassell, 1942)
Cobb, Gerald, *The Old Churches of London* (B. T. Batsford, Winter 1941–2)
Colville, John, *The Fringes of Power: Downing Street Diaries 1939–1955* (Hodder and Stoughton, 1985)
Conn, Stetson, and Fairchild, Byron, *The Framework of Hemisphere Defense* (Washington, Center of Military History United States Army, 1989)
Croall, Jonathan, *Don't You Know There's a War On?* (Hutchinson, 1988)
Cross, Arthur, and Tibbs, Fred, *The London Blitz*, ed. Mike Seaborne (Nishen, 1987)
Cudlipp, Hugh, *Publish and be Damned!* (Andrew Dakers, 1953)
Daniell, A. E., *London City Churches* (Archibald Constable, 1896)
Daniell, Raymond, *Civilians Must Fight* (New York: Doubleday Doran, 1941)
Darwin, Bernard, *War on the Line* (Midhurst, W. Sussex: Middleton, 1984)
Davis, Kenneth S., *FDR The War President* (New York: Random House, 2000)
Davis, Rob, and Schweitzer, Pam (eds), *Southwark at War* (Southwark Council Local Studies Library, 1996)
Deighton, Len, *Fighter* (Jonathan Cape, 1977)
Demarne, Cyril, *The London Blitz: A Fireman's Tale* (Battle of Britain Prints International, 1991)
– *Our Girls: A Story of the Nation's Wartime Firewomen* (Durham: Pentland Press, 1995)
Dickens, Charles, *A Christmas Carol* (Chapman and Hall, 1843)
– *The Uncommercial Traveller* (Chapman and Hall, 1859–70)
Divine, Robert, A. *Roosevelt and World War II* (Baltimore: John Hopkins, 1969)
Doyle, William, *Inside the Oval Office: The White House Tapes from FDR to Clinton* (Kodansha International, 1999)
Eade, Charles, *Churchill by His Contemporaries* (Reprint Society, 1955)
Emerson, Ralph Waldo, *English Traits* (Boston & London: 1856)
Farson, Negley, *Bomber's Moon*, illus. Tom Purvis (Victor Gollancz Ltd, 1941)
Firebrace, Cmdr Sir Aylmer, *Fire Service Memories* (Andrew Melrose, no date)
Fitzgibbon, Constantine, *The Blitz*, illus. Henry Moore (Corgi Books, 1974)
Flanner, Janet, *London Was Yesterday 1934–1939*, ed. Irving Drutman (Viking, 1975)
Fletcher, Hanslip, *Bombed London* (Cassell, 1947)
Foot, Michael, *H. G.: The History of Mr Wells* (Black Swan, 1996)
Foreman, John, *Fighter Command War Diaries Vol. 2* (Air Research Publication, 1998)
Fulbrook, Mary, *The Fontana History of Germany 1918–1990* (Fontana, 1991)
Fuller, J. F. C., *The Decisive Battles of the Western World 1792–1944 Vol.2* (Granada, 1970)
Fussell, Paul, *The Bloody Game* (Scribners, 1991)
Galland, Adolf, *The First and the Last*, trans. Mervyn Savill (Methuen, 1955)
Gellhorn, Martha, *The Face of War* (Granta, 1988)
Gibbs, Philip, *Ordeal in England* (Right Book Club, 1938)

Gilbert, Martin *The Churchill War Papers: Vol. II Never Surrender* (Heinemann, 1994)

– *In Search of Churchill* (Harper Collins, 1995)

– *Winston S. Churchill Vol. VI Finest Hour 1939–41* (Heinemann, 1983)

Goebbels, Josef, *The Goebbels Diaries 1939–41* ed. Fred Taylor (Hamish Hamilton, 1982)

Graves, Charles, *London Transport at War 1939–1945* (Altmark/London Transport, 1974)

– *Women in Green* (William Heinemann, 1948)

Halsey, Margaret, *With Malice Towards Some* (Hamish Hamilton, 1938)

Hanson, Neil, *The Dreadful Judgement* (Doubleday, 2001)

Harrisson, Tom, *Living Through the Blitz* (Penguin, 1978)

Hartcup, Guy, *The Challenge of War: Scientific and Engineering Contributions to World War Two* (Newton Abbot: David & Charles, 1970)

Hay, Ian, *The Post Office Went to War* (HMSO, 1946)

Hennessy, Peter, *Never Again* (Vintage, 1993)

– *Whitehall* (Fontana, 1989)

Henrey, Robert, *The Siege of London* (J. M. Dent, 1946)

Hewison, Robert, *Under Siege: Literary Life in London 1939–45* (Weidenfeld & Nicolson/Readers Union, 1978)

Higham, Charles, *Trading with the Enemy* (New York: Barnes & Noble, 1983)

Hoemberg, Elisabeth, *Thy People, My People* (J. M. Dent, 1950)

Holloway, Sally, *Courage High* (HMSO, 1992)

Hylton, Stuart, *Their Darkest Hour* (Stroud: Sutton, 2003)

'Impresario', *The Market Square* (Imperial War Museum, 1997)

Ingersoll, Ralph *Report on England* (Right Book Club, 1941)

Ingham, H. S. (ed.), *Fire and Water: An Anthology By Members Of NFS* (Lindsay Drummond, 1942)

Ishimaru, Tota, *The Next World War* (Hurst & Blackett, 1937)

Jesse, F. Tennyson, *While London Burns* (Constable, 1942)

Johnson, David, *The London Blitz* (Chelsea MI, USA: Scarborough House, 1990)

Kendrick, Alexander, *Prime Time: The Life of Edward R. Murrow* (Boston: Little Brown, 1969)

Kent, William, *An Encyclopedia of London* (J. M. Dent, 1951)

– *London for Everyman* (J. M. Dent, 1931)

– *The Lost Treasures of London* (Phoenix House, 1947)

Kimball, Warren F., *The Most Unsordid Act: Lend-Lease 1939-1941* (Baltimore: John Hopkins Press, 1969)

Kirkpatrick, Ivone, *The Inner Circle* (Macmillan, 1959)

Kitchen, Martin, *Fascism* (Macmillan, 1976)

Klemmer, Harvey, *They'll Never Quit* (Right Book Club, 1942)

Knoke, Heinz, *I Flew For The Fuhrer*, trans. John Ewing (Transworld, 1957)

Kynaston, David, *The City of London 1914–1945* (Chatto & Windus, 1999)

Laird, Stephen, and Graebner, Walter, *Hitler's Reich and Churchill's Britain* (Batsford, 1942)

Lee, Raymond E., *London Observer: The Journal of General Raymond E. Lee 1940–41*, ed. J. Leutze (Hutchinson, 1972)

Leese, Arnold Spencer, *Out of Step: Events in the Two Lives of an Anti-Jewish Camel-Doctor* (no publisher, no date)

Lenton, H. T., and Colledge, J. J., *Warships of World War II* (Ian Allan, 1973)

Leske, Gottfried, *I Was A Nazi Flier* trans. Curt Reiss (New York: Dell, 1943)

Livesey, Anthony (ed.), *Are We at War? The Times 1939–1945* (Times Books, 1989)

London, Jack, *The People of the Abyss* (Isbister, 1903)

Longmate, Norman, *How We Lived Then* (Pimlico, 2002)

Lukacs, John, *Five Days in London May 1940* (New Haven: Yale Nota Bene, 2001)

Mackay, Robert, *Half the Battle* (Manchester: Manchester University Press, 2002)

McLaine, Ian, *Ministry of Morale* (Allen & Unwin, 1979)

Maclaren-Ross, Julian, *Memoirs of the Forties* (Cardinal, 1991)

Maillaud, Pierre, *The English Way* (Oxford: OUP, 1945)

Matthews, the Very Rev. W. R., *St Paul's Cathedral in Wartime 1939–1945* (Hutchinson, 1946)

Maugham, R. C. F., *Jersey Under the Jackboot* (W. H. Allen, 1949)

Mayhew, Patrick (ed.), *One Family's War* (Futura, 1987)

Medvei, Victor Cornelius, and Thorton, John L. (eds), *The Royal Hospital of St Bartholomew's 1123–1973* (St Bartholomew's Hopital, 1974)

Mee, Arthur, *London, Heart of the Empire and Wonder of the World* (Hodder and Stoughton, 1937)

Meltzer, Albert, *I Couldn't Paint Golden Angels* (Edinburgh: AK Press, 1996)

Mill, John Stuart, 'Of the Liberty of Thought and Discussion' in *On Liberty* (London, 1869)

Miller, Alice Duer, *The White Cliffs* (Methuen, 1941)

Miller, Lee G., *The Story of Ernie Pyle* (New York: Bantam, 1953)

Morgan, Dewi, *Phoenix of Fleet Street: 2000 Years of St Bride's* (Charles Knight, 1967)

Morton, H. V., *Atlantic Meeting* (Methuen, 1946)

– *Ghosts of London* (Methuen, November 16th, 1939)

– *H. V. Morton's London* (Methuen, 1940)

– *Two Englands* (Methuen, 1944)

Muggeridge, Malcolm (ed.), *Ciano's Diary* (Heinemann, 1947)

Murrow, Edward R., *In Search of Light: The Broadcasts of Ed Murrow 1938–61*, ed. Edward Bliss Jr (Macmillan, 1968)

– *This is London* (Cassell, 1941)

Namikas, Lise, 'The Committee to Defend America and the Debates Between Internationalists and Interventionists 1939–41' in *Historian* (Tampa, Florida, Summer 1999)

Nel, Elizabeth, *Mr Churchill's Secretary* (Hodder & Stoughton, 1958)

Newman, Rosie, *Britain at War* (Max Love, 1948)

Nicholls, A. J., *Weimar and the Rise of Hitler* (Macmillan, 1975)

Niemöller, Martin, *The Gestapo Defied* (William Hodge, 1941)

Nixon, Barbara, *Raiders Overhead* (Scolar/Gulliver, 1980)

Opie, Robert, *The Wartime Scrapbook 1939–1945* (New Cavendish Books, 1999)

Orwell, George, *Coming up for Air* (Victor Gollancz, 1939)

– *Down and Out in Paris and London* (Victor Gollancz, 1933)

– *The Road to Wigan Pier* (Victor Gollancz, 1937)

– *The Lion and the Unicorn* (Secker and Warburg, 1941)

Oswell, David, 'Early children's broadcasting in Britain. Programming for a liberal democracy' *Historical Journal of Film, Radio and Television* Vol. 18 No. 3 at http://www.iamhist.org/journal/

Partridge, Frances, *A Pacifist's War* (Robin Clark, 1983)

Pepys, Samuel, *The Diary of Samuel Pepys MA FRS* (George Bell, 1900)

Perry, Colin, *Boy in the Blitz* (Sutton/IWM, 2000)

Pilpel, Robert H., *Churchill in America 1895–1961* (New English Library, 1977)

Price, G. Ward, *I Know These Dictators* (George Harrap, 1937)

Priestley, J. B., *Postscripts* (William Heinemann, 1940)

Pryce-Jones, David, *Paris in the Third Reich* (Collins, 1981)

Pyle, Ernie, *Ernie Pyle in England* (New York: Robert M. McBride, 1941)

Quennell, Marjorie, and Quennell, C. H. B., *A History of Everyday Things in England Vol. 4 1851–1934* (Batsford, Autumn 1934)

Raczynski, Count Edward, *In Allied London* (Weidenfeld & Nicolson, 1962)

Ramsey, Winston G (ed.), *The Blitz Then and Now Volume 2* (Battle of Britain Prints, 1988)

Randoll, Robert, *The Barbican before the Blitz* (Lymne Castle: Harry Margary/Guildhall Library, 1982)

Ranfurly, Hermione, *To War With Whitaker: Wartime Diaries of the Countess of Ranfurly* (Arrow, 1994)

Rasmussen, Steen Eiler, *London the Unique City* (Penguin, 1961)

Ray, John, *The Night Blitz 1940–1941* (Cassell, 1996)

Reith, J. C. W., *Into the Wind* (Hodder & Stoughton, 1949)

Renier, G. J., *The English: Are They Human?* (Fourth Edition, Ernest Benn, 1966)

Reynolds, Quentin, *The Wounded Don't Cry* (Cassell, 1941)

Ricks, Christopher, and Vance, William L. (eds), *The Faber Book of America* (Faber and Faber, 1992)

Robbins, Gordon, *Fleet Street Blitzkrieg Diary* (Ernest Benn, 1944)

Roberts, Denys Kilham (ed.), *Penguin Parade* (Penguin, 1940)

Robertson, Esmonde M., *The Origins of the Second World War* (Macmillan, 1973)

Robinson, W. Heath, and Hunt, Cecil *How to Make the Best of Things* (Hutchinson, 1940)

– *How to Build a New World* (Hutchinson)

Roosevelt, Eleanor, *Autobiography* (Hutchinson, 1962)

Rose, Jonathan, *The Intellectual Life of the British Working Classes* (New Haven: Yale Nota Bene, 2002)

Sansom, William (uncredited), *Fire Over London: The Story Of The London Fire Service 1940–41* (Hutchinson & Co. Ltd for LCC, 1941)

Saunders, Hilary St George, *The Left Handshake* (Collins, 1948) at http://www.pinetreeweb.com

Sebag Montefiore, Simon, *Stalin: The Court of the Red Tsar* (Phoenix, 2004)

Sellar, W. C. and Yeatman, R. J., *1066 and All That* (Methuen, 1930)

Semmler, Rudolf, *Goebbels – the Man Next to Hitler* (Westhouse, 1947)

Sevareid, Eric, *Not So Wild a Dream* (New York: Atheneum, 1976)

Sheean, Vincent, *Between the Thunder & the Sun* (New York: Random House, 1943)

Sherwood, Robert E., *Roosevelt and Hopkins* (New York: Harper & Bros, 1948)

Shirer, William L., *This is Berlin* (Hutchinson, 1999)

Sillince, *We're Still All In It* (Collins, 1942)

Simmonds, Clifford, *The Objectors* (Isle of Man: Times Press, no date)

Simpson, W. Sparrow, *Gleanings from Old St Paul's* (Elliot Stock, 1889)

Sinclair, Andrew, *War Like a Wasp* (Hamish Hamilton, 1989)

Skidelsky, Robert, *John Maynard Keynes* (Macmillan, 2003)

Smith, Karen Manners, 'Father, Son, and Country on the Eve of War: William Allen White, William 'Lindsay White, and American Isolationism, 1940–1941', *Kansas History* Spring 2005 (Vol. 28, No. 1)

Soames, Mary, *Clementine Churchill* (Cassell, 1979)

Somerville, Christopher, *Our War: How the British Commonwealth Fought the Second World War* (Weidenfeld & Nicolson, 1998)

Sorenson, Colin, *London on Film* (Museum of London, 1996)

Spaight, J. M., *Bombing Vindicated* (Geoffrey Bles, 1944)

Stahl, P., *The Diving Eagle, A Ju88 Pilot's Diary* (Kimber, 1984)

Stansky, Peter, and Abrahams, William, *London's Burning, Life Death and Art in the Second World War* (Constable, 1994)

Steinhilper, Ulrich, and Osborne, Peter, *Spitfire on My Tail* (Bromley: Independent, 1989)

Stow, John, *A Survay of London* based on 1598 and 1603 texts, ed. Henry Morley (George Routledge, no date)

Suchitzky, Wolf, *Charing Cross Road in the Thirties* (Nishen, 1988)

Talbot, Godfrey, *Permission to Speak* (Hutchinson, 1976)

Taylor, A. J. P., *The War Lords* (Penguin, 1978)

Thomson, Malcolm, *The Life and Times of Winston Churchill* (Odhams Press, no date)

Thomson Hill, William, *Buried London* (Phoenix House, 1955)

Thorne, Christopher, *The Approach of War 1938–39* (Macmillan, 1973)

Townsend, Peter, *Duel in the Dark* (Arrow, 1988)

Trotsky, Leon, *My Life* (Penguin, 1975)

van Minnen, Cornelis A., and Sears, John F. (eds), *FDR and his Contemporaries* (Macmillan, 1992)

Wadsworth, John, *Counter Defensive* (Hodder & Stoughton, May 1946)

Wagener, Otto, *Hitler: Memoirs of a Confidant*, ed. H. A. Turner Jr. (New Haven: Yale, 1985)

Wakefield, Kenneth, *The First Pathfinders* (William Kimber, 1981)

Walden, H. A., *Operation Textiles: A City Warehouse in Wartime* (1946)

Wallington, Neil, *Firemen at War* (David & Charles, 1981)

Waugh, Maureen (ed.), *Memories of Holborn* (The Holborn Local History Group, 1986)

Wedemeyer, Frederic J. G, Deasy, Daniel A., and Scott, George T. J., *Wartime Fire Defense in London* (Washington: The United States Conference of Mayors, 1941)

Weir, Ron, *Scared, Who Me?* (no publisher, no date)

– *The New Machiavelli* (John Lane and The Bodley Head, 1911)

– *The New World Order* (Secker & Warburg, 1940)

– *The War of the Worlds* (William Heinemann, 1898)

Wheatley, Henry B. (ed.), *The Diary of Samuel Pepys M.A. F.R.S. Vols V and VI* (Bell, 1900)

Wheeler-Bennett, John W., *King George VI* (Reprint Society, 1959)
– *Action This Day: Working With Churchill* (Macmillan, 1968)
Wheen, Francis, *Tom Driberg His Life and Indiscretions* (Pan, 1992)
White, W. L., *Journey for Margaret* (New York: Harcourt Brace, 1941)
Willett, John, *The Weimar Years* (Thames & Hudson, 1984)
Williams, Francis, *A Prime Minister Remembers* (Heinemann, 1961)
Wiskemann, Elizabeth, *Fascism in Italy: its Development and Influence*
   (Macmillan, 1970)
Yeo, Geoffrey, *Nursing at Bart's* (St Bartholomew and Princess Alexandra and
   Newham College of Nursing and Midwifery, 1995)
Young, G. M., *Stanley Baldwin* (Rupert Hart-Davis, 1952)

Newspapers and Periodicals

Issues 24th December–1st January 1940: *Daily Herald, Daily Mail, Daily
Express, Sunday Express, Daily Mirror, News Chronicle, Sunday Pictorial, The
Times, Sunday Times* and *Manchester Guardian.*
Also *Jewish Chronicle,* 3rd January 1941; *Picture Post,* various dates 1940–41;
Radio Times, Christmas Issue 1940; *Virginia Quarterly Review* (Charlottesville),
Issue 15, January 1939

Notes

A fuller version of these notes appears on this book's web page at
http://www.faber.co.uk

Unless otherwise stated, all quotations from and references to the following
come from their Imperial War Museum files: *Felicity Ashbee, Frank Backhouse,
Elizabeth Barnicot, Viola Bawtree, Nancy Bosanquet, Winifred Bowman, Nell
Carver, Stanley Champion, Sidney Chave, Nev Coates, Isabelle Granger, Yvonne
Green, Sergeant H. F. Grey, Miss E. Heller, Frank Hurd, Reverend J. G.
Markham, Win Marshall, Peter Maynard* (under Capt. H. A. Maynard), *Leslie
Paul, Bill and Vi Regan* (under W. B. Regan), *B. J. Rogers, Bert Snow, May
Speed, Ron Weir* (though see also *Scared, Who Me?* in Bibliography).

Unless otherwise stated, details of the St Paul's Watch, including A. S. G.
Butler's letters and his lecture on the geography of the Cathedral, come from the
archives within the Cathedral Library (including research notes kindly shared by
Sally Holloway) or Boxes CF 2–5 and CF 17, held at Guildhall MSS Library.

Introduction

ix Herbert Mason: Fitzgibbon, pp. 213–14.

ix more than half: see for comparison; IWM Photographic: HU 36220A.

xi bulldog-stubborn: purely compositionally, the *Daily Mail* picture – 'it
   symbolises the steadiness of London's stand against the enemy', the paper
   declared, 'the firmness of Right against Wrong' – is strangely echoed in
   Karsh's famous bulldog-grim Churchill, photographed in Canada exactly
   one year later.

xi *Berliner Illustrierte Zeitung:* Ramsey, p. 374.

xi Square Mile: the City is slightly less than the exact 640 acres within the line
   of the long-vanished walls, slightly more in total.

Prelude

3 114th day: by convention counted from 'Black Saturday' (7th September).

3 your odds: perhaps seven million of greater London's eight-odd millions
   'stayed put'; the official London death toll for Sep–Nov 1940 was 12,696
   with about 20,000 seriously injured: *Front Line*, p. 20.

4 daylight-saving: the clocks had not gone back as usual in the autumn; they
   would go forward another hour for summer 1941.

4 'slow footstep': Farson, p. 15.

4 Broadcasting House: Talbot, pp. 29–31; Kendrick, pp. 210–12; Ingersoll,
   pp. 76–81.

5 stiff upper lip: US Military Attaché General Lee bemoaned the BBC's lack of
   showmanship: a dramatic eyewitness broadcast of an air battle over the
   Channel provoked so many protests that it was undignified and un-English
   and sensational that the experiment was not repeated. Lee, p. 33. British

sangfroid was much debated. 'B' wrote to Winnie Bowman in America: 'I suppose it's all pride, we are undoubtedly the proudest race in the world which is a damn good thing because even though one is scared one doesn't show it.' Bowman, Mrs W. C. 85/45/1. Ralph Ingersoll noted the calming influence of being with people who 'do not transmit their fears' pp. 89–90. Vincent Sheean, who had been in Spain and China, did not agree, he wrote, 'with those observers who hold that the English have a monopoly on endurance and tenacity . . . But the English way of resisting terrible adversity is peculiar to the national character . . . A man who had seen his house destroyed and his family's life endangered would have thought himself a sorry knave if he referred to it as anything but "a bit of trouble" . . . when I was sitting in Ed Murrow's drawing room drinking a placid whisky and soda . . . Miss Campbell, the chief of the CBS secretaries, came into the room. "I don't want to disturb you, sir," she said in her cool, trim voice, "but I think the house is on fire."' Sheean, pp. 230–31.

5 Plymouth: Ramsey, p. 35; *Daily Express* 30.12.40. The future held much worse in store for Plymouth. Cities became fiercely protective of their own Blitz – especially in comparison to London's. In 1942, American A. J. Liebling found that the long anonymity of much-bombed Hull had drawn official protests from its sheriff and chief air raid warden: 'It is bad enough to be bombed and anybody who says he likes it is a liar. But one ought at least to get credit for it.' Commenting on an undamaged hotel, he was instantly directed to a devastated department store: "I'll wager you haven't seen anything like that in London," the Councillor said, and when I admitted I hadn't everybody smiled . . . "If you could publish the number of buildings we've had hit," he said solemnly, "it would put Coventry's eye out."' *New Yorker*, pp. 99–101.

5 Indian troops: Newman, p. 7; Getty Images 3326223, 3314650, 3367226. Nehru and Gandhi's Congress Party repudiated the Viceroy's declaration of war without Indian consent, while Mr Jinnah's Muslim League, seeking a separate 'Pakistan' ('a Moslem Ulster' according to Friday's *News Chronicle*!), supported the war. However, more than two million Indians, of all religions and none, fought for the Allies during the Second World War: the largest volunteer army in history.

6 'Very Well, Alone': *Low*, p. 60.

6 loyal subject: Ireland's situation was particularly hotly debated in this weekend's press. A Dominion – linked to Britain only through the monarchy – since 1922, the Irish Free State had in 1937 taken the opportunity of the Abdication to remove all mention of the King from the Constitution of Eire (though it remained part of the Commonwealth of Nations). While the other Dominions of Canada, Australia, New Zealand and South Africa declared war on, or soon after, 3rd September 1939, Ireland remained neutral. However, many individuals from the South as well as the North joined British armed forces, many of London's estimated 60,000 Irish population – notably many nurses – remained throughout the Blitz, and many new Irish immigrants joined the civilian war effort.

6 'little Jamaica': future Jamaican Minister Dudley Thompson, quoted in Somerville, p. 5.

6 Coloured Peoples: *News Letter* (BL) 025NWLT194011, 194012 and

1941o1. Malaya was the first colony to launch a Spitfire Fund and 'the idea spread like wild-fire', according to Issue 22 of the Ministry of Information's *London's Awake*.

6 binoculars: for more Scouting generosity (including £3 from the troop of a Ugandan leper colony), see Saunders, Chapter VI.

7 'city-state': Reith, p. 100.

7 George V: http://www.royal.gov.uk/output/Page3643.asp

7 Cockney woman: Mrs Frank Renton of Dulwich according to *South London Advertiser* 3.1.41.

7 George VI: The Royal Archives, Windsor, Royal Christmas Broadcasts.

8 Ernest Lough: http://betterland.boychoirs.org/bland016.html; *The Times Magazine* 20.5.2000.

8 Goebbels: Goebbels, pp. 182, 185, 220.

9 'odd islanders': Renier, p. vii. Shakespeare, of course, sends Hamlet to England because there 'the men are as mad as he'. Written for a young John Mills to sing in 1932, Noël Coward's 'Mad Dogs and Englishmen' ('It seems such a shame when the English claim the earth/ That they give rise to such hilarity and mirth') showed that the tradition was alive and well.

9 'Psychopaths': Jesse, p. 127. German-controlled Paris radio, meanwhile, broadcast that 'the legend of British self-control and phlegm is being destroyed', with seven million Londoners in the grip of 'hair-raising fear . . . They run aimlessly about in the streets and are the victims of bombs and bursting shells.' *Front Line*, p. 60.

9 'dandy': Goebbels, p. 211.

10 'warmth': Colville, p. 308.

11 'fellow-passengers': Dickens *Carol*, Stave 1. The Dickensian definition of Christmas spirit in *What Christmas Is as We Grow Older* (1851) – 'active usefulness, perseverance, cheerful discharge of duty, kindness and forbearance!' – would certainly not look out of place in any ARP or WVS manual. Though Dickensian villians lurked not too. A cutting from page 9 of the *Evening Standard* (no date, but evidently shortly before Christmas 1940) told of a Barnet couple who opened up their home to a young man who was settling the affairs of his late mother, killed in an air raid. He had 'seemed such a nice young man and spent all the evening telling Bible stories to [their] children' but, after two days, he disappeared with the contents of the gas meter and Christmas savings from the children's money boxes.

11 Scandinavia Sweden, of course, remained neutral throughout the war.

12 French army: the French death toll is not certain (various estimates listed on http://users.erols.com/mwhite28/ww2stats.htm). More than 100,000 French troops were evacuated from Dunkirk: most but not all fought on after the Armistice as Free French under De Gaulle, who was based in London.

12 'curse or cry': Renier, pp. 28–9.

12 'in the final': Churchill *II*, p. 216.

12 'almost happy': Sevareid, pp. 154–5.

12 'long-faced': Daniell, pp. 201–2.

13 'We refugees': Martin Goldenberg, in Croall, pp. 129–31.

13 'better 'ole': Bairnsfather at http://www.firstworldwar.com/poetsandprose/

13 Osterley Park: *Picture Post* 21.9.40; Sevareid, pp. 172–5.

14 'Uncle Basil': Mayhew, pp. 68, 82, 101.

15 'Honestly Winnie': 'Helen' to IWM: Bowman, Mrs W. C. 85/45/1.

15 small meat: 'B' to IWM: Bowman, Mrs W. C. 85/45/1.

15 Storm Jameson: *Times Literary Supplement*, 7.10.39

16 'English viewpoint': Flanner pp. 62–3, 91–2.

16 'Pepys and Dickens': Sevareid, pp. 79.

16 'ketchup bottles': ibid pp. 179–80. Quentin Reynolds, weekending in Kent, found his hostess now spent bridge club meetings making Molotov cocktails: 'the ones we will blow up the tanks with'. ('Molotov cocktails', often linked to Russian resistance to Nazi tanks, were first used by Finns against Russian tanks in 1940; giving rise to the term 'Molotov breadbasket' for canisters of firebombs.)

17 'English epic': Priestley, pp. 1–4. General Lee was fascinated to see defensive forces utilise Martello towers and consult Sir John Moore's defence plans from the Napoleonic era. One regiment even rediscovered a bundle of swords captured at Bidossa. Lee, p. 16.

17 'We British': Mollie Panter-Downes in New York, p.23.

17 'Unaccustomed as we are': IWM: Warner, Miss P. 95/14/1.

18 'the black abyss': Priestley, p. 25.

19 'Yesterday': Goebbels, p. 221.

19 sleeping peacefully: 'Berchtesgaden is the only place where he can get a night's rest without a sleeping-draught . . . whenever his public engagements allow, he stays in bed till noon.' Price, pp. 17–18.

19 'live for millennia': *Der Führer in den Bergen* at http://www.calvin.edu/academic/cas/gpa/booklet1.htm

19 *Bengal Lancer*: British diplomat Ivone Kirkpatrick wrote that Hitler saw the film three times and that it was compulsory viewing for the SS. Kirkpatrick, p. 97.

19 'Shoot Gandhi': ibid, pp. 97–8.

20 'My legacy': Semmler, pp. 20–21.

20 Gareth Jones: *Western Mail and South Wales News* 28.2. 33; 5.6.33; 7.6.33 and 10.6.33 at http://garethjones.org/

21 anti-'Hun' hysteria: humorist Jerome K. Jerome's assessment of the Kaiser's Germany, untainted by either Great War propaganda or appeasement, makes fascinating reading. In the final chapter of *Three Men on the Bummel* (1900), he expressed fears that 'a good people, a lovable people, who should help much to make the world better' were being schooled by a militaristic education system into a faith in authority far beyond what an Englishman felt proper. Duty was, he wrote, 'a fine ideal for any people; but before buckling to it, one would wish to have a clear understanding as to what this "duty" is. The German idea would appear to be: "blind obedience to everything in buttons".' Hitherto the German had been well governed: 'When his troubles will begin will be when by any chance something goes wrong with the governing machine.' http://www.literaturecollection.com/a/jerome/three-men-bummel/14/

21 'Strangely attractive': Gibbs, pp. 206, 372–3.

22 'such friends': Gilbert *Papers,* p. 1284.

23 a report coming via New York: Friday's *Daily Express*, in a report via New

York, envisaged Hitler looking longingly from the chalk cliffs of Boulogne like Napoleon before him. No British dream was more deeply held (nor seemed less likely to be realised) than that Hitler should repeat Napoleon's mistake of marching on Moscow with Britain still undefeated.

23 'doggedly fighting Spitfires': Knoke, p. 36; http://www.battleofbritain.net/bobhsoc/aircrew/pilots.html.

23 'precious jewel': *Richard II*. Shakespeare was a favourite oracle now, with the little-known *King John* much plundered:

> This England never did, nor never shall,
> Lie at the proud foot of a conqueror,
> But when it first did help to wound itself.
> Now these her princes are come home again,
> Come the three corners of the world in arms,
> And we shall shock them. Nought shall make us rue,
> If England to itself do rest but true.

Colin Perry read this in an American magazine: Perry, p. 201; *Come The Three Corners* by Sir Harry Britain was reviewed today in the *Sunday Times*. More pointed lines, from *Henry VI Part 3*, were included in a note to the Prime Minister from one of his Private Secretaries:

> 'Tis better using France than trusting France.
> Let us be back'd with God, and with the seas,
> Which He hath giv'n for fence impregnable. (Colville, p. 181.)

24 '700 square miles': Mee, p. 2. England's population was then forty million.

24 'greater' London sprawl: Hitler may have misjudged his target. 'In works of travel,' wrote G. Ward Price in 1937, 'The maps and plans get most of his attention. He says that if he ever went to London or Paris he would immediately be able to find his way about.' Price, p. 19.

24 Croydon: see Perry, pp. 62–5, 83–4.

24 St Giles bombing: PMGL: 2821; HU86285; Ray, pp. 97–103; Perry, pp. 90–91; http://www.raf.mod.uk/bob1940/august24.html; http://www.battle-ofbritain.net/0029.html.

24 British raids: Ray, p. 98.

25 'raze their cities': Spaight, pp. 43–4; Shirer, pp. 394–5; http://www.battleof-britain.net/0034.html

25 Halifax: memo, Viscount Halifax to Marquess of Lothian, 12th September, 1940, Great Britain Index, Safe Files, Franklin D. Roosevelt Digital Archives at http://www.fdrlibrary.marist.edu/. What Lord Halifax's reply might have been had he instead of Churchill succeeded Chamberlain as Prime Minister is one of the imponderables of history.

26 Operational Training: Deighton, p. 226.

26 'pretty groggy': http://www.battleofbritain.net/0036.html

26 'riots': *Front Line*, p. 39. Nev Coates, meanwhile, noted: 'It is quite wonderful the way London is adapting itself to new conditions, with the people carrying on as best they can, nurses, shop girls, business people, cars stopping at bus stops and the driver asking, "Anyone going to Westminster?" etc. I know this sounds a bit like Priestley's Sunday night *Postscript*, but I'd already noticed it myself.'

26 'Obdurate and cocky': Goebbels, pp. 127, 137, 142, 154, 159, 160, 163, 167.

27 'best in the world': Renier, pp. 43–52

28 'contempt': Goebbels, pp. 143, 186, 214; 191–2; 220.

30 Fire situation (all dates): LMA: LCC/CL/CD/2/13–15. For the operation of Lambeth HQ, see Ingersoll, pp. 131–7; *Picture Post* 1.2.41.

31 'Gentleman' Jackson: Holloway, pp. 166–7. Aylmer Firebrace remained nominal head of the LFB.

31 technically specific: LMA: LCC/FB/WAR/LFR/1/51.

31 twenty-pump fire: Firebrace, p. 176.

32 Stanley Baldwin: Young, p. 174.

32 Haile Selassie: http://www.mtholyoke.edu/acad/intrel/selassie.htm

33 'tolerate this': 'Nightmares of Dead Children . . .' by Cary Nelson, *Cultural Matters* Issue 1 at http://culturalstudies.gmu.edu/

33 'bloody pumps': Demarne, *London* pp. 23, 28; Firebrace, p. 169.

33 thirty or forty times: *Front Line*, p. 25.

33 AFS: Holloway, pp. 149–84; Firebrace, pp. 148–59.

36 'little in the way of smiles': 'B' to IWM: Bowman, Mrs W. C. 85/45/1.

36 three months: Firebrace, p. 171.

37 gallantry: LMA: LCC/CL/CD/1/285.

37 'three vast storeys': IWM: Paul, Dr L. A. 02/57/1.

38 'horrendous': Goebbels, p. 177.

38 'dull in heaven': 'B' to IWM: Bowman, Mrs W. C. 85/45/1.

38 Heavy Rescue: report by Lewis Silkin LMA: LCC/CL/CD/1/114. This was a wholly new craft, said the official Blitz history: 'until our generation, it was hardly a matter of general concern that a house could collapse in three different ways': a collapse into rubble, 'the curving fall of roof and floors, held at one side while the other swung downwards' or floors that split in the centre to form a V that might protect those on the storey below. *Front Line*, 148. Techniques learned in the Blitz are still applied in rescue work around the world.

39 'tin hats': the ironic Great War slang was ubiqitous in London but, Ralph Ingersoll explained to his readers, these were steel helmets, heavy enough to give you a headache just wearing them. Ingersoll, p. 106.

39 Frank and his crew: photograph at IWM: Hurd F. W. 80/30/1.

40 Ralph Ingersoll: Ingersoll, pp. 124–5, 245–6. In the remarkable newsreel clip 'Air Raid Victim' of 29th August 1940 on http://www.britishpathe.com, there is comic contrast between feisty old Mrs Jiggins – who must have been one of the very first Londoners with a 'bomb story' to tell – and the awkward official effort to 'propagandize' her.

40 American General Raymond E. Lee was amused when his valet, bemoaning the tiny tea ration, said coffee was no substitute as it kept you awake all day. Lee, pp. 14–15.

40 'once too often': Kendrick, p. 219.

40 *Traviata:* IWM: Coates, R. N. 98/10/1.

41 'nice impression': Allan, Mrs M. E. 95/8/7 & Con shelf. Another woman felt that this '"Well, this is my last chance" feeling' might account for London's 'magnificent spirit'. Living 'each day as if it were my last' now made her 'more agreeable and more conscientious'. IWM: Warner, Miss P. 95/14/1.

41 'extraordinary lengths': Alan Seymour (1942), quoted Ramsay, pp. 236–49.

42 firewomen: Joan Bartlett, aged eighteen, and Violet Pengelly, nineteen: Debt of Honour Register at http://www.cwgc.org/; LFB: Hickin.

45 'Takoradi': Gilbert *Papers*, p. 1303.

45 the PM: John Colville in Wheeler-Bennett *Churchill*, pp. 50–51. All accounts of Churchill's life in Downing Street are inevitably read against the background of his own account of this time in Volume II of his war memoir.

45 LCC lecturer: IWM: Paul, Dr L. A. 02/57/1. With the co-operation of shelter authorities, the LCC had extended its evening class operation into larger shelters and was currently especially keen to hear from 'those experienced in operating sub-standard cinema projectors and qualified as lecturers in "interest" subjects'. *London's Awake*, No. 22.

46 'Mad fanaticism': Churchill *River War*, pp. 82–164 at http://www.fordham.edu/HALSALL/MOD/1898churchill-omdurman.html

46 'Take one with you': Churchill *II*, p. 232. Sir Auckland Geddes told General Lee: 'You would be surprised . . . to know of how many gentlewomen and old ladies I know who would be happy to die if they could feel that they had killed one German before they went. The women of this country are as belligerent and pugnacious as the men, if not more so.' Lee, p. 40.

46 'Unknown Warriors': BBC Broadcast 14th July 1940.

47 board school education: Police Sergeant Grey, for example, was somewhat erratic in his spelling, but when the Isle of Dogs guns first boomed, it was *The Burial of Sir John Moore at Corunna* that came to mind. Jonathan Rose's *The Intellectual Life of the British Working Classes* rebuts many facile assumptions about cultural poverty among London working people.

47 'phrase-maker': IWM: Warner, Miss P. 95/14/1.

48 'shoes of the other': Emerson, Chapter V.

48 'top nation': Walter Carruthers Sellar and Robert Julian Yeatman concluded their 1930 'Memorable History of England comprising all the parts you can remember including 103 Good Things, 5 Bad Kings and 2 Genuine Dates' with a final one-sentence chapter: 'America was thus clearly top nation, and History came to a .' (The full stop of history, as ever, proving to be barely a comma.) Sellar and Yeatman.

48 Colin Perry: Perry, pp. 56, 119, 124, 128, 199, 224.

48 'shy?': Renier, p. 30.

49 'afraid': Sevareid, pp. 79–80, 173. Ninety years earlier, his countryman had also found that 'every one of these islanders is an island himself, safe, tranquil, incommunicable. In a company of strangers, you would think him deaf; his eyes never wander from his table and newspaper . . . They have all been trained in one severe school of manners, and never put off the harness.' Though Ralph Waldo Emerson did not blame fear, nor shyness: 'I know not where any personal eccentricity is so freely allowed, and no man gives himself any concern with it. An Englishman walks in a pouring rain, swinging his closed umbrella like a walking-stick; wears a wig, or a shawl, or a saddle, or stands on his head, and no remark is made. And as he has been doing this for several generations, it is now in the blood.'

49 '8,000,000 workers': Thomson, pp. 273–4.

50 'good for the figure': IWM: Griffiths, Mrs M. L. C. 86/5/1.

50 'somewhat risky': Nixon, p. 43. To judge from the *Finsbury Weekly News*'s

particularly gloomy wartime diet of inquests and larceny, local ideas of entertainment were quite robust.

50 political uniforms: Public Order Act, 1936.

51 'rompers': Eade, p. 165; Firebrace, 216. Churchill gave George VI a set for Christmas, and to Queen Elizabeth a copy of *Modern English Usage* by H. W. Fowler (who had shared Churchill's love of short, old words). Gilbert *Winston* VI, p. 961.

51 would-be dictator: Renier, pp. 153–4.

51 Joseph Kennedy: this remarkable interview ended Kennedy's ambassadorship and his political career (though not his political ambitions). 'It's just one question,' he said, 'self-preservation for us, England is doing everything we could ask. As long as she is in there, we have time to prepare. It isn't that she's fighting for democracy. That's the bunk. She's fighting for self-preservation, just as we will if it comes to us.' http://www.pbs.org/wgbh/amex/kennedys/filmmore/ps_globe.html

51 'British revolution': Murrow *London*, pp. 112–14; Murrow *Light*, p. 113. Mr Attlee was Lord Privy Seal. Churchill *II*, p. 66.

51 coalition: including not only politicians of other parties but leading trade unionist Ernie Bevin. Churchill *II*, p. 268. Their remarkable rapprochement (Churchill had been Home Secretary during the General Strike only fourteen years before) was celebrated by J. B. Priestley in his *Postscript* of 7th July 1940; Joe Kennedy, on the other hand, told the *Boston Globe* that the inclusion of labour leaders in the Cabinet 'means national socialism is coming out of it'.

52 'Complete liberty': Mill, Chapter 2.

52 Lord Acton: letter to Bishop Mandell Creighton, 3rd April 1887.

53 'Stop that whistling!': Eade, p. 167.

53 buff-coloured: containing top secret 'Ultra' signals from 'Station X'. Colville, pp. 294–5.

53 eyes and ears: John Colville recalled officials forced to justify themselves to an irate PM on issues where the sole source of information was 'a paragraph in *Daily Express* or *Daily Mirror*'. Wheeler-Bennett *Churchill*, p. 90.

54 late into the night: Gilbert *Search*, pp. 160–62. Ingersoll, pp. 158–9.

54 civil servant: Colville, p. 172.

54 'comparatively free': Reynolds, Chapter 10. A Churchill memo to the Minister of Information in July asked that facts be 'chronicled without undue prominence and headlines . . . Localities affected should not be mentioned with any precision. Photographs showing shattered houses should not be published unless there is something very peculiar about them, or to illustrate how well the Anderson shelters work. It must be clear that the vast majority of people are not at all affected by any single air raid, and would hardly sustain any evil impression if it were not thrust before them.' Churchill *II*, pp. 150–51.

55 secret session: 20th June 1940, Churchill *Secret*, pp. 8–16.

55 'half a fool': Reynolds, Chapter 10.

56 scepticism: Churchill *II*, pp. 23–4. Ralph Ingersoll found that, wherever he went in London, people admired Churchill and said they didn't know what Britain would do without him. 'But few felt he would be Prime Minister

after the war. He was simply the right man in the right job at the right time.'
Ingersoll, p. 159.

56 'Winston's speeches': IWM: Carver, N. V. 90/16/1; Cannadine, pp. 104–8.
56 'Victory': House of Commons, 13th May 1940.
57 'Documentary School': one of the most famous graduates of John Grierson's
GPO Film Unit, Humphrey Jennings, later produced *Fires Were Started*, a
detailed, poetic study of a Blitz night, featuring real London firemen and
women and, briefly, 'Gentleman' Jackson himself.
57 *Christmas Under Fire*: Quentin Reynolds took the negative to America himself, *Sunday Times*, 29.12.40.
58 thoughts of fire: Davis, p. 71.
58 'hemispheric defense': Lee, p. 4.
58 Secretary of the Interior: Kimball, pp. 77, 121.
59 'garden hose': Franklin D. Roosevelt Digital Archives at http://www.fdrli-
brary.marist.edu/
59 'a great moral force': IWM: Warner, Miss P. 95/14/1
59 by his friends: Harold L. Ickes and Henry Morgenthau quoted in Doyle at
http://www.insidetheovaloffice.com/excerpt4.htm
60 bankrupt: Lee, p. 25.
61 'Finnish women': 'B' to IWM: Bowman 85/45/1. Finland's spirited defence
against Russian invasion had prompted public sympathy, private donations
and volunteers from both the London Fire Brigade and the Friends
Ambulance Unit, but no British armed support. Kendrick, p. 192.
61 the figures: the first assessment of their need that the British submitted to
FDR, on 30th December 1940, was $15 billion. Kimball, p. 131.
61 'Dominion gone wrong': Van Minnen and Sears, p. 19.
61 stiffed them: the complexities of the Geat War debts question resolved themselves for one US businessman as: 'Every time we've sat in with the family of
nations we've had our pockets picked.' *Western Mail*, 29.11.1932 at
http://garethjones.org/. On Christmas Eve 1940, the *News Chronicle* inter-
viewed an anti-Nazi German-American: 'There's nothing I want more than a
British victory and we should give all support without running the risk of
war,' he said. But, 'England defaulted on war debts. Her Empire is not
democratic. This part of the world is safe from any outside threat, and we
are enjoying a record Christmas.' In 1942 US servicemen coming to Britain
were warned not to discuss war debts (or the Royal Family) with their hosts.
Over There.
61 Congress had passed laws: Kimball, pp. 2–3, 17–22.
61 (including their President): Kimball, pp. 9–10.
61 new plant: Kimball, p. 28.
62 'Short of War': Lee, p. 54.
62 re-election: at the *New York Times*'s election party at the Savoy, every
'Alien' (British) vote went to Roosevelt. The only two Willkie votes from
'Citizens' (Americans) were slipped in after the count by Raymond Daniell
and Bob Post, 'just to make it look a little more like a contest'. Daniell, pp.
181–5.
62 Willkie: 'Wendell Wilkie [sic] spills a bib-ful' 10th October 1940 at
http://www.britishpathe.com

62 'cooling': Daniell, p. 181.

63 Christmas tree: *Daily Mail* 31.12.40.

63 gifts from the King: Matthews, p. 26.

64 King of Kent: Matthews, pp. 10–13.

64 Dean Matthews: ibid pp. 20–25; Butler, pp. 21–25.

64 'the bell tolls': Donne's Meditation XVII , *Devotions Upon Emergent Occasions* (1624).

65 H. V. Morton: Morton *H. V. Morton's London*, pp. 57–8.

65 St Paul's Watch: *Guardians of St Paul's* newsreel at http://www.british-pathe.com. Surveyor to the Fabric was architect W. Godfrey Allen.

68 'acrobatics': Matthews, p. 46.

69 Hitchcock, Williams & Co.: Walden, pp. iii–iv, 3–14, 21–4, 47. Many of the staff also joined the Home Guard.

71 Lieutenant Robert Davies: Walden, pp. 25–9; Matthews, pp. 36–7; both Davies and Wylie at http://www.gc-database.co.uk/

71 heroic gasman: he was, called A. Challess and received a George Medal, according to fellow William Press employee W. G. Howard, IWM: Misc 143 (2228) Miscellaneous 2228.

73 'reredos': Butler, p. 25. This controversial Victorian addition was considered sufficiently damaged by the end of the war to justify its removal.

73 'imprisoned Paris': Pyle, p. 38.

73 'end of the world': Matthews, p. 35.

73 destruction of St Paul's: Norman G. Brett-James in Kent *Treasures*, pp. ix–x. At the time of Dunkirk, Canadian Prime Minister Mackenzie King recalled having a premonition, while walking by St Paul's as a young man, of the Empire's passing. Diary entry 26th May 1940 at http://king.collectionscanada.ca/

73 'dark against the sunrise': Wells *Worlds*, Book 2 Chapter 8.

73 'easy complacency': Wells *Order*, Chapter 1.

74 Plan for Britain: *Picture Post* 4.1.41.

74 high taxes: Raczynski, p. 62.

74 lower-upper-middles: George Orwell so described himself at the start of *The Road to Wigan Pier*: not far from the bottom of the 'mound of wreckage left behind when the tide of Victorian prosperity receded'.

74 'I nearly fainted!': IWM: Warner, Miss P. 95/14/1.

75 'Dutch or Swedish': 'Helen' to IWM: Bowman. Bowman, Mrs W. C. 85/45/1

75 'short lull': Colville, p. 346.

75 'impulse of gratitude': Brittain, pp. 202–4; 216–20.

77 'the world's center': Sevareid, p. 165.

78 'I'll die in Stepney': IWM: Coates, R. N. 98/10/1.

78 'Yes Miss': Nixon, p. 62.

78 'multitudinous things': ibid p. 10.

79 list of the rooms: LMA:LCC/CL/CD/1/114.

79 'normalcy': Ingersoll, p. 48.

79 blackout imposed: 5.27 p.m. Sunday afternoon to 8.39 a.m. Monday morning.

79 'an enormous plain': Orwell *Air*, Chapter 3.

80 banjo: IWM: Wrigley, W. R. 76/10/1.

80 'This is a City': Perry, p. 134.

80 'involved in a conflict': 10th December 1940 at Rheinmetall-Borsig Works, Berlin.

80 'human reef': Wells *Worlds*, Book 2 Chapter 8.
80 'multitudinous littleness': Wells *Machiavelli*, Book the Third Chapter the First Part II.
81 'City of the Absent': Dickens *Uncommercial*, Chapter XXIII.
81 Billingsgate: Lee, p. 109.
82 horseshoe nails: Morton *Ghosts*, pp. 106–9.
82 peculiar square mile: see Colin Perry's October reverie in the bombed Dutch Church for instance. Perry, p. 200.
82 Mr R. H. Lott: from statements made to the Enquiry into the Guildhall Fire.
82 Remembrancer's Office: *Remembrancia*, pp. 24, 51–6, 350–57.
83 or even true: on London's Trojan origins, Elizabethan John Stow judged with Livy that antiquity's mixing of history with gods and demi-gods 'is pardonable . . . to make the first foundation of cities more honourable, more sacred, and, as it were, of greater majesty'. Stow, p. 33.
83 'Captains and the Kings': *Recessional*. Both Kipling and Wells were reacting to the hubris of the Diamond Jubilee of 1897, when cheering crowds had packed the City as troops from around the Empire marched to St Paul's.
83 Falstaff: *Henry V, The Reverie of Poor Susan, A Christmas Carol*.
84 in Washington: Burns, p. 407; Davis, p. 81.
84 Grosvenor Chater: Chater, pp. 42–5.
85 great caned 'wheelers': the autobiography of one-time warehouseman at Bradbury Greatorex, later distinguished biologist, Joseph Webb, obtained privately from Peter Webb, email: webb@math.umn.edu at http://www.math.umn.edu/~webb.
85 GPO responsibilities: most prominent GPO recruit to Station X was computer pioneer Dr Tommy Flowers.
85 Charles II: strictly speaking, Oliver Cromwell launched the GPO, but it soon transferred seamlessly from a republican to a monarchical institution.
86 Benn Brothers: Robbins, pp. 7–8, 24–5, 33. On some days, Mr Robbins mourned, 'No post was received in Bouverie House until just before lunchtime,' though by October the position was 'much improved'.
87 nearby *Punch*: Jesse, pp. 118–32.
87 'anything that protects': Pyle, pp. 39–40.
87 Mr Lillycrop: Walden, p. 9.
87 Surface shelters: Getty Images 3274882. New, stronger shells were eventually built over them. 'Trench' shelters – covered holes in the ground in parks etc. – were also vulnerable. *Daily Mirror* 31.12.40.
88 Lloyd's: *Lloyd's Under Fire* (Lloyd's, no date); City Air Raid Shelters CoL: C46/66 T.1941
88 'Reserved for Lord Halifax': Kendrick, p. 218; Ingersoll. p. 121.
88 Tilbury/Mickey's: Calder *Carry On*, pp. 36–62; Ingersoll, pp. 105–24; Getty Images 3351898.
88 'fireman bold': Calder *Carry On*, p. 20.
89 hair-raising: Firebrace, pp. 153–4.
90 maze: one new straight road, King Street, joined Thames to Guildhall. A man whose land it crossed not only made a killing on the sale, but kept enough of the land to build a house on each side. Pepys, 3rd December 1667.

92 criminal enough: there were harsh penalties for listening to the BBC. Citizens of occupied countries (like enemy aliens in Britain) were not allowed a radio at all.

93 'Chanucah lights': *Jewish Chronicle* 3.1.41.

93 E. I. Ekpenyon: Ekpenyon, pp. 9–11.

94 dark stories: the history of the street still called Old Jewry, in the heart of the City, and the expulsion of Jews in the Middle Ages, being not the least of them.

94 'one religion': Voltaire, Letter VI.

94 'scarcely believe': Trotsky, p. 149. By the end of 1940, his four decades' pursuit of orthodoxy had ended four months ago, with an ice-pick from a Stalinist assassin.

95 'game of cricket': Quennell, p. 90.

95 'annual licence': *England ganz von innen gesehen* (Berlin: Im Deutschen Verlag, 1939) at http://www.calvin.edu/academic/cas/gpa/england.htm

96 'species of freedom': Maillaud, p. 27.

96 Margaret Halsey: Halsey, pp. 244, 208. Americans, like other visitors, offered both bouquets and brickbats. Ralph Waldo Emerson had expressed an American conviction that 'England, an old and exhausted island, must one day be contented, like other parents, to be strong only in her children' and Margaret Halsey, too, felt 'the worn-outness of an old country'. But, also like Emerson, she used England to chastise her countrymen: 'A good deal in England makes the blood boil, but there is not nearly so much occasion as there is in America for blood to run cold' (p. 239). In 1940, when the President of Columbia University called for those who could not agree with the university's pro-British stance to resign, Ed Murrow told listeners it would make strange reading to British scholars, who favoured robust debate – even in wartime. Murrow *London*, p. 216.

96 'another planet': Halsey, pp. 214, 257.

96 Paris: ibid p. 257; Goebbels, pp. 148–9; Getty Images 3062195.

98 drained moat: Getty Images 3325916.

98 food was news: the *Sunday Express* also listed livestock markets closed due to an outbreak of foot-and-mouth disease.

99 Toc H: http://www.toch.org.uk/; http://http://www.wcva.dircon.co.uk/

100 Woodcraft Folk: he left the Scouts for the pacifist Kibbo Kift but split from that over its authoritarian leadership, http://www.kibbokift.org/jhbio.html; http://www.woodcraft.org.uk/

100 'vaguely disappointed': Mayhew, pp. 78–9.

101 'social accomplishment': Simmonds, pp. 11–16. Pacifists before less sympathetic tribunals might go to prison, Croall, pp. 147–73.

101 Friends Ambulance Unit: A. Tegla Davies' interesting history at http://www.ku.edu/carrie/specoll/AFS/library/4-ww2/Friends/fauTC.html

101 'cup of tea': IWM: Ridgway, R 67/347/1.

102 Arnold Spencer Leese: Leese, pp. 51–2.

105 'dead in their dining rooms': Butler, p. 36.

105 'enemy alien': the Home Secretary was distressed about the situation, F. Tennyson Jesse wrote in August, but the military authorities could not otherwise protect refugees if there was an invasion and the populace turned against them. Jesse, pp. 45–6.

106 *Arandora Star:* those lost included Colin Perry's local pet shop owner
    Azario, peaceful resident of Tooting for more than forty years. Perry, p. 13.
    One Frenchwoman claimed (on questionable evidence) Fascist sympathisers
    among the famous Italian restaurateurs lost, Henrey, pp. 13–17.
106 'helpless and lonely': Calder *Lesson*, pp. 72–5.
108 'metropolitan-cosmopolitan': ibid pp. 62–3.
108 'We just have to laugh, Winnie': 'B' to IWM: Bowman 85/45/1.
109 New Zealanders: Madeleine Henrey, who wrote under her husband's name
    of Robert, arrived back from their holiday home in Normandy in June 1940
    to find 'the Strand crowded with burly Australians and small tough Maoris
    who had just arrived'. Henrey, p. 13. May Speed found that 'some of the
    Maoris are very good looking'.
109 Station Master: IWM: Williams, H. T. 02/4/1.
109 Major C. P. Stacey: CMHQ Report No. 1 dated 31st December 1940 at
    http://www.forces.gc.ca/hr/dhh/engraph/home_e.asp
110 'long and glorious': Britain's merchant marine had provided the great major-
    ity of the ships that saw off the Spanish Armada, for instance.
110 Caribbean seamen: *Daily Mirror* 19.12.40.
111 'hypocritical': Orwell *Unicorn*, 'England Your England'.
111 devastated economies: *News Letter* No. 16 (BL) 025NWLT194101.
112 'root difference': *News Letter* No. 15 (BL) 025NWLT194012.
112 Harold Moody: http://www.movinghere.org.uk/galleries/
    histories/caribbean/settling/keys2.htm There were more radical voices than
    Dr Moody's LCP but, working from the heart of Empire, it kept readers of
    first *The Keys*, then the wartime *News Letter*, informed of a wide spectrum
    of opinion around the Empire and beyond. (For Britain's was not the only
    empire in the balance now.)
113 Egyptian doctor: 'soft-voiced' Dr Mustapha Kemal, twenty-seven, and thirty-
    two-year-old Dr Daniel Crawford (*Daily Express* 30.12.40) later received
    the George Medal.
115 funeral: Chamberlain died of cancer on 9th November.
116 'Fear of Japan': Goebbels, p. 214.
116 'gangsters': letter to Bishop Mandell Creighton, 3rd April 1887.
116 'poker game': detail on Nazi-Soviet relations, Sebag Montefiore, pp. 307–60.
    Churchill heard Molotov's joke direct from Stalin in 1942, Churchill *II*, p. 463.
117 hospital porter: Meltzer, pp. 74–110.
117 Party line: in December 1940, remaining Party members were promoting the
    People's Convention to be held in January, with its eight-point plan includ-
    ing better shelters, friendship with the Soviet Union and 'A People's Peace'.
    Life for the *Parti Communiste Français* was, naturally, more complex. On
    Bastille Day 1940, its newspaper was pleased to see 'numerous Paris workers
    striking up friendliness with German soldiers . . . though it may not please
    some bourgeois as stupid as they are mischievous.' Pryce-Jones, pp. 63–6.
    But Saturday's *Daily Express* ran an intriguing story, apparently received via
    Lisbon, of a rank-and-file rebellion at a secret meeting in Nice, in which the
    Moscow line was rejected in favour of propagandising against the Germans
    as well as the French and British plutocracy.
118 coded message: Sebag Montefiore, p. 347; 'Voices in the Wilderness' by

Valery Kalinin, *New Times* May 2005 at http://www.newtimes.ru/eng/; deciphered telegram 16443 reproduced in *Military Parade* JSC, Nov–Dec1997 at http://www.milparade.com/security/24/166.htm

119 national dailies: Londoners had a choice of eleven national daily papers, ten national Sundays and several London evening papers as well as more than a dozen local weeklies. *Newspaper*.

119 St Bride's: Morgan, pp. 139–59.

119 twelve great bells: http://www.inspirewebdesign.com/ringsof12/

120 Cockneys: literature's most famous Cockney family, the Doolittles, came from west London, for instance.

122 'pretty modest maid': Pepys, 18th August 1667.

122 Ye Old Cocke Tavern: only the frontage is original, but nearby 'Prince Henry's Room' and the Wig & Pen Club are Jacobean.

123 fogs: reports about London lack atmospheric 'pea-soupers' only because the weather was now a state secret. Kendrick, p. 191; *Sunday Express* 29.12.40. Weather systems developing from west to east gave British meteorologists a slight theoretical advantage.

123 'like coming home': Sevareid, p. 79.

123 Ernie Pyle: Pyle, pp. xi–29, 45. He wrote to wife Jerry that he had fallen in love with England and, as soon as the war was over, they must drive all round it together: 'all the stuff we've read at home about the people being wonderful doesn't half tell it. I suppose I'll be accused of being taken in by the British, but by God their spirit is just almost unbelievable. They have tough years ahead but I don't believe they will ever crack.' Miller, pp. 129–30.

126 15th September: Fitzgibbon, pp. 129–30.

127 'Fleet Street's merry andrews': Daniell, pp. 290–92.

128 'little or no censorship': ibid, pp. 107–33; Ingersoll, pp. 140–41. Censorship was heavier than US correspondents acknowledged, but for comparison with Berlin censorship, see William Shirer, who had just returned to America because it had become impossible to tell the truth. Shirer, pp. 423–4.

129 Munich: Sevareid, pp. 100–02.

129 'Juden Unerwünscht': 'Jews not wanted.' pp. 104–5. ibid. See also Anton Lang's son Freidl on Nazism in Oberammergau, *Association of Contemporary Church Historians Newsletter* No. 24 Vol. II, No. 12, December 1996 at http://www.calvin.edu/academic/cas/akz/

130 'Silver Shirts': Sevareid, pp. 180–82; the 'Shirtitis Epidemic' was investigated by the McCormack–Dickstein Committee on Un-American Activities. *Forward March!* pp. 479–82.

130 'a clique': See also numerous reports from Dodd to President Roosevelt during 1936–8 in the Franklin D. Roosevelt Digital Archives.

130 'feeling here is intense': Ranfurly, pp. 9–10.

132 'typhoid Mary's': *Harper's Magazine*, pp. 441–444.

132 speechwriters: Robert Sherwood describes the exhausting to-and-fro he and other speechwriters went through with the President before any broadcast, Sherwood, pp. 213–19.

132 'fear itself': First Inaugural Address 4th March 1933.

132 'So many Americans': Wells, *Order* Part II Chapter 7.

133 'a ferry': Daniell, p. 21.

133 'nice letters': Queen Elizabeth to Eleanor Roosevelt, 11th June 1940, King
and Queen July 1939–42 Index, Great Britain Diplomatic Files, Franklin D.
Roosevelt Digital Archives at http://www.fdrlibrary.marist.edu/
133 *The War of the Worlds*: http://www.earthstation1.com/wotw.html
134 'sane people': *Virginia Quarterly Review*, Issue 15.
134 'Mr Hitler': KTSA San Antonio, 28th October 1940 at
http://soundsunknown.nu/mercury/401028.ra
135 The Temple: http://www.innertemple.org.uk/;
http://www.middletemple.org.uk/
135 Tanfield Court: LMA: LCC/FB/WAR/4/10.
135 began to laugh: Lee, p. 109.
136 'No freeman': 'Nullus liber homo capiatur, vel imprisonetur, aut disseisiatur,
aut utlagetur, aut exuletur, aut aliquo modo destruatur, nec super cum
ibimus, nec super cum mittemus, nisi per legale judicium parium suorum vel
per legem terre.
'Nulli vendemus, nulli negabimus aut differemus rectum aut justiciam.'
136 'Our realm': http://www.templechurch.com/pages/church/
137 Verger: Morgan, p. 226.

Fugue

Unless otherwise stated, the story of the next hours is drawn from the following:

RAF documents in the National Archives: AIR16/654, AIR 22/111, AIR 41/17.
Imperial War Museum documents indicated by names in the text.
London Metropolitan Archive documents: LCC/FB/WAR/3/6 Volume 4 (Fire
Returns); LCC/FB/WAR/1/98 (8th January 1941 Conference and Report on the
City Fires at Lambeth HQ); LCC/CL/CD/2/14 (Fires Nov 40–Feb 41 with details
at LCC/FW/WAR/2–3; LCC/CL/CD/2/4 (London Region Situation Report 30th
December 1940); County Hall Fire Picket Log Book LMA:LCC/CL/CD/4/2.
St Paul's Cathedral Library files and St Paul's Watch Boxes CF 2–5 and CF 17 held
at the Manuscripts Section, Guildhall Library.
Corporation of London Records Office: statements made to the Enquiry into the
Guildhall Fire; CD 1.2 B47 671B Control Messages & ARP office; Police Box 2.8.
St Bartholomew's Hospital archives: HA 16/50; HA 16/53–7; *St Bart's Hospital
Journal* Vol. II; *League News* 1939–44.
Hoare's Bank Company Diary, Hoare's Bank, Fleet Street.
Southwark Local History Library: P.940.544.SOU *The Story of Reporting Post
12*; bound volume of *London's Awake*; Southwark Civil Defence Second World
War Incident Reports 5676–84.
Major C. P. Stacey's CMHQ Report No. 1 downloadable at http://www.forces.
gc.ca/hr/dhh/engraph/home_e.asp
Newspaper reports of 30th and 31st December 1940 from the *Daily Herald, Daily
Mail, Daily Express, Daily Mirror, News Chronicle, The Times* and *Manchester
Guardian.*
Published eyewitness accounts attributed to author and written by those present,
as detailed in bibliography: Ritchie Calder *Carry On* and *Lesson*; Aylmer
Firebrace; Philip Henderson in *Fire and Water* (Ingham ed.); The Very Rev. W. R.
Matthews; Ernie Pyle; H. A. Walden; Ron Weir; William L. White.

Other published eyewitness accounts from: Beaman; Brown; Calder *People's;* Darwin; Demarne *Girls;* Demarne *London; Front Line;* Fitzgibbon; Graves *Transport;* Graves *Women;* Hay; Henrey; Kent *Treasures; Lloyd's Under Fire;* Ramsey; Robbins; Sansom; Townsend; Wallington.

Pictorial reference from the Getty Images, British Pathé and Collage websites; Cross & Tibbs collection, Guildhall; and London Fire Brigade Film Unit record LFB 50.

141 Ad Astral House: for a graphic account of its own earlier 'direct hit', http://london.allinfo-about.com/features/joanneblitz.html

142 experimental: Fitzgibbon, pp. 113–15.

142 Peter Stahl: Stahl, pp. 90–94, 98, 105.

143 'Verdun': Goebbels, p. 130.

145 Fighter Command: Lee, pp. 30–31; 42. Due to the practicalities of manufacturing British *matériel* in the US, and in hope of eventual material support from America, the crown jewels of Britain's defence secrets were transferred across the Atlantic from summer 1940, with patent and royalty issues deferred to later discussion (Lee, pp. 157–8; Kimball, pp. 71–2). In September, a British Scientific and Technical Mission had also arrived to exchange information, though a member of the US team told the US Secretary of War that America was getting 'infinitely more' than it could give. Kimball cites as an example of US inexperience the official who arrived at the dockside with a briefcase for the blueprints of Rolls-Royce's Merlin engine – and was directed to two tons of crates in the warship's hold, Kimball, pp. 71–2.

145 Dowding: Dowding's removal as Head of Fighter Command after the Battle of Britain remains one of Churchill's most controversial military decisions.

146 'the Ball Room': quoted in IWM: Ashbee 97/34/1.

147 Spitfires: http://www.raf.mod.uk/history/spit2.html

147 first five stations: Winston Churchill quoted at http://www.spartacus.schoolnet.co.uk/2WWradar.htm

149 15th September: Churchill *II*, pp. 273–6.

150 'most of the girls': Ingersoll, pp. 70–73. The Bentley Priory WAAFs' magazine celebrated this 'double-life':

> Lovely languid debutante going to the Grosvenor
> Smug to the chaperones, seductive to the males;
> With diamonds for shoulder-straps, tiara and ear-rings,
> Blue lids, bare back and bright red nails.
>
> Staid and simple WAAF coming out of the hostel,
> Enveloped in the uniform she couldn't well refuse;
> With grey stockings, gas-mask, beret and comforter,
> Blue shirt, raincoat, and big black shoes.

150 Polish Ambassador: Raczynski, pp. 61–2.

150 'Germany bearing down': Pyle, p. 68.

151 William L. White: Smith; Kimball, p.27n.

152 'Louisiana Purchase': US, Department of State, Publication 1983, *Peace and War: United States Foreign Policy, 1931–1941* (US, Government Printing Office, 1943), pp. 564–7 at

http://www.mtholyoke.edu/acad/intrel/WorldWar2/fdr22.htm

152 one of the 171: Kimball, p. 127.

152 'typical Laval': Namikas. William Allen White resigned from the 'White' Committee on New Year's Day, 1941.

154 deeply disturbing: Churchill II, pp. 312–13.

155 'X-Verfahren': the definitive account of the operation of Kampfgruppe 100 is Kenneth Wakefield's *The First Pathfinders,* including technical details of tonight's attack, p. 215. See also Churchill *II*, pp. 312–19.

157 'afterglow': ibid p. 122.

157 Airborne Interception: while US journalists were alive to the logic of military censorship (Ingersoll, pp. 137–42), Britain's secrets did not weigh heavily with some in neutral Washington. A few days after tonight's raid, General Lee was embarrassed to find that US-based broadcaster Raymond Gram Swing had described AI in a broadcast 'more or less', Lee, p. 203.

158 Uncle Mac: Derek McCulloch. Short sound sample at, http://www.wireless-works.co.uk/info/whoswhoM.htm.

158 *Kindertransport*: http://www.kindertransport.org/

158 potent symbol: LMA: LLC/EO/WAR/2/46

159 'Serious problems': Goebbels, pp. 125–31.

159 babies and toddlers: 'Reassessing the Beginning of the "Euthanasia" Programme' by Ulf Schmidt, *German History*, 17 (1999), No. 4.

161 doughty ladies: something of the remarkable contribution of the Women's Voluntary Service (later Women's Royal Voluntary Service) to the Blitz story is detailed in Beaman, and Graves *Women.*

161 Lord Rothschild: Calder *People's*, p. 499.

161 'sound notions': Oswell.

162 William Brown: in *William Does His Bit* (George Newnes, April 1941) William is sent 'dizzy with rapture' when a fireman addresses him as 'mate' and lets him help clean a trailer pump until sent about his business by an officious Section Officer. '"Well," said William with rising indignation. "I like that. I jolly well like *that.* The street's not his, is it? The whole place isn't his, is it? Who does he think he is? The Lord Mayor of London or Hitler or what?" His creator Richmal Crompton, a member of the Women's Auxiliary Fire Service, was not the only children's favourite on duty in the London Blitz. Noel Streatfeild (*Ballet Shoes*) was both an air raid warden in Mayfair and buzzed around Deptford on a motorbike organising the WVS Mobile Canteen Service.

162 valiant, kindly women: Nixon, pp. 69–71.

163 Conrad Veidt: David K. Bowman for the Conrad Veidt Society at http://members.aol.com/CVSociety/veidtmaster.html. Veidt, of course, went on to play the Nazi Major Strasse in *Casablanca.*

163 'The kids missed us': Demarne, p. 47.

164 F. Tennyson Jesse: Jesse, pp. 30, 67, 369.

164 'police courts': Renier, p. 207. Where, F. Tennyson Jesse informed readers of *The Times* in 1939, they would find: 'Stunted, misshapen creatures, only capable of understanding the very simplest language and incapable of thought . . . when accused and witnesses are of this sub-human sort, it is as though a flat stone in the garden had been raised and pale, wriggling things,

that had never seen the light exposed.' Livesey, p. 28.

165 'mate': London, Chapter 1; Orwell *Down*, Chapter 24.

165 Andrew Butler: Butler, pp. 107–8.

165 'Nanny': Maurice Richardson, *Fire and Water*, pp. 48–51.

166 'dear nan': Weir R. A. 88/49/1.

167 5.20: Ramsey, p. 366.

167 Earlier today: Foreman, p. 123. At 3.12 p.m. a single plane had dive-bombed the Rolls–Royce works at Crewe, dropping two high explosive bombs; one on the No. 16 Erecting Shop and the other near a Balloon Site on open ground, Daily Resume for 30th December 1940, NAPRO: AIR22/111.1. See also Appendix A.

167 calls made few: the Hurricanes of 87 Squadron and Defiants of 141 Squadron were deployed tonight, Foreman, p. 123.

168 London bus: Ingersoll, pp. 61–2. Today's *Sunday Express* reported yet another bus blackout fatality.

168 'Over forty ': Hennessy *Whitehall*, p. 95.

169 Guildhall: Baddeley, pp. 29–33.

169 City of London Police: one element of City independence was its own police force, independent of the Metropolitan force.

169 'The borough' : Ekpenyon, pp. 5–6.

169 'condemnéd English': *Henry V* Act IV. Though Cockney scepticism about their King – 'I believe, as cold a night as 'tis, he could wish himself in Thames up to the neck; and so I would he were, and I by him, at all adventures, so we were quit here' – and their own waverings – 'Would I were in an alehouse in London! I would give all my fame for a pot of ale and safety' – rather lost their edge when Thames and pub were part of the battlefield too.

170 Post 12: Southwark: P.940.544.SOU.

171 Anna Freud: Ingersoll, pp. 143–51.

172 'Tea and Telling about it': *Front Line*, p. 70.

173 'Dear Professor Burn': IWM: Misc 147 (2305) Misc 2305.

174 Stainer Street: Joe French quoted in Davis, Rib and Schweitzer, p. 11.

174 Finsbury: Nixon, pp. 12–72 (Post 2); 74–94 (Post 13).

176 'Go anywhere': Farson, p. 62.

176 'the effing 'orse': Nixon, p. 72. This lady, buried up to the neck at a previous incident (p. 18), kept up a stream of invective at her rescuers that relieved the tension, actress Barbara thought, like the Porter in *Macbeth*.

177 'Anging Round Pubs': IWM: Broadway, Mrs H. 95/13/1.

177 'man of colour': Ekpenyon, p. 8.

178 unlocking: shelters were locked to prevent people camping out in them. Colin Perry witnessed the 'very tragic' sight of a childlike old man, who was frightened of sirens and went out in the dark with a torch to search for Germans whenever they started, pleading for a shelter to be unlocked while his wife tried to persuade him to wait for the '*sireens*'. It was, recorded Colin, 'very tragic'. Perry, pp. 104–5.

179 'time of Munich': Matthews, p. 19.

180 'amber below': Butler, p. 21 and letters.

181 cabbies: many others had joined the AFS along with their cabs.

182 twenty-two-year-old: Bosanquet, Miss N. 81/33/1. For some adventures of

female ambulance drivers, YMCA tea car staff and 'Salvation Army lasses' on duty tonight, see *Daily Mail* 31.12.40.

182 acting in concert: this wartime experience of integration of public, private and charitable institutions had a profound effect on the National Health Service founded in 1948.

183 'the worst journey': AFS veteran Thomas Carter, in conversation with the author.

186 barrage balloons: Wedemeyer, Deasy, Daniel and Scott, p. 70. At full height they were 'three Empire State Building lengths' up (Ingersoll, p. 39) so a trailing cable was a real hazard. 'This morning, poor old C. M. just got indoors when a wire from a Balloon pulled their chimney off. A man arrived and asked to go through to see about it, she said she could not let him in, she was alone, then eight men arrived with ladders etc, so she felt she could not hold out against eight men so she let them through': IWM: Griffiths, Mrs M. L. C. 86/5/1.

186 anti-aircraft fire: 'B' to IWM: Winnie Bowman: /85/45/1: 'God it's a racket, and God, do we love it, they flash and bang and crack and rumble and it's the most wonderful music I know, they make enough noise to wake Joe in Moscow and they positively lull one to sleep.' Fitzgibbon, pp. 113–15

190 multinational team: 1995 interview with Norman Heatly at http://www.sci-encewatch.com/interviews/norman_heatly.htm

191 about a quarter: levels obviously varied over time but a survey in November found only 9 per cent in the LCC area spent the night in any kind of public shelter, 27 per cent in private shelters and 64 per cent in their own beds or on duty. For outer London, percentages were 4, 26 and 70. Mackay, p. 71.

191 'candles would flicker': IWM: Wareham, C. P. 96/31/1. Tonight, young Wareham and fellow-members of the 'Pudden Slingers Quartet' saved the firm when an incendiary crashed through the glass roof of the Bible department.

193 rain shower: Kent, p. 13.

193 autumn leaves: Brown, p. 88.

193 coal-scuttles: the Dean's full account of tonight, Matthews, pp. 44–8.

194 Malcolm Clark: Calder *Carry On*, pp. 19–20. ARP booklet Handbook No 9 LMA: LCC/CL/CD/3/57 gives exhaustive detail on IBs and how to tackle them, as well as rescuing people from burning buildings.

196 'Rather a close one': Mayhew p. 138.

196 St Bride's: hero of the hour was night porter Charles McCarthy, *Daily Mail* 31.12.40 *inter alia*.

197 wedding cakes: local legend credits local baker Thomas Rich with the first tiered 'bride's cake'.

199 Jean Savory: Demarne *Girls*, pp. 79–82; Obituary, *Daily Telegraph* 2.8.2000. Sir Aylmer Firebrace wrote a letter of praise for WAFS to London's Senior Regional Commissioner for Civil Defence Ernest Gowers 15th November 1940 LCC/FB/WAR/LFR/1/10.

200 Observation Posts: Wedemeyer, Deasy, Daniel and Scott, pp. 67–8.

200 'damn near': Miller, p. 130.

207 Major Jackson: *Daily Mail* 31.12.40.

207 Lord Mayor: *Daily Express* 31.12.40.

210 'so-and-sos': IWM: Misc 180 (2706) Miscellaneous 2706.

210 de-gaussing: Hartcup, pp. 35–50. Canadian Charles Goodeve's contribution to this early victory in the 'Wizard War' is discussed at http://www.naval-museum.mb.ca/people/g/goodeve.htm

211 St Pancras: Newbery, C. A. 97/28/1.

213 morphine: *Front Line*, p. 42. One official picture shows a casualty with M 1/4 marked in thick marker pencil on her forehead, a practical message to her eventual destination of dosage already given, Klemmer, pp. 116–17.

213 Trapped survivors: the *Sunday Times* today told of a fourteen-year-old girl in Friday's raid who, with her dead mother beside her and her face near the fire still burning in the grate, directed the rescue workers in their work.

213 official record: Commonwealth War Graves Commission at www.cwgc.org.

215 Moor Lane: the nearby *Jewish Chronicle* building was totally destroyed though, thanks to the maintenance of a parallel office in Queen Victoria Street, the issue in preparation came out on Friday as planned.

216 more than thirty employees: This morning's *Sunday Express* had suggested that this might soon be extended as 'Experience has shown . . . that these premises are often endangered by fires starting in unattended places.'

216 St Stephen's: Daniell, A. E. pp. 285–6.

218 three dollars a day: there were at that point four US dollars to the pound: Miller, p. 129.

218 English accent: http://www.emporia.com/waw/williamlwhite.html

221 Leonard Keyworth VC: http://www.queensroyalsurreys.org.uk/vc/vc06.html

223 withdraw his men: Firebrace, pp. 53–4, 173–83.

226 Noel Mander: transcript of comments by Noel Mander, Winston Churchill Memorial and Library at Westminster College, Fulton, Missouri.

226 firestorm: though obviously not as intensive or sustained as the firestorms later visited on German cities, the mechanics, and the intention, were the same.

230 chandelier flare: Dean Matthews describes their 'weird and terrible loveliness'. In different colours. 'orange and red, perhaps', they presented, 'A constellation of brilliant lights which very slowly fall together, illuminating the whole sky and diffusing vivid and unearthly radiance on the building beneath . . . It may be supposed that we had other emotions than those of pure aesthetic enjoyment, but I believe that few of us were quite unmoved by their beauty. (Matthews, p. 38). In *The Heat of the Day*, Elizabeth Bowen writes of one making 'the street like a mirrored drawing-room'.

232 chased away: the widespread assumption at the time that the RAF night fighters had played a great part in ending the raid early was swiftly rebutted by the Ministry of Information, which correctly credited the weather in later news reports.

232 Friday night's raid: Townsend, pp. 140–42; p. 134 for feelings of impotence during raids on London.

233 'burning history': Demarne *Girls*, p. 79.

233 nothing like it since 1666: the regional record showed six conflagrations needing more than 100 pumps apiece, and twenty-eight fires needing more than thirty pumps. Some 300 pumps were sent in from surrounding regions to assist London's nigh-on 2,000, Firebrace, p. 187.

233 'saw the fire grow': Kent, p. 13.

233 All Hallows Barking: Daniell *Churches*, pp. 15–27.

234 'When wasteful war': Shakespeare Sonnet 55.

234 scorch-marks: Mee, p. 268; Hill, p. 99.

234 darkened church: St Andrew Undershaft survived both the Great Fire and Blitz intact (but lost its seventeenth-century stained glass to an IRA bomb in 1992).

235 braving the flames: *News Chronicle* 31.12.40.

236 'sown the wind': Probert, *Henry Bomber Harris His Life and Times* (Pennsylvania: Greenhill Books & Stackpole Books, 2001) p. 109.

237 ARP boys: who duly noted the UXB, LMA: LCC/CL/CD/2/4.

239 'That was the Prime Minister': Demarne *Girls*, pp. 82–3.

239 'grateful': Matthews, p. 46.

239 'bugbear': Firebrace, p. 178.

240 cracking skulls: Fitzgibbon, p. 206.

240 Half a million: Firebrace, p. 156.

240 water officer: LCC/FB/STA/2/11.

241 Whitbread's: Demarne, pp. 59–60.

241 paddling pools: Firebrace, p. 156.

243 'spring' tide: the low water at three minutes to nine that evening was 0.48m above Chart Datum – that is, only about eighteen inches above the lowest level ever to be expected in normal circumstances. By comparison, low water at London Bridge for December 2005 ranges from 0.8m to 1.8m above CD: (Port of London Authority Hydrographic Service).

244 'some could have been saved': Matthews, p. 47.

245 around a hundred firewatchers: altogether, the crypt gave 'sanctuary' to three hundred tonight, *News Chronicle* 31.12.40.

245 Gordon Papps: Johnson, pp. 138–40, 152.

245 funeral carriage: since moved, but viewable in situ at http://viewfinder.english-heritage.org.uk (reference no: CC97/01637)

246 Leonard Rosoman: conversation with the author April 2005; Sidney Holder, Commonwealth War Graves Commission; another team, *Front Line*, p. 33. Later, a Sub-officer Welsh, ankle-deep in water and still fighting fires after eighteen hours, told a reporter 'one has gone'. He did not know who, wrote the *Daily Express* man: 'There was no time for a roll call. Only the crash of masonry, a shower of sparks, and the thought that there had stood a fireman.'

262 *Ghost on the Stair*: http://www.shadowsradio.com/chronicles.htm. ('Blue Coal' really was blue – anthracite dyed as a marketing technique.)

262 at *The Times*: the famous Letters Page, meanwhile, was set to include a protest from Vera Brittain, Sybil Thorndike and others at the imprisonment of prominent Indian women campaigners; a complaint about the introduction into English of the word 'hospitalize'; and a discussion of whether the Elgin Marbles should be returned to Greece.

263 generous: Klemmer, pp. 165–6. Today's *Sunday Times* had reported that Bundles for Britain sent 100,00 complete knitted outfits and 1,000 crates of clothing and blankets during 1940, with nearly £25,000 in drugs and surgical equipment coming from the Medical and Surgical Supply Committee of America.

263 dollar and gold reserves: sterling payments were consistently rejected by the US administration; they were seen as an investment in Britain's future prospects, which were poor, Kimball, p. 74. Churchill wrote that Britain had entered the war with $4.5 billion in dollars, gold or investments that could be turned into dollars and by the end of 1940 a further $2 billion had been generated by exports; Britain had paid over $4.5 billion in cash for goods received or ordered and needed to place orders well in excess of $2 billion. Churchill *II*, pp. 441–3. Britain's urgent need to husband its dollars and to earn more did not register at even the highest levels of the US administration: the export of whisky and restrictions on imports of American tobacco and fruit became bones of contention. Kimball, pp. 22–3, 31–3.

263 Captain Daw (or Dawe): though mentioned in several records, I have been unable, to date, to discover his exact role – possibly the Hallkeeper.

264 'sprig of holly': Fitzgibbon, p. 212

265 he didn't believe it: Johnson, p. 170.

266 second sortie: ibid, p. 182.

267 light of the burning city: Yeo, p. 78.

271 First Aid Post: CoL: War 1939–1945 CD2.1 (Pt 1).

276 Post 13: Nixon, p. 75.

276 Edward Morgan: information compiled by Mike Pinchen at http://www.eustonfirestation.btinternet.co.uk/EustonFireStation.com.Station History.htm

278 Wordsworth's plane tree: though much of Cheapside was devastated tonight, and St Mary-le-Bow was burnt out in a later raid, the tree miraculously survived – and survives still at time of writing – on the corner of Wood Street and Cheapside.

278 E. T. Wistow and E. T. Smith: British Empire Medal citations at http://www.home-guard.org.uk/bemmmain.html

281 a slight smile: Davis, p. 81.

281 Scarlett O'Hara: *Sunday Express* 29.12.40. Ashley Wilkes (Leslie Howard) was of course already in London, making morale-boosting films.

282 'Hitler knows': House of Commons 18th June 1940.

282 'On National Defense': http://www.fdrlibrary.marist.edu/052640.html

282 desperately sad: General Ismay, quoted in Gilbert *Papers*, p. 160.

282 second term: it was highly irregular for a President to serve more than two terms. A different winner in November, from either party, could have signalled a three-month 'lame duck' period before the inaguration of the new President early in 1941.

282 'every American home': Kennedy to FDR 3.1.39, Secretary's File, Great Britain. Franklin D. Roosevelt Digital Archives at http://www.fdrlibrary.marist.edu/.

283 H. L. Keenleyside: Mackenzie King's diary entries 24th–26th May 1940 at http://king.collectionscanada.ca/

283 just eighteenth: *Peace and War: United States Foreign Policy 1931–1941* (Washington: U. S. Government Printing Office, 1943), p. 56 at http://www.ibiblio.org/hyperwar/Dip/PaW/. On 26th November Secretary of State Cordell Hull told the National Press Club: 'There can be nothing more dangerous for our nation than for the US to assume that the avalanche of

conquest could under no circumstances reach any vital point of this hemisphere . . . should the would-be conquerors gain control of their continents, they would next concentrate on perfecting their control of the seas, of the air over the seas, and of the world's economy . . . ultimately we might find ourselves compelled to fight on our own soil, under our own skies, in defence of our independence and our very lives.' *Keesing's*, p. 4355.

284 already been waiting: Churchill *II*, pp. 35–6. The destroyers were the subject of his first message to the President as Prime Minister on 15th May and many subsequent ones (detailed through that volume of his war memoirs). The speech of 4th June was, wrote Churchill to Lord Lothian, for the wider world, while privately it was important to 'discourage any complacent assumption on United States' part that they will pick up the *débris* of the British Empire by their present policy', ibid p. 326. Was the final bargain a hard one? 'Shrewdly,' writes American historian Warren F. Kimball, 'Roosevelt appealed to the Yankee businessman and the desire to best the English, which lay just beneath the surface in every American', Kimball *Unsordid*, pp. 67–71. And while Winston Churchill averred in 1949: 'The gratitude of the British nation is due to the noble President and his great officers and high advisers for never, even in the advent of the Third Term Presidential Election, losing their confidence in our fortunes or our will', Churchill *II*, p. 215, a rather more embittered Anthony Eden, writing in 1965, claimed: 'At one time the suggestion was put forward in Washington that the entire British West Indies should be handed over for the cancellation of our war debts. I thought this less than friendly bargaining.' Quoted on http://www.spartacus.schoolnet.co.uk/2WWlendlease.htm

284 'less than the requisite': Wheeler-Bennett *George VI* pp. 513–15. The idea that the price of US assistance might be sovereignty over the islands was currently disturbing the King: 'I am the custodian of my subjects.' In 1939 FDR had told him – or at least George VI believed he had told him – that the US would use any bases in British territory to protect convoys. 'If he saw a U boat he would sink her at once & await the consequences,' he informed the Cabinet in London after they met privately during the Royal visit that summer, adding: 'If London was bombed USA would come in. Offensive air warfare was better than defensive & he hoped we should do the same on Berlin.' However, since Roosevelt initiated this conversation while the Canadian Premier Mackenzie King who accompanied the King was taking a nap, there were no other witnesses to this remarkable exchange, ibid, pp. 391–2.

285 'aren't much good': Michael Eden, quoted Gilbert *Papers*, p. 1199.

285 personal and secret: Kimball *Roosevelt* pp. 1296–7, 1308, 1311–12.

285 British Embassy: ibid pp. 118–19, 126–7.

286 'We who are about to die': Merriman had forwarded a letter in which historian G. M. Trevelyan said the British were preparing to 'die in the last ditch, at worst'. Merriman to FDR 10th February 1939; Great Britain Index, Secretary's Files, Franklin D. Roosevelt Digital Archives at http://www.fdrlibrary.marist.edu/; Cannadine, pp. 186–201. For a background to American Anglophobia in the 1930s see John E. Moser's talk on 'The Special Relationship' at http://personal.ashland.edu/~jmoser1/anglophobia.html. For prejudice in the other direction, Margaret Halsey wrote, with a barb that

probably few in England even recognised at the time: 'the people we meet as equals have been trained from childhood to patronise Americans as Americans are trained from childhood to clean their teeth and they do it just as automatically', Halsey, p. 199. Similar sentiments inform Ogden Nash's poem (also published 1938) *England Expects* ('Let us pause to consider the English . . . ') and are tackled in Alice Duer Miller's long, pro-British poem of 1940, *The White Cliffs*.

286 'Britain's broke': Davis, p. 63; Kimball, pp. 96–99.

286 He wasn't sure: the President believed that Britain had $9 billion assets to sell off in the western hemisphere before it needed aid – a figure closer to British and Empire resources worldwide, much of which could not be liquidated. Kimball *Unsordid*, p. 101.

287 'Hitlerism is a tragedy': *Keesing's* p. 4377; Kimball, p. 115.

287 Caribbean cruise: the two-week voyage on the USS *Tuscaloosa* was officially to inspect some of the new British Caribbean bases, but also took in the problematic Vichy French Martinique and the US base at Guantanamo Bay to buy Cuban cigars. For discussion of the motive for this sudden 'vacation' and what transpired, both on board and back in Washington, during this fortnight, see Kimball *Unsordid*, pp. 104–20.

287 'candour and confidence': Churchill *II*, pp. 444–450.

288 'if Britain wins': Navy Department 'Plan Dog' Index, Safe Files, Franklin D. Roosevelt Digital Archives at http://www.fdrlibrary.marist.edu/

Chorale

294 As any fire chief: Firebrace, pp. 173–4.

294 City area consumed: in total it was even greater, though not all confined to the City. 'Half a square mile, from Moorgate to Aldersgate Street and Old Street to Cannon Street' was 'perhaps the largest area of continuous air raid desolation in all Britain' and there were other large patches burnt out, including a quarter of a square mile in the Minories. *Front Line*, pp. 20, 32.

296 rail termini: Fitzgibbon, p. 214.

296 frustration: 'd) Traffic problems – Pedestrian and vehicular traffic attempting to enter and leave the City in the early hours of the morning of 30th December, caused damage to hose and other equipment and greatly hampered the operations of the Brigade.' Conference at LFB Lambeth HQ, LMA: LCC/FB/WAR/1/98.

297 'stopped at all stations': IWM: Woodcock, S. M. S. 87/36/1.

297 get in to work: Dorothy Barton, arriving at her office to find it more or less intact in a street full of rubble, was helping her boss clear up when a policeman rushed in to warn of an unexploded bomb in the backyard. 'Pausing only to grab my handbag *and the ledgers I was responsible for* [my italics], I made my way to the end of the street again, where all the staff gathered with various bits of office equipment in their arms' before they made their way to another firm that had offered them space in their building. *Londoners Remember*, pp. 20–21.

297 One young lad: IWM: Wrigley, W. R. 76/10/1. It was he who had spent his quiet Sunday practising the banjo before the bombing started.

297 Dr Johnson's house: Robbins, p. 35 (pictured opp. p. 32).

297 St Bride's: Morgan, pp. 225–47. Getty Images 3279839, 3316758, 3317641.

298 All Hallows: Hill, p. 99.

298 Sept. 11th: the CTO bombing in the first week of the Blitz.

300 daylight explosions: not all were demolition squads, a delayed action bomb went off in New North Rd, Islington just after ten o'clock.

300 'aliens': *Front Line*, p. 56.

300 'ought to': Calder *Carry On*, pp. ix–xiii.

302 'dull winter daylight': White, pp. 226–9. Though it was a cold day, *The Times* reported unseasonal warm breezes as one passed areas still on fire. Getty Images 3070055, 3071431, 3269580, 3274900, 3296839, 3316760–3316765, 3317644–3317646, 3317651, 3317644, 3336136, 3353288, 3359647, 3422502, 50455782, 52018456, 3312283.

302 Hitchcock, Williams: Walden, pp. 40–44. The spirit of post-raid indomitability was captured in a David Langdon cartoon in which two formally dressed chaps sit in a shattered showroom that might have seemed very familiar to Mr Walden. 'I'd like you to think up something catchy for the window,' one says to the other, 'like "Hitlers may come and Hitlers may go, but Murdoch and Wimpleby were established in 1783 . . . "' Langdon, p. 23. By the end of 1941, it was possible for *Punch* to carry a cartoon in which one person, standing in the wasteland round the Cathedral, assures a friend: 'Actually this is now very much as Wren INTENDED us to see St Paul's.' Sillince, p. 91. And that imp of odd Englishness W. Heath Robinson filled the cover of his book *How To Build a New World* with his trademark little men, straightening spires and readjusting cupolas on a familiar skyline.

302 'Wine Land': *Wine & Spirit Trade Record* 16.1.41.

305 'heart and nerve center': *New York Times 31.12.40,* quoted in Smith.

305 Gog and Magog: Lee, p. 193.

305 smouldering among the bookshelves: CoL: account by John Bromley of damage on 29th December 1940.

305 Zaehnsdorf: Henrey, pp. 56–9. Aylmer Firebrace was wearily familiar with property owners' ungrateful complaints that water often did more damage than fire, Firebrace, p. 57.

305 strongroom: this sporadic rekindling of fires, and repeated rescue of precious books (and library catalogues) at the Guildhall gives a realistic picture of the aftermath of a great fire. In 1666, after the Fire was over, the booksellers of Paul's Churchyard went to collect their stock and valuables from the security of St Faith's Chapel in the crypt of St Paul's. As the doors were opened, the superheated papers burst into flames and a precious record of an age of literary history was lost utterly.

306 Stanley Champion: Stanley was told to stay home for a few days then sacked along with many other members of staff, whereupon he joined the army.

306 Jean Savory: Demarne *Girls*, p. 86.

307 'enormously cheered': IWM: Warner, Miss P. 95/14/1.

309 'When we've beaten 'em': The King, on his first holiday of the war at Sandringham, sent a personal message of sympathy to the Lord Mayor, *Daily Mirror* 31.12.40.

310 Incident 43A: Southwark: Incident Reports 5676–84.

310 in the region of 200 people: compared to around 500 in Manchester's nights
of pre-Christmas bombings, *News Chronicle* 31.12.40.

311 Snow was on the way: a number of diarists and letter-writers greeted the
New Year with frozen pipes.

313 'We are deeply grateful': though dated Tuesday, the text of the message
refers to Sunday as yesterday, strongly suggesting completion in the early
hours. Time difference meant that cables dispatched by 2 a.m. could reach
the White House before the President retired and, in theory, a reply could be
back by the time the Prime Minister woke, Churchill *II*, p. 35; Gilbert
Papers, pp. 1308–14; Kimball *Roosevelt*, pp. 117–27.

314 'Remember, Mr President': Warren Kimball argues that FDR's press confer-
ence and speech 'left absolutely no doubt in anyone's mind about how far
Roosevelt would go in order to save Great Britain', Kimball, pp. 128–9.
Most of 1940 Fleet Street would have agreed but Whitehall was another
matter. For the subsequent development, passing and operation of the Lend-
Lease (and later Reverse Lend-Lease) that put flesh on the bones of FDR's
pronouncements, Kimball's *The Most Unsordid Act* is key. Its title follows
Churchill in slightly misquoting his own eulogy on the death of Roosevelt:
'the most unselfish and unsordid financial act of any country in all history'
becomes, in *Their Finest Hour*, 'the most unsordid act in the history of any
nation'. The phrase first appeared in Churchill's Mansion House speech of
1941: 'about £3,000,000,000 was dedicated to the cause of world freedom,
without – mark this, because it is unique – without the setting up of any
account in money. Never again let us hear the taunt that money is the ruling
power in the hearts and thoughts of the American democracy. The Lease-
Lend Bill must be regarded without question as the most unsordid act in the
whole of recorded history.' (The abrupt cessation of Lend-Lease, and final
settlement at the war's end, brought less rosy assessments from some,
Skidelsky, pp. 818–820.) For the current status of Britain's War Debts to the
United States, see Ruth Kelly's Written Answers to Parliamentary Questions
28th February 2002 Hansard Volume 380 Column 1440–1 and 14th
October 2003 Hansard Volume 411 Column 21W at http://www.publica-
tions.parliament.uk/pa/cm/cmhansrd.htm.

315 'dense and baffling': Churchill *II*, p. 142.

315 removed the paragraph: Gilbert, *Winston VI*, p. 963.

315 hundred to one: Kimball *Unsordid*, p. 129. (Though Gallup found a ratio of
nearer three to one in favour among the three-quarters of respondents who
had heard or read the speech.)

316 'Barbarossa': Churchill *II*, pp. 466–8.

317: God and man: 'St Paul's ARP workers clung jealously to their anonymity,'
reported a *News Chronicle* reporter who was told: 'They all deserve equal
praise . . . no one man can be singled out.'

317 'slacking': Fitzgibbon, p. 218; *Daily Mirror* 31.12.40.

317 Chapter House: let out to another organisation and not guarded by St Paul's
Watch.

319 Quaglino's: renamed after the departure in 1940 of the Italian Quaglino
Brothers, whose establishment had been a byword for glamour when patron-
ised by the Prince of Wales and Mrs Simpson.

323 quarter to ten: John MacSween's report that day for the Canadian Press.

323 burying its war leader: Churchill had been party to the arrangements for his funeral, 'Operation Hopenot', the first state funeral for a commoner since Wellington. Getty Images 3401237, 50544053, 3096780, 3304651.

323 'It All Depends On Me': this phrase was popularised in a letter to *The Times* from the Archbishop of Canterbury in May 1940; the Dean coined the addition, Matthews, p. 32.

324 country churchyard: With his parents at Bladon, near Blenheim Palace.

324 the 'what ifs': as in his alternate Gettysburg in *If it had Happened Otherwise* ed. J. C. Squire (Longmans Green, 1931).

324 unlikely unison: regarding the still-live issue of who, out of the British Empire, Soviet Union and United States of America, really 'won' the War, it is perhaps enough to observe that, without the contributions of all three, the answer would undoubtedly have been Hitler.

325 'jaw-jaw': reported *New York Times* 27.6.54.

325 Bank Tube: Getty Images 2669164.

325 Bullivant's Wharf: IWM: Grey, H. F. 81/10/1.

325 Finsbury's Post 2: Nixon, pp. 142–50.

325 Ernie Pyle: Miller, pp. 387–9. Ernie's friend Ben Robertson, from that first night in the Savoy, was also killed, in a plane crash in Lisbon. Miller, p. 129n.

325 'the lion heart': Westminster Hall, 30th November 1954.

326 in his bath: Hennessy *Never*, p. 56. It was entirely characteristic that this greatest pronouncement should follow hard upon one of his most foolish, in which he told the electorate that any socialist government 'would have to fall back on some form of Gestapo'. To which the electorate had given their answer, ibid p. 82.

326 putting a new face on the City: *Reconstruction,* pp. I–III.

326 May Speed: Gerald G. Swan published at least six Florence Speed novels between 1943 and 1948: *Blossoming Flowers, Butterfly Shoes, Cinderella's Day Out, Exquisite Assignment, Girl Proposes* and *The Love Pedlar.*

327 'never see so much': *King Lear* Act V.

Index

29th December raid 187, 227–8, 244–5, 266–7
aftermath 302, 317
company shelter at 87
and St Paul's bomb 71–2
Hitler, Adolf 10, 19, 20, 33, 132, 134, 325
on America 116
as antidote to Communism 21, 130–1
and the Berghof 19
and the Blitz 23–26, 29, 33, 143
and the British 19–20, 25–6, 28–9, 147, 282, 287, 308
and child evacuation 159
and Italy 22–3, 315
on Japan 116
rise to power 20–22
and Soviet Union 117–18, 315–16
on the war 80
Hoare, Bertram 255–6
Hoare's Bank 14, 122, 151, 192, 241, 255–6
Holder, Sidney 256
Home Guard 11, 13–14, 166, 213, 278–9, 297
Horn, Mary (Dyson House) 213
horses 85, 219, 222, 230, 238, 293, 316
hospitals 182–3
  see also individual hospitals by name
Howard (Jackson Brothers)
  29th December raid 187, 194–5, 197, 199, 222, 265, 266
  aftermath 306
Hurd, Frank 33–4, 90–91, 241
  29th December raid 198
  on City fires 90–1, 256
  essays 39, 90–1, 198, 241
  fate of 310
Hurford, Mr (Guildhall) 264

Ibex House 215
Imperial Fascist League *see* Facists
In Town Tonight (BBC radio programme) 88
India and Indians 5–6, 25, 113, 117
  Hitler's advice to Britain 19–20
  and the war 6
Ingersoll, Ralph 40, 79, 149–50
  interviews Anna Freud 171–2
Inone, Mr (Japanese diplomat) 115

internees (18B and enemy 'aliens') 94, 102–4, 105–6, 106, 136, 164, 295
Invicta Road School 37
Italy
  Americans' relations with 130
  Churchill's speech to 22–23
  declaration of war on Allies (1940) 12
  invasion of Abyssinia (1935) 32
  invasion of Greece (1940) 22
  Italians in London 175, 295
  in North Africa 5, 17, 186
  and Japan 116
  protests at *The Great Dictator* 114
  and Spanish Civil War (1936–39) 32–3

Jackson, Maj. Frank 'Gentleman' 31, 36–7, 43–4, 207, 293–4
Jackson Brothers 187, 194–5, 197, 199, 222, 231, 266, 306
Jameson, Storm 15
Japan
  and America 62, 116, 288, 325
  Japanese in London 115
  and USSR 116
  Three-Power Pact (1940) 116
  war in China 21, 32, 61
Jesse, F. Tennyson 164
Jewish Chronicle 93, 215
Jews
  anti-Semitism 102, 106–7, 161
  in Britain 13, 92–3, 103, 106, 158–9, 161, 164, 190, 218, 304
  children in Britain 158–9
  Hitler and 28
  in Germany 22, 101, 129, 163, 318
  portrayed in *The Great Dictator* 114
Jillings, George (Heavy Rescue) 42–43, 237
John, King 135–6
John of Gaunt 125
Johnson, Dr Samuel 122, 256, 295, 297, 305
Jones, Gareth 20, 21–2
Jonson, Ben 122
'Just William' stories 162

Kampfgruppe '100' *see* Luftwaffe
Keenleyside, H. L. 283
Kennedy, Joseph 51

413